JAMES E. JOHNSON

James E. Johnson
Curriculum & Instruction
College of Education
Penn State University
University Park, PA 16802

Data Collection
and Analysis

DATA COLLECTION AND ANALYSIS

Basic Statistics

Robert M. Thorndike, Ph.D.

WESTERN WASHINGTON UNIVERSITY

GARDNER PRESS, INC., NEW YORK

Gardner Press, Inc.
19 Union Square West
New York 10003

LIBRARY OF CONGRESS CATALOGING IN PUBLICATION DATA

Thorndike, Robert M.
Principles of data collection and analysis.

(Gardner press series on measurement and statistics)
Bibliography: p.
Includes index.
1. Statistics. I. Title. II. Series.
QA276.12.T49   519.5   81-1423
ISBN 0-89876-022-4   AACR2

Printed in the United States of America

Book Design by Sidney Solomon

ACKNOWLEDGMENTS

The manuscript for this book passed through many hands and was affected by numerous people on its way to publication. Preparation of the initial drafts was greatly facilitated by a sabbatical leave from Western Washington University. Typing and artistic support was provided by Western's Bureau for Faculty Research, with Florence Preder valiantly trying to reproduce equations and text from my cryptic scratches and Joy Dabney working with her usual skill and insight to translate my mental images into figures. My colleagues Drs. Carol Diers and B. L. Kintz made helpful and ego-supporting comments on earlier drafts; the book was benefited from their input. Last, but far from least, my wife, Elva, and my daughters, Tracy and Kristi, have managed once again to survive the pain of writing and production with their good humor intact.

PREFACE

Every instructor has her/his own way of selecting, organizing, and presenting the material to be learned in a course. Choosing the textbook is often as much a matter of fit between the approaches of the instructor and author as it is a matter of details of content and production quality.

The decision to write *Data Collection and Analysis* was due in large part to my frustration in trying to find a book that fit my own biases for content and organization. Over the years, I have reviewed dozens of potential texts, have actually used several in my classes, and have always been less than satisfied with the results. The reason has seemed to be that books on research in the behavioral sciences in general, and in psychology in particular, always fall into one of two discrete camps, both of which miss what I want to achieve.

It is my belief, and the principle that has guided me in writing this book, that it is fruitless to separate the analysis of data from the principles underlying the procedures used to collect them. Unfortunately, books dealing with data analysis, generally those with the word statistics in the title, tend to be texts on applied mathematics; they may do an excellent job with the math, but they ignore the source of the numbers. The statistics seem to exist for their own sake rather than to answer important scientific questions.

On the other side are the books dealing with laboratory methods. They usually include the word experiment in the title and cover such topics as the selection and measurement of variables, control and manipulation, and report writing, which they may do well or poorly. But their treatment of data analysis is often so compressed that the beginning student is introduced to complex analysis of variance or multiple correlation in a single chapter.

In this book, I occupy a middle ground. I present the mathematics of data analysis in an accurate and understandable form, always keeping in mind that the purpose of the analysis is to help a human investigator reach a conclusion or decision about a substantive question.

To some readers, this book may seem a little out of step with some of the trends of the times because it generally ignores calculators and computers. The decision not to include material of this kind was based on two factors. First, operating a particular brand of calculator or computer differs from all others, so that a discussion with sufficient generality to apply to a Hewlett-Packard and a Texas Instruments calculator would not prepare the student to use either. Therefore, operating instructions are handled much more efficiently in the owner's manual prepared by the manufacturer for the specific model of calculator. Second, focusing on calculator methods may interfere with the student's attempt to grasp the principles that transcend the particular problem. The component elements of a statistic—how and why they fit together the way they do and what they mean and how they can be interpreted—are more important than how they are computed. In this text, computational procedures are used to highlight the how and why of the meaning.

The coin-toss problems were purposely chosen to strip away unnecessary complexity, so that the student can visualize the process and the relationship between mathematical analyses and actual events. Examples from signal-detection research, test theory, personality research, for example, would have diverted attention from the principle to the particular application, thereby restricting the student's ability to generalize.

With the foregoing conditions as my biases, *Data Collection and Analysis* gradually took form in three parts. The six chapters in Part I deal with individual data points and single sets of data, relating number systems to real-world observations and proceeding through ways of summarizing and condensing sets of data, and finally returning to an augmented meaning of the individual observation in terms of its normative interpretation. Part II treats the relationship between data sets and the use of relationship information in making predictions. Some instructors may wish to skip one or more chapters here if the topics are covered in a measurement course. Finally, Part III presents what is usually called inferential statistics. I have avoided this term because it is confused with the issue of causation. Instead, the presentation focuses on generalization to the population, estimation of parameters, and reaching decisions about the truth of hypotheses. Throughout this portion of the book, the central concept is the sampling distribution and its function in reaching probabilistic conclusions.

It is my belief that the most important feature of a book is that it be useable. Several features have been included in *Data Collection and Analysis* for this reason. The Table of Contents is very detailed to help the reader locate particular topics. The presentation is aimed toward readability and clarity of verbal exposition of concepts while retaining enough mathematical rigor so that the student need not take formulas and statistical concepts on faith. Formal mathematics is deemphasized in the main text, but detailed derivations of important equations are presented step by step in Appendix A for those who wish them. The statistical tables in Appendix B have been arranged in a convenient format for easy use. Indexes have been provided for both appendices. Appendix C contains a summary of the important equations, arranged by chapter. Detailed answers to selected problems are provided in Appendix D, and there is a list of recommended additional sources in statistics, measurement and research design.

Robert M. Thorndike
December, 1981

CONTENTS

Contents

LIST OF FIGURES

Figure 13-4
Rejection region for a two-tailed null hypothesis.   *293*

Figure 13-5
Critical values of z and 5-percent rejection regions for a
one-tailed null hypothesis.   *295*

Figure 13-6
Power and the probabilities of type I (α) and type II (β)
errors for a true μ of 6.   *299*

Figure 13-7
Power and the probabilities of type I (α) and type II (β)
errors for a true μ of 5.5.   *301*

Figure 14-1
Sampling distribution of the differences between means.   *312*

Figure 14-2
t distributions for various degrees of freedom.   *319*

Figure 14-3
Critical values for several t distributions.   *321*

Figure 15-1
Examples of chi-square distributions.   *339*

Figure 16-1
Frequency distribution of data from Table 16-1.   *366*

Figure 16-2
Plot of group means for drug study.   *380*

LIST OF TABLES

xxi

PART I
DESCRIBING DATA

1

THE NATURE AND
PURPOSE OF DATA

INTRODUCTION—WHY YOU ARE BEING SUBJECTED TO THIS

This is a book about information and how to process and interpret it. In general, it is proper to say that information is a set of facts about some aspect of the universe. For the present, equating facts and information is sufficient for our purposes, but we shall see shortly that this is an over-simplification. As we all know from our daily lives, some facts are true and others turn out not to be true; still other facts are only partially true or are true in some situations but not in others. Strategies and techniques for separating true or good facts from untrue or bad facts and for identifying the situations or conditions where these conclusions apply occupy a large portion of this book.

In addition to being a book about information, this is a book about language. All languages are made up of words or concepts and rules for combining these words to produce a communication. Behavioral and social scientists everywhere in the world have a common language that they use to communicate the results of their studies to each other. This language is called *statistics,* and although sociologists, psychologists, and economists may speak different dialects of the language and may deal with very different subjects, they all use the same basic words and rules to communicate about their subjects.

Statistics is a branch of applied mathematics that utilizes mathematical techniques for summarizing quantities of information and for condensing it into a digestible form. We are all bombarded daily by information that has been processed by the techniques of statistics described in later sections of this book. For example, the World Series ended yesterday, and the player voted most valuable had a batting average of 0.400 with seven extra-base hits. The information is its original form would include the batter's performance each time at bat, about 30 separate pieces of information. Knowing about and using statistics for the purpose of summarizing information can be justified simply as a way to save space in your daily newspaper. As we shall see shortly, there are many other reasons for using statistics and being able to understand them.

It would be well to clear up a small semantic matter before we go much further. The singular form, *statistic,* has two meanings in everyday language, but only one in the language of science. Television ads warn us: "Don't become a statistic. Don't drive after drinking." In this case, the term statistic refers to information to which the mathematical procedures of statistics are applied. This is not the meaning used in science, where "statistic" means the number resulting from the application of the mathematical procedures of statistics to a body of information. For example, a batter's batting average is a statistic. The plural form, *statistics,* may refer to more than one statistic or to the branch of mathematics (in which case, it is a singular word!)

WHY COLLECT INFORMATION

The information that is processed by statistical techniques may come in several forms, but before the information is obtained, several questions should be answered, the first is why collect the information. For years, government agencies have been gathering vast quantities of information for the apparent purpose of filling up filing cabinets. However, most information is collected for one of four reasons, all of which involve increasing our knowledge of the world around us.

The most basic purpose for gathering information is *description*. If we want to describe an individual's performance, for example, a baseball player's, we can collect information about the number of times at bat, number of hits, number of fielding chances, number of errors, and so on (almost to infinity in the case of baseball). Our purpose is to describe what has happened or what is presently happening in summary form so that the information can be conveyed to other people. The procedures described in Part I of this book focus on description and are called *descriptive statistics*.

On most occasions involving collection of information, we wish to go beyond merely describing the present. Perhaps the most frequent use of statistical procedures is to *evaluate*. When one outcome or situation is judged to be better than another, the collection of information may have led to an evaluation. Educators use statistical methods to evaluate teaching methods, psychologists use them to evaluate types of therapy, baseball managers evaluate players in terms of batting and fielding statistics. The point to be aware of here is that statistics helps in making value judgements, but that the values themselves are imposed by people. Two different people with different value systems may make quite different judgments from the same information. Since most of the statistical procedures used for evaluation are the same as those used for description, we do not treat the two topics separately but merely note that evaluation generally involves attaching value to a comparison based on descriptive statistics.

There are a number of situations where a person might wish to specify the relationship between two sets of information. In one sense, this is a descriptive problem, that is, we could describe two sets of information in terms of the relationship between them. However, methods have been developed in statistics that allow us to go beyond describing what is in order to *predict* what is likely to happen. For example, colleges use the statistics of prediction when they forecast student performance in college (often in the form of admissions decisions) on the basis of test scores and high-school records. Businesses forecast the acceptability of prospective employees and even the probable success of new products and advertising campaigns. Political candidates forecast the outcomes of elections. Certainly, forecasts of these kinds are not always correct, but the use of predictive statistics can produce a substantial reduction in the number of mistakes. Part II of this book is devoted to the description of relationships and to prediction.

In addition to description, evaluation, and prediction, statistical methods may be used for *research*. By this we mean going beyond the given information to reach conclusions about truth, the laws of nature, or some other abstract principle. For example, the information at hand may show that babies fed an enriched milk substitute are happier than babies fed regular milk. A research approach would ask whether this result is true only for the babies who were studied or is likely to be true for all babies. The mathematical and logical principles involved in this type of generalization are discussed in Part III.

DESIRABLE PROPERTIES OF INFORMATION

Information can be used for many things, but the quality of a description or conclusion resulting from the analysis of information is only as good as the original information. Good decisions cannot be made from poor information. (However, note that it is perfectly possible to make a poor decision from the best information.)

There are two characteristics that information must have if it is to be useful for scientific or social purposes. The first and most fundamental requirement is that each single piece of information must itself be *accurate*. The second is that is must be *representative*.

Accuracy. In many cases, accuracy of information may reasonably be taken for granted. For example, there is relatively little question about the accuracy of the number of hits a baseball player got in a season: The number is publicly verifiable and with the possible exception of controversial calls on fielding errors, not open to question. Congressional voting records, age and sex of children, age and occupation of parents, test scores, and many other pieces of information are assumed to be correct.

Now consider two features of the information gathering situation—first, the source of information and second, the nature of the information itself. Suppose that we are collecting parental age and occupation information from some school children. Whether we can trust our information to be accurate or not depends on whether we are concerned with what the children say or with what their parents' actual ages and occupations are. Information of the former kind is more likely to be accurate than is information of the latter kind. Parental age and occupation are verifiable and knowable pieces of information. Likewise, the child's statement of the parent's age and occupation can be accurately recorded. The problem is that the child's statement may be inaccurate; the child may simply not have the correct information to give us.

The problem here is the source of the information. If we ask the children's parents, we can be reasonably certain of the accuracy of the information. However, if our interest is in the children's beliefs about their parents' ages and occupations, then the best source of information is the children. Careful selection of the best source for our information is the best way to assure that it will be as accurate as possible.

That inaccuracy resulting from the source of information is a problem is shown by the fact that in one published study trained classroom observers showed less than perfect agreement on the sex of the teacher they were observing! If the investigator had asked the teachers themselves, it is highly likely that they would have known and would have given accurate information. In situations such as that, we can only wonder about the accuracy of other, less verifiable observations that were made.

Level of inference. In addition to problems stemming from the source or provider of information, the accuracy of information may be affected by the way in which it is collected. It is often the case in psychology or education, for example, that the information we can collect does not represent exactly the information we want. For example, does your score on an exam in college always reflect how well you have mastered the course material? The number of test items you got right is accurately knowable. However, most teachers assume that answers to test questions give information beyond the questions themselves; that is, test questions give indirect information about learning or mastery of the course content or something else that cannot be known by direct observation. The clinical psychologist who uses a questionnaire to get information about a client's personal functioning is not interested in specific responses to specific items but in what information these responses convey about the person. In both of these examples and whenever we use one piece of information as an indicator of some unobserved characteristic, there is a serious risk that the information we have does not accurately represent the characteristic we wish to know about.

The problem here is the level of inference that we must assume in going from what is actually observed to what we are interested in. In simple cases such as stated age or occupation, the measurement of physical properties like distance, or the price of a stock on the New York Stock Exchange, the result of the observation itself is the extent of our interest. There is no inference required; this information has been obtained by *direct* observation.

In the two examples of test and questionnaire responses, the teacher and the psychologist both wish to infer the existence of a trait underlying the observed behavior. Interest centers not on the observations themselves but on the unobservable characteristic or trait that is *assumed* to be related to the observations. The trait may or may not exist, and if it does exist, the observations may or may not be related to it. There is at best an *indirect* relationship between the information in our observations and the use that we make of it. Therefore, the accuracy of our inferences tends to be relatively low when our information is of this kind.

Please note that we are not suggesting that the situation is hopeless or that the information is without meaning. The point is that there are dangers in being too confident that our conclusions are correct and these dangers are much greater when there is an indirect relationship between the observations and the trait. We should not stop studying such phenomena, but our conclusions about them must be quite tentative in the face of extended chains of inference relating them to our observations.

Representative.   In addition to accuracy, of both the source and the nature of the information, it is desirable to have representative information. That is, if we wish to reach conclusions that extend beyond the available information, the information we have must adequately represent all cases that will be included in our conclusions. Suppose, for example, that we wish to study attitudes toward changing sex roles in American society. In order to gather information, we stand outside the dining hall at a college and ask those students who will speak to us a series of prepared questions about changing sex roles. About whom can we reach conclusions? Our information does not include people who could not speak to us because they do not go to college, do not go to our college, or do not go to the dining hall; it also does not include those people who would not answer our questions.

In addition to those involved, there is another aspect of the problem of inference: Do the questions in our survey cover all facets of the attitudes toward changing sex roles? Each single question may accurately reflect the trait, but a good information gathering procedure will reveal all aspects of the trait. Unless this condition is met, we cannot generalize the information beyond the types of questions asked.

The moral of this little story is that careful planning is necessary to insure that information obtained adequately represents both the topic and the individuals about whom we wish to know. The principles of analysis described in the chapters that follow can be applied to any sets of numbers. In order for the results of an analysis to have meaning, the numbers that go into the analysis must have meaning; unless the numbers are accurate and representative, their meaning is questionable at best. The computer industry has an acronym that well represents the problem: GIGO, garbage in, garbage out.

MEASUREMENT—GIVING MEANING TO NUMBERS

Information must be in the form of numbers if we are to apply mathematics to it. If information has been gathered in some other form, for example, verbal descriptions or videotapes of events or essay responses to test questions, it must be converted into numerical form before it can be subjected to statistical analysis. In any case, numbers are being used to represent something else; the numbers take on meaning beyond numberness. The process of attaching meaning to numbers is known as *measurement,* and numbers that have meaning are often called *data*.

One widely accepted definition of measurement is *assigning numbers to objects or events according to a set of rules.* We are all familiar with many types of measurement that affect our lives daily, and measurements of distance, weight, and time are so familiar that we hardly stop to consider where they come from. But suppose we say that Jane's weight is 50; without some other reference, the number is meaningless. What is missing is the set of rules that led to the assignment of the number 50 to Jane. The set of rules is called a *scale,* and unless the scale is known, the number carries little or no information for us; we must know what rules have been used.

In many areas of the physical sciences and of our everyday lives, the rules for assigning numbers to objects or events are so familiar and well-developed that mere mention of the scale of measurement is sufficient to provide the necessary meaning. For example if we know that Jane's 50 refers to pounds, we have a fairly accurate idea of her weight; likewise, if the 50 refers to kilograms, we have a good, but different idea. Specifying the scale is enough in cases like this.

There are many situations in the social and behavioral sciences where it is necessary to use scales that are quite different in a variety of ways from the scales used for weight and length. In such cases, it may be necessary to specify in some detail what rules were used for assigning numbers to the objects or events that have been observed. Suppose, for example, we wish to measure the gender of teachers in school classrooms and we say that teacher X is a 1. You do not know whether X is a male or female. If we now say that the scale is that males receive a zero and females receive a 1, you know that X is female. Confusion about the scale is one major source of inaccuracy in information, and it may, for example, explain the lack of agreement among observers of classrooms as described before.

It is essential to know the scale before applying statistical analyses to data. Consider a laboratory psychology experiment on maze learning where rat number 7 received a score of 4. Unless we know whether this number reflects the number of correct choices, the number of errors, time to run the maze, or something else, we have no way of interpreting the results of an analysis. The meaning of the number as an index of learning depends on whether it refers to correct or incorrect choices. The mathematics of the statistical analysis does not know or care what the data mean, but unless the investigator remembers (they don't always!), the interpretation of the analysis and the conclusions reached will be useless.

Types of scales. When we consider numbers in the abstract sense of the real number system that is usually used in arithmetic and algebra, the numbers are pure numbers and nothing more. We can add them, subtract them, multiply, and divide them, find squares and square roots, and, in general, perform any mathematical operation. (Note that for some types of number systems, not all of the above operations are permitted. The integer system, for example, does not permit division because the result of the operation many not be an integer.) Numbers that result from measurement and therefore have meaning beyond their numberness can be restricted in various ways. For example, it is reasonable to interpret a batting average of 0.400 as meaning that an individual gets 400 hits per 1000 times at bat (or 40 per 100 or 4 per 10), but it is not reasonable to say that the batter gets 4/10 of a hit each time at bat.

The problem with the second interpretation is that each hit occurs as a whole event and cannot be subdivided. Events that occur in an all-or-none fashion are called discrete events, and the scales used to measure them are called *discrete scales*. Discrete scales are like the integer number system. Except for certain specific applications, such as the first interpretation of batting averages, fractional values are not meaningful. Counting the number of times something happens or the number of objects of a particular kind is the most common kind of discrete scale.

When fractional values are permissible and meaningful, we say that we have a *continuous scale*.[1] The permissibility and meaningfulness of fractional values depend on the characteristic or trait of the object or event and the level of development of measurement scales. If the characteristic of interest is extensive (for example, length, height, width), fractional scale values probably make sense, and the scales available (for example, meter sticks) are sufficiently well-developed that we may reasonably permit and interpret fractional values. Most of the measurements that confront us in our daily lives involve traits that we consider to be continuous and scales that are well-developed, so we are accustomed to thinking in terms of continuous measurements.

It is often difficult to separate a trait from the process used to measure it. However, the student should be aware that while some traits, such as length, weight, and time may be continuous, all procedures used to measure them result in discrete scales at some level of refinement. For every characteristic, there is a point beyond which our current technology does not permit subdivisions, even though they might be possible in theory. We will discuss some consequences of this dilemma after introducing some other properties of scales.

We saw earlier that it was possible to form a scale of gender by specifying that if an individual is male, he is assigned the numerical symbol 0 and if the individual is female, she is assigned the numerical symbol 1. Let us now consider what numerical meaning the numbers that result from this measurement possess.

In most of our experiences with measuring, larger numbers have meant more of something; that is, we normally think of numbers as indicating *quantity*. But what quantity is being expressed by our scale for gender? One rather far-fetched interpretation might be that females have more X chromosomes than do males; on the other hand, males have more Y chromosomes. In fact, our scale of gender is nothing more than a rule that substitutes zero for the word male and the number 1 for the word

---

[1]Strictly speaking, it is the characteristic being measured that is discrete or continuous, not the scale. All scales are discrete in that fractional values of the smallest unit of measurement are not possible in practice.

female. We could then reverse the scale and call males 1 and females zero without affecting the amount or quality of information. In fact, we could use any pair of numbers we choose, 0.005 and 0.006, 8 and 753, and so forth, without gain or loss. All we are doing is substituting numbers for words or names. A scale that substitutes numbers for names is called a *nominal scale*.

Nominal scales are not uncommon in the behavioral and social sciences; gender is one frequent use, as are numerical labels used to designate occupational categories. Another frequent use of nominal scales in psychology is to designate groups in an experiment. Each of these cases involves assigning the same number to people who would otherwise receive the same verbal label (female, securities analyst, latent learning group).

Consider the nominal scale for gender. Does it make any sense to say that the average gender of subjects in an experiment was 0.4? If males are zeros and females are 1's, a value of 0.4 is not a meaningful value on the scale. This is true for two reasons: First, the scale is discrete. (All nominal scales are discrete); thus, values between the named categories are not meaningful. Second, there is no information about amount of anything. The operation $0 + 1 = 1$ is not logical. The only thing we can do with a nominal scale is count the number of times each category occurred. However, nominal scales do deserve to be included as a type of measurement, because they require recognition of categories, and this is the first stage in the development of a science.

Many times it is possible to identify an order in the categories that make up a scale; that is, the different numerical values indicate relatively more or less of the characteristic of interest. Examples of this type of measurement are not difficult to find in sociology and psychology. They generally take the form of rank orders and may involve orderings of preferred activities or individuals, such as those found in measuring interests or friendship patterns or judgments of relative merit of workers, artistic productions, and so forth.

What all of these scales have in common is that the objects or events are ordered according to relative amounts of the trait of interest. Scales that include the idea of order and quantity of the trait and have as one of the rules for assigning numbers that the order of the numbers must preserve the order of the objects or events are known as *ordinal scales*.

Data that come from ordinal scales carry more meaning or information than data from nominal scales, but they still cannot be treated like ordinary numbers. The numbers convey information about relative position *in a group,* but not about amounts of the trait in some absolute sense. Your knowledge of American history might place you third in a class of 20 college sophomores; that is, you might receive a value of 3 on the ordinal scale of history achievement in this group. The same level of knowledge and performance might result in a rank of 20 among 20 college-senior history majors or 200 sophomores. In either case, the numerical value assigned and the meaning of the number depend on the reference group. The same principle applies in ranking friendship choices: The person you most prefer among a group of people that you don't like very well might rank as least preferred in comparison with a group of your closest friends.

Another fairly common type of measurement results in numbers that convey not only information about order but also about magnitudes of differences. Most measurements of human abilities are of this general type. Scale values carry information about order and about *relative amount* of the characteristic in question. The differences or intervals between numbers carry a constant meaning. Scales on which equal numerical differences mean equal differences in characteristics are called *interval scales.*

An example of an interval scale that is familiar to everyone is the Celsius scale of temperature. Water freezes at 0° and boils at 100° under standard conditions, and these two reference points define the unit for the scale; that is, the unit is 1/100th of the difference between the freezing point and boiling point of water. Each unit between these two points is equal, and we may add more units of the same size above 100 and below zero. Equal numerical differences on the scale reflect equal changes in the characteristic being measured.

The most important feature of an interval scale is that it permits definition of a scale that is independent of the particular group on which measurements are being made. Thus, the numbers come to mean amount of something, rather than relative amount of something. The scale or measuring device itself becomes the standard with which comparisons are made. Once this level of meaning has been attained, it is possible to employ more sophisticated mathematical procedures, such as addition and subtraction.

(**Brief Aside.** It is important for the student to remember that numbers do not remember where they come from, and, ordinarily, they will raise no objections, no matter what we do to them. We can add and subtract them, multiply and divide them, take logs and exponentiate and even nominal data will not object. But *data* are both more *and* less than numbers. They are more than numbers because they have been given additional meaning by being assigned to objects or events; they represent those objects or events. Data are also less than numbers because the meaning or nature of the objects or events they represent may not logically permit various numerical operations. Average gender is one example of such a problem; average rank is another example. Suppose George ranks third in verbal ability and fifth in quantitative ability in a group of 50 students. His average rank is fourth, but if the students were ranked in terms of total performance, George's consistency would probably earn him a rank of first or second. The numbers representing the ranks do not themselves object to being averaged, but in most cases, the order that results from averaging does not make sense and does not correspond to the order that would result from a more appropriate procedure.

We shall return to the meaning of numbers from time to time, particularly in Chapters 6, 10, and 12. For the present, it is only necessary to emphasize the intimate relationship between the way the data were collected and how many attributes of numbers they possess. Scales below the interval level are quite restricted in the attributes that they possess.)

Interval scales still have some restrictions; in particular, the definition of zero on the interval scale is arbitrary. The Celsius scale for temperature uses the freezing point of water as an arbitrary zero point. Any other point could have been chosen without affecting calculations very much and without changing the usefulness of the scale at all.

The major consequence of an arbitrary zero point is that statements involving ratios are not meaningful: Stating that 20°C is twice as hot (a ratio of 2 to 1) as 10°C is not meaningful; neither is the statement that 50°C is half as hot at 100°C. In order for these ratio statements to make sense, the zero point on the scale must be defined so that the possibility of negative scale values is ruled out. This is often called an absolute zero. When a scale has intervals and an absolute zero point, it is called a *ratio scale*.

Ratio scales provide the highest degree of measurement and are found in the most well-developed sciences. For example, length and mass are measured on ratio scales. It is generally the case that the numbers resulting from measurements using ratio scales can be treated like the ordinary numbers to which we are accustomed. However, even the numbers on a ratio scale are restricted by their meaning because of the absence of negatives.[2] (Note that the presence of negative values on an interval scale is not an asset of that type of scale over the ratio scale but merely a result of the choice of zero point.)

Each level of scale possesses all of the properties of meaning and numberness of the scales below it, and something more. These properties are summarized in Table 1-1. Because each level of scale builds on its predecessors, each can be converted into a scale of a lower level. This is a desirable and necessary feature for some types of interpretations, such as the normative and ipsative interpretations discussed in Chapter 6, and for some statistical procedures, such as the correlation coefficient discussed in Chapter 9.

TABLE 1-1
Four Major Levels of Scales and Their Properties.

Scale	Properties
nominal	Numbers are names of categories of a variable.
ordinal	Numbers represent the order of categories or individuals.
interval	Equal differences between numbers represent equal amounts of the trait. Negative values are possible.
ratio	Zero means exactly none of the trait. Negative values are not possible.

MORE MEANING IN NUMBERS

Numbers can take on still more meaning beyond their scale properties and the entities or events they represent. These additional meanings are important when the results of measurement are to be used in science. They are frequently discussed under the heading of *experimental design.*

[2]Although some authors (for example, Torgerson, 1958) suggest that negative values can exist in a ratio scale, the definitions given by Stevens (1946) and the name itself imply only positive values. What ratio of positive numbers would be the same as the ratio $-1:2$, for example? The issue is not important for our purposes, but we shall stick with Stevens.

The first feature we must look at is whether more than one numerical value (or verbal label, for that matter) of the scale occurs or should occur in the set of data with which we are concerned. If only one value or type of the trait occurs, the trait is said to be a *constant*. In the process of doing research, it is necessary to keep almost all aspects of the situation constant; this is called *experimental control*. In most situations, it is desirable to keep constant or to control all aspects of the situation except those whose effects we wish to study.

The characteristics we wish to study may occur in more than one form or have more than one scale value; because their values vary, they are called *variables*. Our studies generally involve describing simple variables (counting the ways in which they occur, the frequency of different values), specifying relationships among variables and determining causal effects.

Most research studies in the behavioral and social sciences involve at least two variables. In some cases, the investigator is interested in making observations in a natural setting and seeing which variables seem to go together. In other studies, s/he may choose naturally occurring categories of one variable (for example, sex or age) and measure some other variable (such as mathematical ability or aggression) to determine whether there is a systematic relationship between the first variable and the second.

A third type of study includes those cases where the investigator imposes the value of one variable (for example, type of teaching or drug dose) on the subjects and measures a second variable (learning, reaction time, pupillary dilation, and so forth); this type of study is called an *experiment*. The variable that the investigator imposes on the subjects is called the *independent variable* and the measured outcome is called the *dependent variable*.

It is important to distinguish among the different types of studies and variables because this affects meaning in the data, which in turn determines the type of conclusions we can draw. An experimental study involves an *independent or manipulated* variable and an *outcome or dependent* variable. The independent variable is completely under the investigator's control, while the dependent variable depends upon the manipulation of the independent variable. Studies that involve imposition of an independent variable by the investigator are the only ones that permit us to infer that the change in one variable (the independent variable) caused a change in the other variable.

Many, perhaps most, variables that are of interest to social and behavioral scientists cannot be brought under the investigator's control. Personality and ability variables, gender, attitudes, needs, and a host of other variables can be controlled by the selection of individuals for study, but we are both practically and (often) ethically prevented from imposing values for these variables on our subjects. Variables like these are called *status variables* because they reflect the individual's position or status on some characteristic. Because they cannot be imposed on the subjects, we cannot infer that status variables bear casual relationships with outcome variables; we can infer relationship, but not causation. It is fairly common to refer to status variables as independent variables, and we shall adopt that convention in the remainder of this book, but the student should be aware that we can draw different conclusions depending on whether an independent variable is a status variable or a manipulated variable.

SUMMARY

Statistics is a branch of applied mathematics that provides a language for behavioral and social science communication. Information is collected for the purposes of *description, evaluation, prediction,* and *research.* Useful information must be *accurate,* in the sense that observations must be correctly recorded, and *representative,* in that the observations must reflect variations in the events of interest. *Data* are pieces of information that have been put in numerical form. The process of creating data (that is, putting information into numerical form) is known as *measurement.* A *scale* is the set of rules used in assigning numbers to objects or events. Scales may be *nominal, ordinal, interval,* or *ratio,* depending on the quantitative meaning that the numbers convey. An *experimental control* or constant is a trait that has the same value for all individuals observed. Traits that take on more than one value are known as *variables*; if they are under the investigator's control, they are called *independent variables.* Variables whose relationships to independent variables are being studied are called *dependent variables.* The kinds of inferences we can make about the relationships between independent and dependent variables depend on whether the independent variables are *status variables* or *manipulated variables.*

1. What is the difference between statistics and a statistic?

2. What are the reasons for collecting data?; how do they differ? Describe an example of two different uses of data from your own major.

3. Give two examples each of direct and indirect measurements.

4. Give two examples of data collection situations where the accuracy of the data might be questioned. What are some possible sources of this possible inaccuracy?

5. How could we develop a scale to measure beauty? Is this direct or indirect measurement? How would you make sure the information was representative?

6. What is the difference between a constant and a variable?

7. Can age ever be a dependent variable?; explain why or why not.

8. What is the difference between an independent variable and a dependent variable?; give examples of both.

9. For each of the following types of meaningful numbers, state whether the measurement is direct or indirect; whether the scale represents a discrete or continuous variable; and what level of measurement scale, nominal, ordinal, interval, or ratio is involved:

(a) zip codes

(b) weight in pounds

(c) weight in kilograms

(d) rank in class

(e) intelligence as measured by an IQ test

(f) answer to the question ''Which kind of ice cream do you like better, chocolate or vanilla?''

(g) temperature in degrees Fahrenheit

2

SUMMARIZING DATA IN FREQUENCY DISTRIBUTIONS AND GRAPHS (CIVILIZING THE DATA)

Information does not come to an investigator in neat and orderly packages very often. It was suggested in Chapter 1 that careful planning in the selection of variables is very important for the types of conclusions that can be drawn from a study. Planning in data collection will also facilitate handling the data to be analyzed. For example, it may be possible to arrange for automatic recording of data by an electronic recorder or computer, or it may be possible to prepare a questionnaire so that responses can be read by optical scanning equipment. However, even with the most careful planning and sophisticated equipment, the data, as provided by the real world, come in a organized and incomprehensible mass of numbers, such as those found in Table 2-1.

Table 2-1 presents two types of information. First, there is a series of numbers in order from 1 to 50; this is a nominal variable. Each number identifies a particular individual from whom information was obtained. The second set of numbers represents the information itself, and the qualities of these numbers depend upon the procedures used to collect them. Let us assume for the sake of illustration that the data represent

19

the scores on a test of knowledge of current events of 50 Japanese army survivors of World War II who were just discovered on a remote island in the South Pacific. (They might also represent the scores obtained by 50 second-grade school children on a test of reading achievement or the time 50 monkeys took to solve a puzzle problem.) Whatever the source, it is not unusual for researchers to obtain data in this general form.

What can we say about the data? If there were only very few individuals, we could perhaps take in the whole picture in a single glance and describe our data without further processing. However, any time there are more than a very few pieces of information and every time we wish to progress

TABLE 2-1

Scores of 50 Japanese War Veterans on a Test of Current Events.

Individual	Data Value	Individual	Data Value
1	95	26	81
2	104	27	113
3	111	28	121
4	88	29	97
5	79	30	96
6	96	31	101
7	105	32	117
8	130	33	110
9	100	34	99
10	107	35	83
11	91	36	94
12	102	37	98
13	78	38	90
14	124	39	120
15	99	40	106
16	76	41	113
17	94	42	98
18	92	43	87
19	104	44	86
20	110	45	108
21	99	46	117
22	87	47	93
23	93	48	109
24	101	49	106
25	103	50	116

beyond mere description to evaluation, prediction, or research, it is necessary to put the data into different forms. What form we choose will depend upon how concise we wish our description to be and what types of further conclusions we wish to draw.

Processing data almost always involves trade-offs: We must discard some types of information or lose some detail in the data in order to gain a clearer picture of what remains. (This is a little like saying that to be able to see the entire forest, we must move far enough away so that we can no longer identify the individual trees.) In this chapter, we consider the earliest stages in the process of summarizing data. Frequency distributions and graphs involve a minimal information loss at a considerable gain in perspective.

The student should be aware that computers and pocket calculators have taken over most of the work of statistical analysis. It is unlikely that s/he will ever have to perform by hand many of the operations covered in this book after having learned the basic procedures. For this reason, some books tend to skip the simple, old-fashioned material we cover in this chapter. However, computers do not know where the data came from; the numbers have no meaning for the calculator. Only the mind of the human operator is capable of interpreting the results of an analysis in terms of the meaning of the original data. The computer has tended to separate the investigator from her/his data by doing all the work and making it easy to go directly to a very abstract summary of the data. This has a double disadvantage. First, the investigator may never become aware of some levels of detail in the data. Studying frequency distributions, graphs, and simple descriptive statistics can give a feeling for what the data mean that is hidden by more abstract analyses. Second, operating only with abstract statistical indices can cause the investigator to forget where the numbers came from and reach inappropriate conclusions. It is important that investigators, particularly those just entering a field of inquiry, have available and use data-summarizing procedures that do not discard too much detail.

FREQUENCY DISTRIBUTIONS

The first step in getting to know the data usually involves sorting the data by numerical value and counting the number of times each value occurs. Looking through the data in Table 2-1, we note that individual 16 has the lowest score, 76, and the highest score, 130, belongs to person 8. The scores for the other 48 people lie between these two extremes. A frequency distribution will allow us to tell how many times (how frequently) each of the possible scores in this range occurs.

The task of making a frequency distribution is simple and not too time consuming if done correctly. In Table 2-2, the process is illustrated for our Japanese veterans using the following steps:

1. Find the highest and lowest scores. Write down all possible scores from highest to lowest in decreasing order.

2. Go through the list of individuals, and make a tally mark next to the score each person obtained.

TABLE 2-2
Raw Frequency Distribution of Data from Table 2-1.

X		f	X		f	X		f
130	I	1	106	II	2	82		0
129		0	105	I	1	81	I	1
128		0	104	II	2	80		0
127		0	103	I	1	79	I	1
126		0	102	I	1	78	I	1
125		0	101	II	2	77		0
124	I	1	100	I	1	76	I	1
123		0	99	III	3			
122		0	98	II	2			
121	I	1	97	I	1			
120	I	1	96	II	2			
119		0	95	I	1			
118		0	94	II	2			
117	II	2	93	II	2			
116	I	1	92	I	1			
115		0	91	I	1			
114		0	90	I	1			
113	II	2	89		0			
112		0	88	I	1			
111	I	1	87	II	2			
110	II	2	86	I	1			
109	I	1	85		0			
108	I	1	84		0			
107	I	1	83	I	1			

3. Count the number of tallies for each score value.

Notice that in Table 2-2 the column for score values is labeled X and the column containing the number of tally marks is labeled f. The letter X is widely used in statistics to designate a variable, in this case the possible test scores. The letter f is generally used to label frequencies. These two columns, the values of the variable X and the frequency f with which each occurs, constitute the *frequency distribution*. The column of tally marks is an intermediate step shown for convenience and accuracy and would not be included in the final table.

As stated, preparing a frequency distribution involves some loss of information or detail in the data. In this first stage of data analysis, what is lost is the identification of particular individuals as sources of information. Each separate score appears in the table, but the numbers identifying particular people have been discarded. We shall see as we go along that descriptive statistics involves successively discarding detail in order to develop a broader perspective on the information we wish to analyze. Every gain in condensing and simplifying the data must be paid for with a loss of detail. However, it is important not to throw away the detail too quickly.

Grouped Frequency Distributions. A frequency distribution such as that in Table 2-2 is known as a raw frequency distribution. Every score value is listed, even if its frequency is zero. In many situations, this type of frequency distribution does not provide much simplification; in fact for the example at hand, we have substituted 55 separate score values for the 50 original scores. Many of the possible values of X have zero frequency, and the scores spread so widely that it is hard to discern a pattern to them. There is still too much detail in the data.

The next stage in simplification is to prepare a *grouped frequency distribution* by discarding information about the number of times each particular score occurred and grouping together similar scores; this step is taken to eliminate values of X that have zero frequency. Instead of taking single values of X, we now use *intervals* and count the frequency of scores in each interval.

(**Brief aside.** Before going into the preparation of a grouped frequency distribution, it would be a good idea to recall and expand upon our discussion of continuous variables in Chapter 1. Remember that all measurment involves discrete categories at some level. If a characteristic is truly continuous, its measurement in any particular case involves assigning the number on the scale that is closer to the true amount than any other number on the scale.

The simplest and most obvious example of this principle is the measurement of length. Let us assume that a piece of rope is 12 feet 5.518375 . . . inches long (under standard conditions of temperature, stretch, and so forth). What scale value shall we assign to the rope? It is 4 yards long, 12 feet long, 12 feet 6 inches long, 12 feet $5\frac{1}{2}$ inches long, and so forth. As the units on our scale become smaller, the number we assign changes. In a scale of inches, the true length of rope is 149.518375 . . . inches.

Now assume that we have a second rope measured under identical conditions. Its true length is 12 feet 5.318375 . . . inches, which clearly differs from that of the first rope by 0.2 inches. But by using certain units of length, we can assign both ropes to the same category, since both are 4 yards long and 12 feet long. When the measurement unit is whole inches, rope 1 is 12 feet 6 inches, while rope 2 is 12 feet 5 inches; this is the first unit that differentiates between them. However, notice that when we move to 1/2-inch units, both ropes are again placed in the same category, 12 feet $5\frac{1}{2}$ inches; in units of 1/4 inch or smaller, the two ropes will be placed in different categories.

Each value on a scale actually represents an interval on the scale. An interval covers a region on the continuum from half way between one pair of scale values to half way between the next pair. Each numerical value on the scale falls at the middle of an interval and is used to represent all of the possible values that fall within the interval. For example, on a scale of feet, the scale value 12 represents all values between 11.5000 . . . and 12.5000 . . ., and we do not have a way of differentiating further within this interval. In our rope example, to say that one rope is 12 feet $5\frac{1}{4}$ inches and the other is 12 feet $5\frac{1}{2}$ inches means that one value falls in the interval between 12 feet 5.12500 . . . inches and 12 feet 5.37500 . . . inches, while the other lies between 12 feet 5.37500 inches and 12 feet 5.62500 inches. Both ropes fall in the interval between 12 feet 5.2500 . . . inches and 12 feet 5.7500 . . . inches (1/2-inch intervals) and thus are assigned the value 12 feet 5.500 . . . inches.

Measuring continuous variables always involves approximation, since the measurement scale has categories, and each observation is assigned the label of the category within which it falls. Two students who receive the same score on a statistics test do not have exactly the same level of knowledge statistics; however, they did get the same number of items correct and are, therefore, assigned the same score or scale value. On a longer or more refined test, the differences in their knowledge might have been identified and reflected by different values of the variable.)

Limits of Intervals. It is important to identify two types of intervals when grouping data. As pointed out, a single score represents the midpoint of an interval on the measurement scale of a continuous trait. The interval around each obtainable value on the scale may be called a *real interval* because it represents a fact about the trait itself. The extreme trait values of a real interval are called the *real limits* of the interval; they represent the points on the trait continuum where the scale values change. In the scale of feet from our example, the scale value 12 feet represents a real interval 1 foot wide with real limits at 11.5 and 12.5 feet. The real limits of each interval are always exactly half way between the midpoint of that interval and the next higher and lower midpoints.

Preparing a grouped frequency distribution brings up a new kind of interval, the *score interval.* In contrast to the real interval, which reflects the continuous nature of the underlying trait, the score interval reflects a range of values on the measurement scale itself and its limits, which are obtainable scale values known as *score limits.* The intervals and limits that are used to prepare a grouped frequency distribution are the score intervals and score limits.

In preparing a grouped frequency distribution, it is important to select the intervals carefully. The following principles should guide the selection:

1. It is highly desirable to have each interval contain an odd number of score values. The reason for this is that if the grouped frequency distribution is to be used as a starting point for later computations, the middle value of the interval, its *midpoint,* will be used to represent all scores in the interval. If there is an even number of score values, the midpoint will be half way between two scores and thus a decimal fraction. Using an odd number of scores will result in the midpoint being a whole number.

2. As a general rule, there should be between 10 and 20 intervals in a grouped frequency distribution. The reason for this is that using fewer than 10 intervals often loses too much detail and conceals important information, while having more than 20 intervals presents unnecessary and confusing detail.

With the above principles in mind, we can proceed to prepare a grouped frequency distribution for the data in Table 2-1. First, we must decide on the number of intervals. The best way to do this is to subtract the lowest obtained value on the scale (76) from the highest (130) and divide the resulting value (54) by 10 and by 20. Dividing by 10 shows what interval width will yield ten intervals, and dividing by 20 shows what interval width will yield 20 intervals. This operation shows that an interval width of about 5 will result in ten intervals and an interval width of about 3 will yield 20 intervals. Four is also a possible choice for interval width, but it does not have our first desirable property, an odd number of scores in the interval.

After we have decided on an interval size, the next question is where to start the intervals. One convenient rule of thumb is to choose an interval that has as its lower limit a value that is a multiple of the interval width. Thus if we choose an interval of 5, the lower limit of our bottom interval would be 75. As it turns out, in this case 75 would also be the choice for an interval of 3, but it is not usual for the same value to occur for both choices of interval.

The grouped frequency distributions that would result from using the above procedures on our sample data are given in Table 2-3. Using an interval width of 3 results in 19 intervals, while an interval width of 5 yields 12 intervals. Both of these grouped frequency distributions meet the criteria listed above, so the choice must be dictated by some other factor.

Perhaps the most important factor that would determine our choice between 3 and 5 for interval width is that larger intervals lose more information. We noted earlier that measuring continuous traits always involves some inaccuracy. In the process of preparing a grouped frequency distribution, we are increasing the inaccuracy of our measurement (perhaps it would be better to say that we are using coarser approximations) in the hope of getting a better overall picture of the data. The less we reduce our accuracy, the better; therefore, we would probably choose the left-hand distribution.

The loss of accuracy that results from grouping data is due to the fact that we use the midpoint of each interval to represent all of the scores in that interval. In Table 2-3, the score limits of each interval are given in the column labeled score interval and the midpoint is given in the next column and labeled X; as before, X designates the values of the variable. In a grouped frequency distribution, the midpoints of the intervals are the only values of the X that we retain. All observations that fall in an interval are given the midpoint of that interval as their value X, regardless of the value they had in the original frequency distribution. The three lowest scoring individuals in Table 2-2 had scores of 76, 78, and 79, respectively. In a grouped frequency distribution with an interval of 5, all three are represented by an X-value of 77, which is the midpoint of the interval, but not a score that any of them actually received. The important consequences of grouping the data will become clearer when we see their effects on some computed values in the next two chapters.

Cumulative Frequency Distributions. Another useful way of organizing and summarizing information is in the form of a *cumulative frequency distribution*. It is often useful to know how many scores fall at or below a given scale value, and the cumulative frequency distribution provides this

TABLE 2-3
Grouped Frequency Distributions for Intervals of 3 and 5.

Interval of 3			Interval of 5		
Score Interval	*Midpoint X*	*Frequency f*	*Score Interval*	*Midpoint X*	*Frequency f*
129–131	130	1	130–134	132	1
126–128	127	0	125–129	127	0
123–125	124	1	120–124	122	3
120–122	121	2	115–119	117	3
117–119	118	2	110–114	112	5
114–116	115	1	105–109	107	6
111–113	112	3	100–104	102	7
108–110	109	4	95–99	97	9
105–107	106	4	90–94	92	7
102–104	103	4	85–89	87	4
99–101	100	6	80–84	82	2
96–98	97	5	75–79	77	3
93–95	94	5			
90–92	91	3			
87–89	88	3			
84–86	85	1			
81–83	82	2			
78–80	79	2			
75–77	76	1			

information. To make a cumulative frequency distribution, we must start with a raw or grouped frequency distribution. The cumulative frequency distribution is easily prepared from either of these starting points by listing the values of X in ascending order and counting the number of scores that fall at or below each value of X. In practice, we simply add the frequency in each interval to the sum of the frequencies in the intervals below it. The process is illustrated in Table 2-4 for the two grouped frequency distributions in Table 2-3. Notice that the values of X are the midpoints of the intervals, that the frequencies are the same as those in Table 2-3, and that the cumulative frequency cf in each interval is equal to the sum of the cumulative frequency in the interval below and the frequency in the interval itself. For example in the column with an interval width of 3, the cumulative frequency for an X of 100 includes the 22 people whose scores are below 100 (the cf for 97) and the six people

TABLE 2-4
Cumulative Frequency Distribution for Grouped Data.

	Interval of 3			Interval of 5	
Score X	Frequency f	Cumulative Frequency cf	Score X	Frequency f	Cumulative Frequency cf
130	1	50	132	1	50
127	0	49	127	0	49
124	1	49	122	3	49
121	2	48	117	3	46
118	2	46	112	5	43
115	1	44	107	6	38
112	3	43	102	7	32
109	4	40	97	9	25
106	4	36	92	7	16
103	4	32	87	4	9
100	6	28	82	2	5
97	5	22	77	3	3
94	5	17			
91	3	12			
88	3	9			
85	1	6			
82	2	5			
79	2	3			
76	1	1			

whose scores were 100. The same procedure is followed throughout the distribution: The *cf* for a score of 118 includes the 44 people who scored at or below 115 (its *cf*) plus the two people who earned 118. Cumulative frequency distributions are primarily useful for computing various measures of relative position.

Relative Frequency Distributions. All of the frequency distributions we have discussed have one common shortcoming: They are all specific to a given total number of observations and cannot be generalized to larger or smaller groups. The way to overcome the problem is to report frequencies relative to the total number of observations. Any frequency distribution, whether raw, grouped, or cumulative, can be presented in terms of the relative frequency of each score by the simple process of dividing each frequency or cumulative frequency by the total number of cases observed. Table 2-5 presents the relative frequencies and relative

TABLE 2-5
Relative Frequency and Relative Cumulative Frequency Distributions.

Score X	Frequency f	Relative Frequency rf	Cumulative Frequency cf	Relative Cumulative Frequency rcf
130	1	0.02	50	1.00
127	0	0.00	49	0.98
124	1	0.02	49	0.98
121	2	0.04	48	0.96
118	2	0.04	46	0.92
115	1	0.02	44	0.88
112	3	0.06	43	0.86
109	4	0.08	40	0.80
106	4	0.08	36	0.72
103	4	0.08	32	0.64
100	6	0.12	28	0.56
97	5	0.10	22	0.44
94	5	0.10	17	0.34
91	3	0.06	12	0.24
88	3	0.06	9	0.18
85	1	0.02	6	0.12
82	2	0.04	5	0.10
79	2	0.04	3	0.06
76	1	0.02	1	0.02

cumulative frequencies for the data in Table 2-4. The values in the relative frequency (*rf*) column are obtained by dividing each frequency by 50, while the relative cumulative frequencies (*rcf*) are the *cf* values also divided by 50.

The primary advantage of relative frequency distributions (and *rcf* distributions) is that they are independent of the particular number of entities observed. A frequency of 5 in a group of 50 scores has the same meaning that a frequency of 10 has in a group of 100. This means that we can directly compare two relative frequency distributions, regardless of the sizes of the groups on which they are based. The importance of this will become more apparent as we consider graphs.

GRAPHS—PICTURES OF FREQUENCY DISTRIBUTIONS

One picture is worth a thousand words or so the saying goes; certainly, for some forms of communication, pictures are more useful or persuasive than words. The same principle holds true for some types and purposes of communication involving quantitative information. Pictures that convey quantitative information are called *graphs*. In this section, we shall discuss the advantages and disadvantages of several types of graphs and how to prepare three that are widely used in the behavioral and social sciences.

Everyone who reads newspapers or magazines is familiar with several types of graphs. One common type, called a pie graph, is widely used to illustrate the division of a whole into its parts and is often used by Government agencies to illustrate sources of tax revenues and areas of expenditure. It is called a pie graph because it shows how the revenue pie, for example, is sliced up into various parts or sources. Since this type of graph is used almost exclusively in this way, its value is therefore limited in most behavioral science situations.

A second type that is less limited in its application is the bar graph, which is used to show the frequencies of various nominal categories. For example, schools and colleges often report enrollment information on sex, academic class, and racial or religious composition of the institution in the form of a bar graph. The lengths of the bars in the graph indicate the relative or absolute frequencies of the various categories of the variable. Figure 2-1 shows pie and bar graphs.

By far, the most frequent use of graphs in the behavioral sciences is to

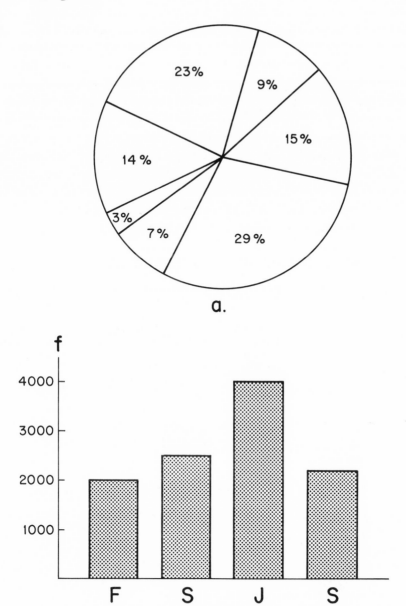

*Figure 2-1 **a.** Typical pie graph showing the division of a whole into its parts. **b.** Bar graph showing the number of individuals in each category. The abscissa is a nominal scale.*

illustrate frequency distributions for continuous variables. Two types of graphs, the *histogram* and the *frequency polygon,* are used with either raw or grouped frequency distributions, while the *cumulative frequency curve* is the graph of a cumulative frequency distribution. Because these three graphs are widely used and because they form the graphic base for many of our later mathematical topics, we shall review their principal features, preparation, and interpretation in some detail.

The Coordinate System. A very large number of topics that we shall discuss can be graphed using two dimensions. What we need first is a system for labeling the dimensions of our space. Mathematicians have given the name *abscissa* to the horizontal dimension of a two-dimensional space, while the vertical dimension is generally called the *ordinate.* As shown in Figure 2-2, the abscissa divides the space in half horizontally, and the ordinate divides it in half vertically, which results in four equal

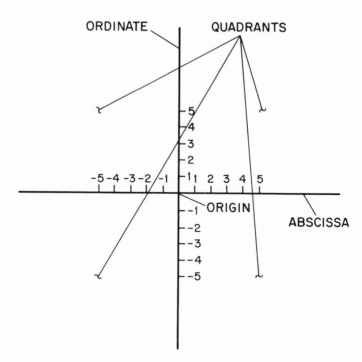

Figure 2-2 The two-variable coordinate system showing the four quadrants formed by the ordinate and the abscissa.

sections or *quadrants*. The ordinate and abscissa are known as the *axes* of the space, and the point where they cross is called the *origin*.

The axes are divided into equal units outward from the origin. On the abscissa positive values are to the right of the origin and negative values are to the left. The ordinate is labeled with positive values above the origin and negative values below it. The values of both axes are zero at the origin. This numerical labeling of the axes is also shown in the figure.

The advantage of labeling the axes in this way is that a single value expresses both direction and distance from the origin along either axis. Using two axes labeled in this way permits us to locate any spot in the space simply by giving the values for the abscissa and the ordinate. These values are generally given in pairs with the value for the abscissa given first. A pair of values given in this way defines the location of a point in the space and is known as the *coordinates* of the point. In Figure 2-3, three points with coordinates (2, 4), (−1, 3), and (−3, −1) are shown.

Each axis can be labeled to represent the different values that some variable may possess. When we wish to express a frequency distribution in the form of a graph, the usual procedure is to label the abscissa with the values of the measured variable and the ordinate with the possible frequencies. Later, we shall find that several other types of graphs in this coordinate system can be quite useful.

Histograms. Graphs of frequency distributions may label the abscissa either with the real limits of the intervals or with the midpoints

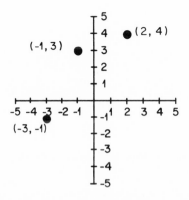

Figure 2-3   Three points plotted in a two-coordinate system.

of the intervals. A *histogram* is a graph of a frequency distribution in which the abscissa is labeled with the limits of the intervals. Each individual whose score places him within that interval may then be represented by a square. The squares are stacked on top of each other until everyone is accounted for. Figure 2-4 shows a histogram for the grouped frequency distribution with an interval width of 3 in Table 2-3. The numbers in the squares refer to individual identification numbers from Table 2-1 and show how a histogram is made from the individuals who have been measured. Ordinarily, the squares representing the individual scores would not be shown, and the histogram would appear as it does in Figure 2-5.

To prepare a histogram, we must first prepare a raw or grouped frequency distribution, then lay out the axes. We label the ordinate f for frequency and mark off enough values to include the largest frequency from our frequency distribution. We label the abscissa with the real limits of the score categories of our measured variable. If the values are all fairly large, as is the case in our example, it is customary to chop out a section of the abscissa and indicate by a broken line that some space has been omitted; Figures 2-4 and 2-5 both use this broken line. Finally, we draw in a bar over each interval so that the top of the bar is even with the fre-

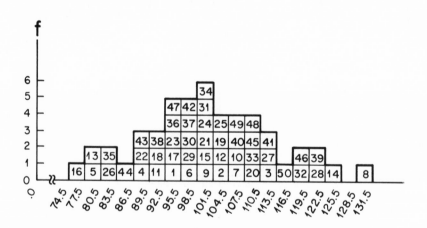

SCORE ON CURRENT EVENTS TEST

Figure 2-4   Histogram of scores. When making a histogram, each person is viewed as a square over the value of her/his score interval.

quency in the interval. The dashed lines in Figure 2-5 may be included as solid lines or omitted entirely from the final graph.

The important thing to remember about histograms is that they indicate the number of people (or objects or events) that fall in each *interval* on the measured variable. Even a histogram of a raw frequency distribution reflects the fact that our measurement is approximate and we are really only sure that the observations fall between two limits, the limits of our interval. The height of the bar indicates the number of observations in the interval.

Frequency Polygons. Instead of labeling the abscissa with the limits of the intervals, we could use the assigned score values. When the abscissa is labeled with the assigned score values, either the raw scores of the raw frequency distribution or the midpoints of the grouped frequency distribution, the resulting graph is called a *frequency polygon*. The frequency polygon shows the number of people (observations, and so forth) that are being represented by each of the listed numerical values.

The procedure for making a frequency polygon is very similar to that for making a histogram. The major difference is in labeling the abscissa. We start by preparing the frequency distribution (or using the one we made for the histogram). We label the ordinate *f* and mark off values as before. Next, we mark off and label the *midpoints* of the intervals from

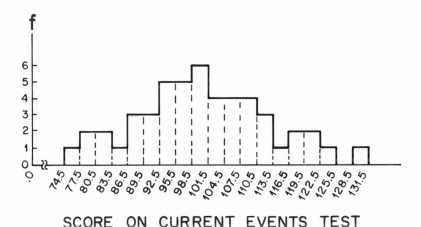

SCORE ON CURRENT EVENTS TEST

Figure 2-5   The squares are not shown in the final histogram.

our frequency distribution; we label one midpoint above and one midpoint below the distribution. Then we find the *point* that has as its coordinates the value of the midpoint of the first interval and the frequency of that midpoint. Since the first midpoint is for the interval below the lower limit of the frequency distribution, its frequency is zero and it falls on the abscissa. For each of the other midpoints, we find the point that has the midpoint and the frequency as it coordinates. These points are plotted and

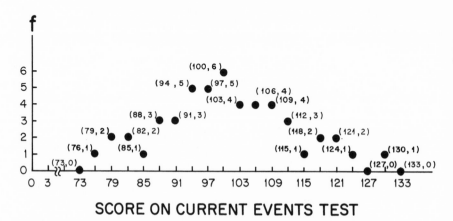

SCORE ON CURRENT EVENTS TEST

Figure 2-6   Frequency polygon of scores. The coordinates of each point are the score value and its frequency.

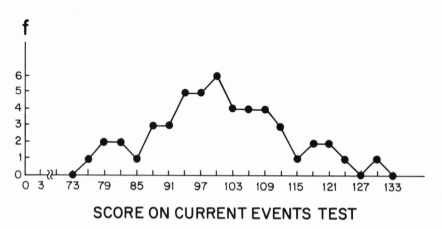

SCORE ON CURRENT EVENTS TEST

Figure 2-7   The frequency polygon is completed by connecting the points with straight lines.

labeled with their coordinates in Figure 2-6. (Ordinarily, we do not include the coordinates but only the points themselves in the frequency polygon.) After all of the points have been located, they are connected with a line, as shown in Figure 2-7. This is what the final frequency polygon should look like.

A frequency polygon and a histogram convey exactly the same information; they are both prepared from the same frequency distribution. The difference is one of focus or emphasis: The frequency polygon emphasizes the numerical values that are used to represent observations, while the histogram emphasizes score intervals. Figure 2-8 illustrates the similarities and differences between them for the second grouped frequency distribution in Table 2-3. Note that both the limits and midpoints have been labeled on the abscissa and that each point for the frequency

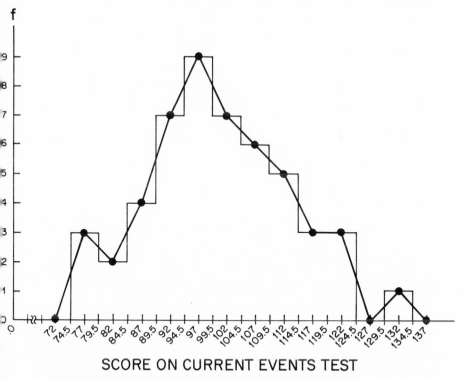

Figure 2-8   The frequency polygon and histogram convey the same information about a set of data.

polygon falls in the middle of the top of the histogram bar for that interval. Notice also the general similarity between the two graphs in Figure 2-8 and those in Figures 2-5 and 2-7, even though the number of intervals is different.

The Cumulative Frequency Curve.   It is also possible to make a graph of the cumulative frequency distribution. Such as graph is called a *cumulative frequency curve,* and it shows how many people scored below a given value in the cumulative frequency distribution.

The procedures for preparing a cumulative frequency curve differ only a little from those for preparing a frequency polygon. First, the axes are laid out and labeled. The abscissa is labeled with the midpoints, and the ordinate is labeled with the cumulative frequency. Then a point is located for each midpoint that has as its coordinates the values of the midpoint and the cumulative frequency of that midpoint. Finally, the points are connected with a line. Figure 2-9 shows the cumulative frequency curve for the distribution of scores in Table 2-4.

There are several important things to notice about the cumulative frequency curve.

1. Like the frequency polygon, it begins with the midpoint of the first interval below the distribution. This means it will start on the abscissa with a *cf* of zero.

2. The cumulative frequency curve never drops back toward the abscissa. While the line of the frequency polygon tends to rise to its highest point near the middle of the distribution and then drops back to the base line, the line for the cumulative frequency curve *never* drops back at all.

3. The curve rises most rapidly where the frequency is greatest (that is, the values corresponding to the highpoints of the frequency polygon) and is horizontal in areas where the frequency is zero. Notice that the curve in Figure 2-9 rises most rapidly over the values between 91 and 109 and that it is flat from 124 to 127.

The curve in Figure 2-9 has a general shape that is very common among cumulative frequency curves. It has the general shape of an *S*, rising slowly at first, then more rapidly, and finally slowly again. Curves with this general shape are known as *ogives.* We shall find these curves useful for estimating some statistical indices in later chapters; however, the major use of this type of curve is in the areas of measurement theory that are beyond our concern.

Curves of Relative Frequency Distributions. Earlier in this chapter, we discussed making frequency distributions where the number of observations in each interval was divided by the total number of

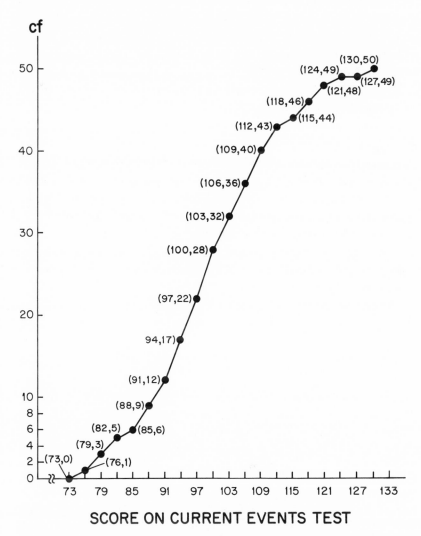

SCORE ON CURRENT EVENTS TEST

Figure 2-9   The cumulative frequency curve is formed by plotting points whose coordinates are the score values and their cumulative frequencies. These points are then connected with straight lines.

observations. Distributions of this kind were called relative frequency
distributions, and the relative frequencies were the *proportions* of
observations falling in each interval. It is possible and often desirable to
prepare graphs of these distributions.

A frequency polygon or histogram is constructed from a relative frequency distribution in exactly the same way as graphs of other frequency
distributions. The only difference is that in the case of relative frequency
distributions, the ordinate is labeled and marked off in proportions. Figure
2-10 shows the relative frequency polygon for the relative frequency distribution in Table 2-5; the shape and size of this figure are exactly the
same as Figure 2-7. The only difference between them is that the height of
the polygon reflects actual frequency or number of cases in Figure 2-7,
while height reflects relative frequency or proportion of cases in Figure
2-10.

Recall the histogram. It may help to look back at Figure 2-4 to see that
the figure is made up of squares representing people or observations. The
area under the figure is 50 units in this example, corresponding to the 50
individuals; similarly, the total area under the frequency polygon is equivalent to the total number of observations. Also, for both of these graphs,
the area of the curve corresponding to a particular interval is equal to the
frequency in that interval, this feature does not characterize the cumulative frequency curve.

In the case of the relative frequency distribution, the total area under

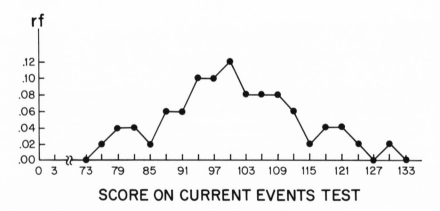

*Figure 2-10   In a relative frequency polygon, the relative frequency f/N of
each score is plotted instead of the frequency.*

the polygon is 100 percent of the group or a proportion of 1.00. Just as the frequencies in the intervals and the areas of the histogram sum to the total frequency, the proportions in the relative frequency distribution and the areas or heights of its frequency polygon sum to the total proportion or 1.00. We shall make extensive use of polygons of relative frequencies or, as they are sometimes called, *unit curves,* in later chapters. All such curves have the properties that the height of the curve above the abscissa indicates relative frequency and the area under the curve is unity (1.00). They have the great advantage of being independent of the number of cases that have been observed and can, therefore, be used to illustrate principles rather than particular examples.

SUMMARY

When data are first collected, they are generally in the form of a list of individuals and their assigned value of some measurable variable. It is usually desirable to simplify and summarize the data by preparing a *frequency distribution.* Observations are grouped by their numerical values, and identification of individual observations is discarded. When there are more than 20 distinct values of the variable, it is often desirable to condense the scores into a *grouped frequency distribution* with 10 to 20 score *intervals.* The number of score values in each interval should be odd, so that the *midpoints* themselves are score values.

Frequency distributions show the number of observations occurring in each category. *Cumulative frequency distributions* show the number of scores that are less than or equal to particular points on the score scale. *Relative frequency distributions* and *relative cumulative frequency distributions* reflect the proportion of observations in each interval and the proportion of scores at or below points on the score scale respectively.

Several kinds of graphs are useful aids for understanding and communicating data. *Pie* and *bar graphs* are used to depict frequencies or proportions for nominal and ordinal variables. Frequency distributions for interval and ratio scale variables take the form of *histograms,* where columns are used to show frequencies in an interval, and *frequency polygons,* which show the frequencies of score values or midpoints of intervals. *Cumulative frequency curves* show the number or proportion of cases falling at or below each score value; these curves are usually *S*-shaped.

*1. While walking through the woods one day, a surveyor made note of the kinds of trees he found along the trail; the observations were as follows:

cedar	pine	dogwood
pine	cedar	cedar
hemlock	hemlock	pine
tamarack	pine	pine
pine	tamarack	tamarack
pine	pine	pine
hemlock	pine	hemlock
tamarack	cedar	pine
pine	hemlock	cedar
pine	pine	dogwood

(a) Summarize these observations with a frequency table.

(b) Construct an appropriate graph for the data.

2. Prepare frequency distributions for the following sets of data. In column one, list the scores, highest to lowest, inclusive, in column two, make check marks for each time a score from the data appears; in column three, list the frequency for the score interval; in column four, list the cumulative frequency.

*(a) 20, 18, 18, 18, 18, 18, 17, 17, 17, 17, 17, 16, 16, 16, 16, 16, 16, 15, 14, 13

*(b) 63, 63, 61, 55, 54, 53, 53, 52, 51, 51, 50, 50, 49, 48, 45, 43, 42, 33, 33, 28

*(c)	35	30	30	30
	29	27	24	23
	21	19		

*(d)	121	115	112	108
	104	104	104	101
	101	100	100	100
	99	96	94	94
	92	92	89	88
	88	88	88	87
	85			

*Answers to starred questions are found in Appendix D.

3. For the data in problem 2, construct a grouped frequency table where it is appropriate to do so.

*4. Construct a frequency polygon from the following table of raw scores:

Score	Frequency
86	*x*
85	*x*
83	*x*
82	*xx*
81	*x*
80	*xxxx*
79	*xx*
78	*xxxx*
77	*xxxxx*
76	*xx*
75	*x*
74	*xxxx*
73	*xxxxx*
72	*xxxx*
71	*xxx*
70	*xxx*
69	*xx*
68	*xx*
65	*x*
60	*x*
59	*x*

5. Construct a frequency polygon from the following frequency distribution:

Score	Frequency
23	1
21	3
19	2
18	2
17	1
16	2
15	3
14	7
13	5
12	1
10	2
9	1
8	2
7	1
6	1
1	1

*6. Construct a histogram from the following table of data:

Score	Frequency
98	x
94	xx
93	x
88	xxxx
87	xxxx
83	xxxxxx
81	xxxx
78	xxxxxxxxx
77	xxxxxxx
75	xxxx
74	xxxx
73	xx
71	xxxx
70	xx
69	x
65	xx
60	x

7. Construct a histogram from the following tabled values:

Score	Frequency
102	1
96	2
93	1
86	2
84	3
80	1
79	4
77	7
76	12
75	14
73	10
72	9
70	5
68	2
67	1
66	2
60	1
59	1

8. From the following frequency distributions, construct a histogram, a frequency polygon, and a cumulative frequency curve:

*(a)

Column 1	Column 2	Column 3	Column 4
29	x	1	35
28		0	34
27		0	34
26		0	34
25	x	1	34
24	xx	2	33
23	xxx	3	31
22		0	28
21	x	1	28
20	x	1	27
19	x	1	26
18	x	1	25
17	xx	2	24
16	xxxxx	5	22
15	xx	2	17
14		0	15
13	x	1	15
12	xxx	3	14
11	xxxx	4	11
10	xxx	3	7
9	xx	2	4
8		0	2
7		0	2
6		0	2
5	xx	2	2

(b)

Column 1	Column 2	Column 3	Column 4
30	x	1	42
29		0	41
28	x	1	41
27	xxx	3	40
26	xxxx	4	37
25	xxxx	4	33
24	xxxxxxx	7	29
23	xxx	3	22
22	xxxxxx	6	19
21	xxx	3	13
20	xx	2	10
19	xxxx	4	8
18	x	1	4
17	xx	2	3
16		0	1
15	x	1	1

9. For the following lists of raw data, a) construct a frequency distribution table with score value, check mark, frequency, and cumulative frequency columns, b) construct a histogram; and c) construct a cumulative frequency curve:

*(a) 66, 67, 68, 68, 69, 69, 69, 69, 71, 71, 71, 72, 72, 72, 72, 72, 73, 73, 73, 73, 74, 74, 75, 75, 76, 76, 76, 76, 76, 76, 76, 76, 77, 77, 78, 78, 79, 79, 79, 79, 80, 80, 81, 81, 81, 82, 83, 84, 86, 89

(b) 1, 5, 6, 7, 8, 8, 10, 11, 12, 13, 14, 13, 14, 14, 14, 14, 15, 15, 15, 16, 16, 16, 16, 16, 17, 17, 17, 17, 18, 20, 20, 20, 21, 21, 28

*(c) 97, 95, 94, 92, 88, 85, 82, 82, 81, 79, 75, 74, 74, 72, 72, 71, 70, 70, 70, 69, 69, 67, 66, 65, 60

(d) For the following data, group the data using 20 intervals: 610, 598, 583, 576, 576, 562, 557, 549, 454, 541, 541, 537, 536, 535, 534, 529, 522, 521, 521, 518, 515, 513, 511, 506, 505, 504, 494, 494, 493, 488, 483, 481, 481, 475, 467, 465, 462, 459, 454, 449, 448, 447, 435, 430, 447, 424, 418, 417, 417

10. With the wholesale price of King Salmon at $2.00 a pound, fishing would be a lucrative business if we knew where to find the fish. Not being old sea salts, let us have numbers help find the fishing grounds. Two friends of ours have returned from fishing last week, and they still have

their sales receipts, which contain number and weight of fish caught. Jim was fishing the Stillaguamish River close by and returned to port every day of the three-day period. Lois was fishing the Samish River farther away; she brought her three-day catch in all at once. From the tabled data, where was the most poundage caught?

Jim—Sept. 7		Jim—Sept. 8		Jim—Sept. 9	
lb	*f*	*lb*	*f*	*lb*	*f*
21	*x*	20	*xx*	19	*xx*
20		19	*x*	18	*x*
19	*xxx*	18	*xxxx*	17	*xxxxx*
18	*xxxx*	17	*xxxxxxxxx*	16	*xxxxx*
17	*xxx*	16	*xxx*	15	*xxxx*
16	*xxx*	15		14	*xx*
15	*x*	14	*x*	13	
14	*xxxxx*			12	*x*

Lois—Sept. 7–9	
lb	*f*
23	*x*
22	
21	*x*
20	*xx*
19	*xxxxxxx*
18	*xxxxxxx*
17	*xxxxxxxxxxxxxx*
16	*xxxxx* ·
15	*xxxxx*
14	*xxxx*
13	*x*

3

MEASURES OF LOCATION

Frequency distributions and graphs are extremely useful for bringing order to a set of data and organizing it so that we can gain an overall picture of the information at hand. These methods of condensing the data work best when it is important to lose very little detail. (No detail is lost with a raw frequency distribution, only individual identification.) Grouping the scores into intervals introduces some inaccuracies, but the pattern in the data may become clearer; however, as methods of summarizing and processing information, both frequency distributions and graphs suffer from two serious faults.

First, they are both extremely inefficient, since they require large amounts of space for presentation and storage, and it often takes a considerable amount of time to study them and compare them with other sources of information. When the amount of information is small or a high level of impact is sought, as is often the case in newspaper and magazine graphs, or it is necessary to retain a high level of detail in the data, as is sometimes necessary in technical research reports, we may be willing to tolerate this inefficiency. However, in daily work and in professional journals, the scientist or scholar has neither the time nor the money (journal space is expensive) to utilize this form of communication.

The second problem with frequency distributions and graphs is that they are an end in themselves. We cannot make quantitative evaluations or predictions or draw statistical inferences from graphs or frequency distributions, although it is certainly possible to make verbal evaluations, predictions, and inferences. We cannot add two histograms together or perform other mathematical operations on them; in fact, we cannot do anything with graphs and frequency distributions except look at them and analyze and compare them visually. Note that this is not to say that we cannot further manipulate and perform analyses on the data (the information-laden numbers that were used to prepare these summaries) but that we must go back to the data.

Our problem, then, is twofold. First, we would like to develop efficient ways to describe the data and communicate their properties; second, we would like these descriptive tools to permit further analysis and comparison. Additionally, we would like to lose as little detail in the information

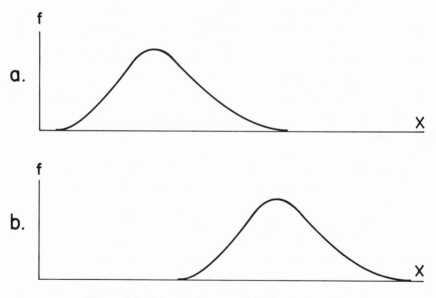

Figure 3-1   Identical curves differing in location.

as possible in the process of summarizing and describing. These conditions, particularly the second, dictate that we seek numerical indices to describe our data.

There are two features of a set of data that are essential in its description; the first of these is the location of the data on the scale of measurement. Figure 3-1 shows two frequency polygons or curves that are the same in every respect except their location on the scale.[1] Location is represented by a numerical index showing where the center of the distribution falls. The second feature of the data that we must describe is the degree of spread or variability among observations. In Figure 3-2, the two frequency curves are centered at the same location on the scale but differ in their variability. In the remainder of this chapter, we cover indices of location or central tendency, while Chapter 4 presents measures of the spread or variability among scores.

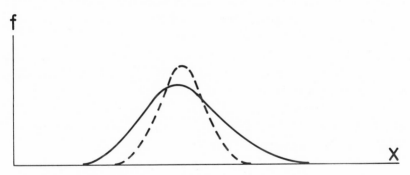

Figure 3-2   Curves with the same center but different variability.

DESIRABLE PROPERTIES OF AN INDEX OF CENTRAL TENDENCY

There are three measures of the location or central tendency of a distribution that behavioral and social scientists have found useful for one or another application; they are the *mode*, the *median*, and the *mean*.

---

[1]Unless a specific set of data is being graphed, we shall use smoothed curves such as those in Figure 3-1 to represent frequency polygons or histograms.

Each of these indices serves certain purposes more or less well than the others. However, it is possible to identify some properties that are generally desirable in a statistical index; they are *uniqueness*, *stability*, *representativeness*, and an *ability to be used in further computations and analyses*.

An index is *unique* if, for a given set of data, one and only one numerical value is possible. An index is *stable* if it does not change much when observing different groups of similar individuals; for example, different first-grade classes in a school district. An index is *representative* if it is close to a large number of the observations in the distribution. In a sense, measures of central tendency are representative by definition; however, we shall see that they satisfy this requirement in different ways and to different degrees. Finally, complete analysis of a set of data, extracting all of the information that the numbers contain, often requires going beyond a single measure of central tendency. An index that permits additional analyses will allow more of the information to be recovered from the data. Without indices that go beyond central tendency, statistics books would be very short!

The Mode.   The *mode* is the numerical value of the score that occurs most frequently in a distribution. From Table 2-2, it is easy to see that the mode of our set of current events scores is 99. This score occurred three times, while other scores, such as 98 and 101, were earned by only two people. Note also that the mode corresponds to the highest point in the graph of a frequency distribution.

This example clearly shows that one of the things to be gained from making a frequency distribution is that the mode immediately becomes obvious. It also shows the primary advantage of the mode as a measure of central tendency: It is easy to determine; no computation is involved. Thus, the mode has two characteristics that make it desirable as an index of central tendency. We are assured that it is representative, since more observations with that value occurred than with any other, and it is easy to obtain.

Unfortunately, the mode does not fare very well on the basis of our other criteria. Since the mode is based only on frequency, only the observations that are at the mode actually determine its value. In this sense, it is not a very representative index because only 3 of 50 observations in our example were used to determine its value.

A second problem with the mode is that it may not yield a unique value. Suppose that three people instead of two had received a score of 106 in our example, so that there are two different score values, 99 and 106, each with a frequency of three. Since there is no way to choose between them, there is no single mode. This problem occurs fairly frequently, and when it does, the resulting distribution is said to be *bimodal*. Figure 3-3 shows some of the possible *multimodal* frequency curves. A frequency distribution that has only one mode is said to be *unimodal*.

Because it is based only on frequency, the mode presents two additional disadvantages. First, it tends to be unstable from one group to another because relatively small shifts in frequency can cause large changes in the mode. Second, the mode is not derived mathematically from the scores themselves, so it cannot be used in any further analyses; it is a dead-end statistic. For these reasons, the mode is seldom satisfactory as the only index of central tendency. It is sometimes reported in conjunction with the median or the mean, but except for cases where the data are clearly nominal, it is seldom reported alone.

The Median. A second way of defining the center of a distribution is to use the point that cuts the distribution exactly in half; this value is called the *median*. The median is defined as the point in the continuous score scale below which exactly 50 percent of the distribution falls.

Sometimes the median can be obtained by counting off cases from the frequency distribution; other times, it is necessary to compute a value for the median. In either case, the first thing to do is determine how many observations there are in 50 percent of the distribution; that is, the first step in determining the median for a set of scores is to divide N, the total number of observations, by 2.

Before going further with the median, let us consider again the idea of a continuous scale, which has infinitely many theoretically possible values. The accuracy of our observations is limited by our techniques of observation and our measurement procedures. Measurements of continuous traits always involve approximations. We might even say that no two people or things are exactly alike on any continuous trait, but we cannot always identify the differences because of the limitations of our measurements.

Suppose that we showed 11 subjects a list of ten words paired with ten symbols and then asked them to recall the words when shown the symbols. The results might be like the scores in Table 3-1. Our subjects recalled up to seven words correctly, with the frequency distribution of

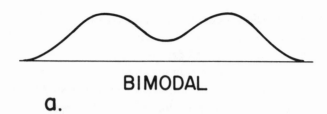

BIMODAL

a.

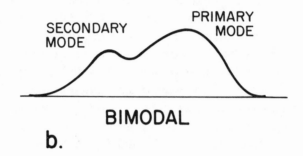

BIMODAL

b.

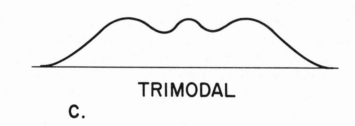

TRIMODAL

c.

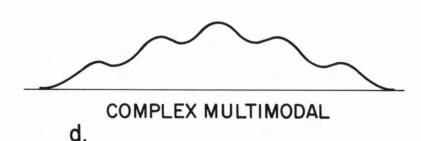

COMPLEX MULTIMODAL

d.

Figure 3-3   Some complex distributions with more than one mode.

scores as shown in the table. If we consider memory to be a continuous trait, we might represent the actual amount of memory of each subject as a position along a line. The true state of affairs might be shown in Figure 3-4, where each individual's identification number has been placed above an X at his position on the line. Individuals 10, 2, 8, and 4 all received a score of 5 because their locations are all between the real limits of the score interval 5; the same is true for the other intervals. (Note that the mode of this distribution is 5.)

To find the median of this set of scores, we must first find $N/2$ or 50 percent of N. Since N is 11, the value we need is 5.5; that is, $5\frac{1}{2}$ of the 11 people fall below the median and $5\frac{1}{2}$ fall above it. The median cuts the middle person in half. Note that if N had been an even number, the median would fall between two people.

The median was defined as the value on the continuous score scale that cuts the distribution in half. Therefore, we have to find the point that corresponds to the $5\frac{1}{2}$th person in the distribution. To do this, we must introduce an assumption about the way the scores are distributed within each score interval. We shall assume that the individual scores are distributed evenly throughout the interval. Thus, the two people in score interval 4 in Figure 3-4 each occupy one-half of the interval; the four

TABLE 3-1
Scores of 11 Research Subjects on a Ten-Item Memory Task.

Individual	Score	Frequency Distribution		
		X	f	cf
1	6	7	1	11
2	5	6	3	10
3	3	5	4	7
4	5	4	2	3
5	7	3	1	1
6	4			
7	6			
8	5			
9	4			
10	5			
11	6			

people in interval 5 each occupy one-fourth of the interval; and the three people in score interval 6 each occupy one-third of that interval.

Now we can find the median; we know that it is the point that splits the sixth person in half. The sixth person is individual number 8. We can see from Figure 3-4 that this subject occupies that part of the score scale from 5.0 to 5.25. Since we must split this subject in half (that is, split the interval in half), the median must be 5.125.

Of course we would never use this graphic procedure to find a median in a real situation. However, the principle underlying the computation of the median follows these steps exactly: First, we must find $N/2$, then locate this point on the score scale as a distance above the lower real limit of the interval containing the point we seek. The formula that is usually used to find the median from a frequency distribution is

$$\text{Mdn} = \text{LL}_i + \left[\frac{N/2 - cf_{i-1}}{f_i} \right]. \tag{3.1}$$

This formula looks much more complicated than it actually is. If we dissect it and examine its parts in light of what we already know, it will not be so formidable.

First, the subscripts i and $i - 1$ are only place indicators for the frequency distribution; they will be used to specify particular score intervals. The symbol LL means lower real limit of a score interval, and f and cf refer to the frequency and cumulative frequency columns of the distribution in Table 3-1. The formula is a sentence that tells us how to combine these values in order to compute the median.

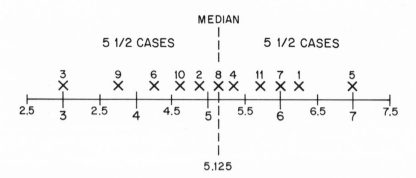

Figure 3-4   Distribution of 11 scores on a memory task; see text for explanation.

As we stated above, the first thing to do is compute $N/2$. This gives us the number of cases we need ($5\frac{1}{2}$ in the present example). Next, we must find the interval that contains the $N/2$th subject; we do this by looking in the *cf* column. The first interval where the value in the *cf* column *equals or exceeds* $N/2$ is the interval that contains the median. Call this interval i (interval i is the score interval 5 in our example). Now we can find all the other values.

LL_i is the lower real limit of interval i.

cf_{i-1} is the value from the *cf* column in the interval immediately below interval i.

f_i is the value from the *f* column for interval i.

By substituting the appropriate values from the data in Table 3-1, formula 3.1 now reads

$$\text{Mdn} = 4.5 + \left[\frac{11/2 - 3}{4}\right].$$

Following these computations through, we get

$$\text{Mdn} = 4.5 + \left[\frac{5.5 - 3}{4}\right]$$

$$= 4.5 + \left[\frac{2.5}{4}\right]$$

$$= 4.5 + .625 = 5.125.$$

This, of course, is exactly the value that we obtained earlier from the graphic approach in Figure 3-4.

There is a direct relationship between what we did in Figure 3-4 and the computations of formula 3.1. In each case, we are, in effect, counting off people until we get to the one we need. In formula 3.1, we locate LL_i as our starting point and as an anchor to the score scale itself. $N/2$ tells us the total number of individuals we need; cf_{i-1} tells us how many we already have by the time we get to LL_i; and the difference, $N/2 - cf_{i-1}$, tells us how many observations we need out of interval i itself. In our example, we need $5\frac{1}{2}$ total observations; we have 3 of them below interval i, so we need $2\frac{1}{2}$ from interval i. Dividing this value by f_i tells us what proportion of the interval we need (remember that we assumed the people spread out evenly throughout the interval). The required proportion for the interval is 0.625, and by adding this to our anchor point, the lower limit of the interval, we obtain 5.125.

As another example, let us take the data in Table 3-2; they are the scores obtained by 340 students on a quiz in an introductory course in sociology. To find the median test score, we first compute $N/2 = 170$. The first interval where cf is greater than or equal to 170 is the score interval 7; this is interval i. We may then compute the median.

$$\text{Mdn} = 6.5 + \frac{170 - 90}{132}$$

$$= 6.5 + \frac{80}{132}$$

$$= 6.5 + 0.606 = 7.106.$$

The median has some definite advantages over the mode as an index of central tendency: It tends to be more stable from group to group than the mode because many more scores must change for the median to shift very much; also, the median must be a single, unique value for a given distribution. Its computation is not really very difficult, and it is representative in the sense that it splits the distribution in half. However, the median does have some drawbacks. First, it may be in a score interval that actually

TABLE 3-2
Frequency Distribution of Scores on a Sociology Quiz.

X	f	cf	
10	8	340	
9	26	332	
8	84	306	
7	132	222	interval i
6	67	90	
5	15	23	
4	6	8	
3	2	2	

contains very few scores; this is most likely to happen in the case of a seriously bimodal distribution. Second, the median is not actually computed from the score values themselves. The only thing that ties the median to the score scale is the lower limit of one interval. No scores are used in its computation, so it cannot be used in further analyses except for a few restricted kinds.

The Mean. When people are asked to give a value that is most typical of a group of observations (for example, what single value would you use to represent the weight of the defensive line of a football team?), the most common answer is the average. The term used in statistics to refer to this concept is the *mean* or, more properly, *the arithmetic mean*, because there are other types of means, such as geometric and harmonic means. We shall restrict our concern to the arithmetic mean and use the single term mean to refer to it.

Most people know how to find an average: Simply add up the values being considered, and divide the sum by the number of things added. For example, if four defensive linemen weigh 255, 265, 270, and 260, respectively, then to find the average weight, find the sum

$$255 + 265 + 270 + 260 = 1050$$

and divide it by the number of things that have been added.

$$\text{Average} = \frac{1050}{4} = 262.5.$$

This basic series of steps is always followed in finding a mean; however, in some cases it will be convenient to express the steps in a slightly different way.

(Brief aside—Notation. Before venturing further, we should become familiar with what statisticians call *summation notation*. Data analysis frequently involves adding up a long list of numbers, and a special way of expressing this process is very useful.

There is a special symbol, sometimes called the summation operator, which looks like an M on its side; this symbol, $\sum$, is the capital Greek letter sigma. It has a particular meaning, just as the symbol $+$ has a particular meaning; $\sum$ means find the sum of the following values. $\sum$ is used in conjunction with the name of some variable; $\sum X$ instructs you to find the sum of the values of the variable X. If X is the weight of our four defensive linemen, then $\sum X$ means find $255 + 265 + 270 + 260$. If X is the score on a test of current events and the values of X are those given in Table 2-1, then $\sum X$ instructs you to find the sum of those 50 scores.

It is often necessary to specify the particular observations that are to be summed; this is accomplished by using *subscripts*. In Table 2-1, each individual was identified by a number that uniquely identified each person. X stands for the test score, and the individual number paired with X specifies which test score we are referring to. The identification number is placed below the letter and is called a subscript; thus, X_{10} refers to the score of individual 10, and the value of X_{10} is 107. Likewise, X_{15} refers to a score of 99, X_{17} has the value 94, and X_{40} is 106. Subscripts are very useful because they allow us to keep track of and refer to long lists of data in a simple shorthand form. (Note that subscripts are also essential in working with computers because they refer to memory locations in the computer. In our work, they refer to locations in the set of data.)

Subscripts are particularly useful when used in a general form; that is, when a letter is used as a variable subscript. The symbol X_i refers to several values of X—those values that could be substituted for i. Used in this way, it is necessary to specify the values of i, and this is done in either of two ways. The most common way is to specify the limits of the subscript on the summation sign.

$$\sum_{i=8}^{15} X_i$$

means to sum those values of the variable X that have subscripts from 8 to 15. In terms of the data from Table 2.2,

$$\sum_{i=1}^{10} X_i = 95 + 104 + 111 + 88 + 79 + 96 + 105 + 130 + 100 + 107$$
$$= 1{,}015$$

and $\sum_{i=8}^{15} X_i = 130 + 100 + 107 + 91 + 102 + 78 + 124 + 99 = 831.$

The other way of specifying subscript limits is to use parentheses following the variable. For example,

$$\sum X_i \qquad (i = 1, 10).$$

In general, the first time an equation is presented and when there might be ambiguity about limits, the limits of each summation will be given. When it is clear over what subscript summation is taking place, only the summation operator, $\sum$, and the subscript on the variable will be given. Thus, $\sum X_i$ means that summation is of the values of X for *all i* observations; the limits $i = 1$, N are assumed.)

Using summation notation (the summation operator and subscripts) allows us to write a very compact expression for finding a mean. We shall use the symbol $\bar{X}$ (X-bar) to stand for the mean of the values of X. Using summation notation, we may then say that

$$\bar{X} = \frac{\sum\limits_{i=1}^{N} X_i}{N}. \tag{3.2}$$

In words, this formula says that the mean of X's equals the sum of the X's, going from the first to the last value of the subscript i, divided by the number of X's that have been summed. We shall use this general formula many times in the remainder of this book, each time changing slightly what we mean by X. We now have a formula for the mean or arithmetic average, (expression 3.2). Applying this short mathematical instruction to the data in Table 2-1, we find that the sum of those 50 numbers is 5027 and that the mean is (5027)/50 or 100.54.

The mean has certain definite advantages over the mode and the median as a measure of central tendency. It shares with the median the feature of being a unique value for any given set of data, but unlike the median, every single score enters directly into the computation of the mean. In this sense, it is more representative of all the data than the median is; however, for exactly the same reason, the mean is more affected by extreme or atypical scores. For example, if the bottom two scores among our 50 Japanese veterans had been zeros instead of 76 and 78, the median would not change, but the mean would be 97.46, a change of over three points.

The mean has two other advantages over the median. First, it is generally less subject to fluctuation from one group to another; it is more stable. Second, and perhaps most important, it is a mathematical function of all of the scores and, therefore, may be used in further computations. It is permissible and useful to add means, subtract means, and treat them just like the original scores. Most of the techniques of data analysis that will occupy our attention in later chapters are based on computations involving the mean.

CENTRAL TENDENCY FROM GROUPED
FREQUENCY DISTRIBUTIONS

We saw in Chapter 2 that it is often useful to group our data into intervals so that the properties of the frequency distribution may be more easily seen. Grouping the data introduces some loss of detail in the frequency distribution because all of the scores in an interval are represented by the midpoint of the interval. We may be willing to pay this price in exchange for the added understanding that grouping provides.

Various ways of finding indices of central tendency from grouped data have been developed. Originally, these procedures were developed to make computations involving large sets of numbers easier and less time-consuming. Modern computers have eliminated the computational drudgery, but learning how to handle grouped data will help the student in two ways: First, data may come to her/him already grouped into intervals, or s/he may not have access to a computer; second, seeing a principle or procedure applied in a similar but not identical context often helps develop a more thorough understanding of the principle or procedure.

Mode. The *mode* for a grouped frequency distribution is the midpoint of the interval with the highest frequency. The *modal class* or *modal interval* is the interval that has the highest frequency. For example, in Table 2-4 for an interval of 5, the mode is 97, the midpoint of the interval, and the modal class is 95–99. Note that it makes a difference how the intervals have been selected: If an interval width of 3 is used for these data, the mode is 99, with a modal class of 98–100.

Median. Computing the *median* from a grouped frequency distribution is almost identical to computing it from the raw frequency distribution. The only difference is that we must adjust for the width of the interval. The formula is

$$Mdn = LL_i + \left(\frac{N/2 - cf_{i-1}}{f_i}\right) \cdot I \tag{3.3}$$

where each of the symbols has the same meaning that it had in equation 3.1, and the symbol I is the width of the interval. Using the grouped frequency distribution with an interval width of 5 in Table 2-4, we first calculate $N/2 = 25$. The first interval where the cf equals or exceeds 25 is the interval 95–99. (Note that in this case the $cf = 25$.) The lower limit of this interval is 94.5; cf_{i-1} is 16; $f_i = 9$; and the interval width (I) is 5.

Therefore, the rule given in formula 3.3 for finding the median may be rewritten for these particular data as

$$Mdn = 94.5 + \left(\frac{25 - 16}{9}\right) \cdot 5$$

$$= 94.5 + \left(\frac{9}{9}\right) \; 5 = 94.5 + (1) \cdot 5$$

$$= 99.5.$$

For this set of data, the median falls at the boundary between two intervals because exactly half of the observations fall in or below the interval 95–99. Since we have assumed that the nine observations in the interval are spread throughout the interval, the upper boundary of the interval is the point on the score scale that has one-half of the observations below it and one half above. Notice that if we had not multiplied by I, our computations would have resulted in a value of 95.5, which is quite in error. Notice also that formula 3.1 is a special case of formula 3.3, where $I = 1$. Thus, formula 3.3 is the proper general formula for the median and may be used either for raw or grouped frequency distributions.

Mean.   The student may have noticed that we did not mention in our earlier discussion computing the mean from a frequency distribution; the reason is twofold. First, the computations summarized in formula 3.2 are widely familiar, so that most people know how to use this formula even though they may have never seen it. We did not need unnecessary complexity at that point. Second, computation of the mean from a frequency distribution uses exactly the same procedure and formula for either a raw or a grouped distribution; therefore, we delayed introducing the former until it was time to handle both.

Let us look once again at the data from the second part of Table 2-3, which are reproduced here as part of Table 3-3. There are three observations in the interval 75–79, each of which is represented by the midpoint value, 77. The procedure for finding a mean is to add together each of the values of X. From the grouped frequency distribution, we have observed a value of 77 for X three times, a value of 82 twice, 87 four times, and so on. One way to find the mean would be to find

$$77 + 77 + 77 + 82 + 82 + 87 + 87 + 87 + 87 + \ldots$$

However, $77 + 77 + 77 = 3(77) = 231$; $82 + 82 = 2(82) = 164$ and
$87 + 87 + 87 + 87 = 4(87) = 348$. In fact, for each interval, the sum of
the observations in the interval j is equal to the midpoint of the interval
(the numerical value of X_j) multiplied by the number of observations in
the interval (the frequency f_j). Carrying out this operation and placing the
products in a column labeled fX gives us the results shown in Table 3-3.
Summing the values in the f-column gives us

$$\sum_{j=1}^{12} f_j = N,$$

the number of scores that have been summed, and summing the values in
the fX column yields

$$\sum_{j=1}^{12} f_j X_j = \sum_{i=1}^{50} X_i,$$

where the X_j are the 12 interval midpoints and the X_i are the scores of the
50 people as represented by the interval midpoints. That is,

$$\sum_{i=1}^{50} X_i = 77 + 77 + 77 + 82 + 82 + 87 + 87 + \dots$$

TABLE 3-3
Computing the Sum of Scores for Grouped Data.

Interval	X	f	fX
130–34	132	1	132
125–29	127	0	0
120–24	122	3	366
115–19	117	3	351
110–14	112	5	560
105–09	107	6	642
100–04	102	7	714
95–99	97	9	873
90–94	92	7	644
85–89	87	4	348
80–84	82	2	164
75–79	77	3	231
		$\sum_{j=1}^{12} f_j = 50$	$\sum_{j=1}^{12} f_j X_j = 5025$

and

$$\sum_{j=1}^{12} f_j X_j = 3(77) + 2(82) + 4(87) + 7(92) + \ldots$$

Either way of performing the operation yields the same value, 5025. Notice that while this value is different from the value 5027 that we obtained earlier from the raw data, the difference is due to grouping, not to multiplication. If we had computed an fX for each score value listed in Table 2-2 and summed across all score values, we would have obtained 5027.

The general equation for computing a mean from any distribution is

$$\bar{X} = \frac{\sum_{j=1}^{J} f_j X_j}{\sum_{j=1}^{J} f_j} . \tag{3.4}$$

The numerator of this formula, $\sum_{j=1}^{J} f_j X_j$, has already been discussed. Here, J is used to indicate the last score value, so the summation takes place across all score values. Those scores with zero frequency are multiplied by zero and thus have no effect on the total. The denominator, $\sum_{j=1}^{J} f_j$ is the sum of all the frequencies or the total number of observations, N. Formulas 3.2 and 3.4 are equivalent. As was the case with the median, the formula for raw data is just a special case of the formula for grouped data.

THE SHAPE OF FREQUENCY DISTRIBUTIONS

Frequency distributions and their graphs were discussed in Chapter 2. We bring them up again here because graphs can sometimes help develop an understanding of the properties of the mode, median, and mean.

First, we must master a little vocabulary. Figure 3-5 shows three frequency curves illustrating the different properties that a frequency distribution may possess. The first of these is called a unimodal symmetric distribution: There is a single mode; it is exactly in the middle of the distribution; and the frequency in each score interval drops off at the same rate on both sides of the mode. In any unimodal symmetric distribution, the mean and median will have the same value as the mode. Distributions with this general shape are quite common in work with psychological tests, anthropometric measures, and educational-achievement test scores. Many of the procedures discussed in Parts II and III are based on the assumption that the data have this type of distribution.

The other two curves in Figure 3-5 represent frequency distributions that are *skewed*. A frequency distribution is skewed when there are more observations at one end of the scale than at the other. Skewed distributions occur when an achievement test has been given that is too hard or too easy for those taking it. Also, such variables as personal income often show skewed distributions when there is a lower limit but no upper limit.

Bunching up the scores at one end and the existence of extreme scores at the other moves the mode toward one end of the distribution and the mean toward the other. When the mean has a numerical value that is higher than the median and mode, the resulting distribution is *positively skewed*. A distribution has *negative skew* when the mean is lower than the median and mode.

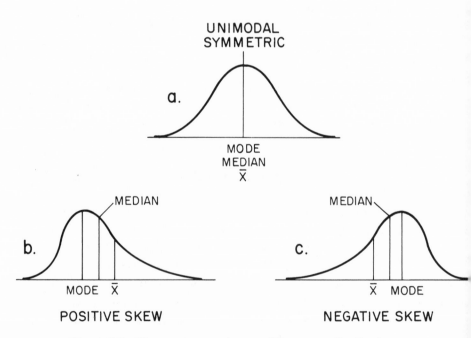

Figure 3-5   Three common shapes of frequency distributions.

CHOICE OF AN INDEX

There are three factors to consider when choosing which index of location or central tendency to use. The first is the level of numerical meaning of the numbers—what type of scale the numbers represent. If the data represent a nominal scale, the mode is usually the only index that makes sense. It is mathematically possible to compute a median or a mean for any set of numbers; the question is whether the resulting value has a meaningful interpretation. For ordinal data, either the mode or the median may be useful, depending on other considerations. When the measurement scale has an interval or ratio level of meaning, any of the indices we have discussed may be used. The second factor to consider is the use to which the index will be put. There are some situations where the only thing that counts is identifying the most frequent event; in other cases, getting an equal number of observations in each side may be important. However, when the scaling properties permit it, we shall find that the mean is the index that satisfies the widest variety of uses.

The final factor to consider is the shape of the frequency distribution. This is closely related to use, because only when the distribution is non-symmetric will the values for the three statistics be different anyway. Remember that the mean will be the highest of the three values for a positively skewed distribution and the lowest of the three for a negatively skewed distribution. Thus, if our use of the index would be benefited by a higher value, we might choose the mean in the case of a positively skewed curve and the mode if the skew is negative. This is just one example of how statistics may be used to support either side of an argument; for others, see *How to Lie with Statistics* (Huff, 1954).

SUMMARY

There are many occasions when it is desirable to use a numerical index to summarize a set of data, since frequency distributions and graphs are inefficient and do not lend themselves to further analysis. Location and spread are two features that should be included in the summary of a frequency distribution. Three indices of location or central tendency are commonly used in the behavioral and social sciences; they are the *mode*, or most frequently occurring score, the *median*, which is the value on the score scale that has exactly 50 percent of the observations below and 50 percent above, and the *mean*, or arithmetic average of the scores. The median and mean can be computed from raw or grouped frequency distributions. The best index to use depends on the type of scale the data represent, the shape of the frequency distribution, and the use the index is to serve.

PROBLEMS

1. Describe two data collection situations where you might expect to obtain a multimodal frequency distribution.

2. State in your own words the steps involved in going from a set of raw data to determining the median.

3. Compute the median and the mean for the following sets of data:
   *(a) 18, 17, 18, 16, 15, 18, 18, 20, 17, 17, 18, 14, 12, 16, 10
   (b) 27, 30, 21, 22, 24, 27, 27, 23, 22, 26, 25, 27, 29, 23, 24
   *(c) 103, 96, 90, 121, 98, 115, 107, 93, 99, 114, 100, 108, 92, 112, 99
   (d) 41, 50, 78, 57, 85, 43, 29, 36, 75, 62, 51, 60, 52, 57, 44

4. Compute the median and mean for the data in problem 8a* and 8b in Chapter 2.

5. What are the median and mean for the following two sets of data?:

*(a)

Score	Frequency
86	x
85	x
83	x
82	xx
81	x
80	xxxx
79	xx
78	xxxx
77	xxxxx
76	xx
75	x
74	xxxx
73	xxxxx
72	xxxx
71	xxx
70	xxx
69	xx
68	xx
65	x
60	x
59	x

*Answers to starred questions are found in Appendix D.

(b)

Score	Frequency
36	xx
35	xxx
34	xxxx
33	xx
32	xxx
31	xxxxxxxx
30	xxxxx
29	xxxxxx
28	xxx
27	xx
26	xxxxx
25	xxx
24	xx
23	xxxxx
22	xx
21	x

6. For the following set of data:

   *(a) Determine the mean and median for the raw data.

   *(b) Prepare a grouped frequency distribution using about ten intervals.

   *(c) Find the mean, median, and mode for the grouped frequency distribution in (b).

   (d) Prepare a grouped frequency distribution using about 20 intervals.

   (e) Find the mean, median, and mode for the grouped frequency distribution in (d).

   (f) Describe the differences you find between the answers to (a), (c), and (e): to what can you attribute these differences?

253	276	320	343
365	383	386	387
393	399	400	425
439	448	449	452
452	452	465	466
470	470	483	483
483	516	523	530
538	538	549	555
559	564	565	587
590	593	596	598
618	624	631	634
643	657	670	674
685	737		

*7. The local flour mill has just installed a new machine for filling 5-pound bags with flour. The first 20 5-pound sacks were weighed to check the accuracy of the machine. From the list of sack weights, calculate the mean and the median. Do the values differ? What is the most frequently occurring weight? Can we tell from the mean value how accurate the machine is? Weight of 5-pound sacks of flour: 5.02, 5.01, 5.01, 5.01, 5.01, 5.01, 5.01, 5.00, 5.00, 5.00, 5.00, 5.00, 5.00, 5.00, 4.99, 4.99, 4.99, 4.99, 4.98, 4.98

*8. In order to run a pharmacological study on the drug caffeine, it is necessary to equate drug dosage with weight, so that each subject gets the same relative dosage. Since it is experimental research, the first population used is animal, for safety's sake, and the most available animal for research is the white rat. From the chart of animal weights determine drug dosage as 1 mg/kg for each animal. What is the average dose given? What is the most frequently prepared dosage? What is the total amount of caffeine we must prepare? What is the average weight of rat? Calculate the median value of rat weight. Which is more representative, the mean or the median?

X *Rat weight*	Y *Drug dose*
267 gm	.267 mg
264	
252	
247	
247	
243	
242	
241	
239	
238	

9. The manager of the local grocery store wants to get an idea of how much each customer spends; a list of the day's sales totals follows. Calculate the average amount spent per customer. What was the most frequent amount spent? Calculate the median amount. Does this value differ from the mean? Which is more representative? In dollars:

3.87, 8.30, 8.42, 8.56, 9.89, 9.90, 10.69, 11.10, 11.48, 11.54, 11.57, 11.63, 11.92, 12.14, 12.39, 12.39, 12.89, 13.20, 13.71, 13.71, 13.84, 13.91, 14.52, 14.65, 14.76, 15.24, 15.28, 15.91, 16.03, 16.13, 16.24, 16.82, 17.51, 17.78, 18.81

Group the data using the rules from Chapter 2; calculate the mean, median, and mode from the grouped data. Do the values from the grouped data differ from the values from the raw data?

The last time the manager went shopping himself, he had the receipt that follows. Calculate the mean amount spent per item. What was the most frequent amount that an item cost? Contrast the total amount of the store manager's grocery receipt with the average spent by customers at his store. What valid conclusions can be made about the differences in amount spent?

Manager Shopping Receipt

0.87
0.99
1.01
1.06
0.99
1.10
1.10
1.11
1.14
1.18

*10. Create a set of ten scores that have a median of 7.5 and a mean of 8.0.

11. Create a set of 25 scores that have a median of 10.3 and a mean of 10.5.

4

MEASURES OF VARIABILITY

In Chapter 3, we described three indices of the location or center of a set of measurements. Using one or more of these statistics, it is possible to specify where on a scale of measurement the center of the distribution falls. This is extremely important information, and a vast body of literature has been developed in psychology and education, for example, based on comparisons of means or medians. However, location is not the only way that groups of measures or sets of scores may differ. In this chapter, we discuss the other major way that two or more sets of measurements may differ from each other; their spread over the scale of measurement or their variability.

The two frequency distributions shown in Figure 4-1 have the same mean, median, and mode. They are located in the same place on the measurement scale, and they are both symmetric, but they are clearly different from each other. In one distribution, the scores cluster tightly around the mean with many scores at or near the mean. A distribution such as this one might be expected on a mathematics achievement test for fifth graders or for the yearly earnings of assembly-line workers in an automobile factory. The other distribution shows relatively fewer observations occurring at any single score value (although scores near the mean still have higher frequencies than those farther away), and the scores spread out across a much wider range of scale values. We might expect a distribution like this for the reading-achievement scores of a fifth-grade class or the earnings of a group of real estate salespeople.

The complete general description of any frequency distribution requires that we specify both its location and its spread. Neither the frequency distribution itself nor its graph are a very efficient means of communication nor very informative. While they both contain all the information that we started with except the identity of individuals, they mask important features with excessive detail. Just as we found it useful to summarize the location of a distribution with a single numerical index, so, too, shall we find it convenient and informative to have a single index that reflects the spread of scores in a distribution. As was the case for central tendency, we shall have a choice of three such indices.

Nominal Scales. Before going any further with measures of variability, we should dispose of the issue of nominally scaled measurements. Remember that nominal measurement does not carry information about more or less of the characteristic. For example, using the nominal scale 1 = baseball, 2 = tennis, 3 = football, increasing numerical values do not mean more or less of any trait. The mode is the only meaningful index of central tendency for such measurements, and it does not indicate location, only the category with greatest frequency. Since the categories of such a scale have no fixed or meaningful order, the concept of the center of the distribution is meaningless. The only summary statement we can

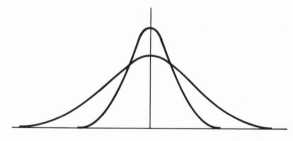

Figure 4-1 *Two distributions at the same location but differing in variability.*

make is that category X (for example, if $X = 3$, X means football) is the most frequently occurring category.

The same properties of nominal scales that prevent interpreting the mode as an index of location on a scale also prevent us from developing any index of variability or spread for a set of nominal measurements. The very idea of spread implies a set of categories with fixed and meaningful quantitative relations to each other. At the very least, the categories of the scale must have a fixed order for even the most crude interpretations of spread. To see that this is the case, remember that the categories on a nominal scale could be designated by letters rather than numbers without losing information. The interpretation of the mode would not be altered, but direction and distance on the scale are not meaningful.

The only way that we can approach the concept of variability for nominal data is to indicate the number of different categories into which our observations are divided. Since the numbers or labels attached to the categories may be completely arbitrary, statistics such as the range are not appropriate. Thus, if we were to collect information about the number of people who play baseball, tennis, and football, we might summarize our findings by saying that we observe three categories of athletics, but not that the range of scores was three scale units. In the discussions to follow, we shall assume that measurements have been made at the level of an ordinal, interval or ratio scale.

THE RANGE

The simplest index of the spread of a set of measurements is called the *range*. It is found by the formula

$$\text{range} = (H - L) + 1 \tag{4.1}$$

That is, find the difference between the highest score and the lowest score and add 1 to that difference. To compute the range for the set of scores in Table 2.2, we find

$$H = 130 \qquad L = 76$$

$$\text{range} = (H - L) + 1 = (130 - 76) + 1 = 54 + 1 = 55$$

There are two interpretations of the range that are useful in many contexts. First, the range specifies the number of unique score values that are covered by a frequency distribution. In our example, there are 55 possible scores between the lowest observed score and the highest observed score. There are several score values that were not obtained by any individual, but these are still unique score values within the range of scores. The second interpretation is that the range is the distance on the measurement scale between the lower real limit of the lowest score interval and the upper real limit of the highest score interval. The upper real limit of interval 130 is 130.5, and the lower real limit of interval 76 is 75.5. We may then state the range as

$$130.5 - 75.5 = 55,$$

which is the same value that we obtained using formula 4.1.

Since this second interpretation of the range implies a distance on the measurement scale, it requires that the data have at least interval scale properties. It is meaningful to use the range when describing variability among the members of a statistics class on a scale of height, on a scale of time to complete an examination, or on the scale of the number of points earned on that examination. Each of these measurements can be thought of as representing at least an interval scale. On the other hand, rank in class is an ordinal scale, so the range could not be interpreted as distance between highest and lowest scores. Note, however, that the first interpretation of the range as the number of unique score values, which in this case is equivalent to the number of individuals in the group, is still appropriate.

The range is a statistic that illustrates clearly a point first made in Chapter 1 and to which we shall return periodically: Numbers by themselves have no scale properties; they can be manipulated by any of the procedures of mathematics, and the results will be meaningful *as mathematical results*. However, the substantive or scientific conclusions that we can draw from any analysis of a set of data are restricted to the meaning that was placed on the numbers by the procedures used to generate them. When a statistic has more than one interpretation, we may be restricted in the interpretations we can make by the scale properties or other aspects of the data. This is quite clearly the case for the range, and we shall see that the principle applies elsewhere as well.

As a measure of the spread of a set of scores, the range has the advantage of being quickly and easily computed; its meaning is also easy to understand. However, certain features of the range make it less desirable than some other indices of variability. First, the range uses very little of the information in a set of measures. It is based on only two scores at the extremes of the distribution and, for this reason, is quite unstable. It can show wide fluctuations from one group to another due to the chance presence of a single extreme individual; for example, if individual number 8 (score of 130) had not been included in the group that provided the data in Table 2-1, the range would have been $(124 - 76) + 1 = 49$, rather than the obtained value of 55. Second, while the range does yield a unique value for any particular set of data, it is a computational dead end; it cannot be used in any additional analyses and does not permit uses or interpretations beyond description of the data at hand.

THE INTERQUARTILE RANGE

A second way of representing the variability or spread in a set of scores is to locate points on the score scale that include some specified percent of the frequency distribution. Two points are of particular interest in this regard: the value that cuts off the bottom 25 percent of the distribution, known as the *first quartile* or Q_1; and the value that cuts off the bottom 75 percent (or top 25 percent) of the distribution, known as the *third quartile* or Q_3. Note that Q_1 and Q_3 bracket or include between them the middle 50 percent of the distribution.

The word *quartile*, of course, means quarter and refers to quarters of the frequency distribution. The first quartile marks off the bottom 25 percent, the second quartile (Q_2) marks off the next 25 percent (or the bottom 50 percent), and the third quartile marks off the next 25 percent (or separates the top 25 percent from the bottom 75 percent). There are four quarters in the distribution but only three quartiles. The second quartile has exactly the same definition and meaning as the median and is computed in the same way. The *interquartile range* is the distance or number of values on the score scale that includes the middle 50 percent of the scores; that is, the distance between Q_3 and Q_1.

The computations needed to find Q_1 and Q_3 are almost identical to those for finding the median. First, we must prepare the frequency distribution and cumulative frequency distribution. We may then use the following formulas to compute Q_1 and Q_3.

$$Q_1 = LL_{0.25} + \left(\frac{0.25\ N - cf_{0.25 - 1}}{f_{0.25}}\right) \cdot I$$

$$Q_3 = LL_{0.75} + \left(\frac{0.75\ N - cf_{0.75 - 1}}{f_{0.75}}\right) \cdot I.$$

(4.2)

In each of these formulas, the terms have meanings very similar to those in formula 3.1.

We can use the data in Table 3-2 that are reproduced here to illustrate the computation of quartiles. To determine Q_1, we must find 0.25 N [0.25(340) = 85], locate the interval that includes this 85th individual, and find the necessary values from the table. Using the rule from Chapter 3 that the interval we seek is the first one where the cumulative frequency equals or exceeds 0.25 N, we select the score interval 6. The 85th person is one of the 67 who received a score of 6. The lower limit of this interval is 5.5, so we compute Q_1 to be

$$Q_1 = 5.5 + \left(\frac{85 - 23}{67}\right) \cdot 1$$

$$= 5.5 + \left(\frac{62}{67}\right) \cdot 1$$

$$= 5.5 + (0.93) \cdot 1$$

$$= 6.43.$$

TABLE 3-2

Frequency Distribution of Scores on a Sociology Quiz.

X	f	cf	
10	8	340	
9	26	332	
8	84	306	interval 0.75
7	132	222	
6	67	90	interval 0.25
5	15	23	
4	6	8	
3	2	2	

Computation of Q_3 for the same set of data proceeds in exactly the same way with the necessary adjustments.

$$0.75 N = 0.75 (340) = 255$$

$$LL_{0.75} = 7.5$$

$$Q_3 = 7.5 + \left(\frac{255 - 222}{84}\right) \cdot 1$$

$$= 7.5 + \left(\frac{33}{84}\right) \cdot 1$$

$$= 7.5 + (0.39) \cdot 1$$

$$= 7.89$$

The interquartile range is the difference between Q_3 and Q_1

$$\text{interquartile range} = Q_3 - Q_1. \tag{4.3}$$

For the data in our present example, this value is found to be

$$Q_3 - Q_1 = 7.89 - 6.43$$

$$= 1.46.$$

The interquartile range may also be computed from a grouped frequency distribution; this is, of course, why the symbol I (interval width) was included in formulas 4.2 and why the value 1 was carried in the two preceding examples. We can use the data in Table 2-3 for an interval width of 5 to illustrate the computations. To find Q_1, we first find

$$0.25 N = 0.25(50) = 12.5.$$

Inspecting the cf column shows that the interval with a midpoint of 92 contains the 12.5th person. Since the score interval is $90 - 95$, its lower limit is 89.5. Then

$$Q_1 = 89.5 + \frac{12.5 - 9}{7} \cdot 5$$

$$= 89.5 + \left(\frac{3.5}{7}\right) \cdot 5$$

$$= 89.5 + (0.5) \cdot 5$$

$$= 89.5 + 2.5$$

$$= 92.0.$$

Because we needed exactly $\frac{1}{2}$ of the cases in the interval, Q_1 turns out to be at the midpoint of the interval.

Using the same general procedure to find Q_3, we get

$$0.75 \, N = 0.75(50) = 37.5$$

$$\mathrm{LL}_{0.75} = 104.5$$

$$Q_3 = 104.5 + \left(\frac{37.5 - 32}{6}\right) \cdot 5$$

$$= 104.5 + \left(\frac{5.5}{6}\right) \cdot 5$$

$$= 104.5 + (0.917) \cdot 5$$

$$= 104.5 + 4.58$$

$$= 109.08,$$

and the interquartile range is

$$Q_3 - Q_1 = 109.08 - 92 = 17.08.$$

Computation of quartiles requires the values of the measurement scale to have a fixed order that is related to the trait or characteristic of interest. However, because the meaning of each quartile value is determined by the number of observed cases falling below that point rather than by how far away those cases are, equal units on the score scale need not be assumed. The data are treated as though they were obtained by using an ordinal scale. Only the observations in the immediate vicinity of the quartile points take part in the calculations.

To illustrate this point, consider the two small frequency distributions in Table 4.1. Each has ten cases and is symmetric around the same median value of 50. The range for distribution A is [(100 − 0) + 1 = 101], while the range for distribution B is only [(53 − 47) + 1 = 7]. The range indicates that the two distributions are very different in spread. Computing the interquartile ranges for the two distributions yields the following results; for distribution A:

$$0.25 \, N = 0.25(10) = 2.5 \qquad 0.75 \, N = 0.75(10) = 7.5$$

$$Q_1 = 48.5 + \frac{2.5 - 1}{2} \cdot 1 \qquad Q_3 = 50.5 + \frac{7.5 - 7}{2} \cdot 1$$

$$Q_1 = 48.5 + \frac{1.5}{2} \qquad\qquad Q_3 = 50.5 + \frac{0.5}{2}$$

$$Q_1 = 49.25 \qquad\qquad Q_3 = 50.75$$

$$\text{Interquartile range} = 50.75 - 49.25 = 1.5$$

For distribution B:

$$0.25\,N = 2.5 \qquad\qquad 0.75\,N = 7.5$$

$$Q_1 = 48.5 + \frac{2.5 - 1}{2} \cdot 1 \qquad\qquad Q_3 = 50.5 + \frac{7.5 - 7}{2} \cdot 1$$

$$Q_1 = 49.25 \qquad\qquad Q_3 = 50.75$$

$$\text{Interquartile range} = 1.5$$

The interquartile ranges for the two distributions are identical! The reason for this result is that extreme cases do not enter into the computation of quartiles; in fact, information from only two score intervals is used to compute any quartile.

The insensitivity of the interquartile range to the presence of extreme scores is perhaps its most appealing feature. We have seen that the range can be greatly affected by a single extreme score and may therefore be quite unrepresentative of the whole distribution and very unstable from group to group. The interquartile range, based on the middle 50 percent of the distribution, is much more stable from one group to another and uses

TABLE 4-1
Two Small Frequency Distributions.

	A			B	
X	f	cf	X	f	cf
100	1	10	53	1	10
52	0	9	52	0	9
51	2	9	51	2	9
50	4	7	50	4	7
49	2	3	49	2	3
48	0	1	48	0	1
0	1	1	47	1	1

more of the information from the entire distribution. Of course, both the range and the interquartile range provide unique values for a given distribution (unlike the problem of multiple modes in expressing central tendency). Like the range and the median, the interquartile range is a statistical dead end in that it does not figure in other more complex analyses of the data.

The major advantage in computing quartiles, beyond the fact that the interquartile range is a measure of the spread or variability for a set of scores from an ordinal scale, lies in the information that they can provide about the skewness of the distribution. To convey the skewness of a distribution, we must compute all three quartiles, Q_1, the median or Q_2, and Q_3. For any symmetric distribution, $Q_2 - Q_1 = Q_3 - Q_2$; that is, the median falls exactly half way between the first and third quartiles for all exactly symmetric distributions. If the distribution of scores is positively skewed, $Q_3 - Q_2$ will be greater than $Q_2 - Q_1$, while for a negatively skewed curve the reverse will be true; for more extreme degrees of skewness the inequality will be greater. These three conditions are illustrated and summarized in Figure 4-2. While there are other more accurate indices of the direction and amount of skewness in a distribution, the differences between quartiles give a sufficiently accurate picture of the distribution for most communications in the behavioral and social sciences. Also, although describing skewness by the differences between quartiles is less precise than other methods and is a computational dead end, there are few, if any, research problems in these areas where accurate information about skewness is of crucial research interest.

THE VARIANCE AND STANDARD DEVIATION

The topic we now turn to is one of the most difficult for students beginning their study of statistics to grasp. However, it is also at the heart of most of the remaining topics in this book; therefore, it is extremely important that the concepts be thoroughly understood.

First, let us do some thinking about the meaning of the concept of variability and our purpose in using statistics. We noted in Chapter 1 that two reasons for collecting information were description of particular phenomena or groups of individuals and prediction of future events or performances. In most situations, it makes sense to say that we would like our predictions or descriptions to be as close to reality as possible. We

SYMMETRIC DISTRIBUTION

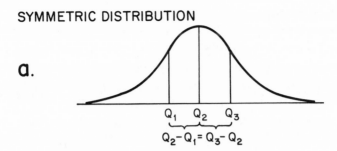

POSITIVE SKEW

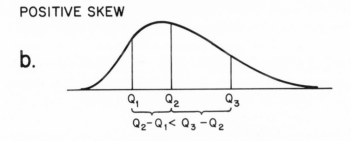

NEGATIVE SKEW

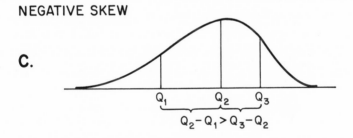

EXTREME POSITIVE SKEW

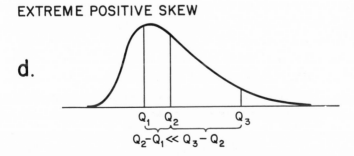

Figure 4-2   Effect of skew on the differences between quartiles.

can, of course, be completely accurate within the limits of our measurement procedures by reporting every observation. However, for reasons discussed in Chapter 3, basically efficiency of communication and insight into the data, it is usually desirable to report a single value to represent the center or location of the set of scores. We have described three statistics that can be used for this purpose: the mode, median, and mean and mentioned some of the advantages and limitations of each.

Any time we use a single value to represent several numerically different scores, that single value will be a better representation of some scores than others in the sense that it will be closer to some scores than others. For example, the median for each set of scores in Table 4-1 is 50. If we use 50 to describe these sets of scores, it will be exactly right for four of the ten individuals in each set and in error by some amount for the remaining six. One way to think about variability is in terms of the errors that we incur in using a measure of central tendency to describe a set of observations; this is probably the most common way that behavioral and social scientists use the term.

A second way to think about variability, one that is common in engineering and business applications of statistics, is the difference between a targeted or intended outcome and what actually occurred. Suppose, for example, that our company manufactures humdingers (whatever they are). Each humdinger is supposed to weigh 16.03215 grams; however, since no manufacturing process is exactly perfect, not all of our humdingers will weigh that exact amount. There will be errors in manufacture resulting in some overweight humdingers and some that are underweight. We might use the same sort of index to describe these errors in manufacturing that we would use to describe errors in description; in each case, the objective is to describe the amount of variation around some point in the distribution.

It is not really necessary to think of variation in terms of error; in the manufacturing example where there is a target, error is an appropriate concept. However, when describing a group of people, we should not think of the fact that people differ from one another as meaning that some are right and others are in error. A century ago, this idea was popular in psychology: The mean was nature's ideal, and data values differing from the mean were viewed as nature's errors; one of the objectives in designing research studies was to reduce or eliminate such errors. While behavioral science has outgrown the idea that the mean is right and variation from the mean is undesirable, the original terms error and deviation continue in the vernacular of statistics. Therefore, when we use the terms error and deviation in what follows, we do so from tradition and for convenience of exposition and do not imply any positive or negative affective value in being at the mean or differing from the mean.

Suppose that we choose to use the mean to describe the location of our group. There are several reasons beyond those already mentioned in Chapter 3 for making this choice. We shall discuss some of them shortly, but for now, we may decide to use the mean more or less arbitrarily. Given that we use the mean to represent the group, our representation of each individual will be in error or inaccurate by some amount except for those few individuals who score exactly at the mean. For each individual, we can represent the magnitude of this inaccuracy by a *deviation score*, which is the difference between an individual's observed score and the mean for the distribution of scores. A deviation score is ordinarily represented by a lower case letter; thus, if an individual's observed score is represented as X_i, the deviation score would be represented as x_i and defined as

$$x_i = X_i - \bar{X}, \tag{4.4}$$

which expresses each score in terms of its distance from the mean of the scores.

Deviation scores have two important properties to which we must pay careful attention. First, deviation scores are *signed numbers*; that is, some of them are positive and some of them are negative (about half of each in most cases). We *must* keep the sign of a deviation score because the magnitude tells us how far from the mean an observation is, and the sign tells us in which direction to go.

The second important property of deviation scores is that for any group of N observations, the sum of the deviations from the mean of the group is zero; that is,

$$\sum_{i=1}^{N} x_i = 0.$$

To see that this is true, we use the definition of deviation scores from equation 4.4 and a little algebra.

$$\sum_{i=1}^{N} x_i = \sum_{i=1}^{N} (X_i - \bar{X})$$

$$= \sum_{i=1}^{N} X_i - \sum_{i=1}^{N} \bar{X}.$$

Because $\bar{X}$ is a constant (that is, it has only one value for a given distribution), summing it N times is the same as multiplying it by N. Using this point and substituting the definition of the mean from equation 3.2, we get

$$\sum_{i=1}^{N} x_i = \sum_{i=1}^{N} X_i - N \frac{\sum_{i=1}^{N} X_i}{N},$$

which gives us

$$\sum_{i=1}^{N} x_i = \sum_{i=1}^{N} X_i - \sum_{i=1}^{N} X_i = 0.$$

This will always be true for the sum of deviations of any set of scores around their mean. It also makes sense intuitively for $\sum x_i$ to be zero, because since the mean is about in the center of the distribution (indeed, it is exactly at the center in terms of deviation scores) and roughly half the scores are positive and half negative, they should average out to about zero. In fact, since $\sum x_i = 0$, the mean of a set of deviation scores must also be zero.

Since a set of deviation scores must sum to zero and their mean must be zero regardless of the shape of the score distribution, the deviation scores themselves do not help us much in describing the spread of a set of scores. Two methods have been suggested to resolve the problem. The first is to find the mean of the absolute values of the deviation scores; that is, chop off the signs and treat all numbers as positive. The resulting statistic, known as the average deviation, has not been found very useful because, like the range and interquartile range, it is a computational dead end.

A much more satisfactory solution is to square each deviation score (multiply it by itself) and find the mean of these squared deviations. This operation results in a statistic called the *variance*, which, for reasons that will become apparent shortly, is given the symbol S^2. The variance is the mean of squared deviations from the mean.

$$S_X^2 = \frac{\displaystyle\sum_{i=1}^{N} x_i^2}{N} \, . \tag{4.5}$$

Notice that we are using *general operations* for finding a mean (summing and dividing by the number of things summed) but that the operations are being applied to something other than observed scores. Since deviation scores can be expressed in terms of raw scores and their mean ($x_i = X_i - \bar{X}$), the variance can also be written

$$S_X^2 = \frac{\displaystyle\sum_{i=1}^{N} (X_i - \bar{X})^2}{N} \, ,$$

where the operation of squaring is performed before summation.

The variance has proven to be an extremely useful and important statistic. Most of the statistical techniques used by educators, psychologists, and many other behavioral and social scientists are based on the concepts of the mean and variance. We shall use these concepts extensively in the chapters that follow. However, the variance in its present form has a drawback for some descriptive purposes. Because it is computed from squared deviation scores, its numerical value will generally exceed the total range of scores in the distribution. In a sense, it is not on the same scale as the original scores. We can correct this problem by taking the square root of the variance. The resulting statistic, which is in the same scale as the original measurements, is called the *standard deviation*.

The standard deviation, which is sometimes referred to as the [square] root mean squared deviation to express the procedures for computing it, is given the symbol S. Obviously, S^2 is used for the variance because the variance is the square of the standard deviation. The definition of S in the form of an equation is

$$S_X = \sqrt{\frac{\displaystyle\sum_{i=1}^{N} x_i^2}{N}}$$

$$\tag{4.6}$$

$$S_X = \sqrt{\frac{\displaystyle\sum_{i=1}^{N} (X_i - \bar{X})^2}{N}}$$

The two equations are equivalent and give identical numerical results if used to compute the standard deviation of the scores of N individuals on variable X.

Using the ten scores from part A of Table 4-1, the steps for computing the variance and standard deviation are shown in columns 1–3 of Table 4-2. In this table, each of the ten scores is listed in column 1, its deviation from the group's mean of 50 is given in the second column, and the squared deviations are given in column 3. The same information for the scores from Part B of Table 4-1 is given in columns 4-6, and the two Ss and S^2s are computed below.

TABLE 4-2
Steps in Computing the Variance and Standard Deviation.

	Part A Scores			Part B Scores	
X_i	x_i	x_i^2	X_i	x_i	x_i^2
0	−50	2500	47	−3	9
49	−1	1	49	−1	1
49	−1	1	49	−1	1
50	0	0	50	0	0
50	0	0	50	0	0
50	0	0	50	0	0
50	0	0	50	0	0
51	1	1	51	1	1
51	1	1	51	1	1
100	50	2500	53	3	9

Calculations

$\sum X_i = 500, \ \sum x_i = 0, \ \sum x_i^2 = 5004$

$\bar{X} = 50$

$S_X^2 = \dfrac{\sum x_i^2}{N} = \dfrac{5004}{10} = 500.4$

$S_X = \sqrt{S_X^2} = \sqrt{\dfrac{\sum x_i^2}{N}}$

$\quad = \sqrt{500.4} = 22.37$

$\sum X_i = 500, \ \sum x_i = 0, \ \sum x_i^2 = 22$

$\bar{X} = 50$

$S_X^2 = \dfrac{\sum x_i^2}{N} = \dfrac{22}{10} = 2.2$

$S_X = \sqrt{2.2} = 1.48$

COMPUTATIONAL FORMULAS

Equations 4.5 and 4.6 are known as definitional formulas for the variance and standard deviation, and they express in a fairly direct way the mathematical meaning of these two statistics. However, we would rarely use these formulas to compute a variance or standard deviation with data from an actual study, the reason being that the mean is seldom a whole number, and when it is not, computations can be extremely tedious and rounding error is introduced. With a little algebraic sleight of hand, which is presented in Appendix A at the end of the book, it is possible to convert these equations into ones that look more complicated but are really much easier to use.

There are two useful computational equations for the standard deviation. Each of them involves finding a quantity

$$\sum_{i=1}^{N} X_i^2,$$

which is found by squaring each individual's score and taking the sum of these squares. If the mean has already been computed or will be needed later, it may be convenient to use the formula

$$S = \sqrt{\frac{\sum_{i=1}^{N} X_i^2}{N} - \bar{X}^2}. \tag{4.7}$$

However, using the mean can still involve decimals and may introduce a very small rounding error. An alternate and equivalent formula that requires only one division step is

$$S = \sqrt{\frac{N \sum_{i=1}^{N} X_i^2 - \left(\sum_{i=1}^{N} X_i \right)^2}{N^2}}. \tag{4.8}$$

This formula is particularly convenient to use with calculators that can accumulate sums of scores and sums of squared scores in a single step or with such tabular layouts as those in Table 4-3. In this table, we illustrate the steps in calculating S and S^2 using formulas 4.7 and 4.8 with Part A scores from Table 4-1. These calculations show that when the mean is a

TABLE 4-3
Computing the Variance From a Frequency Distribution
of Deviation Scores.

X	X^2	Calculations
0	0	$S^2 = \dfrac{\sum X_i^2}{N} - \bar{X}^2$
49	2,401	
49	2,401	
50	2,500	$= \dfrac{30,004}{10} - 2,500$
50	2,500	
50	2,500	$= 3,000.4 - 2,500 = 500.4$
50	2,500	
51	2,601	$S = \sqrt{500.4} = 22.37$
51	2,601	
100	10,000	$S^2 = \dfrac{N\sum X_i^2 - (\sum X_i)^2}{N^2}$
$\sum X = 500$	$\sum X^2 = 30,004$	
$\bar{X} = 50$		$= \dfrac{10(30,004) - (500)^2}{(10)^2}$
		$= \dfrac{300,040 - 250,000}{100}$
		$= \dfrac{50,040}{100} = 500.4$

whole number, the several equations for S and S^2 all give exactly the same results.

COMPUTING S AND S^2 FROM A FREQUENCY DISTRIBUTION

When our data are in the form of a frequency distribution, the computation of the standard deviation and variance require a slight revision in our approach. This revision is exactly the same one we encountered when we computed the mean from a frequency distribution or grouped frequency distribution. Recalling that when dealing with data in a frequency distribution, we multiply each score value by its frequency, we can rewrite equation 4.6 as

$$S_X = \sqrt{\dfrac{\sum\limits_{j=1}^{J} f_j x_j^2}{N}} . \tag{4.9}$$

In this equation, there are J separate score values. Of course, we can substitute $(X_j - \bar{X})^2$ for x_j^2, and N is equal to $\sum\limits_{j=1}^{J} f_j$. The details, using the Part A frequency distribution from Table 4-1, are given in Table 4-4.

We would not ordinarily use equation 4.9 to compute S for the same reason that we would not use equation 4.6. Instead, we note that the following equalities hold for data in a frequency distribution:

$$\sum_{j=1}^{J} f_j X_j^2 = \sum_{i=1}^{N} X_i^2$$

$$\left(\sum_{j=1}^{J} f_j X_j\right)^2 = \left(\sum_{i=1}^{N} X_i\right)^2$$

$$\sum_{j=1}^{J} f_j = N$$

and, by substituting into 4.7 and 4.8, we obtain

TABLE 4-4

Computing the Variance From a Frequency Distribution of Deviation Scores.

X	f	x	x^2	fx^2
100	1	50	2500	2500
52	0	2	4	0
51	2	1	1	2
50	4	0	0	0
49	2	−1	1	2
48	0	−2	4	0
0	1	−50	2500	2500

Calculations

$$\sum_{j=1}^{J} f_j = 10 \qquad\qquad \sum_{j=1}^{J} f_j x_j^2 = 5004$$

$$S^2 = \frac{\sum\limits_{j=1}^{J} f_j x_j^2}{N} = \frac{5004}{10} = 500.4$$

$$S = \sqrt{\frac{\sum\limits_{j=1}^{J} f_j X_j^2}{\sum\limits_{j=1}^{J} f_j} - \bar{X}^2} \qquad (4.10)$$

$$S = \sqrt{\frac{\left(\sum\limits_{j=1}^{J} f_j\right)\left(\sum\limits_{j=1}^{J} f_j X_j^2\right) - \left(\sum\limits_{j=1}^{J} f_j X_j\right)^2}{\left(\sum\limits_{j=1}^{J} f_j\right)^2}}. \qquad (4.11)$$

These equations, particularly 4.11, look formidable indeed, but they really only represent terms from the bottom of a table prepared from the frequency distribution.

We shall use the frequency distribution from Table 3-2, which has been reproduced in Table 4-5, to illustrate the use of equations 4.10 and 4.11. This example demonstrates fairly well the advantages of using frequency

TABLE 4-5

Computing S From a Frequency Distribution of Raw Scores.

X_j	f_j	$f_j X_j$	X_j^2	$f_j X_j^2$
10	8	80	100	800
9	26	234	81	2,106
8	84	672	64	5,376
7	132	924	49	6,468
6	67	402	36	2,412
5	15	75	25	375
4	6	24	16	96
3	2	6	9	18

Calculations

$\sum f_j = 340$ $\qquad\qquad \sum f_j X_j = 2,417$ $\qquad\qquad \sum f_j X_j^2 = 17,651$

$\bar{X} = 7.108823529$

$$S_X = \sqrt{\frac{17,651}{340} - (7.1088)^2} = \sqrt{51.9147 - 50.5350}$$

$$= \sqrt{1.3797} = 1.175$$

$$S_X = \sqrt{\frac{(340)(17,651) - (2,417)^2}{(340)^2}} = \sqrt{\frac{6,001,340 - 5,841,889}{115,600}}$$

$$= \sqrt{\frac{159,451}{115,600}} = \sqrt{1.3793} = 1.174$$

distributions and the appropriate equations for computing S when the number of observations is fairly large. Rather than squaring and summing for 340 scores, we can carry out all computations on only eight score values. Even with the aid of an advanced modern calculator, the computations are easier, and the likelihood of error is less when working with the frequency distribution. The computations in Table 4-5 also illustrate the previously mentioned small rounding error, that can occur when formula 4.7 or 4.10 is used rather than 4.8 or 4.11.

Any of the equations 4.9–4.11 can also be used when the data are presented in the form of a grouped frequency distribution. The only adjustment that we have to make in our thinking is to remember that we are using the midpoints of the intervals as our score values. Applying formula 4.11 to grouped frequency data is illustrated in Table 4-6 for our Japanese war-veteran data with an interval of 5. For the sake of comparison, we

TABLE 4-6

Computing S From a Grouped Frequency Distribution.

X_j	f_j	X_j^2	$f_j X_j$	$f_j X_j^2$
132	1	17,424	132	17,424
127	0	16,129	0	0
122	3	14,884	366	44,652
117	3	13,689	351	41,067
112	5	12,544	560	62,720
107	6	11,449	642	68,694
102	7	10,404	714	72,828
97	9	9,409	873	84,681
92	7	8,464	644	59,248
87	4	7,569	348	30,276
82	2	6,724	164	13,448
77	3	5,929	231	17,787

Calculations

$$\sum f_j = 50 \qquad \sum f_j X_j = 5,025 \qquad \sum f_j X_j^2 = 512,825$$

$$S = \sqrt{\frac{(\sum f_j)(\sum f_j X_j^2) - (\sum f_j X_j)^2}{(\sum f_j)^2}}$$

$$= \sqrt{\frac{50(512,825) - (5,025)^2}{(50)^2}} = \sqrt{\frac{25,681,250 - 25,250,625}{2,500}}$$

$$= \sqrt{\frac{390,625}{2,500}} = \sqrt{156.25}$$

$$S = 12.50$$

note that the standard deviation of the set of scores in Table 2-1 (the raw data) is $S = 12.21$. The difference between this value and the value of 12.50 found in the table is due to inaccuracies introduced by grouping.

Scores are grouped for convenience and in order to obtain a better view of the distribution with the knowledge that grouping may have small and unpredictable effects on the statistics computed from the data. However, the wide availability of modern computational technology has made it possible and relatively painless to have the best of both worlds. Outside the statistics classroom, few people are likely to encounter a situation where a large amount of data must be analyzed by a device as primitive as a modern pocket calculator. Even a small office computer will have sufficient memory to store the original data and can produce both a grouped frequency distribution and a mean and standard deviation computed from the raw data. This enables the user to have the advantageous overview provided by grouping without introducing grouping or rounding errors into the mean and standard deviation.

PROPERTIES OF THE STANDARD DEVIATION

For most situations where a statistic reflecting the spread of a set of measures is needed, the standard deviation is the best statistic to use. It is more stable from one group to another than either the range or the interquartile range; it is more representative of the group in the sense that each score is included in its computation, and it does provide a single index that is unique for the particular set of scores. However, its primary virtue lies in the fact that the standard deviation or its square, the variance, can be used in further computation and in the development of additional statistical concepts. In preparation for our later discussions, we must now introduce two terms that are closely related to the standard deviation.

Sum of Squares. The term sum of squares appears frequently in statistics; it always refers to the *sum of squared deviations*, usually squared deviations from a mean. We have already used the sum of squares in developing the concept of the variance. The symbols $\sum x_i^2$ and $\sum (X_i - \bar{X})^2$ both refer to the sum of squared deviations from the group's mean, where the summation is across all members of the group. The variance may then be defined as the mean sum of squares or the sum of squares divided by the number of observations that are in the group.

One reason for focusing attention on the sum of squares is that sums of squares may be added together for different groups, while variances and standard deviations generally cannot. For example, if we know that two classes took the same final exam in statistics, that the standard deviation in one class with 20 students was 5, and the standard deviation of the other class with 25 students was 10, what is the average standard deviation? To find the answer, we must work backwards. Given $S_1 = 5$ and $S_2 = 10$, we find $S_1^2 = 25$ and $S_2^2 = 100$. The variance is defined as the sum of squares divided by the number of deviations that have been summed. Therefore, the sum of squares (SS) may be found by multiplication

$$SS = N(S^2).$$

In our example, $SS_1 = 20(25)$ and $SS_2 = 25(100)$. We find the sum of squares for the combined group by addition

$$SS_T = SS_1 + SS_2$$
$$= 500 + 2500 = 3000.$$

The resulting sum of squares has been obtained by summing 45 deviations, so to find the combined variance, we compute

$$S_T^2 = \frac{SS_T}{N_1 + N_2} = \frac{SS_1 + SS_2}{N_1 + N_2}$$

$$S_T^2 = \frac{3000}{45} = 66.67.$$

The combined standard deviation is $\sqrt{S_T^2} = 8.16$. Notice that this value differs from what would be obtained either by averaging the standard deviations to get 7.5 or by multiplying each S by its N and finding the average to be 7.78. We may add sums of squares, but we cannot add standard deviations. For the special case where the two groups are the same size, we may average the variances directly, but it is generally better to go through the process of computing the sums of squares and have only one set of steps to remember.

Least Squares. The other important concept related to the standard deviation is least squares. Here we tie together the mean as an index that is generally descriptive of the scores in a distribution and the standard deviation as an index of the accuracy of that description.

Least squares is not a statistic or a numerical value; it is an objective or a criterion that a particular statistic may or may not fulfill. It is a principle that states that we should select as a descriptive value for a set of data the statistic that has the smallest sum of squares. Thus, if we follow the principle of least squares in selecting a single value to describe the test scores of our Japanese war veterans, we must select the value for which

$$\sum_{i=1}^{N} (X_i - A)^2$$

(where A might be anything) is a minimum.

In Appendix A, we show that for any group of scores the mean of the group satisfies the principle of least squares. The quantity $\sum (X_i - \bar{X})^2$ will be smaller than the sum of squared deviations from any other value in the distribution. The fact that the mean satisfies the principle of least squares is a strong argument in favor of using the mean as an index of central tendency. In the least squares sense, it is the value in the center of the distribution and the one most descriptive of each score. The standard deviation is an index of how well the mean fulfills this descriptive function.

SUMMARY

There are three widely used indices of the spread or variability of a set of scores. The *range* is the distance on the scale from the lower limit of the lowest observed score category to the upper limit of the highest observed score category. The range also equals the number of score values covered by the distribution. The range requires an interval scale of measurement for the first interpretation.

The *interquartile range* is the number of measurement units needed to encompass the middle 50 percent of the distribution. The *first quartile* (Q_1) identifies the lowest quarter of the distribution, the *third quartile* (Q_3) cuts off the top quarter of the distribution, and the interquartile range is $Q_3 - Q_1$. The interquartile range is an appropriate index of variation for data that have been obtained by ordinal scale measurement.

The most generally useful and widely used indices of variability are the *standard deviation* and its square, the *variance*. The standard deviation may be used any time it is appropriate to compute a mean. It is computed from the *sum of squares* of deviations from the mean. The mean satisfies the principle of *least squares*, which states that the statistic having the smallest sum of squares should be selected as a descriptive value for a set of data.

PROBLEMS

*1. A teacher measured the heights in inches of 15 students in a class with the following results. What is the range of heights?; the interquartile range? What is the average height?

62, 53, 54, 64, 55, 64, 62, 61, 59, 57, 69, 60, 59, 61, 67

2. A second teacher with a similar class obtained the following measurements. What are the range, interquartile range, and mean of heights in this class?; how do the two classes compare?

59, 63, 70, 57, 59, 53, 55, 62, 61, 66, 59, 59, 60, 62, 61

*3. For the set of data in problem 1, compute the sum of squared deviations and the standard deviation.

4. Compute the standard deviation for the data in problem 2.

5. A statistics teacher has given the class six 25-point quizzes over the term. For each of the following sets of quiz scores, find the range, interquartile range, median, mean, and standard deviation. Do the quizzes seem to be equally difficult?; which, if any, of the distributions seem to be skewed?

   *(a) 8, 10, 10, 12, 3, 11, 7, 8, 11, 8, 5, 7, 12, 15, 14, 9, 10, 13, 4, 7
   (b) 10, 13, 9, 4, 13, 9, 7, 9, 10, 13, 6, 11, 9, 9, 9, 9, 8, 7, 13
   *(c) 17, 7, 10, 5, 8, 11, 21, 16, 13, 18, 6, 8, 11, 5, 16, 22, 20, 13, 2
   (d) 15, 15, 14, 10, 12, 10, 14, 16, 16, 12, 17, 16, 14, 7, 11, 14, 10, 10, 18
   *(e) 13, 17, 9, 15, 7, 10, 11, 11, 12, 9, 14, 8, 16, 22, 17, 15, 16, 8, 12
   (f) 15, 14, 5, 9, 5, 12, 17, 16, 9, 19, 16, 13, 7, 14, 5, 5, 23, 17, 5

---

*Answers to starred questions are found in Appendix D.

6. Construct sets of scores with the following properties:
*(a) $N = 25$, median $= 12$, $Q = 8$.
 (b) $N = 25$, median $= 50$, $Q = 10$.
*(c) $N = 10$, $S = 3$.
 (d) $N = 12$, $S = 4.2$.
*(e) $N = 20$, $X = 8$, $S = 2$.
 (f) $N = 20$, $X = 15$, $S = 3$.

7. Determine the mean, interquartile range, variance, and standard deviation for each of the following frequency distributions:

*(a) X	f	(b) X	f
20	1	35	1
19	0	34	0
18	5	33	0
17	5	32	0
16	6	31	0
15	1	30	3
14	1	29	1
13	1	28	0
		27	1
		26	0
		25	0
		24	1
		23	1
		22	0
		21	1
		20	0
		19	1

8. Compute the interquartile range and standard deviation for the data in the tables that follow:

(a) Interval	x	f	*(b) Interval*	x	f
55–59	57	1	36–38	37	2
50–54	52	4	33–35	34	1
45–49	47	3	30–32	31	4
40–44	42	7	27–29	28	4
35–39	37	10	24–26	25	6
30–34	32	6	21–23	22	5
25–29	27	4	18–20	19	7
20–24	22	5	15–17	16	3
15–19	17	0	12–14	13	2
10–14	12	2	9–11	10	3
			6–8	7	1
			3–5	4	1

9. Calculate the interquartile range and the variance from the grouped frequency table that follows:

Interval	cf
98–100	111
95–97	110
92–94	106
89–91	101
86–88	92
83–85	84
80–82	56
77–79	31
74–76	15
71–73	7
68–70	3
65–67	1

10. Calculate the interquartile range for the data that follow; calculate the variance. Which value is larger, the interquartile range or the standard deviation?

Interval	cf
91–100	90
81–90	81
71–80	73
61–70	62
51–60	50
41–50	41
31–40	27
21–30	12
11–20	12
1–10	3

11. For the following two sets of scores, compute the mean, median, interquartile range, and standard deviation from the raw data. Next, prepare a grouped frequency distribution, and determine the values of the same statistics. Do both methods yield the same value?; why?

*(a) 93, 105, 95, 97, 79, 110, 115, 114, 109, 101, 108, 84, 133, 84, 65, 69, 117, 107, 129, 102, 93, 84, 96, 92, 94, 111, 120, 93, 103, 84, 112, 108, 91, 95, 98

(b) 107, 118, 86, 82, 103, 87, 95, 70, 99, 78, 75, 101, 75, 85, 94, 94, 70, 90, 89, 85, 81, 96, 88, 73, 102, 91, 77, 93, 103, 94, 76, 76, 90, 74, 93, 73, 66, 90, 96, 66

5

TRANSFORMED SCORES

There are many areas of study in the behavioral and social sciences where measurement produces numbers that are quite large; business and financial applications, population geography and demography are only a few of the many areas where analyzing data may involve numbers with three, four, or many more digits. On the other hand, there are research problems in physiological psychology, for example, where very small decimal fractions may result. In this chapter, we shall describe a general procedure for coding or rescaling the data and the effect that such transformations have on computing and interpreting descriptive statistics.

LINEAR TRANSFORMATIONS

The general term for the class of data rescalings in which we are interested is *linear transformations*. It is so named because a graph of the relationship between the original data and the rescaled data is a straight line. If, for example, we show the scale of the original data on the abscissa and place the new scale on the ordinate, we get such a graph as that in Figure 5-1. Each value on the original scale corresponds to exactly one value on the new scale, and these paired values fall on a straight line. The value P on the original scale translates to P' on the new scale, Q translates to Q', R to R', and so on.

One of the advantages of a linear transformation is that it is always possible to write a simple equation to show the relationship between the original scale and the new scale. The general form of the equation for a linear transformation from original scale value X into the paired value X' on the new scale is

$$X' = BX + A \tag{5.1}$$

The value of B is known as the *slope coefficient*; it expresses the relative magnitudes of the units on the two scales. If the new scale requires twice as many units as the original scale, the slope will be 2. For example, if we want to convert from a scale of feet to a scale of inches, it

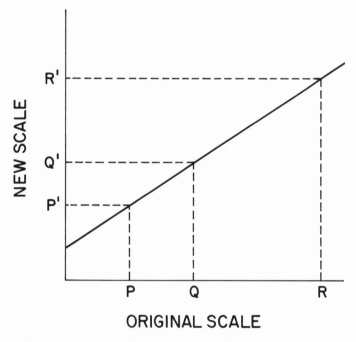

Figure 5-1   In a linear transformation, the relationship between scores on the original scale and scores on the new scale can be expressed as a straight line.

takes 12 times as many inches to express a person's height as it does feet; the slope coefficient is therefore 12. Notice that if we want to go from inches to feet, the slope coefficient is 1/12.

The symbol A in equation 5.1 is called the *intercept*; it gives the value where the graph intercepts the ordinate. When combined with the slope, the intercept completes the definition of a linear relationship, which is illustrated in Figure 5-2. Part **a** shows some of the infinite number of linear relationships passing through the intercept 10, all with different slopes. Part **b** shows just a few of the infinitely many linear relationships with slope 1.5; they are all parallel and have different intercepts. There is, however, one and only one line with slope 1.5 and intercept 10, and the equation

$$X' = 1.5 X + 10$$

specifies this relationship completely and exactly.

One use of a linear relationship that is familiar to most people is the conversion from the Fahrenheit temperature scale to the Celsius or centigrade scale. The temperature of a block of ice or the inside of an oven does not depend on what scale we use to express it. We will burn our hand regardless of whether we express the temperature of boiling water as 100°C or 212°F, but the relationship between the two scales can be expressed as a straight line. Placing the Fahrenheit scale on the ordinate and the Celsius scale on the abcissa, we get the equation

$$F = \frac{9}{5} C + 32$$

which is graphed in Figure 5-3. Using this equation, it is a simple task to compute the value on the F-scale for any temperature on the C-scale and vice versa.

RECENTERING THE DISTRIBUTION

On many occasions, it is desirable to perform the simplest of all linear transformations on a scale: subtracting a constant. This transformation is equivalent to using a slope coefficient of 1.0 and an intercept equal to the constant in equation 5.1 and has the effect of changing the magnitudes of the scores without changing the numerical values of the distances be-

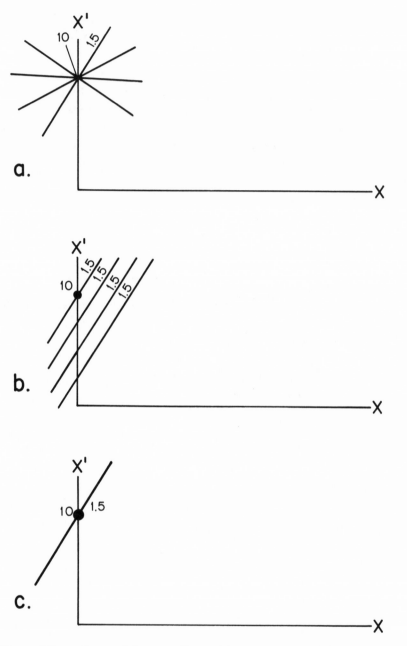

*Figure 5-2   **a.** Some of the many lines with an intercept of 10. **b.** Some of the many lines with a slope of 1.5. **c.** The one line with a slope of 1.5 and an intercept of 10.*

tween score points. Suppose, for example, that two students received test scores of 150 and 170 on a biology test. If we subtract a constant of 100 from both scores, the scores become 50 and 70, but the difference between them is still 20. We could subtract 150 from both scores (getting 0 and 20) or 200 from both (getting −50 and −30), but the difference between the two scores remains 20 units.

There are two reasons why we may wish to perform a transformation of this kind; first, to make computations easier by allowing us to work with smaller numbers. The advantage of this is most obvious when considering calculations involving incomes of countries or major businesses, where the figures may run over eight digits. By subtracting an appropriate value, say 10,000,000, we can make the numbers small enough to fit onto our calculator.

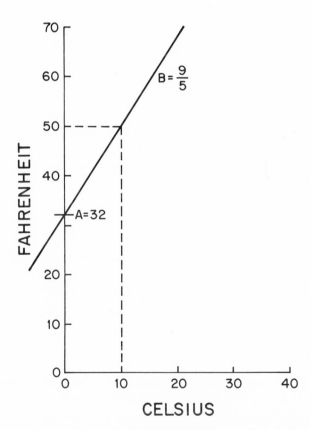

Figure 5-3   Linear relationship between the Fahrenheit and Celcius scales.

The second reason that we may want to subtract a constant from every score is that it may be a necessary intermediate step to an important result. We have already encountered this in Chapter 4, where we developed the idea of deviation scores while obtaining the variance. To compute deviation scores, we subtract a constant, the mean, from every score in the distribution; this has the effect of moving the center of the distribution (considering the mean to be the center) to zero and making roughly half of the scores negative.

Subtracting a constant from a set of scores recenters the distribution at a new point without changing the shape or spread of the distribution. When a constant is subtracted for computational facility, the value of the constant is not crucial and may be chosen for convenience. One common practice is to subtract from every score a value near the lowest score; this means that all scores will be positive numbers but smaller than the original values (we ignore the case where the measurement results in negative numbers on the original scale; in that case, we may wish to add a constant). Of course, if the constant is being subtracted as part of a specific computation, such as to obtain a standard deviation, we must subtract the constant called for. In Figure 5-4, the effects of subtracting the lowest score and the mean are illustrated for a distribution running from 75 to 150 with a mean of 100. Note that neither the positive skew of the distribution nor its range change; all that happens is that the distribution, otherwise unaltered, slides up or down the scale to center on a new point.

Recentering the distribution has a simple effect on the measures of central tendency: Subtracting a constant from each score has the effect of subtracting that same constant from the original values of the mode, median, and mean. That this is so for the mode and median should be obvious from the fact that they are based on the frequencies at one or two score values rather than on the magnitudes of the individuals' scores. The algebra demonstrating the truth of this statement for the mean is given in Appendix A.

To illustrate the procedure, we can take as an example the question of how many pages there are in the average statistics textbook. Suppose we have five books that have 321, 344, 299, 374, and 362 pages, respectively. For a problem this small, it is not too difficult to add up the five numbers and get 1700, which, divided by 5, yields a mean of 340. Let us now subtract a convenient constant, say 300, from every score; this gives us transformed scores of 21, 44, -1, 74, and 62 and a sum of 200. Dividing this sum by 5 yields a mean *of the transformed scores* of 40. If we want to find the mean of the scores in the original scale, we simply add the constant we subtracted from the original scores to the mean of the transformed scores.

The principles for recentering the distribution apply equally when the data have been placed in a grouped frequency distribution. In this case, the constant is subtracted from each interval's midpoint and computations

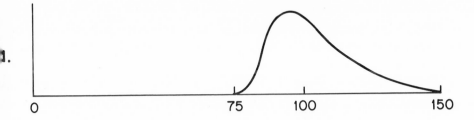

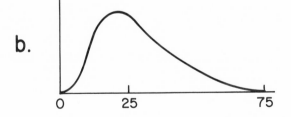

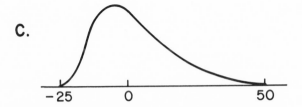

*Figure 5-4   An original distribution (**a**) transformed so that its lowest value is zero (**b**) and so that its mean is zero (**c**).*

proceed in the usual way. Tables 5-1 and 5-2 illustrate the computation of the median and mean using two different constants; the data for both examples come from Table 3-3.

In Table 5-1, the midpoint of the lowest interval, 77, is the constant subtracted from every score. To find the median or the mean, the values in the X' column are used in the appropriate formula from Chapter 3. The values thus obtained are the median (22.5) and mean (23.5) of the distribution of transformed scores that run from 0 to 55. When a constant of 102 is subtracted from each score, the resulting distribution goes from -25 to $+30$, and we find the median and mean to be -2.5 and -1.5, respectively. Note that by adding the constant that was subtracted to the median or

TABLE 5-1

Grouped Frequency Distribution Transformed by Subtracting a Constant of 77 From Every Score.

Interval	X	$X' = X - 77$	f	fX'	cf
130–134	132	55	1	55	50
125–129	127	50	0	0	49
120–124	122	45	3	135	49
115–119	117	40	3	120	46
110–114	112	35	5	175	43
105–109	107	30	6	180	38
100–104	102	25	7	175	32
95– 99	97	20	9	180	25
90– 94	92	15	7	105	16
85– 89	87	10	4	40	9
80– 84	82	5	2	10	5
75– 79	77	0	3	0	3

Calculations

$\sum fX' = 1175$

$\text{Mdn}' = 17.5 + \dfrac{25 - 16}{9} \cdot 5 = 17.5 + \dfrac{9}{9} \cdot 5 = 22.5$

$\text{Mdn} = \text{Mdn}' + 77 = 99.5$

$\bar{X}' = \dfrac{\sum fX'}{N} = \dfrac{1175}{50} = 23.5$

$\bar{X} = \bar{X}' + 77 = 100.5$

TABLE 5-2

Grouped Frequency Distribution Transformed by Subtracting a Constant of 102 From Every Score.

Interval	X	$X' = X - 102$	f	fX'	cf
130–134	132	30	1	30	50
125–129	127	25	0	0	49
120–124	122	20	3	60	49
115–119	117	15	3	45	46
110–114	112	10	5	50	43
105–109	107	5	6	30	38
100–104	102	0	7	0	32
95– 99	97	−5	9	−45	25
90– 94	92	−10	7	−70	16
85– 89	87	−15	4	−60	9
80– 84	82	−20	2	−40	5
75– 79	77	−25	3	−75	3

Calculations

$\sum fX' = -75$

$\text{Mdn}' = -7.5 + \dfrac{25 - 16}{9} \cdot 5 = -7.5 + \dfrac{9}{9} \cdot 5 = -7.5 + 5 = -2.5$

$\text{Mdn} = \text{Mdn}' + 102 = -2.5 + 102 = 99.5$

$\bar{X}' = \dfrac{\sum fX'}{N} = \dfrac{-75}{50} = -1.5$

$\bar{X} = \bar{X}' + 102 = -1.5 + 102 = 100.5$

mean thus obtained, we get the median or mean for the distribution in its original form.

CHANGING UNITS

Adding or subtracting a constant from each score involves only the intercept portion of a linear transformation; the size of the scale units remains the same. It is sometimes useful, though, to change the size of the units on the measurement scale by using a slope coefficient other than 1.0; this is done either to ease computational labors or to reach scale units that have a special meaning. In either case, the transformation now involves both adding or subtracting one constant and multiplying or dividing by another. Each constant may be chosen arbitrarily, but some constants will prove more satisfactory than others.

One very useful choice for a constant comes from the grouped frequency distribution. When the scores have been placed in intervals, dividing each score by the interval width has the effect of making the interval the unit for the new scale. Thus, if there are 15 intervals in the original grouped frequency distribution, there will be 15 score values, one for each interval, on the new scale. When this is combined with a recentering transformation, the result can be numbers that are quite easy to work with. Table 5-3 illustrates the results of two additional transformations for the data in Tables 5-1 and 5-2.

In column 4, the values from Table 5-1 are divided by the interval width 5 to yield a new scale (X'') with values ranging from 0 to 11 in steps of 1 rather than a scale going from 0 to 55 in steps of 5. Column 6 illustrates the consequences of subtracting 102 from the original scores and dividing by 5. Note that in each of these cases, the constant is subtracted first, then division takes place.

The effect on the median and mean of dividing each score by a con-

TABLE 5-3

Two Transformations Involving Both Subtracting a Constant and Dividing by a Constant.

Interval	X	$X' = X - 77$	$X'' = \dfrac{X - 77}{5}$	$X' = X - 102$	$X'' = \dfrac{X -}{5}$
130–134	132	55	11	30	6
125–129	127	50	10	25	5
120–124	122	45	9	20	4
115–119	117	40	8	15	3
110–114	112	35	7	10	2
105–109	107	30	6	5	1
100–104	102	25	5	0	0
95– 99	97	20	4	−5	−1
90– 94	92	15	3	−10	−2
85– 89	87	10	2	−15	−3
80– 84	82	5	1	−20	−4
75– 79	77	0	0	−25	−5

stant is to divide each statistic by that constant; this is shown algebraically for the mean in Appendix A. To obtain the values of the statistics for the data in their original form, it is necessary to perform the transformation in the reverse order: If the transformation involved subtracting 77 from each score and then dividing by 5, the mean of the transformed scores ($\bar{X}''$) can be converted back to the original scale by first multiplying it by 5 and then adding 77; this process is illustrated in Table 5-4. Note that the median and mean of the transformed scores are converted back to the original values by reversing the transformation.

TABLE 5-4
Computing the Mean and Median for Transformed Scores.

X	$X' = X - 77$	$X'' = \dfrac{X'}{5}$	f	fX''	cf
132	55	11	1	11	50
127	50	10	0	0	49
122	45	9	3	27	49
117	40	8	3	24	46
112	35	7	5	35	43
107	30	6	6	36	38
102	25	5	7	35	32
97	20	4	9	36	25
92	15	3	7	21	16
87	10	2	4	8	9
82	5	1	2	2	5
77	0	0	3	0	3

Calculations

$\sum fX'' = 235$

$\text{Mdn}'' = 3.5 + \left(\dfrac{25 - 16}{9}\right)1 = 3.5 + 1 = 4.5$

$\text{Mdn} = [4.5(5)] + 77 = 22.5 + 77 = 99.5$

$\bar{X}'' = \dfrac{\sum fX''}{N} = \dfrac{235}{50} = 4.7$

$\bar{X} = [\bar{X}''(5)] + 77 = 4.7\,(5) + 77$
$\quad = 23.5 + 77 \quad = 100.5$

VARIABILITY OF TRANSFORMED SCORES

We have seen that both portions of a linear transformation affect measures of central tendency and that the same transformation that is applied to the data may also be applied to these statistics. When we come to measures of the variability of a set of data, we find that there may also be both computational and conceptual advantages to certain transformations. However, we shall see that the effects of these transformations are a little less straightforward.

The first thing we may note is that a recentering transformation, adding or subtracting a constant, has no effect on either the interquartile range or the standard deviation because the transformation does not change any of the distances in the distribution. In fact, the definition of the standard deviation involves recentering deviation scores by subtracting the mean from every score. If some other recentering transformation (but not change of units) has already taken place, the new mean is subtracted from each transformed score, resulting in a set of deviation scores identical to what would be obtained from the original scores. We can prove this by subtracting the appropriate means (100.5, 23.5, and -1.5, respectively) from the scores in columns 2, 3, and 5 in Table 5-3. The deviation associated with each interval is the same across all three columns.

The steps in computing the standard deviation and interquartile range from recentered scores are the same as those for the original scores; Table 5-5 shows the steps in the process using the recentered scores in Table 5-2. Note that we have to add the columns for X'^2 and fX'^2 and that the results are the same as those obtained in Chapter 4. When working with data in this form, be careful with negative signs.

Transformations that change the size of the units affect the interquartile range and standard deviation. Dividing each score by a constant has the effect of dividing the interquartile range and the standard deviation by that same constant; this will be true regardless of whether the distribution has been recentered. Once the standard deviation has been computed using transformed scores, its value for the data in the original scale may be obtained by reversing the transformation; the same principle applies to the interquartile range. Note that for the interquartile range, we can proceed either by multiplying Q''_1 and Q''_3 by the chosen constant to obtain Q_1 and Q_3, or we can multiply $(Q''_3 - Q''_1)$ directly.

In the case of the variance, we must proceed in a slightly different way. Since the variance involves squared distances, the effect of the transformation is squared, so the square of the transformation must be applied in reverse to obtain the proper value. The data in the last column of Table 5-3 are used to illustrate the computations in Table 5-6; see Appendix A for the algebra.

TABLE 5-5

Computing Indices of Variability From Scores Transformed by Subtracting a Constant.

X'	f	fX'	X'^2	fX'^2	cf
30	1	30	900	900	50
25	0	0	625	0	49
20	3	60	400	1200	49
15	3	45	225	675	46
10	5	50	100	500	43
5	6	30	25	150	38
0	7	0	0	0	32
−5	9	−45	25	225	25
−10	7	−70	100	700	16
−15	4	−60	225	900	9
−20	2	−40	400	800	5
−25	3	−75	625	1875	3

Calculations

$$\sum fX' = -75 \qquad \sum fX'^2 = 7925$$

$$Q_1' = -12.5 + \frac{12.5 - 9}{7} \cdot 5 = -12.5 + \frac{3.5}{7} \cdot 5 = -12.5 + 2.5 = -10.0$$

$$Q_3' = 2.5 + \frac{37.5 - 32}{6} \cdot 5 = 2.5 + \frac{5.5}{6} \cdot 5 = 2.5 + 4.58 = 7.08$$

$$\text{interquartile range} = Q_3' - Q_1' = 7.08 - (-10.0) = 17.08$$

$$s^2 = \frac{N\sum fX'^2 - (\sum fX')^2}{N^2} = \frac{50(7925) - (-75)^2}{(50)^2} = \frac{396,250 - 5,625}{2,500}$$

$$= \frac{390,625}{2,500} = 156.25$$

$$s = 12.5$$

TABLE 5-6

Computing Indices of Variability From Scores Transformed by
Subtracting a Constant and Dividing by a Constant.

X	$X'' = \dfrac{X - 102}{5}$	f	fX''	X''^2	fX''^2	cf
132	6	1	6	36	36	50
127	5	0	0	25	0	49
122	4	3	12	16	48	49
117	3	3	9	9	27	46
112	2	5	10	4	20	43
107	1	6	6	1	6	38
102	0	7	0	0	0	32
97	-1	9	-9	1	9	25
92	-2	7	-14	4	28	16
87	-3	4	-12	9	36	9
82	-4	2	-8	16	32	5
77	-5	3	-15	25	75	3

Calculations

$\sum fX'' = -15 \qquad \sum fX''^2 = 317$

$Q''_1 = -2.5 + \dfrac{12.5 - 9}{7} = -2.5 + \dfrac{3.5}{7} = -2.0 \qquad Q'_1 = Q''_1 \cdot 5 = -2(5) = -10$

$Q''_3 = +0.5 + \dfrac{37.5 - 32}{6} = 0.5 + 0.917 = 1.417 \qquad Q'_3 = Q''_3 \cdot 5 = 1.417(5) = 7.08$

(Interquartile range) $'' = Q''_3 - Q''_1 = 1.417 - (-2.0) = 3.417$

Interquartile range $= (Q''_3 - Q''_1)5 = 3.417\,(5) = 17.08$

$S''_X = \sqrt{\dfrac{N\sum fX''^2 - (\sum fX'')^2}{N^2}} = \sqrt{\dfrac{50(317) - (-15)^2}{50^2}} = \sqrt{\dfrac{15,850 - 225}{2500}}$

$\qquad = \sqrt{\dfrac{15,625}{2,500}} = \sqrt{6.25} = 2.5$

$S_X = S''_X(5) = 2.5(5) = 12.5$

$S^2_X = S''^2_X[(5)^2] = 6.25(25) = 156.25$

STANDARD SCORES

There is one particular linear transformation that has proven to be extremely useful in the behavioral and social sciences. It is so common that it has been given a special name and symbol, the _standard score trans-_

formation, and it uses the letter z. Scores which have been transformed in this way are known as *standard scores* or *z-scores*.

The standard score transformation involves recentering the distribution at zero and changing the size of the unit to equal the standard deviation. This is accomplished by first subtracting the mean from each score and then dividing the resulting deviation scores by the standard deviation of the original distribution. This may be symbolized

$$z_i = \frac{X_i - \bar{X}}{S_X} , \qquad (5.2)$$

were the standard score for each individual (z_i) is found by subtracting the mean ($\bar{X}$) from the observed score (X_i) and dividing by the standard deviation (S_X).

The reason the standard score transformation is so useful is that it converts any distribution to a new distribution with a mean of zero and a standard deviation of 1. Without regard to the spread or level of the original distribution, the set of z-scores will have $\bar{z} = 0$ and $S_z = 1$ after transformation. The result is that we can take very different distributions and convert them to a comparable metric and then express each observation in terms of a distance in standard score units above or below a standard point. The one reservation that we must always keep in mind is that standard scores are relative to the mean and standard deviation *of the particular group on the particular trait* being measured. Comparisons among groups or traits require the more complex procedures discussed in Chapter 6.

GENERAL EQUATIONS

We have seen that it is possible to compute the mean and standard deviation for a set of measurements either before or after those measurements have been subjected to a linear transformation and arrive at the same result. We now give two equations that present in the most general terms the *processes* involved. The mean of anything may be found by the general process

$$\text{Mean}_T = \frac{\sum_{j=1}^{J} [f_j(T_j)]}{\sum_{j=1}^{J} (f_j)} . \qquad (5.3)$$

That is, the process is one of summation and division by the number of things summed. For raw data that have not been put in a frequency distribution, the f_j at each point is one; T_j is the score for the individual; and the subscript j goes across all individuals. When the data have been put in the form of a frequency distribution, the subscript refers to unique score values; f_j is the number of times a particular value occurs; and T_j is each unique value. For grouped scores, the subscript refers to each interval; f_j to the number of times scores occur in the interval; and T_j is the scale value (mid-point) that represents the interval. Any linear transformation of the data merely assigns new numerical values to T but does not change the computation or meaning of the mean of T.

The same consistency holds for the standard deviation. Using computational formula 4.8 for S in its most general form, we get

$$S_T = \sqrt{\frac{\left[\sum\limits_{j=1}^{J}(f_j)\right]\left\{\sum\limits_{j=1}^{J}[f_j(T_j^2)]\right\} - \left\{\sum\limits_{j=1}^{J}[f_j(T_j)]\right\}^2}{\left\{\sum\limits_{j=1}^{J}(f_j)\right\}^2}}. \tag{5.4}$$

In this formula, each of the letter terms has the same meaning and is used in the same way as in equation 5.3, but the data appear in altered form. The important thing is to pay attention to the exact form in which the data occur and to select the proper values for insertion in the equation. The following equations are all special cases of 5.4. Does the student see that they are all basically the same?

$$S_X = \sqrt{\frac{N\sum X^2 - (\sum X)^2}{N^2}}$$

$$S_X = \sqrt{\frac{(\sum f)(\sum fX^2) - (\sum fX)^2}{(\sum f)^2}}$$

$$S_{X'} = \sqrt{\frac{N\sum X'^2 - (\sum X')^2}{N^2}}$$

$$S_{X''} = \sqrt{\frac{(\sum f)(\sum fX''^2) - (\sum fX'')^2}{(\sum f)^2}}.$$

SUMMARY

It is often useful to perform a *linear transformation* on a set of data. Whether this is done to ease the labor in computing statistics or to recast the data into a form that is more interpretable, all linear transformations may be represented by a straight line when the scale before transformation is placed on one axis of a graph and the scale after transformation is placed on the other. A linear transformation may involve recentering the distribution (adding or subtracting a constant), changing the scale unit (multiplying or dividing by a constant), or both. Recentering changes the value of the mean or median but not the interquartile range or standard deviation. Changing the scale unit will affect both the indices of central tendency and the indices of variability. The value of the mean or median for the scores in the original scale is found by performing the reverse of the transformation on the desired statistic from the transformed scores. Only rescaling transformations (dividing or multiplying by a constant) have to be reversed for the interquartile range and standard deviation. A particularly useful linear transformation is the *standard score* or *z-score* transformation, where the mean is subtracted from each score and the deviation score is divided by the standard deviation. All distributions that have had a *z-score* transformation have a mean of zero and a standard deviation of 1.

PROBLEMS

1. Transform the following distributions by the equation $10X + 3$:
*(a.) 81, 84, 89, 92, 93, 93, 94, 95, 97, 98, 100, 101, 101, 102, 102, 103, 103, 105, 108, 109, 113, 114, 115, 116, 116, 120
(b.) 14, 15, 15, 16, 16, 16, 18, 19, 19, 22
*(c.) 2, 3, 3, 4, 4, 4, 5, 5, 5, 5, 5, 5, 5, 5, 6, 6, 6, 6, 6, 6, 7, 7, 7, 8, 8, 8, 8, 8, 8, 8, 8, 8, 9, 9, 10
(d.) 15, 15, 15, 15, 16, 16, 16, 16, 17, 17, 17, 17, 18, 18, 18, 18, 18, 19, 21, 22
2. Calculate $\bar{X}$ and S for the distributions in 1(a)–1(d) using the raw-score formulas. Also calculate the $\bar{X}$ and S for the transformed distributions; how are the $\bar{X}$'s and S's related?

*Answers to starred questions are found in Appendix D.

3. Transform the following distributions by the equation $5X + 2$:

*(a.) 33, 34, 37, 43, 43, 46, 46, 49, 49, 49, 52, 53, 54, 55, 56, 58, 59, 62, 66, 66

(b.) 47, 50, 58, 66, 67, 68, 69, 71, 73, 73, 74, 74, 75, 76, 78, 78, 79, 80, 80, 85, 86, 86, 87, 88, 89

*(c.) ——————————   (d) ——————————

X	f		X	f
15	2		46	1
14	5		45	3
13	5		44	2
12	6		43	5
11	14		42	4
10	8		41	6
9	6		40	4
8	2		39	2
7	2		38	3
			37	2

4. For each of the sets of data in problem 3, compute the mean, median, interquartile range, and S for the original and transformed scores.

5. A large class in introductory psychology took a final exam. The class mean and standard deviation on this exam were $\bar{X} = 27.3$, $S = 4.7$. Find the z-scores that would correspond to each of the following raw scores:

*(a)	26	(b)	24	*(c)	17	(d)	25
	34		28		20		33
	29		36		27		23
	19		22		32		37

6. Ann, Carol, Mark, and Ted work for the same company. They all arrive at work at the same time, even though they live at different distances from work. It takes each one three minutes to warm up her/his car and five minutes to park and get to the office. Assuming that all of them drive at an average speed of 25 miles an hour, transform the distances that follow into total time it takes each individual to get to work:

Ann	10 miles
Carol	2 miles
Mark	15 miles
Ted	25 miles

6

DESCRIBING THE INDIVIDUAL

Now that we have discussed some of the ways of summarizing a set of measurements and describing a distribution by location and spread, we are in a position to examine in more detail some of the fundamental properties and processes of the measurement operation itself. We have already seen that measurement in the behavioral and social sciences is almost always indirect. We must infer an individual's level of some trait from measures of some manifestation of the trait rather than from observing the trait itself. A positive or "agree" response to the statement "I like most of the people I meet" is not, in itself, the trait of friendliness; rather, it is a response that we would expect from someone who possesses a lot of the trait, and so we infer a high amount of the trait from the response. Measurements of social relationship structures, personality, academic achievement, and a host of other characteristics involve inferences of this kind.

It is the indirect quality of our measurements that presents the greatest problem in the social and behavioral sciences. We have found it impossible to reach general agreement about what constitutes a satisfactory

119

measure of the trait of interest. Two scientists doing research on the effect of having teaching assistants in public-school classrooms may reach different conclusions, and the differences in their results may be due more to the differences in the way they collected their data than to differences in what actually occurred. Until we are able to directly measure the traits of interest or reach widespread agreement on indirect measures, it is unlikely that we shall be able to overcome the problem of defining the traits we study.

Lest the student feel that all is lost and that it would be better to admit perpetual scientific ignorance of social and behavioral phenomena, we should note that there are ways of classifying measurement operations and of manipulating the numbers obtained from the measurements that can help us to draw useful conclusions about the status of an individual. These procedures generally have been developed for educational settings and have seen their most sophisticated application in measuring human ability. However, the ways that they provide for describing observations in quantitative terms that place the individual observation in a meaningful context may prove useful in a broader spectrum of scientific problems.

TYPES OF MEASUREMENT

First, we differentiate between *absolute measures* and *relative measures*. With an absolute measurement, the numbers convey the desired information without further manipulation. For example, the number of words that a child spells correctly from a given list or the number of words that a student can type per minute represent absolute measurement; we need not go beyond the observation itself to obtain useful information about the individual's performance. Knowing that the new typist we hired can type an average of 75 words per minute (including time to put paper in the machine, set margins, and so forth), we can expect that our new employee will complete the typing of a 7500-word manuscript before lunch.

A relative measurement gets its meaning from comparison with something else. We note that Mary spelled 15 words correctly, which is an absolute measurement; however, our interest seldom stops at this point. Is Mary a good speller? This single simple question opens up a whole range of complex issues and answers. To the first question, we must respond, "compared to what or whom?" We might draw one conclusion if

Mary spelled 15 words correctly out of 15 and an entirely different conclusion if she had been given 100 words to spell. Our conclusion could be further modified by Mary's age and by the difficulty of the words she was given. We might want to know whether Mary is a good speller relative to her classmates or relative to students her age from across the country. Of course, the same problems would arise, but to a lesser degree, if we were to inquire whether our new typist was a good typist.

Clearly, the decision whether a measurement is absolute or relative depends upon how it is to be used; however, most of the research that is done on behavior, both human and that of lower organisms, involves some form of comparison with other measures. This is most obvious in educational settings, but it is equally true in psychological and sociological research. We draw the conclusion that a rat has learned to run through a maze by comparing his running time or number of errors on one trial or block of trials with his performance on a previous trial or trials. We conclude that an educational film has improved attitudes by comparing statements made before and after the film.

We shall say more about the comparisons that occur in the research setting in Part III. For the remainder of this chapter, we shall confine our discussion to those particular aspects of relative measurement that involve the description of a single individual or observation. The distinctions and procedures that we now discuss are widely used and misused in public education, industry, and government; they provide the basis for inferring meaning from standardized tests and many academic grading procedures.

Normative and Ipsative Measurement. The definition of some type of standard is fundamental to the measurement process. We have seen that in direct measurement there is widespread agreement about the standard to which a particular entity is compared. In absolute measurement as well, the measuring instrument provides the standard for comparison, and a meaningful numerical value is available without further work. A relative measurement does not provide a meaningful numerical value until the initial result has been compared to some standard other than the measuring instrument itself; that is, the measuring instrument is not itself the standard to which an object is compared. The standard that gives meaning to the numerical result of the measurement operation is other results from the same or similar measurement operations.

We can develop a relative standard from two basic sources of information. Remembering that our task at this point is to describe an individual by using a relative measurement, we may compare the measurement of the individual either with other measurements of the same person or with measurements of other people. When the person's score on one measure is compared to his/her own scores on other measures, the result is called an *ipsative measurement*. Comparison of one person's performance with the performances of other people results in *normative measurement*.

When we ask such questions as is Sally better at basketball than she is at soccer or do you prefer eating ice cream to doing math problems, we are asking for ipsative comparisons. Many measures of vocational interests and of attitudes result in ipsative information, where the individual sets up her/his own standard by providing an ordering for the traits or stimuli. For many purposes, particularly for vocational and personal adjustment counseling, this type of information may be the most desirable. However, there are very few procedures currently in use that provide ipsative information that result in measurements with higher than ordinal-scale properties. Therefore, for some research purposes where it is desirable or necessary to compute more complex statistics in order to answer the research questions, it may be unwise to use ipsative measures because interpreting the results would require the assumption that distance on the scale, as well as direction, has meaning.

Most of the decisions that are made about selecting students for special school programs and employees in industry, for example, involve the comparison of one individual with others. Such questions as is George the best person for this job clearly require comparing George to other potential employees; but the question is Johnny ready to enter second grade also implies a comparison with a standard that is defined by the behavior of others. Tasks are placed at the second-grade level in part because they are things that most children who are about seven years old and have completed one year of school (disregarding kindergarten) can do. An answer to our question requires comparing Johnny with the average beginning second-grader.

NORM GROUPS AND STANDARDIZATION

A normative measurement expresses an individual's status on some trait in comparison with the behavior of other people. The behavior of people defines the standard, and people who are used to provide the standard form the *norm group*. How meaningful a particular normative measurement is depends very much on the quality of the norm group and the extent to which identical measurement procedures were followed in collecting data from the norm group and from this individual about whom we wish to draw conclusions.

The fundamental principle underlying the use of normative measurement is that the person we are now measuring must be compared to a norm group that s/he might belong to. It is not likely to be very useful to compare the behavior of a ten-year-old on some task with that of a group of high-school seniors, since the ten-year-old is not a high-school senior, and their behavior is not going to provide a good standard against which to measure our ten-year-old. The proper standard (except in a few rare cases) would be the behavior of other ten-year-olds. This principle is so important that major commercial producers of educational tests spend millions of dollars on identifying and measuring norm groups, so that adequate normative comparisons will be available for a wide variety of potential test users.

A second factor that is important in all scientific measurements but is particularly acute in normative comparisons is the uniformity of conditions under which the measurements were made. Defining a set of uniform measurement conditions is known as *standardization*. A standardized measure, in particular, a standardized test, is one for which detailed instructions have been prepared covering all aspects of the measurement procedure. The standardized tests that are given throughout the country every year are given to norm groups under carefully specified conditions including verbatim instructions, precise time limits, and as far as possible, quiet and well-lighted surroundings.

When the standard is defined under such conditions, it is necessary to make other measurements under very similar conditions, since the conditions under which the measurement is made are part of the definition of the measurement standard. Measurements using the same questionnaire or set of test items but given under different conditions become measurements with a different scale. Failure to recognize the need to control the conditions surrounding data collection can render the information useless or, even worse, misleading. Much of the meaning that we infer from normative comparisons is based on the assumption that the conditions under which the new measurements were taken replicate quite closely the conditions when the norm group was measured.

The problem of standardization affects many other data collection situations beyond the typical standardized test. Opinion pollsters must be careful to present their questions in the same way every time, or a change in procedure on the part of interviewers may be mistaken for a change in people's attitudes. Experimental psychologists studying avoidance behavior in mice must be certain that changes in heat, light, noise, and so forth do not occur between observations; otherwise, they cannot draw proper conclusions from their data.

Whaley (1973) has defined measurement as a set of procedures for identifying differences. This definition is useful because it draws attention to the importance of standardization in all measurements. Unless a set of standard conditions is specified as part of the measurement process itself, we have no assurance that the differences identified by our measurements represent differences in the trait of interest. In fact, the history of scientific inquiry shows a clear relationship between scientific progress and our ability to control or standardize the conditions under which measurements are made.

INDICES OF RELATIVE POSITION

We have said that the norm group provides the standard for relative measurement. The individual's status on a trait is expressed as the relative position of her/his score on the test or other measuring device in the frequency distribution of scores on that instrument in the norm group. That is, when we are using relative measures, our attention is focused not on the directly observed raw score (such as number of questions answered correctly) but on the relative position of that score in the distribution of scores obtained by an appropriate norm group.

We already have some ways of expressing relative position by using the mean of the distribution or the quartiles. By comparing Johnny's score with the mean of the norm group, we may say that he is average, above average, or below average; that Sally's score of 48 places her in the top 25 percent of her class (it exceeds Q_3). Notice that in the second case, the norm group is Sally's class; this is frequently the case for relative measures in education and is sometimes found in other fields.

It is often desirable to express relative position with greater precision than merely stating that a score is above or below the mean or is in some quarter of the distribution. There are several ways to make more precise statements about a person's relative position. The first two that we shall discuss are ordinal measures very similar to quartiles; the others make use of the mean or the mean and standard deviation.

Percentiles. In Chapters 3 and 4, we described the median and the quartiles, which are special cases of the general concept of a *percentile*. The term percentile refers to the point in a distribution below which some specified portion of the scores fall. In seeking the median, we found the point below which 50 percent of the distribution fell; to locate Q_1 and Q_3, we sought the 25th and 75th percentiles, respectively. In fact, the median (Q_2) and the first (Q_1) and third (Q_3) quartiles are nothing more than points corresponding to special but arbitrarily chosen percentiles. The same general procedure that we used to find these points may be used to calculate any percentile.

Suppose that 59 students in a course in statistics and experimental design were given a 25-point quiz and that the results were as shown in the first two columns of Table 6-1. The instructor has decided that the top 12 percent of the class (and ties) will get As, the next 25 percent will get Bs, the next 40 percent are Cs, and the bottom 5 percent earn grades of F. In order to assign the grades, the instructor must find certain percentiles. If the top 12 percent are to get As, the instructor must find the 88th percentile $(100 - 12 = 88)$; next, the 63rd percentile $[100 - (12 + 25) = 63$ or $88 - 25 = 63]$ must be located. The other required percentiles are the 23rd $(63 - 40 = 23)$ and the fifth.

The general form of the equation that the instructor uses to find percentile P_p is

$$P_p = LL_i + \left(\frac{pN - cf_{i-1}}{f_i} \right) I. \tag{6.1}$$

Each of the terms in this equation has the same meaning that it had for finding the median. The only difference is that we have substituted pN for $N/2$. The letter p in the numerator stands for the desired proportion of the distribution; if we are looking for the 88th percentile, the value of p is 0.88. P_p is the score value that cuts off the desired proportion of the distribution; to find $P_{0.88}$, the computations proceed as follows:

$$pN = 0.88(59) = 51.92.$$

This tells us that we are looking for the 51.92nd person, and by reference to the *cf* column, we find that this individual is one of the four who scored 20; therefore, $LL_i = 19.5$, and we take the other necessary values from the table.

$$P_{0.88} = 19.5 + \left(\frac{51.92 - 49}{4}\right) 1$$

$$= 19.5 + \frac{2.92}{4}$$

$$= 19.5 + 0.73 = 20.23.$$

The scale value 20.23 is the point that cuts off the top 12 percent of the distribution. Because the instructor included ties, all four people who scored 20 plus the six who got higher scores receive As.

TABLE 6-1
Scores of 59 Students on a 25-Point Quiz.

X	f	cf	PR_i	z	IQ
24	1	59	99	1.89	128
23	0	58	98	1.67	125
22	3	58	96	1.45	122
21	2	55	92	1.23	118
20	4	53	86	1.01	115
19	8	49	76	0.79	112
18	6	41	64	0.57	109
17	4	35	56	0.35	105
16	5	31	48	0.13	102
15	3	26	42	−0.09	99
14	4	23	36	−0.31	95
13	3	19	30	−0.53	92
12	4	16	24	−0.75	89
11	2	12	19	−0.97	85
10	3	10	14	−1.19	82
9	1	7	11	−1.41	79
8	2	6	8	−1.63	76
7	2	4	5	−1.85	72
6	1	2	3	−2.07	69
5	0	1	2	−2.29	66
4	1	1	1	−2.51	62

Next, the instructor must find the 63rd percentile. Using the same procedure, we find

$$pN = 0.63(59) = 37.17$$

$$P_{0.63} = 17.5 + \frac{37.17 - 35}{6}$$

$$= 17.5 + \frac{2.17}{6} = 17.5 + 0.36$$

$$= 17.86.$$

The instructor will give Bs to all students who scored 18 or above. The student should now convince her/himself, using the same procedure, that $P_{0.23} = 11.89$ and $P_{0.05} = 6.98$.

Formula 6.1 can be used to find any percentile point for any distribution. If a grouped frequency distribution must be used, it is important to remember to multiply by the interval width (I) before adding the result to LL_i; otherwise, computations always follow the steps outlined. Note that by using $p = 0.25$, $p = 0.50$, and $p = 0.75$, we get the quartiles of the distribution.

Percentile Ranks. Computing percentiles does not actually give us the relative position of each score value in the frequency distribution; that is, percentiles do not provide a relative measurement scale. To obtain such a scale, we must find out *what percent of the distribution falls at or below each observed score value.* The percent of the distribution that falls at or below an observed score is the *percentile rank* of that score.

There are some important differences between percentiles and percentile ranks. It is possible to specify any percentile and compute a point on the *continuous scale* below which that percent of the people fall. Percentile ranks focus on the *discrete scale of obtainable score values.* For example, we could compute an infinite number of percentiles, such as the 36.21835th percentile, for the data in Table 6-1, but there are only 21 score values and, therefore, only 21 computable percentile ranks for the data.

Computing percentile ranks is quite straightforward. We must find the number of individuals whose scores fall below a given observed score value and divide that number by the total number of individuals. Remember that the observed score value is at the middle of each score interval and that we assume that the people whose scores place them in the interval are actually spread throughout the interval. Therefore, to find the number of people in an interval who score below the midpoint of the interval, we must divide the frequency in the interval by 2. The number of people who fall below the particular score value is the number of people who are below the interval entirely plus those people who are in the interval but below its midpoint.

The general formula for computing PR_i is

$$PR_i = \frac{cf_{i-1} + 1/2\, f_i}{N} \,. \tag{6.2}$$

In this formula, PR_i is the percentile rank of observed score i, cf_{i-1} is the cumulative frequency for the next lower score value, f_i is the frequency with which the score i occurs, and N, of course, is the total number of individuals. To find the PR for a score of ten on the quiz in Table 6-1,

$$PR_{10} = \frac{7 + 1.5}{59}$$

$$PR_{10} = \frac{8.5}{59}$$

$$PR_{10} = 0.144.$$

Percentile ranks are almost always given to two places with the decimal point omitted, so this result would be read as a percentile rank of 14.

In the fourth column of Table 6-1, the percentile rank of each score is given. The student should choose one or two score values and convince her/himself that s/he understands how to obtain percentile ranks. Note that PR_5 is not the same as PR_4 even though score value 5 has zero frequency. This occurs because only half of the person who scores 4 is counted as being below 4 and all of her/him falls below 5. Using half of the cases in the extreme score categories and including only score values within the observed score range mean that percentile ranks of 0 and 100 are not possible.

STANDARD SCORES

The most widely used alternative to percentile ranks for creating a relative measurement scale is the standard score transformation. After an appropriate norm group has been measured, the mean and standard deviation of the distribution are found, and every score in the scale can be expressed as a z-score indicating its direction and distance from the mean of the norm group. This series of computations results in a new set of scores, about half of which are negative and half are positive. For our class of 59 statistics students, the mean score was 15.4, with a standard deviation of 4.54. The fifth column in Table 6-1 lists the z-score that is equivalent to each observed score.

Standard scores are seldom left in their original form; they are almost always subjected to some type of linear transformation for final presentation as a relative measurement scale. There are two reasons for this; first, z-scores involve small decimal numbers. Since it is inconvenient to work with numbers like 0.57 as scores, a transformation is used to get rid of the decimal point. Second, about half of the scores in any z-score distribution are always negative, which is undesirable both computationally and socially: Who wants to think of her/himself as a negative quantity?; therefore, the scores are transformed to remove the negative sign.

There are several linear transformations of z-scores that are commonly used in education and psychology; perhaps the most familiar is the so-called IQ scale. This scale uses an arbitrary mean of 100 and an arbitrary standard deviation of 15 (or, for one test, 16). The linear transformation has the general form

$$X_{A_i} = z_i(S_A) + \bar{X}_A. \tag{6.3}$$

The score on the new arbitrary scale is equal to the standard score multiplied by an arbitrary standard deviation and added to an arbitrary mean; for the IQ scale, the equation is $z_i(15) + 100$. The IQ-scale values for each quiz score are given in column 6 for Table 6-1. Notice that we have gotten rid of the decimals and minus signs. The mean of scores on the new scale is 100, and the standard deviation is 15.

Several measures of personality use a transformation with a mean of 50 and a standard deviation of 10; some tests in government and industry are transformed to a mean of 100 and $S = 20$. The College Boards or Scholastic Aptitude Tests (SAT) use a scale with a mean of 500 and a standard deviation of 100. Each has been developed on a norm group and conveys the same general information about the position of an individual's score as some number of standard deviations above or below the mean score of that norm group. Any one of these scales could replace any other without gain or loss of information. They are all equivalent, and they are all equivalent to z-scores.

Let us now compare the information provided by z-scores or their transformations with the information that we get from percentile ranks. The most fundamental difference is the basis upon which the normative scale is constructed. The percentile rank scale is based upon the number of individuals at each score point. If there are more individuals at one place in the distribution than in another, there will be a more rapid change in the percentile rank; the difference in *PR* between two adjacent raw scores will not be the same everywhere in the distribution. In contrast, the standard score scale is based on a single unit of distance on the raw score scale that depends only on the standard deviation, with the zero point determined by the mean. The difference in z-score between any two adjacent raw scores will be the same everywhere in the distribution.

We illustrate this difference using the data in Table 6-1. The difference of one raw score unit is equal to 0.22 units on the z-score scale at all points in the distribution. The change in raw score from 6 to 7 is 0.22 z-units and so is the change from 18 to 19. On the *PR* scale, however, the change of one raw score point from 6 to 7 results in a *PR* change of two points, while the raw score change from 18 to 19 means a *PR* change of 12 points.

The two normative scales are so different because the percentile rank scale changes the shape of the frequency distribution, while the standard score scale does not. If we were to prepare three histograms using the normative scales and the raw score scale on the abscissas, we would get the results shown in Figure 6-1. Histograms **a** and **b** are identical in shape, showing a moderate negative skew; histogram **c**, representing the *PR* scale, is a rectangular distribution showing equal frequency in every interval; this occurs because every interval of ten percent contains 5.9 observations (in our example) without regard for the number of raw score points covered, which results in bars of equal height. In fact, any set of data will yield a rectangular distribution when converted to percentile ranks.

Special Purpose Norms.   There are two additional types of normative scales that are widely used in elementary education and, therefore, have a substantial impact on parents and teachers. They are called *age scales* and *grade scales* and illustrate a third way of developing normative scales. The purpose of these scales is to convey to the user of their information what group of people the measured individual most closely resembles.

The development of age and grade scales requires measuring a large norm group covering a wide range of either ages or grades, depending on

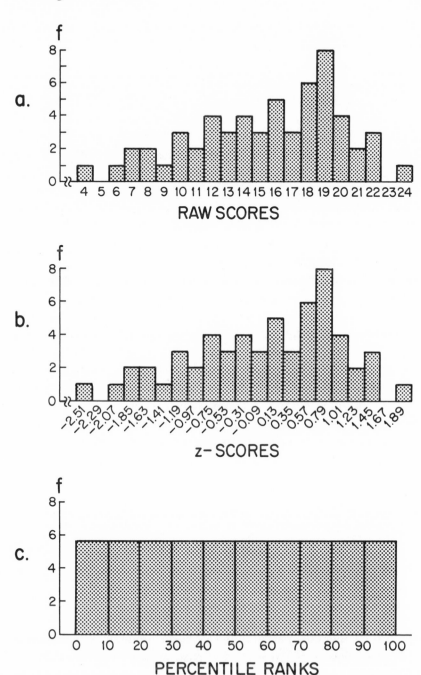

Figure 6-1   Effects of using three different score scales on the abscissa.

the type of scale to be developed. Because these scales are most frequently used with school children, it is not uncommon for both types of scale to be developed from the same norm group.

The principle underlying age and grade scales is that the norm group is subdivided, either by age or by grade, into homogeneous groups. For an age scale, the children are often grouped by age in months, while the division is by years and months of schooling in a grade scale. Then the mean is computed for each of the groups; the raw score that is closest to the mean for children 107 months old is given an age scale value or *age equivalent* of 107 months or eight years 11 months. The raw score that is closest to the mean for students in the seventh month of fifth grade is assigned the *grade equivalent* of 5-7. When new measurements are made, the raw scores for the new individuals are compared to the *tables of norms* from the norm group. The new examinees are assigned age or grade equivalents that indicate the age or grade group that they most closely resemble in terms of score. For example, a grade equivalent of 4-3 on a reading achievement test means that the score of the individual being tested was equal to the mean score obtained on that test by students in the third month of fourth grade.

Age and grade scales are of restricted usefulness outside the period of childhood and adolescence and early formal schooling because they derive their meaning from a common sequence of changes and learning experiences. Such an approach would be useless in an industrial or other occupational setting; however, the scales are mentioned here because they affect almost everyone's life in a test-oriented society and they illustrate an alternative approach to defining a norm-referenced scale of measurement.

INTERPRETING NORMATIVE INFORMATION

There are several factors that must be kept in mind when using normative information. First and foremost, the information gets its meaning from comparison with some norm group; it can be of no higher quality than the basis for comparison permits. If the norm group was poorly defined and/or the measurements of the norm group were carelessly made, no amount of effort on the part of a subsequent user of the scale will ensure high-quality information. This means that the data must be collected from the norm group under uniform conditions that are described in sufficient detail to allow other users of the scale to duplicate the measurement conditions; it also means that the norm group must be described clearly enough to enable other potential users of the scale to decide whether the norm group provides an appropriate standard for the measurements they wish to make.

We have already seen that some scales change the shape of the frequency distribution while others do not; specifically, the information from a percentile rank form of scale is ordinal information. It is important to keep this in mind when choosing which type of scale to use and what analyses to perform on the data in order to answer the questions that prompted the study. Some research questions may be answered using nominal data analyzed by procedures that ordinarily assume an interval level of measurement, while others may require strict adherence to the proper scale level. There is no substitute for careful planning in the choice of variables.

A very common mistake made with normative scales is placing too much faith in the precision of the measurements. Standard scores can be calculated to any number of decimal places, thus giving the impression of high-quality information. In some areas such as business or economic applications, it is quite possible that these numerical values are correct. For example, we may be able to determine the income of a major corporation down to the last penny, and the dollar values of employee benefits, cost of raw materials, and so on may be known exactly. However, in many areas the measurements are not well-defined, and reporting scores or statistics with many decimal values gives a false sense of precision. There is seldom reason to use more than one decimal place in standard score scales in psychology, sociology, or education because the quality of the original information seldom justifies more than this level of precision.

There are a great many other cautions to be observed when interpreting normative scale information for individuals or specific applications; they are thoroughly treated in books that focus on measurement. For our purposes, it is enough to note that for many problems in the social and behavioral sciences, there are two types of standards that can be used in defining a scale to give meaning to the numbers we wish to analyze. One is the data collection procedure itself. Sociologists and psychologists often administer questionnaires and analyze the numbers without reference to any standard other than the verbal content of the questions. The behavior is quantified in terms of the number of errors made, the numerical value the person selects, or some other aspects of the data collection situation. The primary alternative and the main subject of this chapter is using a group's responses as a standard to give meaning to those of an individual. Neither standard is inherently superior to the other, but it is essential to give careful thought to the way that the numerical results will get their meaning *before the data are collected*.

SUMMARY

Measurement scales can be divided into two broad categories, relative and absolute. *Absolute scales* are those where the measuring operation is sufficient to invest the numbers with meaning. *Relative scales* are those where the results of the measuring operation gain meaning through comparison with the results from other measurements. Relative scales may be either *ipsative*, where the comparison is with other measures of the same object or individual, or *normative*, where the comparison is with other objects or individuals. The comparison group is called a *norm group*.

Normative scales may take the form of *percentile ranks*, where the percentile rank of a raw score is equal to the proportion of the scores in the norm group that fall below that point. Alternatively, the raw scores may be converted to standard scores using the mean and standard deviation of the norm group. These z-scores may then be subjected to linear transformation to eliminate decimals and negative values. Age and grade equivalents are other types of normative scales that are used primarily in educational settings.

PROBLEMS

1. For the following distributions calculate the 25th, 47th, and 8th percentiles:
  *(a) 12, 14, 16, 16, 17, 17, 17, 18, 19, 19
  (b) 63, 65, 66, 67, 70, 74, 79, 80, 82, 92
  *(c) 47, 56, 57, 57, 57, 58, 59, 62, 62, 62, 62, 63, 65, 66, 66, 68, 70, 71, 72, 72, 73, 74, 74, 74, 77, 77, 77, 78, 78, 78, 79, 79, 80, 81, 81, 81, 81, 83, 83, 84, 87, 87, 91, 93, 94, 94, 95, 95, 101, 102
*Answers to starred questions are found in Appendix D.

(d) 1, 6, 7, 8, 8, 8, 8, 9, 10, 11, 12, 12, 12, 13, 13, 13, 14, 14, 14, 14, 14, 15, 15, 17, 17, 18, 18, 18, 19, 19, 20, 21, 22, 22, 23

2. For the following distributions calculate the percentile rank of the scores requested:

*(a) 12, 14, 17, 18, 18, 18, 18, 19, 20, 20

$PR_{17} =$

(b) 39, 40, 41, 43, 43, 43, 44, 44, 47, 50, 50, 55, 55, 56, 56, 59, 62, 63, 63, 67, 71

$PR_{63} =$

*(c) 83, 85, 88, 89, 90, 91, 93, 95, 97, 98, 99, 100, 103, 104, 106, 107, 107, 107, 108, 109, 109, 110, 115, 117, 130

$PR_{117} =$

(d) 35, 41, 48, 51, 53, 54, 56, 57, 57, 57, 58, 58, 60, 61, 61, 61, 63, 64, 65, 66, 66, 66, 67, 68, 69, 70, 73, 75, 75, 79, 79, 80, 80, 80, 82, 83, 83, 84, 84, 87, 91, 92, 92, 94, 95, 97, 100, 102, 104, 106

$PR_{57} = \quad PR_{73} = \quad PR_{80} = \quad PR_{91} =$

3. Given the means and standard deviations that follow, find the standard scores corresponding to each score given:

*(a) $\bar{X} = 32$	(b) $\bar{X} = 46$	*(c) $\bar{X} = 5.7$	(d) $\bar{X} = .21$
$S = 4$	$S = 3$	$S = 1.2$	$S = .06$
28	42	8	0.30
31	45	6	0.20
34	48	3	0.10

4. For the data in problem 3, convert to a distribution with a mean of 75 and a standard deviation of 10.

*5. For the following distribution of scores:

(a) Find the 30th-, 45th-, 55th-, and 70th-percentile points.

(b) Calculate the percentile rank for the scores 68, 70, 75, 79, and 87.

(c) Find the mean and standard deviation of the data.

(d) Determine the z-scores of the following raw scores: 68, 75, 79, 87.

(e) Transform these four scores to a distribution with $X = 100$ and $s = 16$.

62, 62, 65, 66, 67, 68, 68, 68, 69, 71, 71, 72, 72, 72, 73, 73, 73, 73, 74, 75, 75, 76, 76, 76, 77, 78, 78, 78, 78, 78, 79, 79, 79, 80, 80, 80, 80, 81, 81, 81, 81, 81, 82, 82, 83, 83, 83, 84, 84, 87

6. Assume that you are an undergraduate sociology major who has obtained a lucrative summer job collecting garbage. Being a particularly well-motivated student, you decide to practice some of the techniques from your spring-term statistics class on your current source of data. To do this, you weigh each garbage can on your route with the following results (in pounds):

58, 28, 25, 51, 31, 35, 47, 37, 38, 38, 43, 29, 37, 45, 33, 37, 37, 35, 37, 42, 42, 34, 26, 33, 31, 41, 20, 41, 32, 25, 30, 29, 36, 40, 31, 38, 28, 23, 32, 39, 42, 39, 31, 54, 41, 29, 35, 33, 54, 36

(a) Find the following percentiles in this distribution: 17, 40, 75, 95.

(b) Find the percentile ranks of the following scores: 20, 30, 40, 50.

(c) Calculate $\bar{X}$ and S.

(d) Determine z-scores for the following raw scores: 20, 30, 40, 50.

(e) If a kilogram is 2.2 pounds, what are the mean and standard deviation of this distribution in kilograms?

(f) Transform the weights of garbage in (d) to IQ scores ($\bar{X} = 100$, $S = 15$).

7. Distinguish between absolute and relative measurement; give two examples of each.

8. Describe a situation where an ipsative measure would be preferred over a normative one, and state why the ipsative measure is more appropriate.

PART II
DESCRIBING RELATIONSHIPS

7

THE NORMAL DISTRIBUTION
AND PROBABILITY

Until now, we have focused on methods for making and describing a set of observations on a single variable. We have been content to summarize the data as they occurred without attempting to impose any theory or explanation on them. This would be sufficient if our objective were merely to describe rather than to predict and understand; however, when we have either of these additional goals, we must go beyond the data we have collected to make predictions about sets of data we have not yet observed (and may never have an opportunity to observe). Note that explaining or understanding a phenomenon implies that we are able to predict its occurrence and its consequences.

The ultimate objective of science is to understand the phenomena under study. Since this implies going beyond the limits of any finite set of observations, it is necessary for all scientists to assume that the entities or events they observed are like those they might have observed but did not. A chemist studying the properties of a complex chemical makes the implicit assumption that the molecules of the chemical that are available for study are not different from all other molecules of the same substance.

139

For the chemist, this assumption is not difficult to justify and is often left unstated; he can generalize the results obtained in a study of substance X to other examples of substance X.

Unfortunately, it is a much more difficult and complex matter to generalize from observed to unobserved entities in the behavioral and social sciences. The entities (particularly people) often have minds of their own and behave in inconsistent ways. There is much more variability among individuals, even when the individuals are microscopic organisms, than there is from one molecule of a chemical to another, and individual organisms change over time.

All of this variability and uncertainty has made it necessary for behavioral and social scientists to develop methods of data analysis that take these factors into account when making predictions and generalizations. In this chapter, we discuss the principles of chance and probability and how they produce a particular frequency distribution, the normal distribution, that has far-reaching significance for statistical analysis; we also discuss methods for rescaling data to produce this distribution.

DISTRIBUTION OF CHANCE EVENTS

Assume that a Las Vegas casino wants to introduce a new gambling game where the players flip Susan B. Anthony silver dollars. The casino owner wants to know what outcomes can be expected if the new game is introduced, so a statistician is hired to forecast the future. Rather than using a crystal ball, the statistician uses logic and computation (crystal balls are very expensive and not too reliable). Let us follow the logical processes that lead to a prediction.

First, our statistician assumes that if a single coin is tossed, it is equally likely to come up heads or tails and it will never stay on edge. Another way to say this is that in a very large number of tosses (call this number T), the coin will come up heads half the time ($T/2$) and tails half the time. (In formal statistical work, T is usually assumed to be infinite.) We now define the *probability* that our coin will come up heads (P_H) as the number of times that a head (N_H) occurred divided by the number of tosses (N)

$$P_H = \frac{N_H}{N} . \tag{7.1}$$

In our example,

$$P_H = \frac{T/2}{T} = \frac{1}{2} = 0.5.$$

The probability that the coin will come up tails is found in the same way

$$P_T = \frac{T/2}{T} = \frac{1}{2}.$$

We note that in this example only two outcomes are possible: Either the coin comes up heads or it comes up tails. The coin toss is an example of what is known as a *binary* event. Since something happens on every toss, the probability of something happening is 1.0

$$\left(\frac{T/2 + T/2}{T} = \frac{T}{T} = 1 \right).$$

In the special case where there are only two possible outcomes, the two probabilities must add to 1.0. The general rule is that the sum of the probabilities of all possible outcomes must add to 1.0, which includes the probability that nothing will happen if that is a possible outcome.

The statistician has now provided the casino owner with the information that the probability that a coin will come up heads is 0.5 and is equal to the probability that it will come up tails (assuming that the casino doesn't tamper with the coins; but that's another story). But the game the casino owner has in mind involves players matching coins with the house: Match and the player wins; fail to match and the house wins. What may we now expect to find?

The house flips a coin that may come up heads or tails and the player does the same; there are now two binary events and four possible outcomes as shown:

	House	*Player*	*Winner*
1	H	H	player
2	H	T	house
3	T	H	house
4	T	T	player

There are two ways for the player to win and two ways for the house to win. Looking at this table, it seems reasonable that the probability of any unique outcome (*HH, HT, TH, TT*) is $\frac{1}{4}$ and the probability that the house will win is $\frac{2}{4} = \frac{1}{2}$.

In this simple example intuition serves us well. However, when the number of events taking place becomes large or the probability of a particular outcome is not 0.5, the matter becomes much more difficult. Suppose, for example, that we have two players against the house (three coins being tossed); there are now eight possible outcomes as shown:

	House	*Player 1*	*Player 2*	*Winners*
1	*H*	*H*	*H*	1 and 2
2	*H*	*H*	*T*	House and 1
3	*H*	*T*	*H*	House and 2
4	*H*	*T*	*T*	House
5	*T*	*H*	*H*	House
6	*T*	*H*	*T*	House and 2
7	*T*	*T*	*H*	House and 1
8	*T*	*T*	*T*	1 and 2

On tosses 1 and 8, both players win and the house loses $2, while on 4 and 5, the house wins from both players. It is still relatively easy to see that the probability of any single outcome is now $\frac{1}{8}$, but things are becoming complex rather quickly. For example, adding another player increases the number of possible outcomes to 16.

Fortunately, there are two simple laws of probability that can help us. The first of these is the *either/or* law or addition law of probability.

ADDITION LAW: The probability that either *A* or *B* will occur is equal to the sum of their separate probabilities. The probability that either *A* or *B* or *C* will occur is equal to the sum of their separate probabilities. A general statement of this law is that the probability that *any one* of several events will occur is equal to the sum of their separate probabilities.

The second law of probability is the *and* law or the multiplication law of probability.

MULTIPLICATION LAW: The probability that both *A* and *B* will occur is equal to the product of the separate probabilities. In its general form, this law states that the probability that *each* of several independent events will occur is equal to the product of their separate probabilities.[1]

The two examples above can be used to illustrate the application of these laws. Remembering that $P_H = 0.5$ and $P_T = 0.5$ for each coin separately, we use the multiplication law to find that the probability of a head on coin 1 *and* a head on coin 2 is

$$P_{H_1 H_2} = P_{H_1} \cdot P_{H_2} = 0.5(0.5) = .25 = \frac{1}{4}.$$

We use the same computations to show that each of the other outcomes also has a probability of $\frac{1}{4}$. The addition law can be used to compute the probability that the house will win. The house wins in case 2 or 3 (*HT* or *TH*), each of which has a probability of 0.25. Therefore, the probability that the house will win is

$$P_{\text{House}} = P_{HT} + P_{TH} = 0.25 + 0.25 = 0.5,$$

which obviously corresponds to our previous expectation.

For the more complex problem of three coins, the same principles apply. The multiplication law tells us that the probability of three heads or any other specific outcome is $\frac{1}{2} \cdot \frac{1}{2} \cdot \frac{1}{2} = \frac{1}{8}$ or $(\frac{1}{2})^3$. The addition law reveals that the probability that the house will win \$2 is $\frac{1}{8} + \frac{1}{8} = \frac{1}{4}$ ($P_{HTT \text{ or } THH} = P_{HTT} + P_{THH}$). The probability that the house will break even (house and one player win) is $\frac{1}{8} + \frac{1}{8} + \frac{1}{8} + \frac{1}{8} = \frac{1}{2}$. If we know the probability of each simple event, we can use the addition and multiplication laws to calculate the probability of any complex event.

The case of three binary events of equal probability is a simple example of a more general and complex problem. Suppose, for example, that the mob has gained control of the casino and substitutes loaded coins for the ones that have been in use. As any good gambler knows, it doesn't take much of an edge for the house to win in the long run, so let us imagine that the new coins have a probability of coming up heads of 0.6 rather than 0.5. We use the addition and multiplication laws to compute the probabilities of the various outcomes as follows:

[1]Strictly speaking, this form of the multiplication law of probability is true only when the events are independent. If one outcome affects another, a more complex form of the law must be used. An excellent discussion of this topic may be found in Hays (1973), but it is beyond our scope. In our discussions, we will assume independence unless otherwise specified.

$$2\text{ coins} \begin{cases} P_H = 0.6 & P_T = 0.4 \\ P_{HH} = 0.6(0.6) & P_{TT} = 0.4(0.4) \\ \quad = 0.36 & \quad = 0.16 \\ P_{TH} = P_{HT} = 0.6(0.4) = 0.24 \end{cases}$$

$$3\text{ coins} \begin{cases} P_{HHH} = 0.6(0.6)(0.6) & P_{TTT} = 0.4(0.4)(0.4) \\ \quad = 0.216 & \quad = 0.064 \\ P_{HHT} = 0.6(0.6)(0.4) & P_{HTT} = 0.6(0.4)(0.4) \\ \quad = 0.144 & \quad = 0.096 \\ P_{HTH} = P_{HHT} = P_{THH} & P_{THT} = P_{TTH} = P_{HTT} \end{cases}$$

For the two-coin case, we see that the probability of a match (either *HH* or *TT*) is $0.36 + 0.16 = 0.52$ rather than the 0.5 that we had earlier. The same thing happens with two players (three coins). The probability that both will match the house (either *HHH* or *TTT*) is $0.216 + 0.064 = 0.280$ instead of 0.25, while the chance that the house will win big (*HTT* or *THH*) is $0.096 + 0.144 = 0.240$. Clearly, if the house leaves the game defined in this way, the odds are in favor of the players, and the house will lose in the long run.

It may seem a little artificial to use gambling examples and coin tosses to discuss statistics, but gambling did provide an early impetus for developing the mathematics of probability. Also, probability estimates are present in many of the games we play and in the news we read and hear: If we play bridge or poker, we use the principles we have been discussing to decide what cards to play or how much to bet. The whole concept of the calculated risk involves specifying more or less clearly the probability of each outcome.

We introduce one last coin-toss example before turning to the other main topic of this chapter, the normal distribution. Let us consider the case of ten coins or, more generally, ten binary, equal-probability events. We have a cocktail shaker with ten coins in it; we shake the coins and dump them out on a table, counting the number of coins that come up heads. Assuming that $P_H = 0.5$ for all coins, what is the most probable outcome? (The response five *H* and five *T* wins.) The next question, what is the probability of this outcome, is a good deal more difficult to answer.

The probability of any *particular* outcome can be calculated by our multiplication rule. A particular outcome is one where we specify exactly which coins come up heads; thus, one particular outcome is that coins 1–5 are heads and 6–10 are tails; another particular outcome is heads on 1–4 and 10, tails on 5–9. Each of these two examples results in the general outcome five heads, but each is itself the conjunction of ten different events; that is, the outcome of heads on 1–5 and tails on 6–10 can occur only if we get H_1 and H_2 and H_3 and . . . T_9 and T_{10}. Therefore, the probability of any particular outcome is computed as the product of the ten separate probabilities or 0.5^{10}. Our handy pocket calculator reveals that $\frac{1}{2}$ raised to the tenth power is $1/1024$ or 0.0009765625.

We can calculate the total number of particular outcomes by multiplication as well. To find the total number of outcomes, we obtain the product of the number of outcomes for each entity (coin in this case). Since there are two possible outcomes for each of ten coins, we obtain $2_1 \cdot 2_2 \cdot 2_3 \ldots \cdot 2_{10} = 2^{10} = 1024$ possible particular outcomes, each of which has the same probability of occurring.

Remember, the question was what is the probability of obtaining five heads? There are several different ways that this can happen, and our problem at this point is to figure out how many different ways ten coins can come up with five heads.

There are two ways to solve the problem; the first is to do what we did with three coins: List all particular outcomes and count the number of these that give us five heads. Unfortunately, with 1024 particular outcomes, this becomes quite an unpleasant task. The alternative is to compute what mathematicians call the *number of combinations*; this is done with the formula

$$_N C_r = \frac{N!}{r!(N-r)!}, \tag{7.2}$$

where N is the total number of objects (coins), r is the number of objects of a particular kind (heads), and the symbol (!) means factorial. A factorial is a successive product where the number is reduced by one at each stage; for example, $3! = 3 \cdot 2 \cdot 1$; $6! = 6 \cdot 5 \cdot 4 \cdot 3 \cdot 2 \cdot 1$; and, in general, $N! = N \cdot (N-1) \cdot (N-2) \ldots \cdot (2) \cdot 1$. In our problem, we want to find the number of combinations of ten coins that will give us five heads

$$_{10} C_5 = \frac{10!}{5!(10-5)!} = \frac{10 \cdot 9 \cdot 8 \cdot 7 \cdot 6 \cdot 5 \cdot 4 \cdot 3 \cdot 2 \cdot 1}{(5 \cdot 4 \cdot 3 \cdot 2 \cdot 1) \cdot (5 \cdot 4 \cdot 3 \cdot 2 \cdot 1)}$$

$$= \frac{9 \cdot 2 \cdot 7 \cdot 2}{1} = 252.$$

This tells us that of the 1024 particular events, there are 252 that give us five heads. Therefore, from formula 7.1, the probability that we get five heads from tossing ten coins is 252/1024 = .246.

Just to complete our assignment for the casino owner, we shall calculate the number of ways that various other outcomes can occur. We find each of these results using formula 7.2 and enter them in Table 7-1 as a frequency distribution; these computations are shown in Appendix A. In addition, we shall calculate the cumulative frequency for each outcome, the probability (P) for each outcome, the percentile rank (PR), and the z-score. Remember to use the correct formula to compute the PR. The mean of the distribution is 5 and the standard deviation is 1.58, yielding the z-scores in the last column.

THE NORMAL CURVE

There are many things in the world of human experience that seem to occur more or less by chance. A variety of games (cards, dice, and so on) use chance events for entertainment, but the pattern of chance events that has been observed in games also seems to fit a variety of naturally occurring phenomena. For example, studies of the distribution of human physical characteristics in the early nineteenth century led scientists to postulate that the mean of each distribution was Nature's ideal and the

TABLE 7-1
Possible Outcomes From Tossing Ten Coins.

X	f	cf	P	PR	z
10	1	1024	0.00098	0.9995	+3.1646
9	10	1023	0.0098	0.9941	+2.5316
8	45	1013	0.0439	0.9673	+1.8987
7	120	968	0.1172	0.8867	+1.2658
6	210	848	0.2051	0.7256	+0.6329
5	252	638	0.2461	0.5000	0
4	210	386	0.2051	0.2744	−0.6329
3	120	176	0.1172	0.1133	−1.2658
2	45	56	0.0439	0.0327	−1.8987
1	10	11	0.0098	0.0059	−2.5316
0	1	1	0.00098	0.0005	−3.1646

variability of people around that mean was due to chance factors in their development. In fact, the model provided by the mathematics of probability fit the observed data so well that the distribution came to be called the normal distribution of error,[1] and the frequency distribution that fit these measurements came to be called the *normal distribution*.

Actually, the normal distribution is a specific mathematical equation that was first published 250 years ago. This equation, whose precise statement need not concern us, gives the height of a theoretical frequency polygon for any possible z-score in the distribution; that is, it is assumed that the trait on the abscissa is a continuous variable and that there are an infinite number of observations. Since these conditions are never met in reality, the mathematical model or distribution that is computed from the equation never fits any set of observations exactly. However, the similarity is great enough, so that the mathematical distribution has been very useful in practical statistical work. In fact, as we shall see in later chapters, much of modern statistical theory and practice is based on the assumption that there is a normal distribution lurking around somewhere.

We begin our study of the normal distribution by looking at the frequency distributions of chance events. Histograms of them have been drawn for the cases of two coins, three coins, and four coins in Figure 7-1. Coin tosses and outcomes are discrete events, but if we assume that the abscissa represents a continuous variable, we can draw a smooth curve through each of the figures. Although the curves have somewhat different shapes, they are all symmetric and unimodal; thus the mean, median, and mode must coincide. Each of the curves is also shaped somewhat like a bell.

The three smooth curves in Figure 7-1 are all normal curves; that is, they satisfy the equation. They are not exactly the same shape because they are plotted on different scales. Also, each theoretical curve only approximates the histogram from which it was drawn. However, as the number of score categories (coins in this case) increases, the similarity between the histogram and the normal curve increases. Figure 7-2 contains the histogram that we would expect for ten coins (the frequencies came from Table 7-1); superimposed on it is the normal curve that approximates the frequency polygon we would get for ten coins. By the time we have the 11 score categories that can occur for ten events, the similarity

[1] See Sir Francis Galton, *Natural Inheritance* (London: Macmillan and Co., 1894).

between the frequency distribution of chance events and the normal distribution is apparent.

As we implied there are many bell-shaped curves that are normal curves. It would be very useful if we could find a way to reduce all of these curves that have the same basic equation to a single curve; then, we would only have to worry about one curve. There actually is a way to reduce all of these curves or theoretical frequency distributions to the same base, and we have already discussed it at some length. We can use a linear transformation to put all of the distributions on a single common

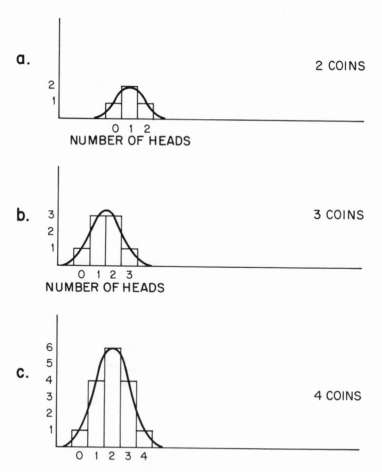

Figure 7-1 *Histograms of expected outcomes from tossing two, three, and four coins.*

scale. The most obvious transformation is the standard score or z-score transformation, which converts each frequency distribution to a mean of zero and a standard deviation of one. The first three distributions we have discussed are converted to z-scores in Table 7-2, and the frequency polygons for all four are plotted in standard score form in parts a.–d. of Figure 7-3, along with the normal distribution; refer to Table 7-1 for the percentages and z-scores of the ten-coin problem.

It is clear from Figure 7-3 that as the number of categories increases from 3 to 4 to 5 to 11, the difference between the coin-toss curve and the normal curve decreases. If we were to plot an example for 25 categories, it

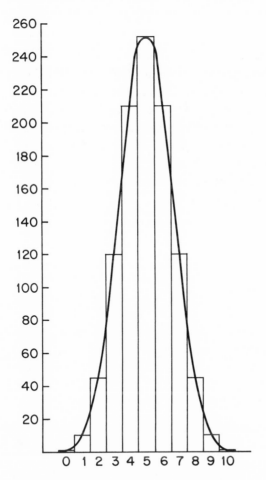

Figure 7-2   Histogram of expected outcomes from tossing ten coins.

would be virtually impossible to see the difference between the normal curve and the frequency polygon of chance events. This increasing similarity between the normal curve and the frequency curve for chance events has enabled statisticians and scientists to use the normal curve, which has known mathematical properties, as a model of many scientific phenomena.

THE UNIT NORMAL CURVE AND PROBABILITY

Look back to Figures 7-1 and 7-2; in these two figures, the frequencies of the various outcomes of our coin tosses are shown as bars in a histogram. Each bar is one unit wide and as many units high as the expected frequency of that particular outcome; that is, if we were to toss two coins four times, we should get zero heads once, one head twice, and two heads once *on the average over a large number of trials*. Another way to look at it is that on a large number of tosses of two coins, we would expect to get two heads 25 percent of the time, one head 50 percent of the time, and no heads on the remaining tosses.

The important point here is that *we can equate the areas of the bars in our histograms with relative frequencies or probabilities of each of our*

TABLE 7-2

Frequency Distributions, Probabilities, and z Scores.
for Expected Outcomes.

Heads	2 Coins			3 Coins			4 Coins		
	f	P	z	f	P	z	f	P	z
0	1	0.25	−1.414	1	0.125	−1.732	1	0.0625	−2.0
1	2	0.5	0	3	0.375	−0.577	4	0.25	−1.0
2	1	0.25	+1.414	3	0.375	+0.577	6	0.375	0
3				1	0.125	+1.732	4	0.25	1.0
4							1	0.0625	2.0

	Calculations		
	$\bar{X} = 1.0$	$\bar{X} = 1.5$	$\bar{X} = 2$
	$S = 0.707$	$S = 0.866$	$S = 1$

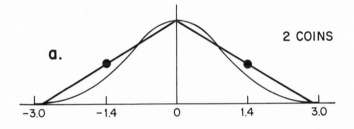

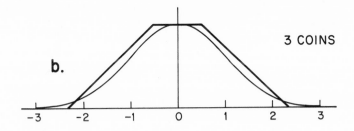

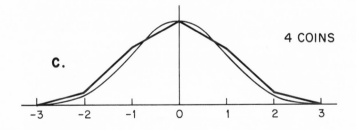

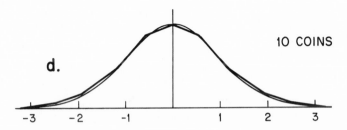

Figure 7-3 Standard score frequency polygons for expected outcomes of coin tosses.

outcomes. Figure 7-4 shows the four histograms we would expect to get from 1000 repetitions of our two-three-four- and 10-coin tosses. The total area under each histogram is 1000 units. The area of each bar can be divided by the total area under the histogram, which converts each bar to

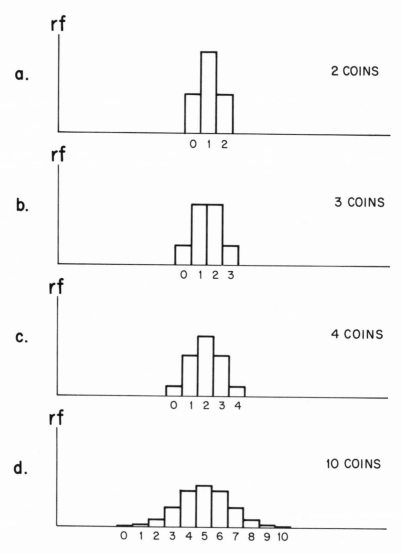

Figure 7-4   Histograms of relative frequencies of coin-toss outcomes. The area of each bar is proportional to the probability of that outcome.

a relative frequency or proportion of the total. Thus, by expressing each histogram in relative frequencies, we have converted the total area under the curve to 1.0. We refer to these as unit histograms because they enclose one unit of area; all unit histograms enclose the same total area.

We have already seen that it is possible to convert all normal distributions to a single curve by transforming them to standard score form. All normal curves in z-score form have exactly the same shape. It is also possible to convert normal curves to unit area by expressing them in relative frequencies. This has the very substantial advantage of reducing all normal distributions to a single curve with precisely known mathematical properties. This single curve or distribution is known as the *unit normal distribution*; some of its properties are presented in Appendix Table B.1.

The most widely used feature of the unit normal distribution is the relationship of area to probability. The primary reference point in the distribution is the mean. Appendix Table B.1 lists the area under the curve between the mean and any z-score. All normal distributions converted to z-score form have the same proportion of their area between the mean and a particular z-score, so the areas listed in Appendix Table B.1 characterize all normal distributions.

There are three questions about area (or probability) that are commonly asked. First, what portion of the area falls between a particular z-score and the mean? This answer may be read directly from the table; for example, what portion of the area falls between $z = +0.9$ and the mean? Referring to the table, we find that the entry under area between z and $\bar{X}$ for a z of 0.9 is 0.3159; that is, 31.59 percent of the area is included in this region. Another way to view this result is to say that we would expect 3,159 out of 10,000 observations to fall in that portion of the normal distribution between the mean and a z-score of $+0.9$.

The second question is what portion of the area falls beyond a given z-score? The answer to this question may be obtained either directly from the column labeled area beyond z in Appendix Table B.1 or by subtracting the area between z and $\bar{X}$ from 0.5000. Note that because the normal distribution is a unimodal symmetric distribution, the mean, median, and mode coincide; therefore, one-half of the distribution is above the mean. The first method yields .1841 and the second does also ($0.5000 - 0.3159 = 0.1841$).

The third question that we may ask is what portion of the area lies between two z-scores? The answer to this question involves adding or subtracting values from the table. For example, we find the area between $z = +0.5$ and $z = +1.5$ by looking up the tabled values 0.1915 ($z = 0.5$) and 0.4332 ($z = 1.5$); the area between them is the difference, 0.2417.

There is one important thing to watch for when computing the area between two z-scores: If they have the same sign, they are on the same side of the mean, and the area is found by subtracting the smaller area from the larger. If the z-scores have different signs, they are on opposite sides of the mean, and the separate areas are added. This principle is illustrated in Figure 7-5.

We do not look up areas under the normal curve for our health or for amusement. The most common use of the normal curve is in making statements about probabilities, and the relationship between area and probability is used in forecasting what will happen. The normal curve is

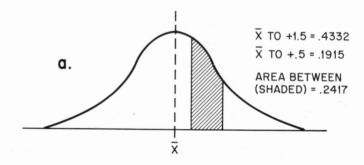

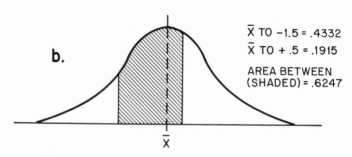

Figure 7-5   Proportion of the normal distribution between z scores.

used because it is simple, widely available, and it seems to fit reasonably well many of the probability problems that scientists encounter.

We can illustrate the use of the normal curve in calculating probabilities with our coin-toss example for ten coins. The exact probabilities given to four places are reproduced in Table 7-3; also given are the z-scores for the various outcomes. However, these z's are of little use to us because they represent midpoints of the intervals that would exist if the coin tosses were truly continuous. Recall from the discussion of the histogram in Chapter 2 that the score values represent the midpoints of score intervals when a scale is being used to measure a continuous trait. The bar for six heads can then be viewed as covering the interval that has real limits of 5.5 and 6.5, and it is the z-scores for these points that we have to

TABLE 7-3
Using the Normal Distribution to Estimate Probabilities.

X	P	Midpoint z	Limit z	Area z to $\bar{X}$	Area Interval
			3.4810	0.4998	
10	0.00098	3.1646			0.002
			2.8481	0.4978	
9	0.0098	2.5316			0.0112
			2.2152	0.4866	
8	0.0439	1.8987			0.0436
			1.5823	0.4430	
7	0.1172	1.2658			0.1141
			0.9494	0.3289	
6	0.2051	0.6329			0.2058
			0.3165	0.1231	
5	0.2461	0.0			0.2462
			−0.3165	0.1231	
4	0.2051	−0.6329			0.2058
			−0.9494	0.3289	
3	0.1172	−1.2658			0.1141
			−1.5823	0.4430	
2	0.0439	−1.8987			0.0436
			−2.2152	0.4866	
1	0.0098	−2.5316			0.0112
			−2.8481	0.4978	
0	0.00098	−3.1646			0.002
			−3.4810	0.4998	

use with Appendix Table B.1. The z's of these interval limits are listed in the fourth column of Table 7-3 under limit z. The next column of the table contains the portions of the normal distribution between these z-scores and the mean. In the final column are the portions of the normal curve that lie in each interval. These entries are the estimates that we would make of the probabilities of each of the possible outcomes of tossing ten coins using the normal distribution approximation rather than calculating the exact probabilities from the number of combinations.

The most striking feature of the approximate probabilities in the last column is that they are so close to the exact values in column 2 of the table. The largest discrepancy, which occurs in the extreme cases of 1 and 9, is only 0.0014. The normal distribution provides a very close fit to the data for ten coins; as the number of coins or different outcome categories increases, the fit gets better.

PERCENTILES AND CONFIDENCE INTERVALS

The relationship between standard scores in the normal distribution and the probability of various outcomes is also widely used for forecasting continuous traits. Scores on achievement tests, personality and interest inventories, for example, are often assumed to fall in a normal distribution; that is, if we were to administer an appropriate test of reading achievement to all high-school students in our state, we might expect the frequency distribution of scores to be very nearly normal in shape. Although we know that the scores actually come from a scale with discrete units in the form of test items, there are enough different scale values so that we can treat the resulting measurements as forming a continuous scale. Suppose that students' scores on the reading test ranged from 10 to 150 with a mean of 80 and a standard deviation of 20 and a frequency distribution in the shape of the normal curve. It is conventional to say that the scores are normally distributed with mean 80 and standard deviation 20.

We can use Appendix Table B.1 and information about the frequency distribution of test scores to make some general probability statements about people's performances on the test. As described in detail in the next section, there is also a consistent relationship between percentiles and z-scores in normal distributions. These features allow us to do two things. First, we can translate z-scores directly into percentiles. This is accomplished by determining the portion of the distribution that falls below a given z-score; for negative z's, the percentile is simply the area of the distribution beyond the z-score. Thus, a person with a z-score of -1.30 falls at the tenth percentile. Positive z-scores are above the mean, so their percentiles are found by adding 0.50 to the area between the mean and z. A z-score of $+0.60$ falls at the 73rd percentile. Of course, both of these z-scores can be transformed back into the original scale. The z of -1.27 becomes a raw score of 54 or, stated the other way, a raw score of 54 falls at the tenth percentile of a normal distribution that has a mean of 80 and standard deviation of 20.

The second widespread use of the normal distribution and Appendix Table B.1 is in making statements about the probability of outcomes that fall within particular ranges of scores. The same general procedure that we describe here will come up again in prediction in Chapter 8 and is the basis for all of our discussions in Part III.

Suppose that we write down on separate slips of paper the scores obtained by each of the students who took our reading test and placed the slips in a large drum. If we mix the slips well and reach into the drum, what is the probability that we will draw a score that is less than 75?; what is the probability that the score we draw is between 50 and 110? We can use the normal distribution to answer these questions.

The solutions to these problems are found by first converting the raw scores to z-scores and then using Appendix Table B.1. In the first situation, we have $z_{75} = -0.25$; since we want to know the probability of a score below 75, the answer is given by the area beyond a z of -0.25. This is found to be 0.4013, so we can say that the probability of drawing a score of less than 75 is 0.40. Note that a more precise answer is obtained if we use a raw score of 74.5, the lower limit of the score interval; in this case, $z_{74.5} = -0.275$, and the probability of a score below this point is 0.39. However, it is almost always sufficiently accurate to use the raw scores themselves when the distribution has a range exceeding 25.

The answer to the second problem is also found by converting the raw scores to z's; the difference is that we use the area between the two scores to find the desired probability. We find $z_{50} = -1.50$ and $z_{110} = 1.50$. The area between each z-score and the mean is 0.4332, so the area between the two z's is 0.8664, and the probability of obtaining a raw score between 50 and 110 is 0.87. Again, a more exact procedure would be to use the interval limits of 49.5 and 110.5, which yield an area between the two scores of 0.8726, but in this case, our 0.87 probability does not change.

Sometimes it is also useful to reverse the question and ask between what two scores does some specified percent of the distribution fall. When the question is asked in this way, we have the first of several kinds of *confidence intervals*. A confidence interval is that portion of the frequency distribution that is centered on the mean and contains the specified percent of the distribution. We might ask for the 50 percent confidence interval, or the 75 percent, 90 percent, or 95 percent confidence interval; whatever confidence interval we are seeking, the answer will be in units of the original raw score scale.

Appendix Table B.1 is used in reverse to find confidence intervals. Because a confidence interval is symmetric around the mean, we divide the desired percent in half and look up that value in the table. To find the 50 percent confidence interval, we look up the z that has 25 percent of the distribution falling between itself and the mean; this value is about 0.675, so we know that 50 percent of the distribution falls between $z = -0.675$ and $z = +0.675$, and the 50 percent confidence interval is from 66.5 to 93.5. We find the 90 percent confidence interval in the same way; we now need 45 percent of the distribution on each side of the mean. Referring to Appendix Table B.1 shows the necessary z to be 1.645; therefore, the 90 percent confidence interval is from 47.1 to 112.9.

There are several useful ways in which confidence intervals are used or interpreted. First, as we have seen, the p percent confidence interval includes p percent of the normal distribution; thus, p percent of the distribution falls within that range. Also, the probability of drawing a score from our drum that falls within that range is p. Second, the probability is p that the confidence interval covers or includes a particular individual's score. We shall return to each of these uses of the confidence interval as it comes up in the course of our discussion.

NORMALIZING A DISTRIBUTION

As stated above, the principal use of the normal curve is not for estimating how many heads will occur in coin tosses. The coin toss is merely a simple example that permits us to see the relationship between area, frequency, and probability. The principal features of the normal curve that permit the interpretations described in the last section are that many different frequency distributions can be reduced to one common distribution and that for this distribution *there is an exact and known relationship between z-score and percentile rank.*

In Table 6-1, we saw that percentile ranks and standard scores could both be used for creating normative scales. Unfortunately, there was no necessary relationship between the two scales because one was based on score units ($\bar{X}$ and S), the other on relative frequencies. It would be difficult to compare two frequency distributions that differed in shape (for example, one positively skewed and the other negatively skewed) because the results of the comparison might depend on which scale was used. Two distributions could have the same mean and standard deviation and, therefore, the same z-score scale, but the percentile rank scales might be quite different.

The known relationship between percentile ranks and z-scores makes the normal distribution particularly useful. We have the advantage of a scale in score units that can be treated like an interval scale. We can add and subtract z-scores, just as we do raw scale scores; in addition, we also have frequency information. We can interpret scores in a normal distribution as representing positions in a relative frequency distribution. In other words, in a normal distribution, z-scores possess both linear transformation information and relative frequency information; both interpretations of the scores are possible, and we can move from one to the other without difficulty.

While the normal distribution appears to provide a good approximation for many distributions encountered by social and behavioral scientists, the data that are collected in a particular study seldom form a perfect normal curve. Several factors may be responsible for this. First, the characteristic may not have a normal distribution; for example, the tendency to psychopathology may not be normal in shape (no pun intended), the number of miles that employees commute to work, or the number of children per family may not have normal distributions in nature. When there is reason to believe that the natural distribution of a trait departs substantially from normal, it may be necessary or desirable to analyze a set of data with methods other than those described in this book. Appropriate procedure for analyzing such data are given in Tukey (1977) and Segel (1956).

The other major reason that the data collected in a study do not fall in a normal distribution is chance. The particular group of individuals we measured may have been biased in some way; there may have been some errors in data collection, or any one of a large number of random effects may have caused the departure from normality. If it can reasonably be assumed that unimportant and nonsystematic factors were responsible, then it is often desirable to normalize the distribution.

It is common practice among the publishers of widely used psychological and educational measures, particularly measures of ability, to normalize the distribution of scores of their norm groups. This is accomplished in two stages. The first phase is a nonlinear transformation that puts the scores into a normal distribution of z-scores; then, a linear transformation is applied to eliminate negatives and decimal values.

The most widely used two-stage normalizing transformation was first suggested by McCall in 1922. He called the resulting scores T-scores. These T-scores form a normal distribution and have a mean of 50 and a standard deviation of 10. We can use the data presented in Table 6-1 to illustrate the conversion to T-scores. The raw scores, percentile ranks accurate to four digits, and z-scores from this table are reproduced in the first three columns of Table 7-4.

The process of normalizing the distribution involves determining percentile ranks and using the table of areas under the normal curve to *assign* new z-scores. After computing the percentile ranks (remembering that they are calculated for the midpoint of the interval), look in the column of Appendix Table B.1 labeled area Beyond z for a value equal to the percentile rank of the lowest score. Doing this for a *PR* of 0.85, which is a proportion of 0.0085, we find the value 0.0084 is the closest listed value to 0.0085. The z-score associated with this proportion is 2.39, and since we are below the mean, it is negative; that is, the z-score -2.39 has a percentile rank of 0.84 in the normal distribution. Since we wish to normalize our obtained distribution in order to eliminate its negative skew, *we assign the z-score* -2.39 *to our raw score of* 4 because this is the z-score that 4 would have if the distribution were normal.

The same process is repeated for each of the other scores. For the *PR* of 1.69, we look in the table and find, next to the entry 0.0170, a z-score of 2.12. The z-score -2.12 is then assigned to a raw score of 5. Each other raw score is treated in the same way: Its *PR* is found in the table; the z-score for that *PR* in the normal curve is read and is assigned to the raw score. Of course, once the percentile ranks exceed 50, the z-scores become positive, and we must switch to the second column of the table as steps 1–5 for a score of 18 illustrate, but the basic process remains unchanged.

1. $PR_{18} = 64.41$. As a proportion, this is 0.6441.
2. Subtract 0.5000 for the bottom half of the distribution:
   $0.6441 - 0.5000 = 0.1441$.
3. Look up 0.1441 under area between z and $\bar{X}$.
4. 0.1443 is the closest value; its z is 0.37.
5. Assign $z = +0.37$ to the raw score 18.

Careful comparison of the z-scores computed from the raw data with those assigned on the basis of percentile ranks reveals the effects of a normalizing transformation. In areas where the frequency is below what would be expected for a normal distribution, the scale is compressed. Note that the minimum z is not as extreme for the assigned z's and that the differences between z-scores are generally smaller in the lower portion of the distribution. In contrast, in areas where the observed frequencies

TABLE 7-4

Normalizing Transformation Applied to 59 Quiz Scores.

Raw Score	Percentile Rank	z	Assigned z	Normalized Raw Scores	T-score
24	99.15	1.89	+2.39	26.3	74
23	98.31	1.67	+2.12	25.0	71
22	95.76	1.45	+1.72	23.2	67
21	91.53	1.23	+1.37	21.6	64
20	86.44	1.01	+1.10	20.4	61
19	76.27	0.79	+0.72	18.7	57
18	64.41	0.57	+0.37	17.1	54
17	55.93	0.35	+0.15	16.1	52
16	48.31	0.13	−0.04	15.2	50
15	41.53	−0.09	−0.21	14.4	48
14	35.59	−0.31	−0.37	13.7	46
13	29.66	−0.53	−0.53	13.0	45
12	23.73	−0.75	−0.72	12.1	43
11	18.64	−0.97	−0.89	11.4	41
10	14.40	−1.19	−1.06	10.6	39
9	11.01	−1.41	−1.23	9.8	38
8	8.50	−1.63	−1.37	9.2	36
7	5.08	−1.85	−1.64	8.0	34
6	2.54	−2.07	−1.95	6.5	30
5	1.69	−2.29	−2.12	5.8	29
4	0.85	−2.51	−2.39	4.6	26

exceed those expected in a normal distribution, the scale is expanded. For example, the difference between z_{19} and z_{20} is 0.22 for the computed z's and 0.38 for the assigned z's, indicating a stretching of the scale by over $1\frac{1}{2}$ times.

The fifth column of Table 7-4 contains the normalized raw scores. This column represents a linear transformation of the assigned (normal curve) z-scores using the mean and standard deviation of the original distribution; these values were 15.4 and 4.58, respectively. By applying the transformation

$$X' = (4.58\ z) + 15.4$$

to each assigned z-score, we obtain the values in column 5. Like the raw scores, this distribution will have a mean of 15.4 and a standard deviation of 4.58, but like the assigned z's, the lower portion of the scale has been compressed and the upper portion has been expanded. The results of the T-score transformation (mean $= 50$, $S = 10$) are given in the last column of the table. Of course any other linear transformation ($\bar{X} = 100$, $S = 15$, $\bar{X} = 500$, $S = 100$, and so on) could be applied to these normalized z-scores, and the resulting distribution would still be normal in shape.

Figure 7-6 illustrates the effect of a normalizing transformation on the frequency distribution. The raw data are plotted in the upper portion of the figure. Here, each interval is one unit wide, yielding bars that are all the same width. The area of each bar (frequency) is directly proportional to its height and unrelated to its width. The smoothed curve reveals a distribution with definite negative skew.

In part b of the figure, the abscissa is marked off in the same units as in part a, but the histogram bars cover the real limits of the *normalized score intervals*. In fact, the expansion at the top of the scale has resulted in one normalized raw score that exceeds a perfect score on the test. We have used values half the distance between adjacent normalized score values as the real limits of each interval. Each histogram bar represents the same frequency in part b as in part a, but the intervals vary in width. The result is that area and frequency are the same in both graphs, but they are no longer related only to the height of a bar. The varying widths of the bars reflect the compression and expansion of parts of the scale by the normalizing transformation. The smoothed curve through the histogram is a normal curve.

Normalized scores are particularly useful for conveying normative

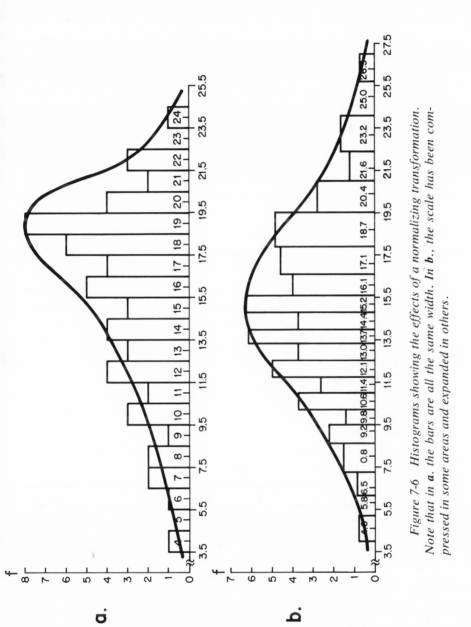

Figure 7-6   *Histograms showing the effects of a normalizing transformation. Note that in **a**. the bars are all the same width. In **b**., the scale has been compressed in some areas and expanded in others.*

information about individuals. Once the norm group has been measured, the normalizing transformation, and probably some linear transformation as well, is applied to the distribution. Typically, a table listing each possible raw score and its transformed equivalent is prepared. When a new individual is measured, her/his raw score is looked up in the table and the normative score is read off. The resulting scores may be used in further computations such as finding means of groups (which is not possible with percentile scores), and they also give percentile information directly. For example, a normalized score of 125 in a distribution with a mean of 100 and a standard deviation of 15 (that is, our IQ transformation from Chapter 6) would be equivalent to a normalized z of $+1.67$ and would imply a percentile of 95. In the same scale, a score of 100 would have a percentile equivalent of 50, and a score of 80 would be at the ninth percentile.

SUMMARY

The concept of *probability* was introduced with examples of binary events; for example, the probability of event A, obtaining three heads on a toss of five coins, is equal to the number of ways that event A can happen divided by the total number of things that can happen. The probability of event A may also be viewed as the number of times that we can expect A to occur over a long series of trials. In this sense, probability is the relative frequency of event A in the distribution of all possible outcomes.

The *normal distribution* is a precisely defined mathematical function that closely approximates the distribution of many chance events. The frequency polygon of the normal distribution is called the *normal curve* and is a unimodal symmetric curve. When a normal distribution is expressed in terms of the relative frequencies of z-scores, a single curve can be used to fit any distribution. This curve is called the *unit normal curve* because the area enclosed by the curve is 1.0. The area between the mean of this curve and any z-score can be found in Appendix Table B.1. The values in this table can be used to find the area of the curve between any two z-scores.

The area under the portion of the unit normal curve that lies between two z-scores can be viewed as the probability that an event with a value in that range will occur, which makes it possible to state consistent relationships between z-scores in a normal distribution and the percentile ranks of those z-scores. Any distribution, regardless of its original shape, can be converted into the shape of the normal distribution by finding the percentile rank of each raw score and assigning the z-score with that *PR* from the normal distribution to the raw score. These normalized z-scores can be given further linear transformations, including the *T*-score scale that results in a normal distribution with a mean of 50 and a standard deviation of 10.

PROBLEMS

1. Suppose we want to study human-concept formation and we are going to obtain our research subjects from a large lecture class with the following characteristics: There are 225 males and 275 females; there are 40 freshmen, 180 sophomores, 275 juniors, and 5 seniors. Assuming that we select subjects at random, what are the probabilities that the first person selected will be

*(a) male

(b) female

*(c) a freshman or a sophomore

(d) a sophomore or a junior

*(e) a male sophomore

(f) a female junior

What condition must we assume is true for the probabilities in (e) and (f) to be correct?

2. Friar Tuck is teaching a course in medieval statistics. Unfortunately, you have to take the class and, since you speak no Latin, it is all Greek to you. The final exam, also in Latin, has 100 questions, each of which is a 4-alternative multiple choice item. You decide that your best strategy is to select your answers at random.

*(a) What is the probability that you will get item 10 correct?

(b) What is the probability that you will get item 11 correct?

*(c) How likely is it that you will get either item 10 or 11 correct?

*(d) What are your chances of getting them both right?

*(e) What is the most likely score you will receive?

*Answers to starred questions are found in Appendix D.

(f) Using the normal distribution approximation with a mean of 25 and a standard deviation of 4.33, what is the probability that you will get a score:

*(1) below 20
(2) above 20
*(3) above 22
(4) above 28
*(5) between 22 and 28
(6) between 20 and 30
*(7) below 22 or above 28
(8) below 24 or above 27
*(9) below 19 or above 24
(10) between 20 and 24
*(11) between 30 and 33
(12) above 35

3. Sketch a typical normal distribution. Indicate the position of the mean, the whole value z scores (0, +1, +2, and so on) and the proportion of the distribution between each pair of z-scores.

4. Find the area under the unit normal distribution that lies:

*(a) above $z = 1.00$
(b) below $z = 2.00$
*(c) above $z = 1.64$
(d) below $z = -1.96$
*(e) between $z = 0$ and $z = 3.00$
(f) above $z = -0.50$
*(g) between $z = -1.50$ and $z = 1.50$
(h) between $z = +.25$ and $z = +1.25$

5. Find the z-scores that are exceeded by the following proportions of the area under the unit normal distribution:

Proportion of area above z-score

*(a)	0.50	*(e)	0.005
(b)	0.16	(f)	0.995
*(c)	0.84	*(g)	0.10
(d)	0.05	(h)	0.90

6. Find the standard score of a normally distributed variable such that 49 percent of the distribution falls between the mean and this particular value (hint: There are two answers).

*7. Find the value of the normally distributed random variable X such that 60 percent of the distribution lies to the left of this specific value when $\bar{X} = 150$ and $S = 20$.

8. The general population of children's Stanford-Binet IQs have a nearly normal distribution with a mean of 100 and standard deviation of 16. Find the percentile equivalent of each of the following IQs:

IQ	Percentile equivalent
*100	
120	
*75	
95	
*140	

9. Final-exam averages in statistics are typically approximately normally distributed, with a mean of 74 and a standard deviation of 12. If the top 10 percent of the class receive As, the next 20 percent receive Bs, the next 40 percent Cs, the next 20 percent Ds, and the bottom 10 percent Fs:

  *(a) What average final-exam score must you exceed to obtain an A?

  (b) What average must you exceed to receive a grade better than a C?

  *(c) What average must you obtain to pass the course? (You'll need a D or better.)

10. If a typical Detroit car lasts 6 years before "burning out," with a standard deviation of 6 months, when should everyone buy a new car so that only 5 percent of the cars will "burn out"? (Remember 1 year = 12 months.)

*11. If the distribution of intelligence-test scores is normal in shape, with a mean of 100 and a standard deviation of 15, what two scores form the boundaries of the middle 75 percent of scores?

12. Given the conditions in question 11, what interpretation can be made of an IQ score of 120? of 70?

8

PREDICTION

We have already seen that predicting chance events had an important role in developing applications for the normal distribution. In this chapter, our concern shifts to a much more practical problem, prediction in the individual case. There are many times in everyone's life when s/he is affected by statistical prediction: Schools use tests to predict academic success and to assign students to classes; colleges and universities use tests and grades to select the students who will be admitted. Tests are widely used in business, industry, and government service to select the best prospective employees or to place people in the jobs they are most likely to perform satisfactorily.

There is also widespread controversy in the media about the propriety of prediction. Articles have appeared in magazines and newspapers criticizing many of the instruments that are widely used for prediction. Television programs and specials with much the same message have been broadcast, and at least one state has passed a law seriously restricting the use of tests for predicting educational achievement. Thus, there are several practical reasons for developing an understanding of what statistical prediction is and how it works.

TYPES OF PREDICTION

Prediction generally involves forecasting. Given certain information that is available at the present time, what is the most likely outcome at some future time?; which outcome has the highest probability of occurrence, or, more generally, what is the probability for each of several possible outcomes? For example, we know from our discussion in Chapter 7 that the probability of getting five heads on a toss of ten coins is 0.246. Any sound prediction strategy seeks to use best the available information in determining the probability of each of several possible outcomes. However, a very important point to keep in mind and one that is often overlooked is that different individuals and groups have different purposes in making predictions and different prediction procedures may be appropriate for these different purposes.

A prediction usually results in a decision of some kind. There are three categories of decisions. *Selection decisions* are those decisions that involve picking out some individuals from a larger group. The individuals may be selected in, as when a college accepts some applicants but not others, or they may be selected out or identified for exclusion; in either case, there is some organization, a school or a college, a company, and so on that is doing the selecting. Usually, the organization has limited resources and wishes to realize the highest return from its prediction decisions. A college selects those students it believes are most likely to complete degrees or those students who are likely to earn the best grades. A company wishes to select people who will be good workers and remain with the company for a long time.

Certain features characterize selection decisions. First, they are made by the organization for the benefit of the organization. (In the case of a state university, for example, the organization may be the taxpayers of the state.) Second, the organization usually makes many such decisions, some of which will be correct and others incorrect. The organization seeks to maximize the number of correct decisions *on the average*. Of necessity, attention is focused on the results of a group of predictions. The procedures described in later sections are those widely used to obtain the best selection decisions.

A second type of decision is the *classification decision*. This is also a decision made by an organization, but it differs from the selection decision in that no one is excluded. In a classification problem, each individual is assigned to a category, treatment, or job. The objective is to obtain maximum results across the average of all categories. The major example of classification is in military-duty assignments. Procedures for making and evaluating classification decisions are beyond our scope but are treated in books on decision theory.

Placement is the third type of prediction decision; here, attention focuses on benefit to the individual. A placement decision involves assigning each individual to the category that suits her/him best. These decisions are made both by the organization and by the individual and often involve such subjective factors as preferences and role perceptions in addition to more objective information about past performance and probable success; the eventual accuracy of the decision may be difficult or impossible to assess. From the point of view of the individual, very few placement decisions will be made in a lifetime, so each decision is very important.

A great deal of misunderstanding and confusion occurs because people fail to identify the differences between the various types of prediction. Educational institutions have been severely criticized for using tests as part of their selection procedures because the predictions made from the tests are sometimes in error by a large amount. Similar criticisms have been leveled against industrial selection procedures. What seems to be missing in many of the discussions is a realization that almost all attempts to predict future events are in error to some degree. It is not possible to eliminate errors of prediction; all that we can hope to do is to minimize the errors and the negative impact that they may have.

THE PRINCIPLE OF LEAST SQUARES

While predictions are made for the individual, those predictions are based on the past behavior of a group; this is generally true whether we are predicting the behavior of people, animals, or the stock market. There are some cases, such as stocks, where detailed information about the entity is available over a long period of time, so that we might predict that the present trend or direction of movement for that individual entity will continue. However, forecasting a change in the present trend requires reference to the group. The predictions that are made in education, psychology, sociology, and personnel work generally involve people and their behavior. For these situations, we seldom have a long and detailed history of the individual's behavior, so we must rely on the behavior of previous groups in similar conditions.

The basic principle on which prediction operates is quite simple. We have an individual, call him Ishmael, for whom a prediction is to be made; by collecting some current or past information about Ishmael, for example, age, education, and score on the *XYZ* test, he is identified as a member of a group of similar individuals whom we have encountered in the past. The group is defined as those who are like him in age, education, and test score and for whom outcome information is available. If Ishmael is an applicant for admission to our university and we wish to predict his grades, we use the performance of previous applicants who were like him in age, and so forth. Our prediction is that Ishmael will behave on the outcome variable like the group that he most resembles based on the information we have available.

The information that we collect in order to identify groups is called *predictor* information; Ishmael's age, education, and test score are predictor information. The variables of age, education, and *XYZ* test are known as *predictor variables*. The behavior that we wish to predict is called the *criterion variable*; in Ishmael's case, grade average is the criterion variable.

Let us take a closer look at the prediction process by examining a specific example. Suppose that we wish to predict scores on the next weekly quiz in a statistics course. The information that we have as a predictor is the number of homework assignments completed prior to taking the quiz. We also have the performance of last year's class both on the homework and on the quiz. These data are given in Table 8-1, where the 30 members of last year's class are listed along with their scores on the two variables.

A little quick calculation reveals that last year's class taken as a whole had a mean score on the quiz of 6, and the standard deviation was 1.37. If we wished to choose a single score to describe the performance of last year's class, the score to choose would be 6. Why? Because 6 is the mean, and the mean, as we know from our discussion in Chapter 4, is the center of the distribution in a least squares sense. That is, the mean is the point or score that is closest to every score; it is the score with the smallest sum of squared differences between it and the other scores in the distribution.

The standard deviation is an index of the inability of the mean to represent every score in the distribution. Remember that most scores are not exactly at the mean; they deviate from the mean, and these deviations can be viewed as errors. If we use the mean to describe each of the 30 people in last year's class, our description will be in error by some amount for all but eight class members; for example, our description of individual 1 is in error by one point. Using the mean of the group will result in smaller errors than for any other value, but there will still be errors. The standard deviation is an index of how large these errors tend to be.

Charlie is a member of this year's class; what is our prediction, our best guess about what his score on the quiz will be? If we have no further information about Charlie, our best guess is that his score will be 6. We would make this prediction because we want our errors to be as small, on the average, as possible. Although we make only one prediction for Charlie himself, we must view him, at least potentially, as a member of a group. It is the average error for the group that we must minimize in order to make the best prediction that we can for Charlie. We know that our

TABLE 8-1
Quiz Scores and Homework Assignments for 30 Students.

Individual	Homework Completed	Quiz	Individual	Homework Completed	Quiz
1	1	5	16	3	7
2	2	7	17	2	8
3	1	6	18	2	5
4	3	5	19	1	4
5	3	9	20	2	6
6	1	5	21	2	7
7	2	4	22	3	8
8	2	6	23	1	5
9	1	4	24	3	7
10	1	7	25	2	5
11	3	6	26	1	6
12	3	8	27	3	6
13	2	6	28	3	7
14	3	7	29	1	5
15	1	3	30	2	6

prediction is likely to be in error, but we have no way of knowing whether our prediction is too high or too low. In choosing the mean, we have selected the value where the mean error is zero (remember that $\sum(X - \bar{X}) = 0$), and the sum of squared errors is minimized. This is what we mean when we speak of least-squares prediction.

Now suppose that we have some additional information about Charlie; we know that he handed in all three homework assignments. This is predictor information, information that allows us to put Charlie in a group of people who are like him in some way. If we sort the people from last year's class into groups defined by the number of homework assignments completed, Charlie can be identified as a member of the group that completed all three assignments.

As luck would have it, a third of the class falls in each of the three groups. Computing the mean quiz score for each group reveals that those who handed in only one assignment earned an average of five points on the quiz, while the other two groups had means of 6 and 7, respectively. Since Charlie's group has a mean of 7, this should be our new prediction for him. The standard deviation of the group is 1.1, indicating that the average error is smaller, which means that using our predictor information has reduced the size of our errors. We shall still make errors, but they will tend to be somewhat smaller.

Predictor information is useful if it reduces our errors; in fact, we generally reserve the term predictor for the information that reduces our errors. In the example above, knowing the number of homework assignments completed reduced our errors; therefore, we would say that this variable predicts quiz performance. On the other hand, the color of Charlie's socks is probably not useful in reducing our error in guessing his quiz score; sock color would not be considered a predictor variable.

The principle underlying the use of a predictor variable is illustrated in Figure 8-1 for our homework-quiz score example. The vertical dimension is test score and the abscissa represents homework assignments. It is standard practice when preparing a graph of a predictor variable and a criterion variable to place the predictor on the abscissa and the criterion on the ordinate. The frequency distribution on the axis labeled test score is the distribution for all 30 members of the class. The three smaller frequency distributions contain the people who handed in one, two, and three homework assignments, respectively; the three smaller distributions can be summed to yield the larger one.

ERRORS IN PREDICTION

The mean is always a least-squares predictor for a given amount of information. If no predictor information is available, the overall mean of the
criterion variable is the best we can do, and the standard deviation is an
index of the amount of error we are likely to make on the average. When
there is a predictor variable that we can use to form groups, the mean of
each group is a least-squares prediction for the members of that group,
and the standard deviation of the group-members' scores around the
group's mean is the index of error. This standard deviation of observed
scores from their predicted value is given a special name; it is called the
standard error of estimate.

Although the mean of the smallest group with which an individual can
be identified is the best prediction of her/his score on the criterion variable, it is important to realize that this is best in terms of the whole group

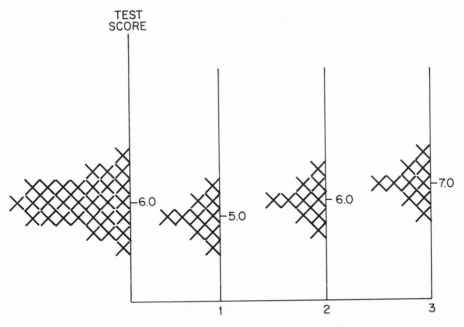

*Figure 8-1   Frequency distributions of quiz scores for total group and for
subgroups based on homework completed.*

and may not be accurate for the particular individual. For example, Charlie may earn a score of 6 on the quiz; if this happens, our prediction would have been more accurate if we had ignored the predictor entirely. There is no way to know ahead of time what score an individual will earn, but over a series of predictions, the least-squares prediction will result in the smallest average error.

It is often useful to know how large we may expect our errors to be; another way of phrasing this is to ask what the probability is that our prediction will be in error by some specified amount. For example, what is the probability that Charlie will get a score below 6 on the quiz? To answer this question, we can use the standard error of estimate and the relationship between probability and the normal distribution. There are two conditions that we must assume are true in order to do this: First, that the standard error of estimate is the same for each group; otherwise, it would be necessary to compute a separate one for each group. Second, we must assume that each of the groups forms a normal distribution. To the extent that this is not true, the relationship between probability and z-score described in Chapter 7 and Appendix Table B.1 will not hold exactly.

If our two assumptions are reasonably well met by the data we have at hand (in this case, the data from last year's class), then we can proceed to answer the question, what is the probability that Charlie will score below 6? Charlie handed in three homework assignments; therefore, our best prediction of his quiz score is 7 because this is the mean of his group. The standard error of estimate is 1.1, and the lower limit of the score category 6 is 5.5; we calculate the z-score as

$$z_{5.5} = \frac{5.5 - 7}{1.1} = \frac{-1.5}{1.1} = -1.36.$$

Looking up the area below a z of -1.36 in Appendix Table B.1, we find the value 0.0869, which we round to 0.09; that is, our calculations tell us that there is a 9 percent chance (or about 1 in 10) that Charlie will actually get a score below 6 on the quiz. Notice that this conforms very closely to our frequency distribution where one of the ten people who handed in all three homework assignments actually received a quiz score of less than 6. Using exactly the same procedure, we can determine the probability that someone who handed in only one homework assignment will get a score above 6.

Notice that once again we must be careful to use the real limits of the score interval in our computations using the normal distribution; otherwise, our probability estimates will not be so accurate. If we had forgotten or ignored the fact that a score value of 6 is used to represent an interval on the continuous trait from 5.5 to 6.5, we would have found a z-score of -0.91. The area of the normal curve that falls beyond this point is 0.1814 or 0.18, which is just double our previous answer. Had we made this mistake, we would have overestimated the probability of a score below 6; of course, as the number of score categories in the distribution increases, the importance of this distinction is diminished.

The most widespread use of the standard error of estimate is to place what are called *confidence intervals* on our predictions. A confidence interval is a range of values selected so that we have some specified level of confidence or assurance that the interval includes the unknown value we are estimating or predicting. Confidence is stated in terms of probability; a 95 percent confidence interval is one where the probability is 0.95 that the interval includes the unknown value. In our example, 9 percent of the distribution of quiz scores of people who had completed three homework assignments would be expected to fall below the score category 6; likewise, 9 percent would be expected to score above 8 ($z_{8.5} = +1.36$). Therefore, 82 percent will fall in the range 5.5 to 8.5, or the score values 6 and 8 are the score limits of the 82 percent confidence interval, and 5.5 and 8.5 are the real limits. We can also expect about 82 percent of the people who have handed in three homework assignments to earn scores between 6 and 8. In addition, the probability is about 80 percent that Charlie will earn a quiz score between 6 and 8.

Confidence intervals are extremely useful in making predictions for individuals because they allow us to make approximate predictions (range predictions) with a specified probability of being wrong. We can adjust the limits of the interval in order to take into account the difference in value of overpredicting or underpredicting. We shall say more about confidence intervals after discussing linear prediction.

LINEAR RELATIONSHIPS

Two variables are said to be related or to have a relationship when the value of one variable changes as the value of the other is changed. There are always two or more variables involved, and the relationship may be simple or complex. Our discussion will be restricted to the case of two variables and to the simplest form of relationship.

A relationship between two variables is known as a *bivariate relationship*; one of the variables is given the label X and the other Y. When prediction is involved, it is customary to use X for the predictor variable and Y for the criterion variable. In our previous example, the number of homework assignments would be the X-variable and quiz score would be Y. In cases where prediction is not involved, it makes little difference which variable is called X, but it is conventional when graphing the relationships to put the X-variable on the abscissa and the Y-variable on the ordinate. Y is then treated as the criterion variable even if no predictions are to be made.

The relationship between X and Y is expressed in the form of an equation. Since Y is the variable to be predicted, the equation has the general form

$$Y = f(X),$$

where the right-hand term, which is read "function of X," can assume any form needed. Some possible forms for $f(X)$ are

$$X^2 + 2X + 96$$

$$17X^3 - 386X^2 + 0.0037X + 23.$$

By far the most common form of relationship used in the social and behavioral sciences is the *linear relationship*. The equation for a linear relationship is the same one we have already encountered for a linear transformation,

$$Y = BX + A. \tag{8.1}$$

GRAPHING RELATIONSHIPS

As we noted, it is customary to present the graph of a relationship with the Y-variable on the ordinate. With both axes marked off in appropriate units the graph of equation 8.1 is a straight line that intercepts the Y-axis at a value A and increases B units of Y for each unit of increase on X; B is the *slope* of the line and A is its *intercept*.

A set of observations never follows a straight line perfectly; the graph of a set of observations is called a *scatter plot*. It is formed by plotting a point to represent each person. Every member of the group is observed on both variables, and we follow essentially the same procedure in making a scatter plot that we followed in preparing a histogram, with the difference that we have to consider both variables simultaneously.

The steps in making a scatter plot are outlined in Figure 8-2 using the set of scores in Table 8-2. In part a of the figure, the coordinate axes are laid out with the proper numerical labels, since the data show scores from 1 to 6 on each quiz. If data on one or both variables are to be grouped, the axes reflect this; in other words, each axis is labeled just as it would be in preparing an ordinary (univariate) histogram.

Part b of Figure 8-2 illustrates the major difference between a bivariate and a univariate graph. There is an axis representing frequency that is perpendicular to a plane surface formed by the X- and Y-axes. The

TABLE 8-2
Scores of 20 Students on Two Quizzes.

Individual	Quiz 1(X)	Quiz 2(Y)
1	2	3
2	4	4
3	6	5
4	4	2
5	5	4
6	5	3
7	3	4
8	4	4
9	2	3
10	6	4
11	3	2
12	3	1
13	4	2
14	2	3
15	2	2
16	2	1
17	3	3
18	4	3
19	3	4
20	5	6

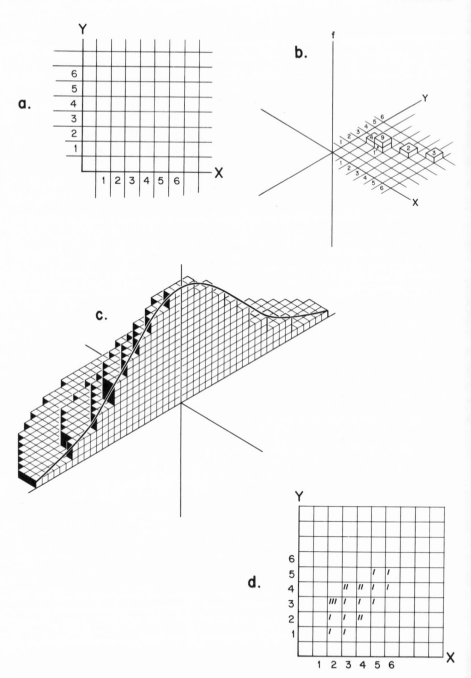

Figure 8-2   Preparation of a bivariate (two-variable) histogram and scatter plot; see text for explanation.

squares on the plane are equivalent to the intervals in the ordinary histogram; each represents a unique combination of X- and Y-scores. The bivariate histogram is then formed by placing a cube on the appropriate square for each person. Individual 1 has the score combination $X = 2$, $Y = 3$, so the cube representing her/him is placed on the square with coordinates 2, 3. The cubes for individuals 2, 3, and 4 are shown in their proper places. Individual 9 has the same score combination as 1, so the cube for this person is placed on top of that for individual 1. We continue adding cubes, one for each person, until the entire group has been placed; a hypothetical histogram for a large group is shown, cut in half, in part c.

We seldom use a bivariate histogram; rather, the most common form for a scatter plot is that shown in Figure 8-2d. In this figure, the X- and Y-axes are shown with tallies used to indicate the number of individuals who received each possible combination of scores. Here, three people got the score combination $X = 2$, $Y = 3$, so there are three tallies in this square. Each of the other squares has a number of tallies equal to the number of people in that square. Figure 8-2d is a bivariate frequency distribution; most scatter plots are presented in this form.

LINEAR PREDICTION AND DESCRIPTION

We saw in Chapter 4 that the mean provides a least-squares description of a group of observations, and our discussion in the first part of this chapter extended the concept of least squares to prediction. Actually, the distinction between the two is one of purpose, since the same set of observations can be used for either of them. We measure two variables for a group of people, and if we want to describe the degree of relationship between the two variables, the same indices are computed that would be used for prediction, but a new set of observations is not obtained. When prediction is the objective, we describe the relationship between the two variables and by assuming that the relationship is the same for other, as yet unmeasured people, use that description to make forecasts.

Observations of the real world seldom if ever form a perfect linear relationship; instead, they form an ellipse like the scatter plot in Figure 8-2d. For each value of X, several different values of Y are observed. In a perfect linear relationship, only one value of Y would occur for each value of X, and the scatter plot would form a straight line.

The data in Tables 8-1 and 8-2 are typical of the kind obtained in social and behavioral science research. In the first case, there is a clear grouping of the observations on the X-variable, and it is possible to use X-group means on the Y-variable as least squares predictors of Y-scores. In the latter case, however, we can reasonably consider both of the quizzes to be continuous variables. It is necessary, therefore, to introduce some assumptions in order to obtain least squares predictions.

Linearity Assumption. Our first and most important assumption is that if it were possible to form groups on the X-variable and compute the mean Y for each group, those Y-means would fall on a straight line. Another way to say this is that we assume it is possible to find a straight line that passes through the Y-means of any possible groupings on the X-variable. Thus the straight line so determined provides a least squares prediction of Y for any value of X. It does so because it passes through the value that the mean of Y would have if we were to compute it for all individuals who have that value of X.

It is difficult to overstate the importance of understanding that there is a straight line that provides a least-squares prediction of Y from X. This is what is meant in statistics by the term linear relationship. If the data satisfy the linearity assumption, then it is possible to find a straight line of the form $Y = BX + A$ such that for every value of X, the value Y is a least squares predictor for the individuals who have that value of X. The linear relationship is a straight line that is fitted to the observed data so that it satisfies the principle of least squares. Several of the concepts we discuss later and many that are beyond the scope of our discussion are based on the linear bivariate relationship.

Brief Aside. When we say that we are making an assumption about the data or that a particular condition or principle is assumed to be true, our assumption may be strictly correct or it may be false in varying degrees. Mathematicians in general and statisticians in particular must make certain assumptions or set down certain guidelines and ground rules in order to develop their logical systems. These logical systems can be viewed as mathematical models that may be applied to real-world problems. The degree to which the model's assumptions are met by the data determines how well the properties of the model represent reality. The data will never fit the assumptions of the model exactly, but if the fit is close, the model will provide a good representation. Failure of the data to fit the model's assumptions means that computations based on those assumptions will give poor results.

For example, suppose that the assumption of linearity is not met. This does not mean that we cannot use a straight line to make predictions or describe the relationship between our variables. The data don't know anything about assumptions; they are ignorant; in fact we can still find the best or least-squares straight line. What the failure of our assumption means is that there is some line other than a straight one that provides a better model for the data and predictions that are more accurate than can be made from a straight line.

An Example. Fitting a line to a set of observations does not involve identifying groups or computing means. Rather, the points, each of which represents an observation, are used directly, and the least-squares criterion is applied directly to the line; this is illustrated in Figure 8-3 for a set of ten points.

Suppose that the data plotted in Figure 8-3 represent the number of errors made by ten students on each of two lab reports in a course in experimental design. We are interested in whether there is a relationship between errors on one assignment and errors on another. We do not have enough people with each score to form groups, but by assuming a linear

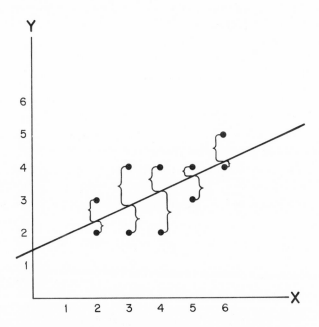

Figure 8-3 Bivariate scatter plot of ten scores and least squares regression line showing errors of prediction from the line.

relationship and using procedures to be described shortly, we can still find a least-squares linear predictor equation.

The least-squares criterion is applied to the Y-scores, which means that the line is located in order to minimize the sum of squares of the distances of the points from the line in a direction parallel to the Y-axis. The distance of an individual's data point from the line is the error of prediction. These errors are indicated in the figure by brackets. The line is chosen so that the sum of squares of these errors is minimized.

Normality Assumption. Our second important assumption when we make predictions is that the group or individual about whom we are predicting is not different in any but chance ways from those on whom the prediction equation was based. This implies that the errors of prediction form a normal distribution, because, as we have seen, chance events tend to follow the normal curve. Stating this another way, we assume that the errors of prediction form a normal distribution. Looking back at the bivariate histogram (Figure 8-2c), the assumption that the distribution of errors or deviations from the line is normal suggests that if we were to slice the histogram at any point parallel to the Y-axis, the surface of the slice would yield a normal distribution.

Homogeneity Assumption. The third assumption goes by the interesting name of homoskedasticity. What this word, derived from Greek, means is that the variance of scores in any slice through the bivariate histogram and parallel to the Y-axis is equal to the variance of the scores in any other such slice. Another way of saying this is that the variances of errors of prediction are homogeneous. The standard deviation of Y-scores for those people who received a score of X_1 is the same as the S_Y of people who earned a value of X_2 on the X-variable. We also note that the linearity assumption implies that the mean of each slice is a point on the line. Therefore, we are assuming that the variance of observations around any point on the line is the same for every point on the line. We shall see shortly that this assumption permits us to place confidence intervals on our predictions.

MAKING PREDICTIONS

In our earlier prediction problem, we computed group Y-score means and used these as our least squares predictors of Y for the several values of X (groups). We have now seen that for continuous predictor variables, it is possible to find a line that will serve the same function but will yield a predicted value of Y for any value of X without the need to form groups.

Predicted values of Y are determined for any value of X by using the equation for the line. When predictions are to be made, the equation for the line is generally written

$$\hat{Y}_i = BX_i + A, \tag{8.2}$$

where the caret (^) over the Y indicates a predicted score. The symbol indicates that the relationship between X and Y is not exact and that the observed data points spread out around the line. The values of $\hat{Y}$ all fall on the line.

If we know the slope B of the line and its intercept A, we can use equation 8.2 to compute a $\hat{Y}$ for any X. The data plotted in Figure 8-3 are listed in Table 8-3 and will be used to illustrate the computations. By procedures we shall discuss shortly, the slope of the least-squares or best-fit line is found to be 0.45 and its intercept is 1.5. Placing these values in equation 8.2 gives us the equation for the line.

$$\hat{Y} = 0.45X + 1.5.$$

By inserting any value of X in this equation, we can compute the predicted value of Y; for example, if $X = 2$

$$\hat{Y} = 0.45(2) + 1.5$$

$$= 0.9 + 1.5 = 2.4.$$

Similar computations for each of the other observed values of X yield $\hat{Y}$'s of 2.85 for $X = 3$; 3.3 for $X = 4$; 3.75 for $X = 5$; and 4.2 for $X = 6$.

Once we have predictions for each person, we can compute the errors of prediction. They can then be used to compute a standard error of estimate, which is the standard deviation of the distribution of distances of points from the line. Remember that our least-squares principle located the line so that the standard error around this line is less than it would be if we used any other line to make our predictions.

Column 4 of Table 8-3 contains the predicted values $\hat{Y}_i$; the errors of prediction $(Y_i - \hat{Y}_i)$ are given in column 5, and the squares of these errors appear in the last column. Note that the sum of errors (but not the sum of squares) is exactly zero. This is the same thing that we observed about the sum of deviations from the mean in Chapter 4 and illustrates the fact that the line is just like a mean that runs all the way through the frequency distribution. At the end of Table 8-3, $\sum Y$, $\sum Y^2$, and S_y, are given. The value of S_y (1.005) is, of course, an index of the average amount of error that we would incur by using $\bar{Y}$ as our prediction for each individual. Also included in the table are $\sum(Y - \hat{Y})$ $(=0)$, $\sum(Y - \hat{Y})^2$, and the standard error of estimate, which is computed as

$$S_{y \cdot x} = \sqrt{\frac{\sum\limits_{i=1}^{N}(Y_i - \hat{Y}_i)^2}{N}} \tag{8.3}$$

$$= \sqrt{\frac{6.05}{10}} = \sqrt{0.605} = 0.778.$$

The standard error of estimate is an index of the average amount of error that would result from using the line to make our predictions.

The symbol $S_{y \cdot x}$ is used for the standard error of estimate. The letter S indicates that it is a standard deviation, and the subscript $Y \cdot X$ is read "Y given X," which means that we are talking about the standard deviation of Y's around the best prediction that we can make from X. Since the regression line is the best prediction that we can make, $S_{y \cdot x}$ is the standard deviation of Y's around the regression line.

We have said that the regression line is like a continuous mean of Y-scores for each value of X. However, the data in our example show that

TABLE 8-3
Computing the Standard Error of Estimate.

Individual	X	Y	$\hat{Y}$	$Y - \hat{Y}$	$(Y - \hat{Y})^2$
1	2	3	2.4	0.6	0.36
2	4	4	3.3	0.7	0.49
3	6	5	4.2	0.8	0.64
4	4	2	3.3	-1.3	1.69
5	5	4	3.75	0.25	0.0625
6	5	3	3.75	-0.75	0.5625
7	3	4	2.85	1.15	1.3225
8	6	4	4.2	-0.2	0.04
9	2	2	2.4	-0.4	0.16
10	3	2	2.85	-0.85	0.7225

	Calculations	
$\sum Y = 33$	$\sum(Y - \hat{Y}) = 0$
$\sum Y^2 = 119$	$\sum(Y - \hat{Y})^2 = 6.05$
$S_y = 1.005$	$S_{y \cdot x} = 0.778$

the value on the line $\hat{Y}$ is not equal to the mean of Y-scores for any value of X. At $X = 2$, $\bar{Y}$ is 2.5, but $\hat{Y} = 2.4$; similar discrepancies occur at each value of X. The reason for this is that the data do not fulfill our assumption of linearity precisely. The regression line is determined for a particular set of data in such a way that, for that set of data,

$$\sum_{i=1}^{N} (Y_i - \hat{Y}_i) = 0$$

$$\sum_{i=1}^{N} (Y_i - \hat{Y}_i)^2 = \text{minimum.}$$

If the mean Y at one or more values of X does not fall on the line, our assumption of an exactly linear relationship for this set of data is false. For reasons that we shall discuss in Part III, this assumption and all others are never exactly true for any set of observations. The question we must answer is whether the departure from our assumptions is too great. The experience of over 75 years is that there are very few occasions when social and behavioral data cannot be analyzed more fruitfully with the assumption of a simple linear relationship than with any other kind.

FINDING B

Slope coefficients (B) and intercepts (A) do not grow on trees, nor are they obtained from divine revelation. They are computed from the observed data using some relatively simple formulas. First, remember that we defined the line as the least-squares line, which means that the line we seek is the one for which errors are minimized. The errors are $(Y_i - \hat{Y}_i)$, and the least-squares criterion states that the line we seek is the one that yields the smallest possible value of $\sum(Y_i - \hat{Y}_i)^2$.

Developing an equation for the regression line will be simpler if we first convert everything to deviation scores. In Chapter 4, we found that subtracting the mean (or any constant) from every score in a distribution did not change the sum of squares. Thus, if we subtract $\bar{Y}$ from all Y's, call predicted Y's $\hat{y}$'s and use $x_i = (X_i - \bar{X})$, we can cast our problem in the form

$$F = \sum_{i=1}^{N} (y_i - \hat{y}_i)^2 = \text{minimum.} \tag{8.4}$$

One of the advantages of expressing the regression line in terms of deviation scores is that the intercept is zero; that is, the regression line always passes through the coordinates $(\bar{X}, \bar{Y})$ in the scatter plot. If we convert to deviation scores, which we can do without loss of information, the coordinates $(\bar{x}, \bar{y})$ are $(0, 0)$ or the origin. The regression line passes through the origin and therefore must have an intercept of zero. Under these circumstances, the equation of the regression line becomes

$$\hat{y}_i = bx_i. \tag{8.5}$$

(It is widely used, but not universal, notation to let b represent the slope of the regression line when deviation scores are used and to have B symbolize the slope for raw scores. The two slope values are numerically equivalent, but we shall follow the tradition.)

Substituting equation 8.5 into 8.4, the function to be minimized is

$$F = \sum_{i=1}^{N} (y_i - bx_i)^2.$$

By a series of manipulations presented in Appendix A, this expression yields the deviation-score equation for b.

$$b_{y \cdot x} = \frac{\displaystyle\sum_{i=1}^{N} x_i y_i}{\displaystyle\sum_{i=1}^{N} x_i^2} \tag{8.6}$$

The symbol $b_{y \cdot x}$ denotes the slope of the regression line for predicting y, given the value of x. The numerator of the right-hand term is called a sum of cross-products and requires us to multiply each individual's y by her/his x (remembering that they are deviations) and find the sum of these products. The denominator is the sum of squares of x.

It is important to note that it can matter a great deal which variable is called x and which is y in computing the slope of the regression line. Suppose we wish to predict x from y. We could then write the equation of the regression line as

$$\hat{x}_i = b_{x \cdot y} y_i,$$

with the constraint that $\sum(x_i - \hat{x}_i)^2$ be minimized. Applying the same steps as before, we find that

$$b_{x \cdot y} = \frac{\sum\limits_{i=1}^{N} x_i y_i}{\sum\limits_{i=1}^{N} y_i^2} . \tag{8.7}$$

The only difference between this equation and 8.6 is the denominator, but this means that unless $\sum y^2 = \sum x^2$, the two regression lines will have different slopes. Of course, predictions made from the wrong regression line can be worse than no predictive information at all, so care is required.

Deviation-score equations are not convenient to use when computing the slope coefficient. By substituting raw scores and means into equation 8.6, we can obtain a computational formula for $b_{y \cdot x}$ that uses only raw scores.

$$B_{y \cdot x} = \frac{N(\sum X_i Y_i) - (\sum X_i)(\sum Y_i)}{N(\sum X_i^2) - (\sum X_i)^2} . \tag{8.8}$$

The equivalence of equations 8.6 and 8.8 is shown in Appendix A. The computational form has the double advantage of being easier to use and less prone to rounding errors, even though it does look more complex.

The raw data from Table 8-3 are reproduced in Table 8-4 to provide an example of computing $b_{y \cdot x}$ using either the deviation (8.6) or the raw score (8.8) formula. In this example, the numbers are simple enough so that the slope of 0.45 works out quite easily either way. However, it is generally the case that the computational formula 8.8 will be easier to use and give a more accurate answer because it involves no rounding.

COMPUTING A

Deviation scores are often more convenient for algebraic derivations, but with practical prediction problems, it is almost always preferable to work with raw scores. This means that we shall use the regression equation

$$\hat{Y}_i = B_{y \cdot x} X_i + A_{y \cdot x}.$$

The value of $A_{y \cdot x}$ is, of course, the value of Y, where the regression line crosses the Y-axis (when the value of X_i is zero). For a given set of data, we can then find the intercept by

$$A_{y \cdot x} = \bar{Y} - B_{y \cdot x} \bar{X}. \tag{8.9}$$

The development of this equation is given in Appendix A.

The intercept can easily be computed for the data in Table 8-4. With $\bar{X} = 4.0$, $\bar{Y} = 3.3$, and $b_{y \cdot x} = 0.45$, we get

$A_{y \cdot x} = 3.3 - (0.45)\,(4)$

$\quad = 3.3 - 1.8 = 1.5.$

This, of course, is the same value we used to plot the regression line in Figure 8-3 and to compute predicted scores for use in finding $S_{y \cdot x}$, the standard error of estimate.

TABLE 8-4
Computing the Slope From Deviation Scores.

X	Y	x	y	XY	xy	x^2
2	3	−2	−0.3	6	0.6	4
4	4	0	0.7	16	0	0
6	5	2	1.7	30	3.4	4
4	2	0	−1.3	8	0	0
5	4	1	0.7	20	0.7	1
5	3	1	−0.3	15	−0.3	1
3	4	−1	0.7	12	−0.7	1
6	4	2	0.7	24	1.4	4
2	2	−2	−1.3	4	2.6	4
3	2	−1	−1.3	6	1.3	1

Calculations

$\sum X = 40 \qquad \sum Y = 33 \qquad \sum XY = 141$

$\bar{X} = 4.0 \qquad \bar{Y} = 3.3 \qquad \sum xy = 9.0$

$\sum X^2 = 180 \qquad \sum Y^2 = 119 \qquad \sum x^2 = 20.0$

$$B_{y \cdot x} = \frac{\sum xy}{\sum x^2} = \frac{N(\sum XY) - (\sum X)\,(\sum Y)}{N(\sum X^2) - (\sum X)^2}$$

$$= \frac{9}{20} = \frac{10(141) - 40(33)}{10(180) - (40)^2}$$

$$= 0.45 = \frac{1410 - 1320}{1800 - 1600}$$

$$= \frac{90}{200} = 0.45$$

INTERPRETING THE REGRESSION EQUATION

As we have said, the regression equation, or the equation of the regression line, is used in making least-squares predictions. This equation gives one basic piece of information about the nature of the relationship between the two variables, the direction or sign of the relationship. The algebraic sign ($+$ or $-$) of the slope coefficient tells us whether the value of $\hat{Y}$ gets greater or smaller as the value of the predictor is increased. A positive sign on $B_{y \cdot x}$ means that the line rises as we go from left to right, as shown in part a of Figure 8-4; we call this a positive relationship between

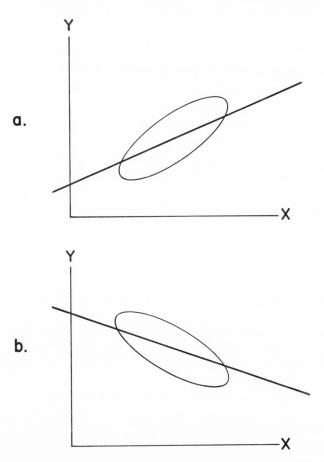

*Figure 8-4 Meaning of the sign of a regression coefficient showing a positive slope (**a.**) and a negative slope (**b.**).*

the two variables. A negative sign on $B_{y \cdot x}$ tells us that the value of $\hat{Y}$ decreases as the value of X increases; this situation, shown in part b of the figure, is called a negative relationship.

It is important to recognize the limited significance of the information conveyed by $B_{y \cdot x}$: The sign indicates the direction of the relationship, but not its strength or value. A positive relationship between two variables is no better or worse than a negative one, and its meaning depends entirely on the meaning of the variables themselves. There are some situations where the direction of measurement (which end of the scale is up) may be more or less arbitrary. For example, a scale that measures the trait political liberalism (high score is liberal) might show a negative relationship with chronological age. The same scale, but rescored as a measure of political conservatism (high score is conservative), might be positively related to age. The most important thing to remember in interpreting regression slopes is which end of the original scale is up.

Except in certain restricted situations, one of which is discussed in the next chapter, the numerical value of $B_{y \cdot x}$ conveys little information of interpretive value. A large B does not indicate a better or stronger relationship. In fact, the value of B is unrelated to the accuracy of prediction or the usefulness of the predictor information, except in the one special case where the value of $B_{y \cdot x}$ is exactly zero. When $B_{y \cdot x}$ is exactly zero, we make the same prediction for everyone ($\hat{Y} = A$), but in all other cases the value of B tells us little beyond the information in its sign.

Likewise, A has no interpretive significance by itself. There are situations where it is useful to compare intercepts and slopes for different groups, and we discuss them in Part III, but the intercept for a single group tells us nothing beyond what is needed to compute the most accurate predictions possible for this set of data.

CONFIDENCE INTERVALS

The standard error of estimate is the standard deviation of errors of prediction from the regression line. It may be used just like any other standard deviation to compute z-scores because under the assumptions that we have made about the bivariate distribution, the regression line is always a mean Y-score for people with a particular value of X. That is, if

$\hat{Y}_p = BX_p + A$, then $\hat{Y}_p$ is the mean Y-score for those people whose X-score was X_p. Since $\hat{Y}$ is a mean,

$$\sqrt{\frac{\sum (Y - \hat{Y})^2}{N}}$$

is a standard deviation (which we symbolize $S_{y \cdot x}$) and the value $(Y - \hat{Y})/S_{y \cdot x}$ is a z-score.

Given the truth of our assumption of a bivariate normal distribution (we always assume that our assumptions are true), we can use the normal curve and its associated probabilities just as we did in our earlier example of homework and quiz scores. For any value of X, we compute a $\hat{Y}$ and a confidence interval around the predicted value. Once we have $\hat{Y}$, there are two ways to set the confidence interval. The first way is to ask how likely it is that the prediction will be in error by more than K points. The second is to specify some probability (P) of error and set our confidence interval so that the probability of an individual's actual score falling outside the interval is only P.

Suppose that Dr. Numbercruncher is giving her statistics class a final exam. She has been teaching the course for several years, and each year she computes the regression equation for the relationship between midterm and final-test scores. This year, she tells her class that on the basis of years of experience she has concluded that the appropriate regression slope is 0.84, the intercept is 37, and the standard error of estimate is 4.15 and the minimum score on the final to get at least a C is 60.

Joyce is worried about her performance; she got a score of 34 on the midterm and would like to know what her chances are on the final. What can we predict from the information given? First, we compute Joyce's predicted final score. Using the instructor's regression equation, we get

$$\hat{Y} = 0.84(34) + 37$$

$$= 65.56.$$

Since the critical score for a C is 60, we find z_{60} to be

$$z_{60} = \frac{60 - 65.56}{4.15} - \frac{-5.56}{4.15} = -1.34.$$

Looking in the table of the normal curve, we find that the probability of a z beyond -1.34 is 0.09, so we conclude that there is only about one chance in ten that Joyce will get a *D* or less. (Note that Joyce might be able to alter this probability by a little studying.)

This example does not involve a true confidence interval, although it does involve a kind of problem that is frequently encountered. We might rephrase the question: What is the probability that a student will obtain a score more than five points above or below the predicted value? Finding the *z* of +5 or −5 to be

$$z = \frac{5}{4.15} = 1.20,$$

we use Appendix Table B.1 to find that the probability of a score more than five points above the predicted one is 0.1151, and the same is true for the lower side. Therefore, we can say that the probability is 0.23 (or 23 percent) that our prediction will be in error by at least five points for any given individual. Looking at it from the other point of view, we can conclude that 77 percent of our predictions are likely to be in error by five points or less. The crucial problem for which there is no adequate solution at the present time is how to identify the people for whom the error will be large.

The second and more conventional way of expressing a confidence interval is to specify a probability and work backward to the score limits. For example, Joyce still has a predicted score of 65.56, but she would like to know a range that she may be 90 percent certain will include her score. She is willing to accept a 5 percent chance of being too low and a 5 percent chance of being too high.

The solution to this problem is to look up the *z* beyond which 5 percent of the normal distribution falls; from Appendix Table B.1, we find this value to be 1.645. Five percent of the distribution falls above +1.645 and another 5 percent falls below −1.645. We convert these *z*-scores to deviations by multiplying by $S_{y \cdot x}$ (4.15) to get ± 6.83. That is, 90 percent of our errors will be less than 6.83 units, or Joyce with her predicted score of 65.56 can be 90 percent certain that the interval from (65.56 − 6.83 =) 58.73 to (65.56 + 6.83 =) 72.39 includes the score that she will actually earn. In other words, the 90 percent confidence interval for Joyce's score is 58.73 to 72.39.

It may be helpful at this time to review our discussion of *z*-scores, probability, and the normal distribution in Chapter 7. The student should be able to see how the same principles are at work in the two kinds of problems. Of course, if our assumption of a normal distribution for the errors of prediction from the regression line is not met, the confidence interval and its associated probability will not be correct. However, for most practical work, the discrepancy would have to be fairly large for the inaccuracies to be important.

SUMMARY

Predictions occur in many facets of our lives. Prediction decisions may involve *selection, classification*, and *placement*. We usually find that applying the *least-squares principle* to the relationship between a *predictor* (*X*) and a *criterion* (*Y*) results in the best overall prediction.

When the predictor variable is a discrete group-membership variable, the group mean on the criterion variable is the least-squares prediction for each individual in the group. The standard error of estimate ($S_{y \cdot x}$) is the standard deviation of errors of prediction. It can be used to compute a confidence interval around the prediction.

We generally assume that the relationship between two continuous variables is best described by a straight line. The scores of individuals are represented in a scatter plot that is usually elliptical in shape. Predictions are made from a straight line of the form $\hat{Y} = BX + A$. If the assumption of a linear relationship is met, the value of $\hat{Y}$ is a least squares prediction of *Y* for every value of *X*, and the standard error of estimate is the standard deviation of deviations from the line. Using $S_{y \cdot x}$, it is possible to determine a confidence interval for any prediction or to state a probability that the criterion score of a person with a given predictor score will be above or below a particular value. We pointed out that the slope of the regression line indicates the direction of a relationship between two variables but gives no information about its strength or about the accuracy of predictions made from the regression line.

PROBLEMS

1. Give two examples for each of the three types of prediction decisions.

2. For each of the following situations state whether the decision is selection, classification, or placement:

*(a) A prison warden is making work assignments for new prisoners.

(b) A counselor is helping a student choose a major.

*(c) A college department chairman is making teaching assignments.

(d) A large company is hiring new secretaries.

*(e) An agricultural worker is identifying those plants to be used for next year's seed.

3. A social psychologist has collected the following data on student attitudes toward the college dean. The numbers 1 through 4 indicate class (freshman, and so on) and the second number of each pair is attitude score:

2, 3	4, 7	1, 9	2, 4
1, 7	4, 5	4, 6	1, 8
3, 3	3, 2	1, 7	4, 6
1, 6	2, 5	3, 2	4, 8
2, 6	2, 7	2, 6	3, 4
1, 5	1, 8	4, 6	
3, 3	4, 7	3, 5	
2, 5	3, 1		

(a) Assuming that we treat college class as a discrete variable, explain the application of the principle of least squares to predicting attitude scores for additional students.

*(b) What is your least-squares prediction for each class?

*(c) What is the standard error of estimate for juniors?

*(d) What is the 75 percent confidence interval for juniors?

*(e) Why is it inappropriate to use a regression line for these data?

4. The sailing instructor at an exclusive yacht and sailing club is interested in finding a way to predict how well new students will do in his course on learning how to sail. By comparing scores of 25 students on a quiz he gave them before instruction with their total points at the end of the instruction, he obtained the following results:

*Answers to starred questions are found in Appendix D.

Student	Quiz Score (X)	Total-course Points (Y)
1	78	81
2	84	80
3	82	77
4	92	86
5	83	89
6	78	80
7	86	84
8	85	90
9	83	77
10	79	78
11	84	84
12	89	84
13	93	89
14	88	88
15	86	75
16	81	81
17	84	84
18	84	82
19	92	80
20	89	85
21	88	83
22	80	76
23	87	85
24	79	75
25	78	83

(a) Plot these data with quiz scores on the X-axis and total points on the Y-axis. Just by "eyeballing" the data, sketch where you think the best fitting regression line should go.

(b) Calculate the regression line. What is the slope? intercept?

(c) Three new students have just taken the quiz but have not yet started the course. Their scores are 90, 89, 76; what are their predicted total-course points?

*5. In order to ensure enough on-duty personnel for oil-spill cleanup, the Coast Guard has kept a record of amount of tanker traffic and the amount of oil spilled.

Day	Number of Tankers	Size of Oil Spill in Yards
Sept. 8	3	100 yd^2
Sept. 10	7	800
Sept. 20	2	90
Oct. 3	5	500
Oct. 12	8	850
Oct. 15	6	600
Oct. 20	2	100
Nov. 11	1	50
Nov. 12	7	800
Nov. 20	5	650

(a) Plot these data with tanker traffic on the X-axis and oil spilled on the Y-axis. Eyeball the best fitting regression line and sketch it in.

(b) Calculate the regression line. What is the slope? intercept?

(c) If one man is needed for every 100 yd^2 of cleanup, how many men should be on duty if five tankers are due in port? 10? 3?

6. Calculate $B_{y \cdot x}$, $A_{y \cdot x}$, and $S_{y \cdot x}$ for the following distributions:

(a)	X	Y		(c)	X	Y
	118	20			21	75
	87	13			23	74
	99	15			14	91
	101	16			29	55
	114	19			21	82
	111	19			26	72
	99	15			16	83
	106	19			28	63
	110	20			28	66
	110	20			20	76

*(b)	X	Y		*(d)	X	Y
	14	78			83	18
	20	117			81	18
	16	88			73	15
	14	85			75	17
	20	118			81	17
	17	100			86	19
	17	104			85	18
	19	114			73	17
	17	105			77	17
	18	108			84	18

(e)

X	Y	X	Y
78	99	68	95
54	79	72	97
56	87	83	105
93	122	73	96
79	99	84	103
79	106	88	117
59	90	84	105
90	119	84	104
81	100	86	104
83	103	76	96
67	94	77	99
77	97	85	109
88	110		

*7. A developmental psychologist doing research on age and finger dexterity has found the following results for 15 subjects (finger-dexterity scores are number of errors made on the task):

	Age	F.D.		Age	F.D.
1.	7	5	9.	10	3
2.	5	3	10.	7	7
3.	4	7	11.	8	5
4.	6	6	12.	4	4
5.	8	2	13.	7	2
6.	5	6	14.	9	1
7.	10	1	15.	6	4
8.	9	2			

(a) Make a scatter plot of the results.

(b) Compute the equation of the regression line for predicting finger dexterity score from age.

(c) Johnny is 5 years 7 months old; what is his predicted score?

(d) What is the standard error of estimate?

(e) What is the 90 percent confidence interval for Johnny's score?

9

STRENGTH OF A RELATIONSHIP

In the last chapter, we saw that the mean of a group was the least-squares predictor of the criterion scores for members of that group. In addition, it was possible to fit a regression line through a scatter plot of two continuous variables in such a way that the line served as a least-squares predictor for any value of X; however, we had no index of how good our prediction was. The standard error of estimate, which is the standard deviation of errors of prediction, can be used to put confidence intervals on our predictions, but it does not indicate how much useful information the predictor is giving us.

In the present chapter, we discuss the predictable and unpredictable portions of a score and use this idea to develop indices of the strength of a relationship between two variables. These indices are particularly useful because they apply to situations where we have no interest in predicting anything but wish to discuss the degree of association between two traits. After presenting the basic concepts, we show how such indices may be applied and interpreted in several situations.

PARTS OF A SCORE

We use the example from Figure 8-1, reproduced here as Figure 9-1, to illustrate the parts of an individual's score. First, there is the whole score as we actually observe it; let us call this score Y_i, the score on variable Y of individual i. It is circled in the large Y-distribution and has, in this particular case, a numerical value of 8. We can express the score as the sum of two pieces, the overall mean, $\bar{Y}$, and the deviation of Y_i from $\bar{Y}$. In the form of an equation, this reads

$$Y_i = \bar{Y} + (Y_i - \bar{Y}). \tag{9.1}$$

Suppose that we know to which group i belongs (it might be our friend Charlie). Let us say that i handed in three of the homework assignments and is, therefore, a member of group 3 in the figure. The score of 8 can now be viewed as being composed of three parts, the overall mean, the deviation of i's group mean $\bar{Y}_3$ from $\bar{Y}$, and i's deviation from the mean of her/his own group. Figure 9-2 illustrates these parts of i's score, which may also be expressed as

$$Y_i = \bar{Y} + (\bar{Y}_3 - \bar{Y}) + (Y_i - \bar{Y}_3). \tag{9.2}$$

By removing parentheses and rearranging terms, it is easy to see that this expression is an identity. However, what is useful about equation 9.2 is that it shows clearly that $(\bar{Y}_3 - \bar{Y})$ is the added information supplied by the predictor variable. Without the predictor, $\bar{Y}$ itself would be our least-squares prediction, and our error would be $(Y_i - \bar{Y})$, as it was in equation 9.1. If $\bar{Y}_3$ is not equal to $\bar{Y}$, then $(Y_i - \bar{Y}_3)$ must, on the average, be smaller than $(Y_i - \bar{Y})$ by an amount equal to $(\bar{Y}_3 - \bar{Y})$, which, as we said, is the amount of information added by the predictor.

Now let us subtract $\bar{Y}$ from both sides of equation 9.2; this gives us

$$Y_i - \bar{Y} = (\bar{Y}_3 - \bar{Y}) + (Y_i - \bar{Y}_3),$$

or the deviation of Y_i from the overall mean is composed of two deviations; the deviation of the group mean from the overall mean and the deviation of i's score from the group mean. Actually, each of the 30 Y-scores is composed of the three basic pieces in equation 9.2, and each deviation is composed of two pieces.

It is now convenient to introduce a second subscript to help us keep track of our observations. The data for Figure 9-1 are presented in Table

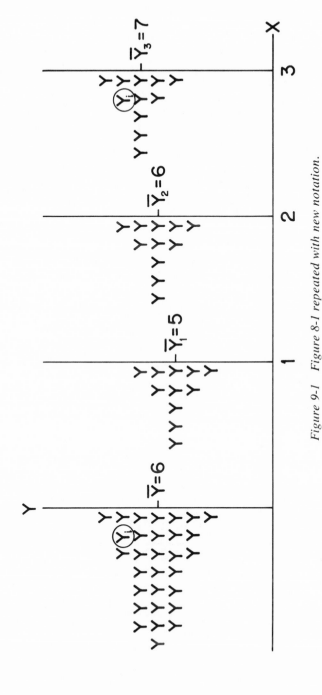

Figure 9-1   Figure 8-1 repeated with new notation.

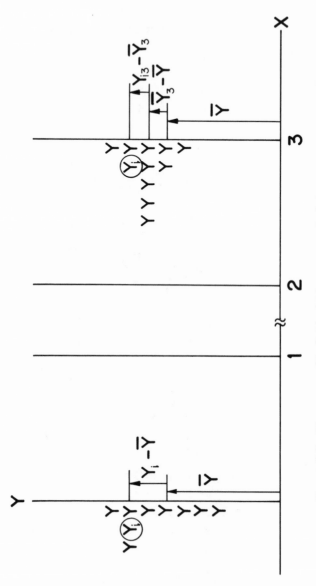

Figure 9-2   The score of individual i is composed of three parts; see text for explanation.

9-1. Note that these are the same data that were presented in Table 8-1 but they now appear in a different form. There are ten rows to the table and three columns; the columns identify which group an individual is in and the rows refer to individual within group. We use the symbol i as a subscript to indicate individual within group, the symbol j as a subscript designating group, and the general symbol Y_{ji} to refer to the ith individual in group j. In any particular example, Y_{ji} has a specific numerical value, the score of a particular person. $Y_{2\,5} = 8$, as do $Y_{3\,4}$ and $Y_{3\,7}$. The score $Y_{1\,10}$ has the numerical value 5 in this set of data.

We now rewrite equation 9.2 in the more general form

$$Y_{ji} = \bar{Y} + (\bar{Y}_j - \bar{Y}) + (Y_{ji} - \bar{Y}_j). \tag{9.3}$$

A particular deviation from the overall mean is

$$(Y_{ji} - \bar{Y}) = (\bar{Y}_j - \bar{Y}) + (Y_{ji} - \bar{Y}_j). \tag{9.4}$$

Each of the terms has the same meaning as before, but they are now general. The deviation of any score from the overall mean is composed of the predictor information contained in the group mean's deviation from the overall mean and the error that is left after we have made our best prediction.

The next step is to consider the variance of the scores around the overall mean. Remember that the variance, the square of the standard

TABLE 9-1

Data from Table 8-1 Broken up into Groups by Number of Homework Assignments Completed.

i	$j = 1$	$j = 2$	$j = 3$
1	5	7	5
2	6	4	9
3	5	6	6
4	4	6	8
5	7	8	7
6	3	5	7
7	4	6	8
8	5	7	7
9	6	5	6
10	5	6	7

deviation, is an index of the variability of a set of scores around a mean. We find the variance by summing the squared deviation scores and then dividing by the number of things summed. The general formula is

$$\text{Variance} = \frac{\sum_{i=1}^{N} (Y_i - \bar{Y})^2}{N}.$$

But, we have already seen that the term in parentheses can be broken down into two parts. By applying the operations for obtaining a variance (squaring, summing, dividing by the number of things summed, and simplifying the result [see Appendix A]) to equation 9.4, we obtain

$$\frac{\sum_{j=1}^{J} \sum_{i=1}^{n_j} (Y_{ji} - \bar{Y})^2}{\sum_{j=1}^{J} n_j} = \frac{\sum_{j=1}^{J} \sum_{i=1}^{n_j} (\bar{Y}_j - \bar{Y})^2}{\sum_{j=1}^{J} n_j} + \frac{\sum_{j=1}^{J} \sum_{i=1}^{n_j} (Y_{ji} - \bar{Y}_j)^2}{\sum_{j=1}^{J} n_j}. \tag{9.5}$$

Equation 9.5 looks much more complicated than it really is, but it is presented in this form because we shall have occasion to use it again later. Remember that in our example we are dealing with three groups and there are ten people in each group. The double summation signs

$$\sum_{j=1}^{J} \sum_{i=1}^{n_j},$$

simply take this fact into account and tell us to sum within each group first

$$\left(\sum_{i=1}^{n_j} \right)$$

for as many people (n_j) as there are in group j. Once this is done for all groups, we sum the group results to a total. For the data in Table 9-1, we sum the squared deviations down the first column, do the same for the second and third columns, and then sum the three column totals.

It is important to understand the terms in equation 9.5. When there is more than one summation, the summation closest to the variable is carried out first over its subscript dimension, then we move to the left of each term, summing over the next subscript dimension. There is an exact correspondence between the layout of the data in the table and what the summation notation tells us to do. In the left-hand term

$$\frac{\sum_{j=1}^{J} \sum_{i=1}^{n_j} (Y_{ji} - \bar{Y})^2}{\sum_{j=1}^{J} n_j},$$

we are instructed to subtract the overall mean from each of the $n_j (=10)$ observed scores in column $j(=1)$, square this deviation, and sum the $n_j (=10)$ squared deviations; this is repeated for the columns $j = 2$ and $j = 3$. The second, or left-hand, summation sign tells us to sum the J column totals. Of course, the term

$$\sum_{j=1}^{J} n_j$$

in the denominator is simply N, the total number of individuals. It is included in this form in equation 9.5 because there are times when we do not use all N cases. There are also times when there are different numbers of individuals in each group, causing the limit of summation in the numerator to vary from column to column.

The first term on the right in equation 9.5 tells us to subtract the overall mean from the predicted score for each person. The predicted score $(\bar{Y}_j)$ is the group's mean, and it is the same for every member of the group. Notice, however, that this term looks very much like the variance term on the left. It involves finding a squared deviation for each person, but the deviation on the right is of the *predicted score* from the overall mean. The deviation for each person is that part of his deviation from the overall mean that is "due to" his group. In fact, the term

$$\frac{\sum_{j=1}^{J} \sum_{i=1}^{n_j} (\bar{Y}_j - \bar{Y})^2}{\sum_{j=1}^{J} n_j}$$

is a variance (the variance of the predicted scores around the overall mean), and it is often called the variance due to group membership or the predictable variance.

The second term on the right of 9.5 should look familiar; it is the square of the standard error of estimate that we developed in Chapter 8. For each individual, we find the square of her/his deviation from the subgroup's mean and use this to find a total *variance error of estimate* by summing across all individuals and dividing by the number of individuals summed across.

Equation 9.5 is extremely important because it shows that the total variation in a set of scores can be broken down into two pieces. Total variance is equal to predictable variance (variance due to our predictions) and error variance (what we cannot predict with the predictor variables available). We use this *partitioning* of the variance to develop measures of the strength of association or relationship between two variables.

CORRELATION RATIO

For convenience, we can rewrite equation 9.5 using variance symbols. Substituting appropriately subscripted S^2 terms in 9.5, we obtain

$$S_y^2 = S_{\hat{y}}^2 + S_{y \cdot x}^2. \tag{9.6}$$

This equation says again that the total variance in a set of Y-scores is composed of predictable variance ($S_{\hat{y}}^2$) and variance error of estimate ($S_{y \cdot x}^2$).

We can convert equation 9.6 into proportions by dividing both sides by S_y^2. The left-hand term becomes 1.0, and the two terms on the right become the proportion of the total variance that is predictable from X and the proportion that remains error, respectively

$$\frac{S_y^2}{S_y^2} = 1 = \frac{S_{\hat{y}}^2}{S_y^2} + \frac{S_{y \cdot x}^2}{S_y^2}. \tag{9.7}$$

In order to obtain an index of the degree of relationship between the two variables, X and Y, we solve equation 9.7 for the proportion of variance that is predictable or is due to the association. Note that because these values are proportions, they are not affected by the absolute sizes of the variance terms, only their relative magnitudes

$$\frac{S_{\hat{y}}^2}{S_y^2} = 1 - \frac{S_{y \cdot x}^2}{S_y^2}. \tag{9.8}$$

The left-hand term in equation 9.8 has been given the name *correlation ratio* and the symbol η^2 (eta squared)

$$\eta^2 = \frac{S_{\hat{y}}^2}{S_y^2} = 1 - \frac{S_{y \cdot x}^2}{S_y^2} \; ; \tag{9.9}$$

η^2 is an index of the degree or strength of association between two variables and expresses directly the proportion of variance in Y that is predictable from X. Of course, we cannot put an individual's score under a microscope and remove the portion that is predictable. The index is the result of observations of a group and summarizes the relationship for the group. Because it is a proportion, it yields comparable information for variables that differ widely in their standard deviations.

The interpretation of η^2 is fairly simple and fairly limited. It is the proportion of variance in Y that is predictable from a knowledge of X in the group of individuals on whom we have data. Alternatively, we can say that it is an index of the degree to which our error in predicting, or estimating, a person's score on Y is reduced by a knowledge of her/his score on X.

One of the features that makes the correlation ratio a particularly useful statistic is that it can be used with most sets of data. The only requirements or assumptions are that the Y-variable must be an interval variable, that it must have an approximately normal distribution, and that each of the subgroups must also have approximately normal distributions and approximately equal (homogeneous) variances. These assumptions are the same ones that we had to make when we used the standard error, or estimate, to set up confidence intervals. Notice that we do not have to assume that the subgroup means fall on a straight line or that X is anything more than a nominal variable.

Failure to meet the assumptions about Y does not have any important mathematical consequences: Our calculator will not start flashing lights or error messages, nor will we give the computer a case of indigestion; however, we may make practical mistakes or draw illogical conclusions. For example, $S_{y \cdot x}$ and η^2 are the result of averaging across all of the groupings on X. If the subgroup variances are not homogeneous, the confidence intervals will be too wide for some predictions and too narrow for others. Also, our statements about the degree of relationship will not be accurate across the entire set of data. A violation of the interval-scale assumption may lead to such conclusions as 50 percent of the variance in gender (sex) is related to eye color.

Computational formulas for the correlation ratio can be obtained by substituting the appropriate terms from equation 9.5 into equation 9.9 to yield

$$
\eta^2 = \frac{\sum\limits_{j=1}^{J} \sum\limits_{i=1}^{n_j} (\bar{Y}_j - \bar{Y})^2}{\sum\limits_{j=1}^{J} \sum\limits_{i=1}^{n_j} (Y_{ji} - \bar{Y})^2} = 1 - \frac{\sum\limits_{j} \sum\limits_{i} (Y_{ji} - \bar{Y}_j)^2}{\sum\limits_{j} \sum\limits_{i} (Y_{ji} - \bar{Y})^2}. \tag{9.10}
$$

We can compute η^2 from either of these ratios of sums of squares. These formulas have the advantage of using values that are intermediate steps in some of the computations we encounter in Chapter 16. Of course, it is also possible to use either form in equation 9.9 when $S_{\hat{y}}^2$ and $S_{y \cdot x}^2$ have already been computed for other reasons.

There is an additional shortcut that we can use in computing η^2 from equation 9.10. The value of $(\bar{Y}_j - \bar{Y})^2$ is the same for all members of group j. Adding a constant n_j times is the same as multiplying the constant by n_j (see Appendix A, summation rule I). Therefore, we can replace the second summation sign in the numerator with n_j, giving us

$$
S_{\hat{y}}^2 = \frac{\sum\limits_{j=1}^{J} n_j (\bar{Y}_j - \bar{Y})^2}{\sum\limits_{j=1}^{J} n_j}.
$$

The data in Table 9-1 provide an example of the computation of η^2 and the various sum-of-squares terms. The deviation score of each person from the overall mean is listed in the three columns of Table 9-2 under $(Y_{ji} - \bar{Y})$. The sum of squares of each of these columns is given at the bottom, as are the total sum of squares (56) and the overall variance (1.87). The next three columns contain the deviation of each person from the mean of her/his group, and below the column, the overall sums of squares and the variance error of estimate (1.2). In the last column, the three group-mean deviations, the sum of squares $[10(-1^2) + 10(0^2) + 10(1^2) = 20]$, and the variance due to groups are given. The value of η^2 may be computed using equation 9.9

$$
\eta^2 = \frac{0.67}{1.87} = 0.358
$$

TABLE 9-2

Computing S_y^2, $S_{\hat{y}}^2$, and $S_{(y \cdot x)}^2$ for data in Table 9-1.

i	$Y_{ji} - \bar{Y}$			$Y_{ji} - \bar{Y}_j$			$Y_j - \bar{Y}$
	$j=1$	$j=2$	$j=3$	$j=1$	$j=2$	$j=3$	
1	-1	1	-1	0	1	-2	$(\bar{Y}_1 - \bar{Y})^2 = -1$
2	0	-2	3	1	-2	2	$(\bar{Y}_2 - \bar{Y})^2 = 0$
3	-1	0	0	0	0	-1	$(\bar{Y}_3 - \bar{Y})^2 = 1$
4	-2	0	2	-1	0	1	
5	1	2	1	2	2	0	
6	-3	-1	1	-2	-1	0	
7	-2	0	2	-1	0	1	
8	-1	1	1	0	1	0	
9	0	-1	0	1	-1	-1	
10	-1	0	1	0	0	0	

Calculations

$$\sum_{i=1}^{n_j}(Y_{ji} - \bar{Y})^2 \quad 22 \quad 12 \quad 22 \qquad \sum_{i=1}^{n_j}(Y_{ji} - \bar{Y}_j)^2 \quad 12 \quad 12 \quad 12$$

$$\sum_{j=1}^{J}\sum_{i=1}^{n_j}(Y_{ji} - \bar{Y})^2 = 22 + 12 + 22 = 56 \qquad \sum_{j=1}^{J}\sum_{i=1}^{n_j}(Y_{ji} - \bar{Y}_j)^2 = 12 + 12 + 12 = 36$$

$$S_y^2 = \frac{56}{30} = 1.87 \qquad\qquad S_{y \cdot x}^2 = \frac{36}{30} = 1.2$$

$$\sum_{j=1}^{J} n_j(\bar{Y}_j - \bar{Y})^2 = 20$$

$$S_{\hat{y}}^2 = \frac{20}{30} = 0.67$$

or

$$\eta^2 = 1 - \frac{1.2}{1.87} = 1 - 0.642 = 0.358.$$

Using equation 9.10 gives us

$$\eta^2 = \frac{20}{56} = 0.357$$

or

$$\eta^2 = 1 - \frac{36}{56} = 1 - 0.643 = 0.357.$$

The difference 0.001 between these two pairs of equations is due to the effects of rounding in computing the variances.

A final observation that we can make about η^2 is that it can never be negative, which should be obvious if we keep in mind the following points:

1. η^2 is a ratio of two variances. No proper variance can ever be negative. All ratios of positive numbers are positive.

2. $S_{\hat{y}}^2$ and $S_{y \cdot x}^2$ must each be less than or equal to S_y^2; that is, it is not logical for more than all of Y's variance to be predictable, nor is it possible for more than all of it to be error. The inequalities

$$S_{\hat{y}}^2 \leq S_y^2 \qquad \text{and} \qquad S_{y \cdot x}^2 \leq S_y^2$$

assure us that equation 9.9 can never yield a negative value.

CORRELATION COEFFICIENT—PREDICTABLE VARIANCE

The idea of a regression line was developed in Chapter 8. When it is reasonable to consider both X and Y to be interval variables having approximately normal distributions, we can determine a line that provides a least-squares prediction of Y from X. The relationship has the general form

$$\hat{Y} = BX + A$$

and is determined so that

$$\sum_{i-1}^{N} (Y_i - \hat{Y}_i)^2$$

is a minimum.

It is possible to break up an individual's score into three parts for a linear relationship in the same way that we did when the predictor was group membership. Consider the scatter plot in Figure 9-3. The Y-score of individual i is composed of a portion due to $\bar{Y}$, the mean of all Y's; a portion due to the difference between her/his predicted score and $\bar{Y}$, $(\hat{Y}_i - \bar{Y})$; and a portion that is the difference between predicted and observed scores, $(Y_i - \hat{Y}_i)$. That is,

$$Y_i = \bar{Y} + (\hat{Y}_i - \bar{Y}) + (Y_i - \hat{Y}_i). \tag{9.11}$$

This partitioning is identical to that in equation 9.3, except that we are

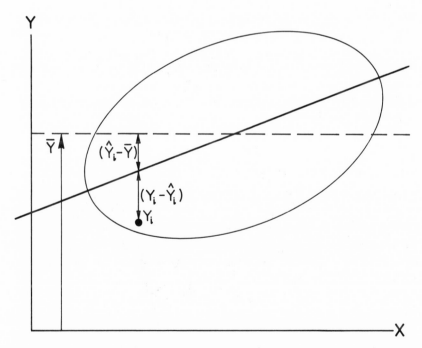

Figure 9-3 Parts of a score in a scatter plot. The observed score Y_i is composed of the mean $\bar{Y}$, the deviation of $\hat{Y}$ from $\bar{Y}$, and the deviation of Y_i from $\hat{Y}$.

using the predicted score from the regression line ($\hat{Y}_i$) rather than the subgroup mean ($\bar{Y}_j$); of course, both are predicted scores for individual i.

We follow the same steps with equation 9.11 that we used to go from equation 9.3 to η^2 in order to develop an index of the strength of a linear relationship between continuous variables. By subtracting $\bar{Y}$ from both sides, squaring and summing across the N individuals, we obtain

$$\sum_{i=1}^{N} (Y_i - \bar{Y})^2 = \sum_{i=1}^{N} (\hat{Y}_i - \bar{Y})^2 + \sum_{i=1}^{N} (Y_i - \hat{Y}_i)^2, \tag{9.12}$$

which says that an individual's deviation from $\bar{Y}$ is composed of a portion that is due to the difference between the predicted score and $\bar{Y}$ and a portion that is due to error. (Note that in the absence of specific group membership information we need only use one subscript.) If we now divide both sides by N, we obtain an equation with three variance-like terms, just as we did in equation 9.5.

$$\frac{\sum_{i=1}^{N} (Y_i - \bar{Y})^2}{N} = \frac{\sum_{i=1}^{N} (\hat{Y}_i - \bar{Y})^2}{N} + \frac{\sum_{i=1}^{N} (Y_i - \hat{Y}_i)^2}{N}. \tag{9.13}$$

This equation shows that the total variance of Y can be divided into a portion of variance that is due to prediction and a portion that remains error after we have used our predictor information. Writing equation 9.13 in terms of variances, we get

$$S_y^2 = S_{\hat{y}}^2 + S_{y \cdot x}^2, \tag{9.14}$$

where $S_{y \cdot x}^2$ is the same variance-error-of-estimate term that we encountered in equation 9.6 and $S_{\hat{y}}^2$ is the variance in Y that is predictable from knowing a person's score on X. $S_{\hat{y}}^2$ is an index of the amount that our error in predicting Y is reduced by knowing X.

The one last thing we must do is convert equation 9.14 into a proportion, so that we obtain an index that is not directly dependent on the size of S_y^2. Dividing both sides of equation 9.14 by S_y^2 yields

$$1 = \frac{S_{\hat{y}}^2}{S_y^2} + \frac{S_{y \cdot x}^2}{S_y^2}, \tag{9.15}$$

which is identical to equation 9.7 but had been derived for predictions made from a regression line. The first term on the right is the proportion of variance due to prediction, and the second term is the proportion that is due to error.

Again, we solve for the first term, obtaining

$$\frac{S_{\hat{y}}^2}{S_y^2} = 1 - \frac{S_{y \cdot x}^2}{S_y^2}.$$

The left-hand term in this equation is given the label r^2 (*r*-square) and is the square of the *correlation coefficient*.

$$r_{xy}^2 = \frac{S_{\hat{y}}^2}{S_y^2} = 1 - \frac{S_{y \cdot x}^2}{S_y^2}. \tag{9.16}$$

This equation asserts that the *square of the correlation coefficient* (whose computation and other interpretations we discuss shortly) is the proportion of variance in *Y*-scores that is linearly related to *X* or is linearly predicted from *X*.

CORRELATION COEFFICIENT—PREDICTION

The regression line that we developed in Chapter 8 could be used for either raw scores or deviation scores. In either case, the value of b was the slope of the regression line and the intercept was A for raw scores or zero for deviation scores. Now, let us consider the regression line for standard scores.

The deviation score form of the regression line was

$$\hat{y}_i = b_{y \cdot x} x_i,$$

where we found that the value of b that minimized $\sum (y_i - \hat{y}_i)^2$ was given by

$$b_{y \cdot x} = \frac{\sum x_i y_i}{\sum x_i^2}. \tag{9.17}$$

Standard scores are a special kind of deviation score. All deviation-score distributions have a mean of zero and standard scores fulfill that condition; however, they have the additional property that $S_z^2 = 1$ for all standard-score distributions. If we insert standard scores into equation 9.17 for x_i and y_i, we obtain

$$b_{z_{y \cdot x}} = \frac{\sum_{i=1}^{N} z_{x_i} z_{y_i}}{\sum_{i=1}^{N} z_{x_i}^2}.$$

Because

$$\sum_{i=1}^{N} z_{x_i}^2 = N$$

(see Appendix A for proof), we can rewrite the equation for the *slope of the least squares regression line for standard scores* as

$$b_{z_y \cdot z_x} = \frac{\sum z_{y_i} z_{x_i}}{N} .$$

Sir Francis Galton gave the name *coefficient of co-relation* to an earlier form of this equation in 1886.[1] The symbol **r** was given to this statistic and now, in the last quarter of the century, r or the correlation coefficient is one of the most widely used statistical indices.

The correlation coefficient has all the properties of a slope coefficient and some additional ones as well. For example, recall that there are two different slopes, $b_{y \cdot x}$ and $b_{x \cdot y}$, for raw or deviation scores. The slope for z-scores is

$$r_{yx} = \frac{\sum z_y z_x}{N} . \tag{9.18}$$

The numerator of the right-hand term is the same regardless of which variable is doing the predicting and so is the denominator. This means that for a given set of data, there is only one correlation coefficient, while there are two regression slopes for raw or deviation scores.

The reason for this difference is shown in Figure 9-4. When raw or deviation scores are put in a scatter plot, the shape of the scatter plot is affected by the variances of the two variables. Part a illustrates the situation when the predictor has the larger variance, and a criterion with larger variance is shown in part b. The case for standard scores is shown in part c; here, because the variables have equal variances, the scatter plot is the same regardless of which variable is the predictor.

The correlation coefficient can be used in a regression equation to make predictions. The equation is

$$\hat{z}_{y_i} = r_{xy} z_{x_i}. \tag{9.19}$$

[1]Sir Francis Galton, "Family likeness in stature," *Proceedings of the Royal Society of London*, 40, (1886) 42–73. The derivation of equation 9.18 was provided by Karl Pearson, one of the foremost English statisticians of the late nineteenth and early twentieth centuries, in 1896.

Because it is the slope of a regression line, the correlation coefficient can be positive, as is the case in Figure 9-4, or it can be negative. The sign has the same interpretation as the sign of $b_{y \cdot x}$, and the magnitude of r_{yx} is also the number of units increased in $z_{\hat{y}}$ for each unit of increase in z_x. How-

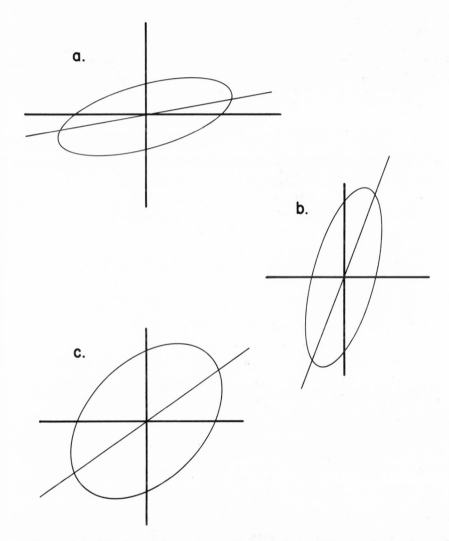

*Figure 9-4   Which variable is the predictor makes a difference in the slope of the regression line for deviation scores (**a.** and **b.**), but not for standard scores (**c.**).*

ever, because it is often inconvenient to convert observed scores to z-scores, equation 9.19 is seldom used to make predictions.

Equation 9.18, which is sometimes called the definitional formula for the correlation coefficient, shows quite clearly what the slope of a regression line means in terms of observed scores. The denominator N is always positive, so the sign that results from the calculation must be determined by the numerator. Because z-scores are deviation scores, roughly half of them will be positive and half negative for each variable. The numerator in equation 9.18 consists of cross-products of z-scores, and these cross-products will be positive when both z's have the same sign. For individual i, if both z_x and z_y come from above the mean (positive) or both come from below the mean (negative), their cross-product will be positive. A negative cross-product occurs when the two scores fall on opposite sides of their respective distributions. Thus, a positive correlation indicates that there is a tendency for people to obtain similar z-scores on the two variables. A negative correlation reveals a tendency for individuals who scored above the mean on one variable to score below the mean on the other.

RELATIONSHIP BETWEEN r AND b

We have seen that both the correlation coefficient and b are slopes of regression lines. Both can be computed from the same basic data, but they are not, in general, equal. There is a fairly simple principle governing the relationship between them that may be demonstrated by substituting deviation score equivalents for the z-scores in equation 9.19. Remembering that because $x_i = X_i - \bar{X}$, one of the forms of a z-score is

$$z_{x_i} = \frac{x_i}{S_{x_i}},$$

we substitute to obtain

$$\frac{\hat{y}_i}{S_y} = r_{yx} \frac{x_i}{S_x}.$$

Multiplying both sides by S_y yields

$$\hat{y}_i = \left(r_{yx} \frac{S_y}{S_x}\right) x_i.$$

Substituting $b_{y \cdot x}$ for the quantity in parentheses gives us the deviation-score regression equation. Therefore,

$$b_{y \cdot x} = r_{yx} \frac{S_y}{S_x} . \tag{9.20}$$

A similar series of steps shows that

$$b_{x \cdot y} = r_{yx} \frac{S_x}{S_y} ,$$

which clearly shows that the relationship between r and b is determined by the ratio of the standard deviation of the predicted variable to the standard deviation of the predictor variable. Also, $b_{y \cdot x}$ can only equal $b_{x \cdot y}$ if the two variables have equal standard deviations. Otherwise, they will differ by an amount that depends on the relative magnitudes of their standard deviations. (Note that $r_{xy} = r_{yx}$, so the order in which the subscripts are written does not matter in most cases.)

COMPUTATIONAL FORMULAS FOR r

Except in some rather unusual circumstances, we would not expect to compute z-scores in order to obtain the correlation coefficient. We can proceed by some fairly simple steps from the definitional formula to any of several computational forms. Starting with

$$r_{xy} = \frac{\sum z_x z_y}{N} ,$$

we can substitute for the z's to get

$$r_{xy} = \frac{\sum_{i=1}^{N} \frac{x_i}{S_x} \frac{y_i}{S_y}}{N} = \frac{\sum x_i y_i}{N S_x S_y} . \tag{9.21}$$

This is the deviation-score form for the correlation coefficient. Although it is not very useful by itself, it does lead to an important and useful concept. If we solve equation 9.21 for the *mean cross-product of deviation scores*, the result is a quantity called the *covariance*. That is, the covariance is

$$r_{xy} S_x S_y = \frac{\sum xy}{N} . \tag{9.22}$$

The covariance has an important place in more advanced statistical procedures. We shall have occasion to use it briefly in a few places later in this book; it is mentioned here because it is parallel in form to r. The correlation is the mean cross-product of z-scores, while the covariance is the mean cross-product of deviation scores. Of course, the difference between them is that r is independent of the standard deviations of the variables, and the covariance, as its name implies, is not.

We can move from equation 9.21 to a raw-score formula for r by substituting raw-score equivalents for each of its terms and by performing an algebraic sleight of hand; the details are given in Appendix A. They lead us to the following raw score equation for r:

$$r = \frac{N[\sum(XY)] - \sum X(\sum Y)}{\sqrt{N\sum X^2 - (\sum X)^2} \sqrt{N\sum Y^2 - (\sum Y)^2}} ; \tag{9.23}$$

While it looks imposing, this formula is not difficult to use and gives better results from raw data than either equations 9.19 or 9.21 because it involves much less rounding of numbers.

The 20 pairs of quiz scores from Table 8-2 can be used to illustrate the use of all three equations for computing r. The raw scores are reproduced in the X and Y columns of Table 9-3. These are followed by the deviation scores x and y and the standard scores. Then the cross-products XY, xy, and $z_x z_y$ are given in the last three columns. Finally, the necessary sums and sums of squares are shown at the bottom of the table. To reduce the apparent complexity of the formula, subscripts and summation limits have been omitted. It should be understood that cross-products are computed and summation takes place for all N individuals.

Selecting the appropriate values from the table, we find that equation 9.19 yields an r of

$$r = \frac{\sum z_x z_y}{N} = \frac{11.5}{20} = 0.5750.$$

This can be compared to the value that we get from equation 9.21,

$$r = \frac{\sum xy}{NS_x S_y} = \frac{16.8}{20(1.14)(1.28)} = \frac{16.8}{29.184} = 0.5757$$

Finally, using 9.23, we find r to be

$$r = \frac{N\sum XY - \sum X(\sum Y)}{\sqrt{N\sum X^2 - (\sum X)^2} \sqrt{N\sum Y^2 - (\sum Y)^2}}$$

$$= \frac{20(240) - 72(62)}{\sqrt{20(292) - (72)^2} \sqrt{20(218) - (62)^2}}$$

$$= \frac{4800 - 4464}{\sqrt{5840 - 5184} \sqrt{4360 - 3844}} = \frac{336}{\sqrt{656} \sqrt{516}}$$

$$= \frac{336}{581.8} = 0.5775.$$

All three values are quite similar; the differences are due to errors introduced by rounding in the calculation of the deviation and z-scores. That

TABLE 9-3
Quantities needed to compute the correlation coefficient.

i	X	Y	x	y	z_X	z_Y	XY	xy	$z_X z_Y$
1	2	1	−1.6	−2.1	−1.25	−1.84	2	3.36	2.30
2	2	2	−1.6	−1.1	−1.25	−0.96	4	1.76	1.20
3	2	3	−1.6	−0.1	−1.25	−0.09	6	0.16	0.11
4	2	3	−1.6	−0.1	−1.25	−0.09	6	0.16	0.11
5	2	3	−1.6	−0.1	−1.25	−0.09	6	0.16	0.11
6	3	1	−0.6	−2.1	−0.47	−1.84	3	1.26	0.86
7	3	2	−0.6	−1.1	−0.47	−0.96	6	0.66	0.45
8	3	3	−0.6	−0.1	−0.47	−0.09	9	0.06	0.04
9	3	4	−0.6	0.9	−0.47	0.79	12	−0.54	−0.37
10	3	4	−0.6	0.9	−0.47	0.79	12	−0.54	−0.37
11	4	2	0.4	−1.1	0.31	−0.96	8	−0.44	−0.30
12	4	2	0.4	−1.1	0.31	−0.96	8	−0.44	−0.30
13	4	3	0.4	−0.1	0.31	−0.09	12	−0.04	−0.03
14	4	4	0.4	0.9	0.31	0.79	16	0.36	0.24
15	4	4	0.4	0.9	0.31	0.79	16	0.36	0.24
16	5	3	1.4	−0.1	1.09	−0.09	15	−0.14	−0.10
17	5	4	1.4	0.9	1.09	0.79	20	1.26	0.86
18	5	5	1.4	1.9	1.09	1.67	25	2.66	1.82
19	6	4	2.4	0.9	1.88	0.79	24	2.16	1.49
20	6	5	2.4	1.9	1.88	1.67	30	4.56	3.14
$\sum$	72	62	0	0	0	0	240	16.8	11.5

Calculations

$\overline{X} = \ \ 3.6$	$\overline{Y} = \ \ 3.1$
$\sum x^2 = 292$	$\sum y^2 = 218$
$S_x = \ \ 1.28$	$S_y = \ \ 1.14$

is, the value 0.5775 is the most accurate because rounding errors can only occur in the square root and division steps of the computation.

Of the three examples, the amount of computation appears to be greatest in the third. However, the raw score equation requires only columns 1, 2, and 7 from Table 9-3, with only the cross-product column requiring any computation. Either of the other two formulas requires five columns of the table, three of which involve computation. Therefore, even if the other two did not involve rounding error, they require enough additional intermediate computation to make them more time-consuming and cumbersome than equation 9.23.

RELATIONSHIP BETWEEN r AND $S_{y \cdot x}$

We have now completed two separate definitions or conceptualizations of the correlation coefficient. On one hand, the slope of the best-fit regression line for a scatter plot of standard scores is

$$\frac{\sum_{i=1}^{N} z_{x_i} z_{y_i}}{N}$$

and this we labeled r. On the other hand, we have seen that it is possible to partition the variance of a criterion variable into two parts, that which is related to the predictor and that which is error. When the predictions are made from a regression line, the ratio of the variance due to predictions to the overall variance was called r^2. This implies a relationship between the two concepts, a relationship that we shall demonstrate in this section.

First, recall that in the development of the regression coefficient there was a function

$$S_{y \cdot x}^2 = \frac{1}{N} \sum (y_i - bx_i)^2$$

that we wished to minimize. We determined b such that the function was minimized, and this was the slope of the least-squares regression line. Using the relationship in equation 9.20, we can substitute to get

$$S_{y \cdot x}^2 = \frac{1}{N} \sum \left(y_i - r_{xy} \frac{S_y}{S_x} x_i \right)^2.$$

Squaring, distributing the summation, dividing by N, and combining terms (see Appendix A), we obtain

$$S_{y \cdot x}^2 = S_y^2 - r_{xy}^2 S_y^2,$$

which may be rewritten as

$$S_{y \cdot x}^2 = S_y^2(1 - r_{xy}^2). \tag{9.24}$$

This equation is the usual expression for the variance error of estimate. Solving equation 9.24 for r_{xy}^2 yields

$$r_{xy}^2 = 1 - \frac{S_{y \cdot x}^2}{S_y^2},$$

which is exactly the same as equation 9.16. Thus, we have started from two different ways of viewing correlation and arrived at the same place. The single index provides both the slope of the regression line (for z-scores) and, when squared, an index of the strength of the relationship between two variables. In addition, we can take the square root of equation 9.24 to find the standard error of estimate for computing confidence intervals.

We use the data in Table 9-3 to illustrate these points. The student may wish to verify that the raw score regression equation is

$$\hat{Y}_i = 0.512 \, X_i + 1.256.$$

This equation was used to compute the $\hat{Y}$-values in Table 9-4. The errors of prediction $(Y_i - \hat{Y}_i)$ are given in the third column. At the bottom of each column, the sum, sum of squares, and variance of the scores in the column are listed. The variances are S_y^2, $S_{\hat{y}}^2$ and $S_{y \cdot x}^2$, respectively. Employing the two forms of equation 9.16 to compute the correlation coefficient, we obtain

$$r_{xy}^2 = \frac{S_{\hat{y}}^2}{S_y^2} = \frac{0.4313}{1.29} = 0.3343$$

$$r_{xy} = 0.5782$$

or

$$r_{xy}^2 = 1 - \frac{S_{y \cdot x}^2}{S_y^2} = 1 - \frac{0.8589}{1.29} = 1 - 0.6658 = 0.3342$$

$$r_{xy} = 0.5781.$$

Both of these results differ very slightly from 0.5775, obtained from the raw-score equation; we can reasonably attribute the difference to rounding errors incurred in calculating the predicted scores. There are few, if any, situations in the social and behavioral sciences where a difference between two correlations of 0.001 (the size of the rounding error in this example) would be considered worth noticing. The important thing for the student to see is that the results of computations with real data conform exactly to the results predicted by the algebraic manipulation of symbols.

TABLE 9-4

Predicted scores and errors of prediction for scores from Table 9-3.

Y_i	$\hat{Y}_i$	$Y_i - \hat{Y}_i$
1	2.28	-1.28
2	2.28	-0.28
3	2.28	0.72
3	2.28	0.72
3	2.28	0.72
1	2.79	-1.79
2	2.79	-0.79
3	2.79	0.21
4	2.79	1.21
4	2.79	1.21
2	3.30	-1.30
2	3.30	-1.30
3	3.30	-0.30
4	3.30	0.70
4	3.30	0.70
3	3.82	-0.82
4	3.82	0.18
5	3.82	1.18
4	4.33	-0.33
5	4.33	0.67

Calculations

$\sum Y$	62	61.97	0.03
$\sum Y^2$	218	200.64	17.1775
S^2	1.29	0.4313	0.8589

In an actual research or prediction problem, we would seldom compute the variance error or estimate $S_{y \cdot x}^2$ in this way. The more usual course is to compute the correlation and then use equation 9.24, rather than compute a predicted score for each person. From our previous example, equation 9.24 should yield a value of about 0.8589, and we find that it does.

$$S_{y \cdot x}^2 = 1.29 \, (1 - 0.5775^2) = 1.29 \, (1 - 0.3335)$$

$$= 1.29 \, (0.6665) = 0.8598.$$

Again, the small difference of 0.0009 is due to rounding.

The standard error of estimate is then $\sqrt{0.8589} = 0.927$. To find the 95 percent confidence interval for a predicted score, we would use Appendix Table B.1 to look up the z that includes 95 percent of the normal distribution or leaves $2\frac{1}{2}$ percent in each tail. This value is 1.96, so the 95 percent confidence interval for these data is 3.63 units wide.

SUMMARY

An observed Y-score can be partitioned into a portion that is predictable from X and a portion that is error. Likewise, the variance of a set of Y-scores can be partitioned into variance that is related to X or is predictable from X and variance that is independent of X. The variance in Y that is unrelated to X is called the *variance error of estimate*, and its square root is the *standard error of estimate*. This quantity is the standard deviation of the errors of prediction that would result from using X-scores to predict Y-scores for a group of individuals.

An index of the strength of relationship or degree of association between two variables may be obtained from the ratio of the predictable variance of Y to the total variance of Y. When X is a discrete variable and the group means of Y are used as least squares predictions, the resulting ratio is called η^2, or the *correlation ratio*. It is interpreted as the proportion of variance in Y that is related to X.

It is also possible to partition Y-scores and their variance when both X and Y are continuous variables. In this case, the nature and degree of their association is expressed by the *correlation coefficient r*. The correlation coefficient is the slope of the regression line for predicting z_y from z_x. It is related to $b_{y \cdot x}$ by the ratio S_y/S_x. The square of the correlation coefficient is the proportion of variance in Y that is linearly related to X. r can be computed directly from raw scores and used to obtain the standard error of estimate without computing predicted scores.

PROBLEMS

*1. Mrs. Jones' sixth-grade spelling class is divided into three groups: high, medium, and low. Calculate an eta² as an index of strength of relationship between group membership and results on this week's spelling test.

Spelling Test		
High	*Medium*	*Low*
20	17	15
19	20	14
11	16	12
16	12	6
19	18	19
20		

Mrs. Jones would also like to find out if there is any relationship between spelling group and score and the weekly math test. Calculate an eta² for spelling-group membership and the math test. Can the same conclusions be drawn about math and group membership in spelling as were drawn about membership and spelling-test results?

Math Test		
High	*Medium*	*Low*
98	67	62
76	82	76
61	74	84
86	95	100
79	91	89
81		

*Answers to starred questions are found in Appendix D.

2. The following data are from problem 3 in Chapter 8:

Freshman	Sophomore	Junior	Senior
7	3	3	7
6	6	2	5
9	5	2	6
7	7	4	6
8	6	3	8
5	4	1	7
8	5	5	6

(a) Plot the data
(b) Calculate eta^2
(c) Calculate r^2
(d) Why are the two values so different?
(e) For this research problem, what is the proper interpretation of r^2? of η^2?

3. Calculate r, r^2, and $b_{y \cdot x}$ for the following distributions. State whether the relationship is high, medium, low, or none. For each set of data find $S_{y \cdot x}$ and $S_{x \cdot y}$. Are they different? Why?

*(a)	X	Y	(b)	X	Y
	100	25		25	56
	26	15		16	60
	37	17		17	61
	42	16		21	40
	56	18		25	52
	94	22		11	63
	67	19		12	67
				18	54
				19	53

*(c)	X	Y		(d)	X	Y
	506	16			33	37
	521	17			37	32
	604	24			41	38
	702	12			56	42
	733	21			25	36
	409	16			37	42
					18	81
					24	17

*(e)	X	Y		(f)	X	Y
	21	22			3	6
	42	16			9	5
	67	17			7	2
	81	18			17	11
	17	25			8	14
	16	11			3	5
	58	16			10	15
	62	21			8	2
	21	22			4	4
	14	15			9	9
	98	12			14	9
					18	14

(g)	X	Y
	13	13
	11	0
	6	6
	9	9
	9	7
	17	5
	14	10
	13	8
	5	1
	12	10
	4	0
	3	8

4. The following data were collected by a teacher studying the relationship between level of motivation and test performance. The motivation variable has scores from 1 (very low motivation) to 10 (very high motivation). Test performance is measured as the number of items *missed*. Perform an appropriate analysis of these data and state your conclusions.

	Motivation	Performance		Motivation	Performance
1.	2	17	19.	5	18
2.	4	17	20.	1	19
3.	8	16	21.	7	15
4.	10	18	22.	9	16
5.	1	18	23.	3	16
6.	5	14	24.	10	17
7.	3	18	25.	6	17
8.	6	16	26.	9	14
9.	8	14	27.	2	16
10.	5	16	28.	4	15
11.	2	19	29.	10	16
12.	6	15	30.	1	16
13.	10	15	31.	7	13
14.	2	17	32.	6	15
15.	7	16	33.	3	17
16.	9	17	34.	8	15
17.	3	15	35.	6	14
18.	4	14			

5. Create a set of 15 pairs of scores that illustrate a correlation between 0.25 and 0.35. Create a second set where the correlation is between 0.45 and 0.55, and a third set where r is between 0.65 and 0.75.

10

QUALITY OF DATA

Educators and psychologists who use standardized tests have devoted considerable thought and effort over the last 80 years to the quality of the information their measurements produce. Their procedures, findings, and concerns are typically confined to books with words like measurement or testing in the title, with the unfortunate consequence that researchers and students who are not directly concerned with the use of standardized tests on humans frequently overlook some important aspects of measurement theory. The present chapter provides a brief overview of some of the major issues in evaluating the quality of data as they have arisen in the testing area. In a later chapter, we shall discuss some concerns that are more specific to the laboratory setting.

It is possible to state quite simply the two desirable properties that high-quality measurements should have: They should be accurate representations of the property being measured, and they should be easy to interpret. Accuracy implies that it is possible to divide the measurement scale into units small enough for the scientist's purposes and that an observation receives the correct scale value. Ease of interpretation means

231

that there is general agreement among users or potential users of the scale about the information contained in the number that results from a measurement.

The physical sciences have been very successful in developing scales and measurement procedures that yield high-quality measurement. There is now universal agreement on a standard unit of distance, the meter, that is defined with sufficient precision so that the accuracy and meaning of a physicist's measurement of this property is seldom in doubt. The same is true for such properties as time and temperature. The quality of measurement is so high in the physical sciences that there are usually only two reasons for a difference in measurements: human error in reading the scale or a real change or difference in the trait or entity being observed.

Unfortunately, social and behavioral scientists have been unable to develop measurement procedures of this quality. Certainly, one of the reasons is that they have only been at the task for about 100 years. Measurement procedures for time and space have been under development for more than 20 times that long. Another reason is the number of assumed relationships between the measurement and the property. In the measurement of time, the interval between two ticks of the clock is defined as the unit of measurement and is equivalent to the property of interest without further extrapolation. What is called the operational definition of the property, the procedure used to measure it, is equivalent to the property itself; in the social and behavioral sciences, this is seldom the case. For example, we generally use responses to a series of test items to measure something we call intelligence. But, getting a test item correct is not itself intelligence; it is *assumed to be* intelligent behavior, which is *assumed* to occur because there is intelligence around somewhere. (The somewhere is ordinarily assumed to be between the ears.)

A third reason for the lack of high-quality measurements in the social and behavioral sciences is that the entities themselves, usually humans, are constantly changing. It is very difficult to develop a high-quality scale on something that is undergoing change, because it is hard to know whether it is the object or the scale that is unstable. Consider, for example, trying to develop a procedure for measuring length when the only rulers you have are made of soft rubber. Are two people the same height, or have you stretched the ruler more for one observation than the other?

All of these problems have led testing specialists to develop a vocabulary for measurement quality and a series of procedures to estimate the accuracy and usefulness of particular measurements. In the first section of this chapter, issues related to accuracy are discussed under the general heading of reliability of measurement. The second section, validity, covers the problem of usefulness from the philosophical-scientific side and from the practical-prediction side.

RELIABILITY

The term reliability is usually used when we are concerned with the stability, consistency or reproducibility of measurement. The question is whether a set of measurements of trait T on group G remains the same over time or over repeated measurements of the same trait. A measuring instrument is said to be reliable if it yields the same scale value for an individual each time the measurement is made. The fundamental concepts in reliability partion observed variance into different components in much the same manner that we have already done. We shall consider these partitions after having examined an example.

Consider some learnable and repeatable act such as throwing darts at a circular dart board. Let us assume that Charlie (the same fellow who handed in all three homework assignments) is throwing darts. As a budding scientist, Charlie reasons that it should be possible to measure a person's status on the trait of dart-throwing ability. His scientific training has led him to a firm belief in the value of controlled conditions for measurement, so he carefully sets up a measurement procedure. A standard board is used, as are standard-weight darts with properly sharpened points and combed feathers. The people to be measured stand in a fixed location, and temperature, humidity, and air movement are carefully controlled. Everything is perfect.

Enter Charlie with his first candidate, one Annie Oakley. A premeasurement interview has revealed that Annie has never thrown a dart in her life before, but she is willing to help Charlie develop his measurement procedure. She takes her place and tosses a dart; bull's-eye! Charlie can be heard mumbling to himself that it must be luck: Annie could not have a 20 on his scale of 0 to 20. This measurement must be wrong; a second measurement is taken (score of 8) and a third (17) and a fourth (0). Now Charlie is really confused. He has four different measurements of Annie's ability, each quite different from the others, with no way of telling which is the right one.

While this example is obviously contrived, it serves to point out a major factor of measurement in the social and behavioral sciences. Repeated measurements of the same trait on the same people often show a great deal of variability. Sometimes it is reasonable to attribute this variation to changes in the person over time. For example, one's expressed interest in eating or the time needed to fall asleep should vary throughout a single day; other characteristics such as moods can be expected to fluctuate from day to day. However, there is always some amount of variation that cannot be explained in this way.

Let us return to the dart board for a moment to take a look at the variation in performance. Remember that we are measuring dart-throwing ability and that each toss is a measurement of that ability. Suppose that Annie has been practicing diligently for several weeks now and has reached a fairly uniform level of performance. It would be reasonable to think of measuring her true level of ability; we could even say that the average of her scores on ten darts was her true ability. With this in mind, we ask her to throw ten darts, and, then, just to be sure, we have her throw ten more. Imagine our dismay when the first measurement and the second disagree.

Our dart example is not too unlike what seems to be going on in many measurement situations. It is reasonable to assume that the individual possesses a relatively stable amount of a quantifiable characteristic. Our experience with direct measurement of physical attributes suggests that we should obtain fairly consistent measurements. However, we find that repeated measurements of behavioral or social characteristics can give results showing much more than the expected degree of variability. For example, a student's knowledge of statistics could be assumed to be constant over a period of half an hour. But if we give two 15-minute, ten-item quizzes on statistics, the student may not get the same score on each. Is it that the student changed, the instruments are measuring different things, or the student's behavior is just inconsistent? The *measurement model* has been devised to account for this variability in observations.

The measurement model is an outgrowth of what used to be called the *true-score model*. In its earlier form, this model held that each observation was composed of two parts, the individual's true level on the trait of interest, known as the *true score* (T_i for individual i) and some error of measurement that occurred in this particular measurement of this particular person (e_{ij}). A person's true score was assumed to be constant across all measurements of the same trait within a reasonable time span, and errors were assumed to be completely random chance events. Over a large number of measurements, the distribution of these errors was assumed to be normal in shape with a mean of zero.

The major difference between the true score model and most current formulations of the measurement model is that true score is seen as being partitionable into several sources of variance. The notions of true score and error have been replaced by consistent or between-persons variance and inconsistent or within-persons variance. An early formulation of this model (Thorndike, 1949) identified five major categories of variation; later contributors (cf. Cronbach et al., 1972) have suggested many more factors that need to be considered. The particular sources of variance proposed under the measurement model would depend on the research context. There is the possibility of real differences in what is measured by two procedures or tests that seem to measure the same thing. There is the possibility of real differences between classrooms or schools that are due, not to characteristics of the children who are measured, but to physical or social differences in the school environment or the way the teacher administered the test. It is sometimes quite important to identify such sources of variance as these as different from either true scores or random errors of measurement. Our present discussion will be phrased in terms of the true-score model because it is the simplest approach to the problem and the principle of partitioning observed variance into parts remains the key concept in more complex versions.

In the form of an equation, then, the true-score model says that the measurement of individual i on trait X at occasion j is

$$X_{ij} = T_i + e_{ij}. \tag{10.1}$$

That is, an observed score X_{ij} is composed of two parts, the individual's true score T_i, which is constant, and an error of measurement e_{ij}, which is a random or chance event. The model predicts that we can expect to find some variations among repeated measurements of the same individual.

Consider our dart-throwing example again. It would be possible to measure Annie a very large number of times and get a frequency distribution of her scores. The mean of the distribution of observed scores is her true score (current authors use the term universe score instead of true score), because the mean of the e_{ij} is zero. The variance in scores can be found by subtracting the mean from each score, squaring, summing, and dividing by N (see Appendix A) to obtain

$$S^2_{x_{ij}} = S^2_{e_{ij}}.$$

The variance in observed scores of an individual is entirely due to errors of measurement according to the true score model. The standard deviation of the distribution of an individual's observed scores is known as the *standard error of measurement*.

The standard error of measurement, sometimes abbreviated SEM and sometimes S_e, is a standard deviation. It is the standard deviation that we get from the distribution of repeated measurements of a single individual on a single trait; it is the standard deviation of the distribution of errors of measurement.

In the real world, it is seldom possible to calculate the *SEM* directly because its definition requires a constant true score. Repeated measurements tend to change the person being measured, therefore confusing error of measurement with true changes. Even in a situation as simple as our dart-throwing example, our subject will probably show some changes over time. In more complex measurement situations such as the measurement of human ability, it is clear that we cannot retest people many times and expect them to remain unchanged.

We attempt to overcome this problem by making a small number of measurements on a group of people and letting the large number of individuals substitute for the repeated measurements that we cannot make. For example, we may make two measurements of each of N people, in which case each person's score on first testing is expressed as

$$X_{1i} = T_i + e_{1i}. \tag{10.2}$$

The second score is expressed in the same way,

$$X_{2i} = T_i + e_{2i}.$$

Using the same steps that we have used several times before, we determine that the variance in X_1 is composed of two parts. First, subtract $\bar{X}_1$ from both sides and square the result

$$(X_{1i} - \bar{X}_1)^2 = (T_i - \bar{X}_1)^2 + (e_{1i} - \bar{X}_1)^2.$$

Now, by summing across the N individuals and dividing by N, we get three variances,

$$S^2_{X_1} = S^2_T + S^2_{e_1}. \tag{10.3}$$

The total variance in X-scores at time 1 is composed of variance due to differences among people in their true levels on the trait (S_T^2) and variance due to errors in measurement at time 1 $(S_{e_1}^2)$. The same form of equation also holds for scores at time 2; that is,

$$S_{X_2}^2 = S_T^2 + S_{e_2}^2.$$

Unfortunately, we have no way of knowing at this stage what values to place on S_T^2 and S_e^2. All we know are the values of $S_{X_1}^2$ and $S_{X_2}^2$. We also know that both S_T^2 and S_e^2 must be smaller than S_X^2, but we do not know their relative magnitudes. The solution to the problem is to compute the correlation of X_1 and X_2. First, let us simplify the problem by putting equation 10.2 in the form of deviation scores

$$x_{1i} = t_i + e_{1i} \qquad (10.4)$$
$$x_{2i} = t_i + e_{2i}.$$

Then we can express the correlation of x_1 with x_2 as

$$r_{x_1 x_2} = \frac{\sum\limits_{i=1}^{N} x_{1i} x_{2i}}{N S_{x_1} S_{x_2}} = \frac{1}{N} \frac{\sum x_1 x_2}{S_{x_1} S_{x_2}}. \qquad \text{(see 9.21)}$$

By substituting from equation 10.4, we get

$$r_{x_1 x_2} = \frac{1}{N} \frac{\sum (t_i + e_{1i})(t_i + e_{2i})}{S_{x_1} S_{x_2}},$$

which, when we multiply the numerator, yields

$$r_{x_1 x_2} = \frac{1}{N} \frac{\sum (t_i^2 + t_i e_{1i} + t_i e_{2i} + e_{1i} e_{2i})}{S_{x_1} S_{x_2}}.$$

Distributing the summation sign and $\dfrac{1}{N}$ produces

$$r_{x_1 x_2} = \frac{\dfrac{1}{N} \sum t_i^2 + \dfrac{1}{N} \sum t_i e_{1i} + \dfrac{1}{N} \sum t_i e_{2i} + \dfrac{1}{N} \sum e_{1i} e_{2i}}{S_{x_1} S_{x_2}}. \qquad (10.5)$$

Now we must remember an assumption that we made and introduce another one. First, we assumed that the errors of measurement were chance events. If they are, then they should be uncorrelated with each other and with true scores because chance events are unrelated to anything. Noting that each of the terms in equation 10.5 is a variance or covariance (see equation 9.22 and Appendix A), the last three terms must be zero. Therefore, equation 10.5 becomes

$$r_{x_1 x_2} = \frac{\frac{1}{N} \sum t_i^2}{S_{x_1} S_{x_2}} ,$$

and since $\frac{1}{N} \sum t_i^2$ is the same as the variance in true scores S_T^2

$$r_{x_1 x_2} = \frac{S_T^2}{S_{x_1} S_{x_2}} . \tag{10.6}$$

Our new assumption is that since the two tests really are measures of the same thing, they have equal standard deviations. If $S_{x_1} = S_{x_2}$, then $S_{x_1} S_{x_2} = S_x^2$, which we can substitute in equation 10.6 to get

$$r_{x_1 x_2} = \frac{S_T^2}{S_x^2} . \tag{10.7}$$

The correlation coefficient in equation 10.7 is a special type of correlation known as a *reliability coefficient*, which we symbolize r_{xx}; it is the correlation between two measures of the same thing. Note carefully that we have made some assumptions in its development and that its interpretation is different from that of other correlations. First, we assumed that an observed score could be broken down into two nonobservable parts. Second, true scores were assumed to be constant, identical from one testing to the other. In addition, errors of measurement were assumed to be chance events uncorrelated with anything, and the standard deviations of the two sets of measures were assumed to be equal.

A reliability coefficient is interpreted as the proportion of variance in observed scores that is due to true-score differences among people. In this respect, it is quite different from other correlations because it is a direct variance ratio. Remember that in Chapter 9 we found the *square* of the correlation coefficient to be a ratio of two variances (see equation 9.16). The key to the difference is that the reliability coefficient involves the unobservable true score that is constant in both measuring instruments.

As noted, we never observe true score or error directly; all we ever see are observed scores and their correlations, but with the aid of equations 10.3 and 10.7 we can get estimates or best guesses about S_T^2 and S_e^2. From equation 10.7, we find that

$$S_T^2 = r_{xx} S_x^2 .$$

The variance in true scores is the observed score variance multiplied by the reliability. Substituting this result in equation 10.3 and solving for S_e^2 yields

$$S_x^2 - S_x^2 r_{xx} = S_e^2,$$

which is equivalent to

$$S_x^2(1 - r_{xx}) = S_e^2.$$

By taking the square root of both sides, we obtain

$$S_e = S_x \sqrt{1 - r_{xx}} \qquad (10.8)$$

as an expression of the standard error of measurement.

The important thing about equation 10.8 is that it is in terms of observable quantities. Without an equation like this, it would not be possible to get a value for the standard error of measurement for most variables of interest because repeated testings are not possible. The reason that S_e, or *SEM*, is important is that it allows us to express our level of uncertainty about an individual's performance. It functions like any other standard deviation in forming confidence intervals at whatever level we choose.

Perhaps an example will help clarify the situation. Let us assume that reading text X has a standard deviation of 20 and a reliability of 0.91. (A reliability of 0.91 is about what we might expect from a carefully developed and standardized test of this type. Most measurements in the behavioral and social sciences have reliabilities well below this level.) From the information given, we calculate

$$S_e = S_x \sqrt{1 - r_{xx}} = 20 \sqrt{1 - 0.91}$$

$$= 20 \sqrt{0.09} = 20 (0.3) = 6$$

The standard error of measurement of this test is six points. This means that we would expect the standard deviation of observed scores around true score for a person to be six points if we could collect those repeated measurements. Using the table of the normal distribution, we find that 95 percent of observed scores can be expected to fall in a band $11\frac{3}{4}$ points on either side of the true score.[1] The 95 percent confidence interval is $23\frac{1}{2}$ score points wide! This means that there is about one chance in 20 that a person with a true ability of 100 would earn an observed score above 112 or below 88.

The standard error of measurement is an important piece of informa-

[1] $z_{0.475} = 1.96$, $1.96 (6) = 11.76$

tion to consider whenever indirect measurements are involved. It reflects our degree of uncertainty about the exact value of a measurement and should lead to caution in interpreting the results of a measurement. This caution should be greatest when dealing with the scores of single individuals rather than groups because the errors of measurement tend to cancel each other out when scores are averaged for a group.

The problem of unreliability in our measurements is probably one of the major reasons that research in the behavioral and social sciences has depended heavily on group averages rather than the scores of individuals. If a measuring device yields highly reliable measurements, each individual will retain the same relative position in a group on first and second measurements. Few measurements accomplish this very satisfactorily for individuals, but averaging the scores for the group yields results that are quite stable or reliable. The larger the group over which the average is taken, the more reliable the result will be. Thus, we have tended to overcome the problem of unreliability or instability in our measurements by focusing attention on group averages. Unfortunately, this trend may often mask situations where we can say things that are true for a group but less than true for any individual in the group.

VALIDITY

The reliability or unreliability of a set of measurements is an important issue when considering the quality of data. Unreliable data, data where all or most of the observed score variance is due to error of measurement, are not likely to advance scientific understanding. Because of the random nature of errors of measurement in the model (random deviations around true scores), unreliably measured variables are unlikely to show relationships with other variables. Unreliable measurements will probably result in frustration but will probably not lead to serious misdirection.

A far more serious question in data quality is whether a measuring procedure actually measures the property of interest; this is the general issue in the *validity* of measurement. We can say for the purpose of starting our discussion that a measurement is valid if it in fact measures the property or trait that we think it measures. The consequence of using an invalid measurement, then, can be a serious misdirection of the investigator's thinking and consequently drawing erroneous conclusions.

We can think of the difference between the reliability and validity of data as the difference between random errors and inherent lack of relationship. A measure that is unreliable will not have a high correlation with anything, not even itself. A reliable measure is consistent, it shows a high relationship with itself, but it still may not be related to anything else.

The key to validity is that a measurement has validity *for some purpose*; the measurement is related in some way to something other than itself. That something may be scholastic or job performance, voting behavior, mental or physical health, or learning a maze, for example. In each case the measure is valid for purpose X.

Because there are a very large number of uses for measurements, there are a number of different types of validity. Each type has its own particular features and ways in which it is assessed, but all types of validity are concerned with the relation of a measurement to something other than itself. We describe three major types of validity. While there are many others that we do not cover, these three are sufficiently general and of widespread concern to cover most situations.

Empirical Validity. Empirical validity covers those situations where there is a measured predictor variable or group of predictors and a measured criterion variable or (in very rare cases) group of criterion variables. The empirical validity of the predictor is its correlation with the criterion. The numerical value of the correlation coefficient is considered to be the validity of the predictor; a high correlation is equated with high validity.

It soon became obvious to researchers and test users that there was not just one type of empirical validity, but rather a continuum based on the time relationship between the predictor measurement and the criterion measurement. A rough but useful distinction has been drawn between *predictive validity* and *concurrent validity*. Both are empirical validities, but predictive validity involves collecting predictor information, waiting for a period of time, and then collecting criterion information. Concurrent validity refers to those situations where both measurements are made at essentially the same time.

Over the years, some other important restrictions on empirical validity have been identified. A predictive measure may have quite different levels of validity (magnitudes of correlation) for different but similar criteria: Test X may be a good predictor of performance as a plumber but not as an electrician. Also, the test may be a good predictor in one company but not in another. Perhaps even more important has been the finding that measures may have different levels of validity for different identifiable groups of people. A test may have one level of validity for men and a different level of validity (higher or lower) for women; there may be different correlations and different least-squares regression lines for various subgroups within the population.

Such findings as these have led most psychologists and educators to reject the notion of a single validity for any measurement. We must now speak of a test, or other measurement procedure, as having a validity for a particular purpose (job, school achievement) with a particular group of people. It is important to make these qualifications because the empirical validity of a measure for an individual is directly related to the accuracy of our prediction for that person. The standard error of estimate increases as the empirical validity drops, so predictions may be more accurate for members of one group than another.

Content Validity. Educators have long been concerned with tests measuring such specific domains of content knowledge as principles of statistics. To a lesser extent, other social and behavioral scientists may be concerned with well-defined content areas. The extent to which a measure covers a domain of content is known as its *content validity*. Content validity is not a concern of all measuring instruments; it is important only for those topics where it is possible to specify in considerable detail the elements of a domain. The clearest and most obvious examples come from education. For example, we might consider that our domain includes the 144 multiplication facts for the numbers 1-12. It is possible to state for any behavior whether it is in this domain or not.

There are two fundamental features that a measure must have in order to be considered to possess content validity. First, each element of the measurement operation (usually a test item) must come from the domain. If there are elements included that are not in the domain, they detract from the content validity of the instrument. Second, the elements must cover all aspects of the domain. To the extent that there are subareas of the domain that are not represented by elements of the measurement, the instrument lacks content validity. For example, the multiplication fact $13 \cdot 13 = 169$ is not in the domain we defined, so including it in a measurement of that domain would detract from content validity. Likewise, failure to include any items covering the numerals 11 and 12 would constitute incomplete coverage of the domain.

As we noted, content validity is primarily a concern for educational achievement tests. However, there may be other areas where the idea of a domain of content is appropriate or can help in instrument construction. For example, some work in attitude measurement has utilized the basic idea of content validity. As knowledge expands in any area of research on behavior, the possibilities of specifying a domain of content or of behavioral manifestations of a trait of interest increase.

Construct Validity. In the 1950s, psychologists and educators began to focus their attention on an important philosophical issue that had not been widely addressed by behavioral and social scientists. The issue was the place of measurement operations in science, and it arose from the work of P. E. Meehl and his associates (Cronbach and Meehl, 1955; Mac-Corquodale and Meehl, 1948). It is probably the most important link between thought and observation in the conduct of science.

Let us begin by considering what a science is. Recall that early in Chapter 1, we discussed collecting information; science involves collecting information. The conditions under which information is collected, for example, proper controls, is known as the scientific method. The tightness of controls and other research conditions vary from one science to another, as do reliance on formal and agreed-upon measurement procedures. However, all sciences contain three basic elements; the real world of events to be observed; a set of more or less abstractly derived principles to explain the events in the real world; and a set of measurement operations that connects the real world with the abstract principles.

We can take an example from experimental psychology to illustrate the structure of a scientific inquiry. Suppose that we are interested in measuring and studying learning. Learning is an abstract principle that we use to explain real world events. It is not, at the present stage of our knowledge, possible to observe learning directly; we cannot even prove that it exists in a formal sense. What we can do is observe behavior, manipulate the environment, and measure what happens. We put a hungry rat in a maze and record the amount of time taken and the number of errors made before the rat reaches food. Repeating this process, we record shorter times and fewer errors on later trials in the maze.

Note the three parts of a science at work here. We have the real world of rat behavior (substitute people or cockroaches, if you wish), the abstract principle of learning that we wish to use to explain a change in behavior, and the measurements of the real world (time and errors) that tie the two together. We develop our science by making predictions about the real world and confirming those predictions with measurements.

So far, so good. The abstract principles that form the scientific theory are called *hypothetical constructs*. They are constructs (entities or processes) that are hypothesized to exist and to account for the events we observe. The problem that was identified by Cronbach and Meehl is that our measurement procedures may or may not actually involve the constructs. They coined the term *construct validity* to refer to this issue. A measure possesses construct validity or is construct valid if it is a measure of the hypothetical construct it is supposed to measure.

Let us take an example from education. Suppose we have a hypothetical construct that we label mathematics aptitude. Our theory of human performance says that aptitude precedes achievement; that is, the theory says that someone may possess an aptitude for mathematics without any experience or training. Achievement is the result of aptitude and experience and is manifest in actual performance of mathematical behavior. The aptitude could exist even if the opportunity for experience never arose.

Now, consider a measure of mathematical aptitude. Since our construct does not require performance of mathematical behavior, our measuring instrument probably should avoid such behavior. Suppose that this leads us to devise a measure that requires a lot of reading and other verbal skills as well as whatever it is that is mathematics aptitude. We now measure an individual and find a low level of aptitude, but the low score may also be due to lack of reading ability, not mathematics aptitude. To the extent that the measurement procedure depends upon, or is affected by, things that are not part of the construct, it will not be a measure of the construct.

Construct validity is an essential quality for any measuring procedure to have if it is to be used for scientific purposes. In those situations where prediction of a criterion is the only thing that matters, we need not worry about what the instrument measures, only whether it correlates highly with the criterion. However, when scientific understanding is the objective, it is necessary for the measuring procedure actually to measure what we assume it measures. Otherwise, the causes or constructs that we infer to be operative may not be present at all.

A measure that possesses construct validity will probably satisfy other validity requirements as well. A construct-valid instrument will demonstrate predictive validity for criteria that are related to the construct. If there is a domain of content relevant to the construct, the instrument should have content validity for that domain. Construct validity is an issue when the instrument is being used to measure a trait that is part of a scientific theory. Since we can only know about the construct through measurements that should be related to it, we infer simultaneously the existence of the construct and the validity of our measures of it; neither can be separated entirely from the other. Both grow and gain credibility to the extent that predictions made from them are confirmed. For example, confirmation of a prediction that faster running times in the maze and fewer errors should both occur on later trials in the maze adds an increment of credibility to the construct learning and to running time and errors as measures of that construct.

SUMMARY

There are two primary qualities that measurement procedures should have in order to produce data of high quality; these are *reliability* and *validity*.

Reliability refers to the consistency or stability of measurements. In the behavioral and social sciences, tests and other measures of behavior tend to show variation in repeated measurements of the same individual. If it is reasonable to assume that the person's status on the trait has not changed, the variation in score is attributed to error of measurement. Because it is seldom possible to obtain many repeated measurements on a person, consistency of measurement is assessed by partitioning the variance in a group of people on two measurements into a portion that is between-persons variance, or true score variance, and a portion that is within-persons, or error, variance. The *reliability coefficient* is the correlation between two measurements of the same thing and is the ratio of between-persons variance to total variance. The *standard error of measurement* is the square root of the error variance and can be used to obtain a confidence interval for a person's score.

Validity is the relationship of a measure to something other than itself. The *empirical validity* of a predictor is its correlation with a criterion. *Content validity* is the relationship between a test and a domain of content. A content valid measure includes all aspects of the domain. *Construct validity* relates to the scientific value or appropriateness of a measure. Science consists of *hypothetical constructs*, the real world, and measurement operations that relate the constructs to the real world. To be construct-valid, a measure must relate constructs to real world observations.

*1. Mr. Smith gave a test of mathematical reasoning to her sixth-grade class in the fall and again in the spring. Discounting effects of learning in the interim, is Mr. Smith's test a reliable index?

	Fall	*Spring*
Tom	17	18
Bob	21	23
Sarah	56	40
Jane	27	31
Joe	15	16
Tom	17	22
Sam	20	24
June	25	31
Joanne	30	29

2. Mr. Smith split the spring test of mathematical reasoning into halves. Calculate the split-half reliability; is the test reliable?

	First Half	*Second Half*
Tom	9	9
Bob	20	3
Sarah	20	20
Jane	15	16
Joe	6	10
Tom	10	12
Sam	10	14
June	15	16
Joanne	15	14

*3. Mr. Jones is trying out a new English test that is shorter than the one he currently uses. Calculate the concurrent validity coefficient for the two tests. Does the shorter test accurately predict performance on the longer test? Should Mr. Jones use the shorter test to save time?

*Answers to starred questions are found in Appendix D.

	Short Test	*Long Test*
Jim	21	117
Tom	22	156
Gretchen	15	141
Max	16	136
Jane	21	137
Robert	27	126
Richard	15	152
Janice	22	142
Doug	27	113

4. Mrs. Beach is caught in a bind; grades are due tomorrow and she hasn't had time for a spelling test. She does have spelling errors from an English assignment, however. Should Mrs. Beach use the English paper as a spelling grade? Mrs. Beach has last quarter's spelling grades for the pupils; calculate the validity for the English paper used as a spelling test.

	English Paper	*Spelling Grade*	
Jim	−6	A	(4)
Joe	−2	B	(3)
Fred	−12	D	(1)
Mike	−1	C	(2)
Larry	−16	A	(4)
Sue	−3	C	(2)
Bev	−17	C	(2)
Jill	−12	A	(4)

5. For each of the following situations, state what type of validity is involved.

*(a) A questionnaire about occupational interests is compared to stated job perference.

(b) Final scores in a typing class are correlated with supervisor ratings after six-month's employment.

*(c) The correlations among three different measures of maze learning for a group of rats are determined.

(d) Scores on an intelligence test are correlated with teachers' ratings of student ability.

*(e) Workers on an assembly line are given a manual-dexterity test and the correlation between test scores and supervisor ratings is found.

(f) The correlation between an algebra pretest and final-exam scores in a statistics course is 0.62.

PART III
GENERALIZING TO UNMEASURED CASES

11

SAMPLES AND POPULATIONS

Up to this point, we have carefully avoided using the terms *sample* and *population* in our discussions. The reason is that these two terms have very precise meanings in the field of statistics, and since we were not yet ready to make use of the distinction, the neutral term group was used. It is now necessary to make the distinction and attend to it quite carefully.

The primary unit is the population. The population is composed of all of the individuals about whom we want to make statements or draw conclusions. We are free to define the population in any way we choose; it can include the members of a statistics class, all freshmen at college X, all students at college Y, the residents of city P, state Q, or nation Z. There is a population of white rats, a population of common stocks, and a population of nations.

What is important to realize here is that the definition of the population consists of two parts and both are determined by the investigator. The first part is the definition of the entities being studied; these entities may be people, animals, plants, social institutions, or anything else of interest.

What is the population in one study may be the single entity (often called a subject) in another. For example, a psychologist might study the attitudes of individuals to learn about changing birth rates within a country; the people in that country are the population. A demographer might well use the same country as one subject in a study of worldwide birth rates. In the latter case, nations are subjects, and the population is all nations.

The second part of the definition of population is the limit for inclusion in the population. Once we have defined the general type of entity (for example, people, white rats, molecules of calcium chloride) that we want to study, we must specify in more detail who qualifies for membership in the population. This step is very important because it defines the individuals to whom we can apply the conclusions of our study. If the proper definition of the population is college students, then it would not be appropriate to say that the results of our study are applicable to middle-aged business executives.

Issues in defining the population will become clearer after we introduce the concept of a sample. The most fundamental definition of the term sample is those entities from whom data are collected. The individuals or subjects who take part in a study are the sample. This is not a very satisfying definition, but it is probably the one that most frequently applies in research in the behavioral and social sciences. A much better definition of a sample, but one that is seldom appropriate to describe the current practice of research, is a subgroup of a population. A sample is taken from a population. This implies that the population has been defined, that individuals have been chosen from the population by some means, that these subjects have been measured in some way, and that we can draw conclusions about the sample and, hopefully, about the other members of the population.

The key difference between the two definitions is explicit reference to the population. A sample is always a sample from some population. In the first definition of sample, we allowed the sample to define the population. That is, if the sample is measured without prior definition of the population, then the only possible definition of the population is the group of entities that could have yielded the sample that we observed. From a logical point of view, this definition is circular. However, the circularity can be avoided by identifying two separate populations.

TWO KINDS OF POPULATIONS

The interpretation and application of research findings in the social and behavioral sciences may actually involve two different kinds of populations. The first of these we shall call the *statistical* or *sampling population*. This is the population whose definition depends upon the investigator and which should be determined prior to sampling. This is also the population from which the sample is drawn and the group that is most frequently referred to in statistical discussions of populations. The discussion of sampling later in this chapter primarily concerns this type of population.

A second kind of population that is particularly useful in interpreting research results is what we shall call the *outcome* or *treatment population* (Lindquist, 1953). The treatment population is hypothetical; it is an extension of the results from the study of the sample. It does not actualy exist as a population, but it is the population that would exist if all members of the sampling population received the treatments to which the sample was exposed.

An example may help to clarify the differences between these two ways of viewing populations. Suppose we want to study the effects of vitamin E on spelling achievement in school children. Our research design might involve giving one group a pill that contained vitamin E, while a second group received a sugar pill. We could define our sampling population as all elementary school children in the local school district. Using procedures described shortly, we draw a sample from this population and assign half of the sample (which we shall now call the vitamin E group) to the vitamin condition of our study, while the other half (the sugar group) receives the sugar pill.

Note that the sampling population is what we start with. We draw our sample from the sampling population. However, suppose we measure the spelling achievement of the children; expose the two groups to the vitamin and sugar conditions, respectively, along with normal school work for a period of six months; measure them again and using the independent samples *t* test described in Chapter 14, conclude that the vitamin E group members are now better spellers than the sugar group members. We know that the two groups came from the same sampling population, but now they are different. Each of the two groups is now *a sample from a treat-*

ment population. The vitamin E group is a sample from the hypothetical population that *would exist* if the members of the sampling population were given the vitamin E treatment. Likewise, the sugar group is a sample from a hypothetical population of students who received the sugar pill.

Having now defined treatment populations, it is important to identify research situations and purposes that do and do not involve these hypothetical entities. There are two broad categories into which we can divide research studies; those that attempt to estimate what the present parameters of the sampling population are; and those whose objective is to estimate the consequences of *doing something* to the members of the sampling population. The former involves only the sampling population. We estimate the population mean, standard deviation, correlation coefficient, and so forth, or we estimate the differences between the parameters of two definable populations. We are generalizing to other members of the sampling population, and, in general, we can say that this is the type of generalization that occurs with status variables. Generalization to a treatment population occurs when one or more of the variables in the study is a manipulated variable. We want to conclude from this type of study that what we have done to the subjects, our treatment, changed the sample so that it is now a sample from a new population, and it is to this new hypothetical population, the treatment population, that we want to generalize the effects of our manipulation.

It is important to define a sampling population and then draw a sample from that population because the relationship between the two is the foundation of scientific inference as it is practiced in the behavioral and social sciences. We shall go into the details of the logical system in the next chapter, but the basics of the reasoning process are summarized here.

In addition to assuming that the universe is a lawful place, we assume that there are populations of entities or populations of possible observations. The populations are usually too large for us to measure each member, but we would like to be able to say something, such as state a scientific law, that would be true for the population. We draw a sample from the population, measure the sample, and conclude that what is true for the sample is true for the population. We generalize the result from the sample to the remaining unmeasured members of the population.

Note that in the absence of some type of measurement error, such as using an invalid measure or misreading the measurement, the results we obtain from the sample are true and correct *for the sample*. No generalization to unmeasured cases is involved. However, in the absence of a population that has a definition independent of the sample, no unmeasured members of the sampling population exist. It is at this point that reference to the treatment population is particularly useful. Were it not for this hypothetical population, many studies could not be generalized. When no generalization is possible, the study becomes a scientific dead end unless it is rerun on a sample from a defined population.

PARAMETERS AND STATISTICS

There is a distinction in numerical indices that parallels the difference between populations and samples. A numerical index that applies to a population is known as a *parameter*; it is usually represented by a Greek letter, and *its value is true and unvarying for the population*. It is the value of the index, for example, the mean or the correlation coefficient, that we would obtain by appropriate computation from measurements taken on every member of the population.

The numerical index that applies to a sample is called a *statistic*. The mean computed from a sample is a statistic, as is the standard deviation. Statistics are usually symbolized with Roman letters. *Their values are true and correct for the sample* from which they were computed, but may not be the same as the population parameter. *Statistical inference* is the logical and mathematical system for relating observed sample statistics to unobserved population parameters.

The student should note the close relationship between the statistic-parameter distinction and the sample-population issue. When the population has a proper prior definition and the sample is drawn from it, the logical processes described in Chapter 12 and the mathematical principles developed in Chapter 13 can be applied to generalize from the observed statistic to the unknown parameter. In the absence of a properly defined population and a properly drawn sample, such generalizations from statistics to parameters cannot properly be made. If the individuals we have measured are the only ones in whom we are interested, statistical inference and the procedures discussed in this and following chapters are not needed. The sample and the population are the same thing, and the conclusions reached are, within the limits of measurement errors, known to be accurate; however, this is not scientific inquiry.

TYPES OF SAMPLES

In the last 50 years, great strides have been made in using samples to represent populations. The considerable success of public opinion polls, sometimes using samples of about 1000 to represent as many as 100,000,000 people, testifies to the accuracy with which population parameters can be estimated from sample statistics. While a detailed treatment of sampling techniques is beyond our scope, a brief discussion of the major categories of samples will help us with later developments.

One of the most common types of samples found in research literature is what is called the *sample of convenience* or the *available subjects sample*. We have already alluded to this type of sample; it is one where there is no prior definition of the sampling population. While the issue of population is not mentioned, the implicit definition is "whatever group might have given us a sample like this one." The available subjects sample is the one that a student of psychology would obtain by standing outside the dining hall, handing out questionnaires to whoever will take them, and tabulating the results of those that are returned. It is the sample tested by the educator who tests only those students whose teachers are willing to donate class time for testing. It is the sample that anyone obtains when there is no prior definition of who the members of the sampling population are and when there is no definite plan for sampling.

Notice that the implications of using an available subjects sample are quite different for the sampling and treatment populations. The sampling population is undefined and probably unknown when the sample is a sample of convenience. The treatment population, on the other hand, is unaffected by the type of sample that is used. The treatment population can still be viewed as the hypothetical population that would reasonably have produced a sample with the characteristics that we observed at the outcome of our study; it is neither more nor less real and neither more nor less well-defined.

The alternatives to the available subjects sample all require that the sampling population be defined so that it would be possible to state for any given entity that it does or does not belong in the population. The population can be small (all female, sophomore engineering students at university X) or large (all those holding United States passports), but it is necessary to be able to determine for every entity or observation whether it is a member of the population or not. For some sampling procedures, it is even necessary to identify every member of the population.

The problem of sampling and defining the population is particularly acute for research on human beings: Researchers are usually restricted to using volunteers in their studies, and this has an immediate effect on the population definition. For example, we can very carefully define the population and select people to take part, but then find that when we ask them to serve as subjects many refuse. White rats and other nonhuman subjects seldom do this, so generalizations are straightforward. With humans, we never know what the effect of having to use more or less willing volunteers will be on our results.

Random Sampling is the simplest method of drawing a sample from a defined population. We define a random sample as one where every member of the population has an equal chance of being included in the sample, which means that every member of the population starts with the same chance of being selected for the sample. Suppose, for example, that we want to draw a random sample of ten people from a statistics class with 100 members. Before anyone is selected for the sample, each member of the class has an equal chance of 10/100, or 0.10, of being included in the sample. Each member of the class is given a number between 00 and 99. We then consult a table of random numbers.[1] Since each class member is represented by a two-digit number, we read pairs of digits from the table, and include each individual whose number comes up until we have ten people. If a person's number comes up twice before we have completed our sample, we skip the number the second time. When we are finished, we have a random sample of 10 from our defined population of 100.

The advantage of using a table of random numbers for selecting our sample is that the probability that an individual's number will come up remains constant at 1/100 throughout the sampling process; thus, each member retains a 10/100 chance of being included in the sample. If we had drawn names out of a hat, the probability of inclusion on the first draw

[1]Such tables are included in many statistics books, and there are a number of computer programs that generate random numbers. The most extensive table is provided in Rand Corp. (1955).

would have been 1/100, on the second 1/99, on the third, 1/98, and so on; that is, the chance of inclusion changes as the sample is drawn and is not independent of the order of drawing.[2] For most research purposes, this difference is not very important compared with other effects such as error of measurement. Also, it can be overcome by what is called sampling with replacement: putting each person back in the population after s/he has been drawn. However, since random number tables are easy to use, assure random sampling, and can be applied to almost any situation, it is a good idea to use a table of random numbers when the research plan calls for drawing a random sample to assure that the requirements of equal and independent probability of inclusion in the sample are met as well as conditions allow.

Virtually all statistical procedures for generalizing from a sample to a population involve an assumption that the sample is a random sample from the population. Unfortunately, the conditions necessary for the simple type of random sampling we have just described seldom exist outside statistics books. In the real world (wherever and whatever that is), we are seldom confronted with a clearly defined and randomly sampleable population. Even when we can sample randomly, a random sample of manageable size (our budget is only $100,000) may not be a good sample.

What is a good sample? For most purposes, it is one that is *representative* of the sampling population; that is, the individuals in the sample possess many of the same characteristics in the same relative degree as do members of the population. A random sample of white rats or pigeons or fruit flies may be quite satisfactory because there is little variability among rats, pigeons, or flies (unless you are one). The random sample, in this case, resembles the population closely because there are few dimensions where the individuals differ; however, when people are the entities being sampled, the problem becomes more complex.

The problem with people is that they vary on so many dimensions, and the status of individuals on those dimensions affects their behavior. Age is often an important dimension; so are social status, level of education, number of parents living at home, for example. Some of these dimensions may be important for one study, others for another.

Remember that our purpose in using statistical procedures for inference is to generalize the findings on a sample to a population. Generaliza-

---

[2]The details of changing probabilities in sampling are beyond our scope and are more complex than the simple example presented here would indicate. Hays (1973) presents a discussion of probabilities and random sampling.

tion *requires* the sample to be drawn from the population. If the population shows variation in some characteristic but the sample does not, then the sample is not drawn from the population *with respect to that characteristic*. We must redefine the population as a new population (a subpopulation of the original one) where the characteristic is constant. That is, we cannot generalize across levels of a variable trait in the population unless that trait is represented as a variable in the sample.

An example will clarify this important point. Suppose we want to do research on teaching methods: We want to compare the effectiveness of teaching reading using phonics with the look-say method. There are two teachers available to teach two first-grade classes. Teacher *A* uses phonics for a year, while Teacher *B* uses the look-say method. At the end of first grade, we measure reading achievement and find that the children in the class with Teacher *B* obtained higher scores. What conclusions can we draw?

Once again, our treatment population is not affected in the same way by the limitations of our sampling procedure as the sampling population is. The effect that we observe is the effect that we would expect to get if all members of the sampling population that yielded these two first-grade classes received either of the treatments we have administered. That is, if the sampling population were given phonics instruction by Teacher *A*, we would expect it to become the treatment population that would yield a sample like the class we measured. Treating the sampling population to look-say instruction by Teacher *B* would make it the treatment population that would yield the other class. Thus, the difference that we observe between the two classes is the difference we would expect to find between the two treatment populations. However, we must be careful how we talk about the treatments as well. In this study, the definitions of the treatments included the personalities and abilities of the teachers themselves as well as the teaching methods they used. We cannot generalize the results to other teachers because each teacher used only one method, so therefore, we cannot tell whether the results were due to the teacher or the method or a combination of the two. We cannot generalize to other grades because only one grade was represented. Even if the students were randomly sampled from all the first graders in the district, we cannot generalize to other districts because this one may be unique. Such factors as the ethnic mixture of the classes, parents' socioeconomic status, for example, have been ignored.

The point, which is crucial for good research studies in the behavioral and social sciences, is that generalizations can be made only to those segments of the population that are represented by the sample. Research with humans is particularly difficult in this regard because the population of interest is so diverse in so many important ways. It is seldom necessary to consider variables like hair color when defining the population because hair color, although a variable, does not seem to be related to most of the behavioral variables of interest to psychologists, sociologists, and educators. However, many other variables such as age, gender, height, weight, number of siblings, area of residence, for example, may be related in important ways to the variables under study. Unless the sample varies on some of these traits, the results of the study cannot be generalized across them.

In a sense, where studies of complex organisms are involved, the characteristics of the sample always place constraints on the definition of the sampling population. We can never generalize except to a population that might reasonably have yielded the sample we have measured. A sample of white Anglo-Saxon Protestant males between 18 and 22 is unlikely to have resulted by random selection from the general American population, but there have been attempts to draw conclusions about the nature of man from such groups. This is not to say that using such groups for research is illegal, immoral, unethical, or in any way improper. What is improper is claiming that the results necessarily apply to other groups that differ in systematic ways from the group that was measured.

We must be completely clear about one other aspect of the generalization problem. The fact that we have obtained a sample of convenience and are using a limited selection of treatments conditions does not mean that the effect we have found in our study does not apply to individuals who are not members of the sampling population and to treatment combinations we have not included. Such individuals may very well be members of the treatment population; that is, had they or people like them been exposed to treatment condition X, they might have responded as the subjects in our study did. However, in the absence of being able to claim that such people were included in the definition of the sampling population, we would be on shaky ground were we to include them in the treatment population. Thus, while all adults might respond to treatment X as college students do, we should conduct a study of treatment X with other age groups before concluding that the effect we have found with college students is true for all people.

Now that we have given a list of don'ts pertaining to sampling and generalizing we shall consider the general strategy for obtaining samples that do permit us to generalize to the population of interest. Remember, there are two broad conditions that we have to meet: The sample must be representative of the population, and there must be a random element in selecting an individual member of the sample.

Stratified random sampling refers to the class of procedures that are used to obtain representative samples from diverse human populations. There are a variety of special procedures that can be used in one application or another, but there are two basic elements that are common to them all: The first is stratification of the population into subpopulations, and the second is a systematic (but at least partially random) sampling of entities within subpopulations.

The first part of the procedure, stratification, requires identifying important dimensions of variability in the population. For example, if we want to do research on voting behavior (or perhaps take a political poll), it is necessary first to identify important variables, or dimensions, that are related to voting; those that come readily to mind are age, sex, and social status. There are, of course, many others that would be included by a political research firm, but these will suffice to describe the process. The dimensions are called *stratification variables*.

Once a set of stratification variables has been identified, the next step is to determine the relative frequency of each category of each variable in the population. In our example, let us assume that age has been divided into four categories, social status into three, and sex into two. A hypothetical set of relative frequencies for each category might be

Age	Rel. Freq.	Soc. Stat.	Rel. Freq.	Sex	Rel. Freq.
18–22	0.15	high	0.15	M	0.50
23–29	0.20	middle	0.50	F	0.50
30–49	0.40	low	0.35		
50+	0.25				

That is, 15 percent of the population of interest is in the 18–22 age range, 35 percent is of low social status, and so on. These frequencies might characterize the population of voters in a city or congressional district in which we are interested. Local records or the most recent census data for the area could be used to obtain the population frequencies.

The three stratification variables divide the population into 24 unique categories or combinations. There are, for example, some females of middle-social status who are in the 23–29 age range, and there are 23 other combinations of our three stratification variables. Our problem now is to determine the relative frequency of each combination, and this is also done with census records or information from other appropriate sources. If information about the frequency of each category is not obtainable, it is necessary to assure that the relative frequencies of each of the categories of the stratification variables themselves are properly represented in the sample.

A sample that is representative of the population will contain the same relative frequency of each type of individual as the population. Thus, if the relative frequency of 23- to 29-year-old, middle-status females is 0.06 in the population and we want to draw a sample of 100 individuals, six of our 100 subjects should be middle-class women between 23 and 29. Each unique combination of the stratification variables is represented in the sample by an appropriate number of people. Stratification ensures that the sample is representative of the population on the stratification variables and other variables that are related to them.

Once the relative frequency of each category of the population and the number of individuals of each type needed for our sample have been determined, we can proceed to draw our sample. There are many different ways of doing this. One simple way that can be used when the population is small is to sort all members of the population into their respective categories and draw a random sample of the needed size from each category. We take small random samples from defined subpopulations that are homogeneous with respect to our stratification variables. When these small random samples are combined, the result is a stratified random sample that is representative of the population in terms of the stratification variables and, hopefully, also in terms of the variables of interest in our study. It is not a true random sample, but stratification has assured representativeness with a smaller sample size. Thus, using stratification variables is a more efficient sampling procedure that sampling at random from the entire population.

There are many other ways of drawing stratified samples, some random and some not so random. Television networks report voting results from carefully selected precincts that have particularly representative voting histories. There is nothing random about their methods, but the predictions can be very exact. Other sampling procedures use school districts or city blocks as sampling units and then measure all individuals in the unit. Whatever the method, the objective is a sample that is representative of the population, so the results from the sample can be generalized to the population.

Careful selection of the stratification variables is crucial to the success of a sampling plan. It is these variables that assure the representativeness of the sample in heterogeneous human populations. It is often necessary to use the published reports of other studies to identify variables that are related to the variable we want to study. These reports can also help determine the relative frequencies of the categories of the stratification variables in the population we want to study. After identifying and defining the population, we can proceed with the study, confident that we shall be able to generalize the results to the population we have defined.

SUMMARY

The primary unit for research is the *population*, which includes all individuals to whom we want to apply the results of a study. There are two kinds of populations, the *sampling population* from which the sample is drawn and to which generalizations about status variables are made and the *treatment population*, which is hypothetical and to which generalizations about manipulated variables are made. A *sample* is a subgroup of a population. The sample is the group on whom the study is conducted with the intention of generalizing the findings in the sample to the appropriate population. A summary index such as the mean, when computed for a sample, is called a *statistic*. The same index computed for the population is called a *parameter*.

Samples may be obtained in several ways. A poor, but frequently used, approach is the *available subjects sample*. This method uses those subjects who are most readily available and is poor because there is no defined population to which the results can be generalized other than the treatment population. One preferred alternative is the *random sample*, where the population is defined and all members have an equal chance of appearing in the sample. Several *stratified random sample* methods have been developed to ensure representative samples, and some nonrandom representative procedures have also proven useful. The most important feature of the sample is that it must be representative of the sampling population from which it was drawn.

1. Give three examples of sampling populations.

2. For each of the following situations describe an appropriate sampling population and, if appropriate, the treatment population:

*(a) Two groups of male white rats learn to run through a maze; the groups differ in amount of food reward.

(b). Dr. Median has two statistics classes. One class is taught by the lecture-only method, while a second class has lectures and laboratory exercises; the two classes are compared on a common final exam.

*(c) A social psychologist compares the attitudes of men and women toward abortion for a random sample of students at college *X*.

(d) A statistics student hands out questionnaires about welfare programs to people coming out of a department store.

3. State the difference between a parameter and a statistic.

*4. What are the characteristics of a random sample? What is the most important characteristic for a sample to have?

5. You are planning a study of student attitudes toward athletics and you wish to be sure your sample is representative of the student body. You obtain the following information about the population from the registrar (all values are frequencies):

Sex		Class		Athlete Status	
Males	1,056	Freshman	921	Varsity	427
Females	2,375	Sophomore	882	Intramural	1,540
		Junior	846	None	1,464
		Senior	782		

Assume that you are going to draw a sample of 100.

*(a) How many should be male?

(b) How many varsity athletes should be in your sample?

(c) How many sophomores should you include?

*(d) How many women should be juniors?

(e) What proportion of the sample should be senior nonathletes?

*(f) How many of your subjects should be sophomore women who participate in intramural athletics?

*Answers to starred questions are found in Appendix D.

12

HYPOTHESES AND DATA COLLECTION

In our discussion in Chapter 1 of the reasons for collecting information, we made a distinction between research and evaluation. We noted that the difference primarily depends upon the use that is to be made of the results. However, as we shall see shortly, this difference in purpose has an important effect on the logical structure that underlies what we are doing. In this chapter, we shall first define some terms and discuss the way that an evaluation study may be conducted. Then we shall tackle what is for many students the most difficult part of a course in statistics, the logical structure underlying the test of an hypothesis.

INDEPENDENT AND DEPENDENT VARIABLES (AGAIN)

Both evaluation and research share an interest in the relationship between variables. In fact, we could even say that determining the presence (and perhaps magnitude) of a relationship is the primary reason for performing a study. We collect data on two or more variables to see whether a relationship exists between them.

It is common practice in the social and behavioral sciences to select the values for one variable and leave the other variable free to vary. For example, we can select certain shock levels in an avoidance study and record the number of trials needed to learn the avoidance response. Or we can select particular teaching methods and measure educational achievement after instruction by these methods. In each of these cases, one variable has its values defined by the investigator and the other is left free to assume any appropriate value.

The variable whose values are selected by the investigator is known as the *independent variable*. The investigator is free (independent) to choose the levels of this variable that will occur in the study. The characteristic must be a variable; it must have more than one value. For example, gender can be an independent variable when both males and females are included in the study; if only females are included, gender is a constant or controlled condition, not an independent variable. The defining feature of the independent variable is that the investigator exercises direct control over its values.

The variable that is left free to vary is known as the *dependent variable*; it is given this name because its values are seen as depending upon the independent variable. In the two examples given above, we can say that speed of learning the avoidance response (number of trials) depends upon level of shock, and educational achievement depends upon method of teaching; at least, this is probably what the investigator would like to be able to say.

The distinction between independent and dependent variables has proven very useful in closely controlled studies in the natural sciences. One sample is exposed to one level of the independent variable; the other sample is given a different level; and the dependent variable is measured. In younger and less-well developed areas of investigation, the distinction is often less appropriate because many characteristics that are studied as independent variables are not really under the investigator's control. That is, the investigator may not be able to obtain a representative sample of subjects from the population and assign each subject to a level of the independent variable. Gender, age, height, weight, ability level, political preference, and a host of other characteristics that are often studied as independent variables are actually *status characteristics* of the subjects and are not subject to the investigator's control. The investigator may choose to select subjects on the basis of their level on one or more of these status variables, thereby making them function like independent variables, but the subjects have predetermined membership in one group or another. This makes it difficult to draw certain kinds of conclusions. We shall have more to say about the importance of the nature of the independent variable for the kinds of conclusions we can draw about the relationship between the independent and dependent variables after we have discussed some other aspects of conducting the study.

EVALUATION STUDIES

Over the last several years, there has been an increasing awareness that many studies are conducted to determine whether some social or government program had the desired effect and that these studies may be different in important ways from more traditional scientific studies. The term *evaluation* has been used to refer to studies of the former type, while *research* is the term suggested for the latter. The difference in purpose between the two types of studies means that some rules and procedures may be required for one and not the other.

There is actually a continuous gradation of studies from pure, or basic, research to the most socially oriented evaluation. At one extreme is the pure research study whose ultimate objective is to discover truth. This is dispassionate, amoral science, unaffected by anything outside the laboratory and conducted without regard to its potential uses or consequences. This type of study, which provides the model for scientific logic, is becoming rare in an increasingly technological world.

At the other extreme is what we might call a pure evaluation study where we find out whether we have done what we set out to do. Questions are not phrased in terms of the nature of the universe but as whether our manipulation of the physical or social environment had the desired effect. For example, a school district might increase class size for some of its classes and not others and conduct a study to compare the level of achievement of students in the larger classes with those in the smaller classes. If students in the larger classes perform just as well as students in the small classes, the school district may increase the size of all classes in order to save money.

This example points out one of the most common differences between pure evaluation and pure research. Pure evaluation usually leads to direct consequences in terms of action: A program is started, increased, decreased, or canceled as a result of the outcome of the evaluation. Pure research seldom has such effects. Another difference concerns the investigator's ability and desire to generalize his results to a population. It is frequently the case in pure evaluation that every member of the population has been included, so that there are no additional cases to which to generalize. Thus, data analysis may stop at the descriptive level because this form of data summarization provides answers to the investigator's questions. An investigator engaged in pure research on the other hand, will usually wish to generalize the findings of the study to the widest possible population. Most studies conducted by social and behavioral scientists fall between these two extremes: They are motivated both by a desire to understand some phenomenon and by the prospect of having social or policy consequences.

Because of their different contexts and objectives, evaluation studies and research studies are conducted under somewhat different sets of rules. While *careful planning and the best possible measurements are essential for useful results in either case*, studies done for research purposes are, in general, more carefully controlled and more restricted in the types of conclusions that are drawn. A loose, but not entirely unfair, characterization of the way an evaluation study may be interpreted is that it does not contradict what its designers set out to show, which may mean that the variable under study is cost-effective, that it achieves the same results in less time than do competitors, for example. The interpretation of an evaluation study may be quite casual and informal, in contrast to the rigidly prescribed logical structure of a research conclusion, as we shall now see.

LOGIC OF RESEARCH

For the student who is just beginning to study the way research is done in the social and behavioral sciences the process often seems backward: The investigator makes a statement of belief about the phenomenon under study (called an hypothesis) and then sets out to prove that the hypothesis is wrong. Why can't we simply say what we believe will happen and if our expectation is confirmed, conclude that we were right?

The source of the apparently illogical logic of research in all scientific disciplines lies in philosophy. For centuries philosophers have struggled with ways of discovering truth and ways of knowing about causal effects. The general trend of their thinking, as it applies to scientific inquiry, is that we can never conclude that something, an hypothesis for instance, is true, but we can conclude that it is false. We can never know what something is, but we can reach conclusions of reasonable certainty about what something is not. There are two reasons for this. The first, which we have already encountered, is the approximate nature of measurement operations: All measurements are only approximations of reality. The second, which extends beyond the bounds of measurement and science, is the nature of the reasoning process itself.

Approximations in Measurement. Let us take a simple example to illustrate what the philosophers are saying. Suppose that we have a table and we want to measure its length. (We could equally well use intelligence, weight, creativity, or any other continuous variable as an example.) We can use the best measurement procedures yet devised and still never be certain of the exact length of the table. Our measurements can rule out most of the possible values; we may, in fact, be able to rule out values below 59.9995 inches and above 60.0005 inches, but so long as the trait (not the measurement scale but the trait itself) is continuous, we can never say that any one value is *the* length of the table. Of course, beyond some point, our ignorance loses its importance for practical applications of measurement; however, this principle governs all scientific applications of measurement.

The reasoning process. It is useful to distinguish two quite different logic processes when trying to understand the nature of scientific inquiry. The first of these is called *deduction*. Deductive reasoning proceeds from a set of facts to a necessary consequence. In its simplest form, the deductive reasoning chain is as follows:

fact	All members of this class understand the mean.
fact	Mary is a member of this class.
conclusion	Mary understands the mean.

Given the facts, the conclusion must follow. Of course, one or more of the facts may actually be false, but that is not a part of the reasoning process itself.

Contrast the example of deduction with the following set of statements that form an *inductive* chain of reasoning:

fact	Mary understands the mean.
fact	Mary is a member of this class.
conclusion	All members of this class understand the mean.

The three sentences are identical, but even given the truth of both facts, the conclusion does not necessarily follow; it could be either true or false.

The difference between these two examples lies in the nature of the facts and conclusions. Deductive reasoning involves going from a general fact (all students) to a particular conclusion (Mary understands). The particular case is deduced from the general principle, and the conclusion can be correctly identified as *either* true or false. Applications of scientific findings, for example, gravity and resistance in the ballistics of rocket flight, involve this kind of process. However, since the objective of scientific inquiry is to find the principles themselves, science cannot use the deductive reasoning process.

When, as in the case of scientific investigation, we apply inductive reasoning, we reason from the particular case (Mary understands) to the general principle (all students). The only type of valid conclusion from this type of reasoning is a negative conclusion; that is, given the facts,

> Mary *does not* understand the mean.
> Mary is a member of this class.

the conclusion, "*Not all* members of the class understand the mean," is a proper logical conclusion. Note that the location of not is crucial: The conclusion, "All members of the class do not understand the mean," is an improper conclusion.

At this point, we can state two general principles about inductive reasoning. First, no number of confirming particular facts can assure that the general principle is true, except for the trivial case where every member of the population is included as a fact. Second, a single disconfirming fact, or exception to the rule, proves the principle false. Therefore, the only way that science can make progress is by ruling out incorrect alternatives. There are many possible explanations for any phenomenon, and a scientific study is designed and conducted to rule out some of the possible explanations. All scientific research, whether in physics, biology, sociology, or psychology, is part of an ongoing process of excluding incorrect explanations for phenomena.

HYPOTHESES

In order to rule out, or eliminate, an explanation as true, we must phrase the explanation in terms of its possible consequences. That is, if the explanation is *untrue* or *false*, we must observe that certain events occur. This means that the explanation must be stated in such a way that it is possible to observe and measure the events related to it. The proposed explanation of the phenomenon is called a *theory*, and statements that specify observable consequences of the theory are called *hypotheses*.

An hypothesis usually takes the form of an if-then statement. If theory X is untrue, then under conditions A, B, and C, using measurement procedure Y, we should observe Z. If the theory that the world is flat is untrue, then a boat sailing west from the Strait of Gibraltar should, after dodging various land masses that may be in the way and avoiding assorted sea serpents, arrive back at its starting point.

The important point here is to realize that no amount of research could ever *prove* that the world is flat. The theory may state that you will fall off the edge of the flat world if you get too close, but failure of your ship to return does not permit the conclusion that the theory is true, only that you were unable to prove it false. There are a variety of other reasons why you may fail to return, including shipwreck, being eaten by sea serpents, and deciding to settle on a delightful island in the South Pacific. The test of the hypothesis *failed to disconfirm the theory*.

Let us suppose that I observe you sailing west from Gibraltar, and some months later, I observe you approaching the same point from the southeast. Can I conclude from these observations that the world is not flat? Not necessarily, because there are other explanations, other theories that would cause us to expect to see you approaching from that direction. One possibility is that you cheated and, circling back out of sight, are now approaching as though having sailed around the world. There may be others.

This little example contains several types of hypotheses that are important in scientific investigations. First, there is the hypothesis that comes from the theory of interest; this is often known as the *research hypothesis*. The theory that the world is flat leads to the hypothesis that you will not return. Next, there is the opposite of first hypothesis. This second hypothesis, often termed the *alternate hypothesis*, arises from an alternate theory. The alternate theory that the world is not flat leads to the alternate hypothesis that you will return. Finally, there are the other explanations that are consistent with either or both of the possible outcomes. These other explanations, that you are a cheat, that you were shipwrecked or devoured by sea serpents, and so on, lead to *plausible rival hypotheses*. Plausible rival hypotheses provide other reasonable explanations for why the study turned out as it did.

DESIGNING A RESEARCH STUDY

In any area of scientific inquiry there are theories. Often there are competing theories that offer different explanations for the phenomena. There are always plausible alternative theories that no one has yet considered. The goal of anyone who is conducting research is to plan the study so that the information collected will lead to a clear and unambiguous conclusion. No study ever reaches this ideal stage of clarity, but there are various things the investigator can do to rule out some of the wrong alternatives. Carefully planning the study to rule out as many of the competing explanations as possible is essential to scientific progress. No amount of elaborate analysis can recover information from data when the planning of the study was inadequate. Statistical analysis cannot eliminate plausible rival hypotheses; only good research design can do that.

There are several approaches that we can use to rule out various types of plausible rival hypotheses; one that has had a long and honored tradition in many scientific disciplines is using *controlled variables* or *experimental controls*. This principle is employed, for example, by the physicist who takes all experimental measurements at the same temperature. Because the temperature is controlled and not allowed to vary, this rules out differences in temperature as an explanation for differences in the dependent variable. Experimental control is also employed when a psychologist uses only female subjects in a learning experiment or an educator studies teaching methods only in third-grade classes. Any characteristic that represents a constant condition across all observations can be ruled out as an explanation for any differences that are found and thus is eliminated as a plausible rival hypothesis.

A second way of eliminating alternate explanations is called *randomization* or *random assignment* of subjects. This procedure is used to eliminate systematic differences between groups of subjects. For example, suppose we want to compare the effects of two teaching methods, a traditional rote-memory approach and an insight approach, on third graders learning the multiplication tables. If we let the parents determine which method their child will use, there is the danger that systematic differences among the parents will result in two groups of subjects who also differ in systematic ways. By assigning each child to one teaching method or the other randomly, we rule out the possibility that systematic, or selective, differences will exist between the groups. Random assignment of subjects is the most powerful method that social and behavioral scientists have of eliminating plausible rival hypotheses.

There are many other procedures that have been devised to rule out various undesirable factors in a research study—so many, in fact, that we cannot begin to cover them here. A number of books have been written on the topic, some of which are listed at the end of this book; the student who will be designing an original research study should consult one of them *before beginning the study* because there is no way to use statistical analysis to salvage meaning from a badly designed study. It is the design of the study and the quality of the measurements that permit us to isolate the research hypthesis from plausible rival hypotheses and test the research hypothesis against its alternative.

As previously suggested, quality measurement procedures are equal partners with good research design in evaluating the research hypothesis. It is essential that the measures be reliable, thus reducing random errors of measurement that would make testing the hypothesis more difficult. The measures must be valid, or the subjects' scores will not mean what we think they mean; thus, our conclusion would almost certainly be wrong because it would be drawn about something we were not measuring. Quality measurements of the trait or traits of interest coupled with good research design and careful data collection are necessary prerequisites if statistical analysis is to lead to proper conclusions.

DRAWING CONCLUSIONS

We noted earlier that according to the thinking of most philosophers, we can only reach the conclusion that something is false, not that it is true. As we shall see in the next chapter, statistical analysis never permits us to *prove* anything, only to reach a conclusion that something is unlikely to be true, with a specifiable probability that our conclusion is in error. We must always remember that statistical procedures have this limiting feature and view with considerable caution some of the more grandiose conclusions that are based on statistical analyses.

The conclusions that we can reach as a result of our study are of two basic kinds. Remembering that even in the most simple study there are at least two measured variables, we can conclude that there is a relationship between the variables under study or that there is not. In the natural sciences and in a few of the more highly developed areas of behavioral and social science, the hypothesis may specify the degree of relationship; in that case, our conclusion would be that the relationship is of that specified degree or it is not. In either case, we have (hopefully) designed the study so that the data permit us to choose between one of two alternatives.

Sometimes it is possible to draw stronger conclusions than that the variables are related; some research designs permit a statement about the nature of the relationship. The most popular of these statements is that the relationship is casual; that is, that changes in one variable cause changes in the other.

This is not the time to get into a philosophical discussion of causation. Regardless of whether we can ever infer causation or not, many investigators reach the conclusion that there is a causal relationship between the variables in their study. Some even go so far as to say that the type of statistical analysis performed determines whether we can conclude that a relationship is causal. There is a timeworn saying in statistics that we cannot infer causation from a correlation, implying that such inferences are permitted only when we use the procedures described in Chapters 13 through 16. Unfortunately, this saying has been misinterpreted as referring to statistical analyses rather than to the data collection procedure. It is the design of the study, the choice of variables, the way they are used and measured, that determines whether causal inferences are warranted. Causation, if it occurs, occurs at or before the time of measurement, not at the time of data analysis. Careful study design and execution *may* permit the inference that a relationship *revealed* by statistical analysis is causal, but the statistical analysis itself can only reveal meaning and information that are already in the data.

There are two major factors in determining whether we can infer that a relationship is causal or not. One that we have already discussed at some length is a design that rules out other noncausal alternatives. The second is the nature of the variables under study. Some of the variables that are of great interest to social and behavioral scientists cannot be separated from a complex of other variables. Such a situation makes casual inferences impossible.

The major useful distinction is between variables that can be manipulated, or assigned, by the investigator and variables that are status characteristics of the individual subjects. *Manipulated variables* are those whose values are chosen by the investigator, and their values can be changed by the investigator. If under appropriately controlled conditions, a change in variable X from value 1 to value 2 is consistently followed by a change in Y from Y_1 to Y_2, we can infer that there is a causal relationship between the change in X and the change in Y. For example, if a given amount of a gas at constant volume is exposed to a heat source, we observe a rise in both temperature and pressure. The manipulated variable is the presence or absence of a source of heat. We can infer that the addition of that heat caused both the increase in temperature and the increase in pressure.

Status variables are nonmanipulable characteristics possessed by the entities under study. The investigator has no control over these variables; they include such obvious properties as the age, height, weight, and gender of subjects. But as mentioned earlier, variables such as intellectual ability, psychomotor ability, motivation, cultural background, personality, for example, should also be considered status variables. While their values may change systematically (we are all getting older at a constant rate) or erratically (the social interactions we experience may have quite unpredictable effects), the investigator can do little about them other than attempt to hold them constant by subject selection or observe the presence or absence of relationships among them. It is seldom, if ever, possible to conclude that a relationship between status variables is causal because the variables cannot be isolated from their context.

Consider again our package of gas. When we first observe it, it is at a given temperature, pressure, and volume. These are status characteristics of this particular package of gas. If we observe other packages of the same type of gas, or of different gases, each package will have its own amount of temperature, pressure, and volume. We can, after extensive observation of packages of gas, conclude that there is a highly consistent relationship among these three variables, but we cannot without manipulation conclude that the relationship is causal.

Inability to manipulate variables does not necessarily mean that a science lacks power or importance. For example, astronomers have never been able to manipulate the variables they study, but they have determined the quantitative properties of the relationships they study to a very high degree, and they borrow freely from other physical sciences and mathematics. Consequently, they are able to predict very accurately the type and magnitude of future extraterrestrial events. Well-documented and stable relationships can be very useful and important even when causation cannot be inferred.

SUMMARY

In this chapter, we drew a distinction between independent and dependent variables. *Independent variables* are those that the investigator manipulates during the course of a study or those for which s/he selects the values to be used. Variables of the latter type are often status characteristics of the subjects. *Dependent variables* are those that are measured as an outcome of the study. The same variable may be an independent variable in one study and a dependent variable in another.

Evaluation studies usually attempt to determine whether some treatment has a desired effect. The investigator often has an interest in one of the possible outcomes, and decisions based on study outcomes may include cost-effectiveness and other social values. Formal testing of hypotheses derived from theories is often of secondary interest. *Research* studies are generally independent of social or monetary values. Their primary goal in testing hypotheses derived from theories is advancement of knowledge.

A research study is conducted to test a hypothesis. The hypothesis is a statement of the expected outcome of the study derived from a set of beliefs (called a theory) about the phenomenon of interest. There are three types of hypotheses: the research hypothesis derived from the theory; the negation of the research hypothesis, called the alternate hypothesis; and a potentially very large set of plausible rival hypotheses, which are alternate ways of explaining the study's results. Scientific progress is made through a continuing process of disproving research hypotheses, thus eliminating incorrect alternatives and theories.

Careful research design is necessary to rule out plausible rival hypotheses and provide a clear test of the research hypothesis. Experimental controls and random assignment of subjects are two ways to focus the study on the research hypothesis. Careful selection of reliable and valid measures of the variables is also an essential feature of good research design.

The conclusions that we draw from a research study usually involve the presence or absence of a relationship between the independent and dependent variables. Manipulated independent variables may allow us to infer a causal relationship with the dependent variable, while status independent variables do not. Highly accurate descriptions of the relationship between variables have proven very useful even when causal inferences cannot be drawn.

PROBLEMS

1. Find four studies in your major area at the library, two of which involve control variables and one or more manipulated independent variable and two of which involve status independent variables. For each study, list each variable and state whether it is a manipulated or status independent variable, a dependent variable or a control.

2. For each of the studies you used in question 1, state the author's research hypothesis and alternate hypothesis. What steps were taken in the research design to eliminate plausible rival hypotheses? What others might have been taken?

13

SAMPLING DISTRIBUTIONS AND STATISTICAL INFERENCE

In the last chapter, we discussed the general problem of testing hypotheses and drawing conclusions. This chapter is devoted to the particular problems encountered when statistical analysis is used to test hypotheses. As we shall see, it is necessary to state our hypothesis in the proper form of a *statistical hypothesis* in order to be able to test it. But first, we must bring together the idea of summary indices discussed in Part I with that of samples from a population in order to develop a new type of frequency distribution known as a sampling distribution.

SAMPLING DISTRIBUTIONS

Consider a theoretically infinite population. For example, there is a population of outcomes from tossing ten coins that is theoretically infinite. There are 11 possible kinds of outcomes, but there is no limit to the number of tosses that could occur. If we think of each toss as an observation in an experiment, it is possible to draw a sample from the population that is made up of N individual observations, each observation independent of all the others. It is not unreasonable to consider this sample to be a random sample of size N with each individual receiving a score between 0 and 10 based on the number of coins showing heads.

Tossing coins is not an inherently interesting activity for most people, and the student may wonder why we spend so much time that way. The reason is that examples such as this provide the clearest view of what is actually going on in an analysis. We can design our study with confidence that the assumptions essential to valid statistical inference are met and that the population will conform to our requirements. When doing research on real problems, the considerations of research design are paramount, and in most cases, the statistical analysis should flow logically from the design. By eliminating for a while the problems of design, we can get an undistracted view of the logical and mathematical processes underlying statistical inference.

Back to our coins. Assume that we toss our ten coins, count and record the number of heads, and repeat the process ten times. We have drawn a random sample of size 10 from an infinite population of coin tosses; compute the mean, median, and standard deviation of the sample; and record these. Now repeat the process nine more times. (If you actually try this yourself you may find it instructive.)

We now have ten samples of size 10, each with a mean, median, and standard deviation. These samples have been drawn randomly from a population with a known mean ($\mu = 5.0$) and standard deviation ($\sigma \doteq 1.58$). (The Greek letter μ (mu) is the symbol usually used to denote the mean of a population. The symbol σ (lower case Greek letter sigma) stands for the population standard deviation.) However, if we actually perform this little experiment, we find that not all of the samples have means ($\overline{X}$'s) of 5.0 nor standard deviations (S's) of 1.58. In fact, it is unlikely that the statistics from any sample will exactly equal the parameters of the population; instead, they will show a distribution of values around the parametric value.

Now, let us take some more samples, an infinite number of them. If we were to do this and compute some summary statistics ($\overline{X}$, Mdn, and S) for each sample, we could prepare a frequency distribution for each type of sample statistic. We would get a frequency distribution of means, one of medians, and another of standard deviations. Each of these frequency distributions will have a mean, median, and standard deviation of its own; these frequency distributions of sample statistics are called *sampling distributions of the statistic.* The frequency distribution of sample means is the sampling distribution of the mean. The frequency distribution of standard deviations is the sampling distribution of the standard deviation, and so forth.

The notion of sampling distributions is fundamental to the entire logical structure of statistical inference. We reach conclusions about statistical hypotheses on the strength of probabilities based on sampling distributions. We shall see shortly how this miracle is accomplished, but first we must explore some of the characteristics of sampling distributions.

We noted that the means of several samples will not, in general, be equal and will not equal the population mean μ; they form a sampling distribution around the population mean. It can be shown[1] that the mean of the distribution of means of random samples from a defined population is the mean of the population. That is, the population mean μ is the mean of the sampling distribution of $\bar{X}$. This is a very important fact because it allows us to specify the location of the sampling distribution on the measurement scale. If we know the population mean, as we do in the case of our coin tossing example, we know that the distribution of sample means will center on this value.

If we use the symbol $(\bar{\bar{X}})$ to indicate the mean of sample means, we can say that

$$(\bar{\bar{X}}) = \mu_X, \tag{13.1}$$

which merely states our assertion from the preceding paragraph in the form of an equation. When the mean of the sampling distribution of a statistic is equal to the population parameter, we say that the statistic computed from a random sample from that population is an *unbiased estimate* of the parameter. The mean of any random sample from a population is an unbiased estimate of μ because of the equality in equation 13.1.

Not all sample statistics are unbiased estimators of their population parameters. Even when a sample is randomly drawn from the population, some of its statistics are biased; that is, the mean of the sampling distribution is either larger or smaller than the parameter. This is a feature of several statistics, most prominent of which is the sample standard deviation S. The mean of the sampling distribution of S (call it $\bar{S}$) is not equal to the population standard deviation σ. $\bar{S}$ is always smaller than σ, and the

[1]Statisticians' jargon for "the proof is too complex to be included in this book."

amount of bias is determined by the size of the sample. We shall return to the problem of bias in S shortly, but now we must focus our attention on other aspects of sampling distributions in general.

STANDARD ERRORS

Every sampling distribution has a mean, but every sampling distribution also shows some degree of spread, or variability, around its mean. The standard deviation of the sampling distribution of a statistic is known as the *standard error* of the statistic. The standard deviation of sample means around μ is known as the standard error of the mean and is given the symbol $\sigma_{\bar{X}}$. The subscript $\bar{X}$ indicates that we are talking about the standard deviation of the means of samples. There is also a standard error of the median (σ_{Mdn}) that is the standard deviation of the sampling distribution of the median; a standard error of the correlation coefficient (σ_r), called the standard error of r, and so on. The worst tongue twister of the lot is the standard error of the standard deviation σ_S. This, of course, is the standard deviation of the sampling distribution of standard deviations.

Each sample value we compute is an estimate, either biased or unbiased, of the population parameter. As sample size increases, we tend to find less variability among the statistics from various samples. In fact, the standard error of a statistic is, in part, a function of the size of the sample on which it is based. Assuming that we know σ, the standard deviation in the population, it can be shown that the standard error of the mean is

$$\sigma_{\bar{X}} = \frac{\sigma}{\sqrt{N}}. \tag{13.2}$$

In our coin-tossing experiment, we had a sample of size 10 ($N = 10$) and a known standard deviation of 1.58. Using these values, the standard error of the mean is

$$\sigma_{\bar{X}} = \frac{1.58}{\sqrt{10}} = \frac{1.58}{3.16}$$

$$= 0.4996.$$

If we were to take a very large number of random samples from the population, compute their means, and calculate the standard deviation of the distribution of these means, we would expect to get a value of about

0.4996. Equation 13.2 states that as sample size increases, the standard error of the mean decreases. Taking samples of 100 tosses of ten coins will reduce the value of $\sigma_{\bar{X}}$.

$$\sigma_{\bar{X}} = \frac{1.58}{\sqrt{100}} = 0.158.$$

When samples are larger, we see less variability among their means. Increasing sample size has the same general effect on the sampling distributions of all statistics. The equations for the standard errors of several statistics are listed in Table 13-1. Every one of them is an inverse function of sample size. As N increases, the standard error decreases. Note the limitations on σ_S and σ_r, the reasons for which will be discussed shortly.

THE CENTRAL LIMIT THEOREM

We have seen that increasing sample size has the effect of decreasing the standard error of a statistic. However, sample size has an important effect on another characteristic of the sampling distribution, its shape. This

TABLE 13-1
Standard Errors of Some Common Statistics.

Sample Statistic	Standard Error
$\bar{X}$	$\sigma_{\bar{X}} = \dfrac{\sigma}{\sqrt{N}}$
Mdn	$\sigma_{\text{Mdn}} = \dfrac{1.253\,\sigma}{\sqrt{N}}$
S	$\sigma_S = \dfrac{\sigma}{\sqrt{2N}}$ [a]
Q	$\sigma_Q = \dfrac{0.7867\,\sigma}{\sqrt{N}}$
r	$\sigma_r = \dfrac{1 - r^2}{\sqrt{N-1}}$ [a]

[a] Approximate value to be used only with $N > 30$.

effect is specified by the *central limit theorem*, which states that as sample size increases, the sampling distribution of a statistic approaches the normal distribution. This effect is not strictly true for all statistics, but it is close enough so that we can handle the exceptions fairly easily.

The central limit theorem is based on a very important assumption that is easy for statisticians to meet but is seldom satisfied in social and behavioral science research. This assumption is that the sampling procedure is random (see Chapter 11). Strictly random sampling is hardly ever the case in actual research situations; however, if the investigator can be reasonably certain that the sample is representative, the statistician's assumptions can usually be considered to have been met.

The central limit theorem is usually applied to the sampling distribution of the mean because most research attention has focused on sample means. As sample size increases, the sampling distribution of $\bar{X}$ approaches a normal distribution with a mean equal to μ and a standard deviation of $\sigma_{\bar{X}}$, *regardless of the shape of the population distribution*. It is this last phrase that gives the central limit theorem its importance. Not all populations are normal in shape; some are definitely nonnormal, being seriously skewed or bimodal. The central limit theorem states that the sampling distribution of $\bar{X}$ approaches the shape of the normal curve as sample size increases even when the samples are drawn from populations that are known to be nonnormal. This principle also holds for the sampling distributions of several other statistics as well.

The central limit theorem is so important because it makes it possible for us to apply the properties of the normal curve in making statements about sampling distributions. (Remember: Areas under the normal curve can be equated to probabilities.) If the sampling distribution of a statistic is known to be normal, we can specify the probability that a sample with a mean, or standard deviation, in a particular range will occur.

Again, we focus our attention on the mean because this is the most widespread application, but keep in mind that the same logic can be applied to other statistics with only minor modifications. Recall that our sample of ten coin tosses was drawn from a population with $\mu = 5$ and $\sigma = 1.58$. Since $\bar{X}$ is an unbiased estimate of μ, the mean of the sampling distribution is also 5, and the standard error is 0.4996. The fact that the population is known to have a nearly normal distribution means that we do not have to worry about the normality of the sampling distribution. If we had reason to suspect the possibility of nonnormality, we might want to collect a larger sample (use 50 tosses, for example) to be reasonably confident of a sampling distribution with normal-curve properties.

Given the information in the preceding paragraph, what is the probability that a sample of $N = 10$ tosses of ten coins will have a mean greater than 6? We know $\mu = 5$ and $\sigma_{\bar{X}} = 0.4996$, so we can determine the proportion of the sampling distribution that lies beyond the point $\bar{X} = 6$. We do this by computing the standard score for the given $\bar{X}$ in the sampling distribution of $\bar{X}$.

$$z_{\bar{X}} = \frac{\bar{X} - \mu}{\sigma_{\bar{X}}} . \tag{13.3}$$

With the values given,

$$z_6 = \frac{6 - 5}{0.4996} = +2.002.$$

Looking this value up in Appendix Table B-1, we find that the proportion of the normal curve beyond $z = +2.00$ is 0.0228. We can therefore say that the probability of getting a mean of six heads in ten tosses of ten coins is about 0.023 or about 23 in 1000.

The same series of logical steps can be used to determine the probability that a sample mean will fall between two values. For the same set of conditions $\mu = 5$, $\sigma_{\bar{X}} = 0.4996$, the probability that we would get a sample with a mean between 4.5 and 5.2 is determined as follows:

$$z_{4.5} = \frac{4.5 - 5}{0.4996} = -1.00$$

$$z_{5.2} = \frac{5.2 - 5}{0.4996} = +0.40.$$

The area between $z_{4.5}$ and zero is 0.3413, and the area from zero to $z_{5.2}$ is 0.1554. Therefore, the area between $z_{4.5}$ and $z_{5.2}$ is $0.3413 + 0.1554 = 0.4967$, and the probability of obtaining a sample whose mean is in this range is about 0.50.

The way that we phrase our statements about these probabilities is very important because we are about to apply them to testing statistical hypotheses. We must remember that the population has a mean that is what it is and does not vary or change; the same thing is true of each particular sample. The population mean and each particular sample mean are fixed, and each has a probability of 1.00, or 100 percent, of occurring in that population or in that particular sample. What is uncertain, and therefore open to probabilistic statements, is which sample we shall get.

The importance of this point for the logic of statistical inference cannot be overstated. In a greatly simplified example, consider a population with four possible samples, each of which is equally probable (0.25) and each of which has a different mean. Suppose $\bar{X}_1 = 1$, $\bar{X}_2 = 2$, $\bar{X}_3 = 3$, and $\bar{X}_4 = 4$. If we reach into the population to obtain a sample and get sample 2, the mean of this sample is certain to be $\bar{X}_2(=2)$, whether we ever measure the subjects and compute the mean or not. There is a 25 percent chance that we shall draw this sample, but once it is drawn, only measurement and computational errors can affect the outcome. Therefore, when applying normal curve procedures and the principles of probability to problems involving sampling distributions, statements or conclusions about probability must be restricted to the sampling phase.

TESTING STATISTICAL HYPOTHESES

At the most fundamental level, a statistical hypotheses is a hypothesis about sampling. The hypothesis is that our sample was drawn from a population with certain stated parameters. We know the shape of the sampling distribution of our chosen statistic (usually the mean) around the parameter, so we can determine the probability that we would draw a sample with the observed value of the statistic from a population with that sampling distribution. If the probability is small that we would get such a sample from that population, we reach the conclusion that the hypothesis is not true. We conclude that the sample was not drawn from a population with the stated parameters.

Let us take our population of coin tosses one more time. The population in our hypothesis has the parameter characteristics $\mu = 5$ and $\sigma = 1.58$. For random samples of size $N = 10$, the sampling distribution has $\mu = 5$ and $\sigma_{\bar{X}} = 0.4996$ as its characteristics. Draw a sample of size 10 and compute its statistics. Suppose we find that $\bar{X}$ is 6.3. Our hypothesis is that this sample was drawn from the population specified. We can use the sampling distribution and the areas of the normal distribution to determine the probability that we would obtain a sample of 10 with $\bar{X}$ as great as 6.3 from a population with $\mu = 5$ and $\sigma = 1.58$ by computing a standard score for the sample mean in the sampling distribution. We obtain

$$z_{6.3} = \frac{6.3 - 5}{0.4996} = +2.60.$$

The proportion of the normal curve that lies at or beyond a z of 2.60 is 0.0047. If we were to draw 10,000 independent random samples from the population specified in our hypothesis, we would expect to obtain about 47 samples with a mean of 6.3 or greater. Another way of saying it is that the odds are about 200 to 1 against getting a sample like this from our specified population.

NULL AND ALTERNATE HYPOTHESES

Statisticians have a special term that they use to designate the hypothesis that includes the specification of the population and the sampling distribution; it is called the *null hypothesis*. The null hypothesis may be expressed in many forms, but all can be reduced to one essential sentence. The null hypothesis states that sample S was drawn from population P, which has the parameters μ, σ, ρ (Greek letter rho standing for the population correlation coefficient), and so forth.

In Chapter 12, we saw that inductive reasoning (reasoning from the particular to the general) can only proceed by negation. For example, if we observe three people and all of them are female, it does not logically follow that all people are female; however, if we observe three people and one of them is not female, it does logically follow that not all people are female. It is precisely this line of reasoning that we must apply in testing statistical hypotheses.

The null hypothesis is the hypothesis under test in any analysis involving statistical inference. Since inductive reasoning is the only avenue open to us, we can only proceed by negation. The only strong conclusion that we can reach is that the null hypothesis is false; that is, we can reach the conclusion that sample S was *not* drawn from population P. Statistical inference never permits the conclusion that sample S was drawn from population P. Even if $\bar{X}$ is exactly equal to μ, we cannot say that S was drawn from P because there are many other populations that could also yield sample *S*. For example a population of coin tosses with $\mu = 4.75$ would yield samples with means of 5 or greater about 31 percent of the time; there is no way of telling whether our sample is one of these.

Statisticians use the term *alternate hypothesis* to refer to negation of the null hypothesis. Note carefully that this alternate hypothesis is different from the hypotheses discussed in Chapter 12. There we discussed hypotheses from alternate, or competing, theories and plausible rival hypotheses that provided alternatives to any theory. Here, the alternate hypothesis contains no substance; it is merely the negation of the null hypothesis. It is not an hypothesis in the same sense that the null hypothesis is because no population is specified, but it does state a general belief in the nontruth of the null.

REACHING A DECISION

The data collected in an investigation permit us to reach a decision regarding the null hypothesis. We can come to one of two decisions: We may decide that the null hypothesis is false; this is called rejecting the null.[2] Or, we may conclude that the evidence does not justify rejecting the null; that is, we may reject the null, or we may fail to reject the null. We can not conclude that the null is true because to do so would violate the rules of inductive logic.

Our decision that the null is false is based on the probability that a sample such as ours would be drawn by random sampling from the population specified in the null. If the probability of such a sample is small, we say that the difference between the sample and the hypothesized population is *statistically significant*, and we reach a decision to reject the null hypothesis.

It is important to understand exactly what these terms mean and exactly what conclusions can be drawn from a statistical analysis, because the terms are often misinterpreted and the conclusions are frequently overdrawn. The term *statistically significant* does not mean *important*; it does not mean *meaningful*; it does not even mean *true*. All that the term *statistically significant* means is that the results are unlikely to have occurred by chance if all of our assumptions are true. We conclude, therefore, that one of our assumptions, the null hypothesis, is false.

[2]It is customary to use the term null, or the symbol H_0, to refer to the null hypothesis. The term alternate, or H_1, is used to indicate negation of the null hypothesis.

When do we say that the difference between the sample and the population specified in the null hypothesis is significant? Mathematical statistics does not have an answer, but editors of scientific journals have adopted some minimum values as conventions. When the probability of the sample occurring under the null hypothesis is less than 5 percent, the result is said to be significant at the 0.05 level. A result that would occur less than one time in 100 is significant at the 0.01 level.

Any time we reach a decision on the basis of statistical analysis, there is some chance that our decision is incorrect. Somewhere out there, there is a true state of affairs. From the point of view of testing statistical hypotheses, the true state may be that the null hypothesis is true or that the null is false. Our decision may be to reject the null or to not reject the null; this yields the four possible outcomes listed in Table 13-2. When the null is true and our decision is to not reject it, we have reached a correct decision. Likewise, when the null is false and we decide to reject it, we are correct; otherwise, our decision is in error.

There are two types of errors that we can make. We can reject the null when it is true; this is called an error of the first kind or a *Type I error*. Conversely, we can decide not to reject the null when it is false; this is a failure to detect a false null hypothesis and is called a *Type II error*.

Statistical significance relates to the probability of making a Type I error. In reaching a statistical decision, we can specify in advance the risk that we are willing to run of making a Type I error; this probability is given the symbol α (Greek letter alpha). We can specify any values we choose for α, but convention tends to dictate the use of 0.05 and 0.01.

As we stated, the null hypothesis specifies a population with particular parameters, which, in turn, define the sampling distribution of the mean (or other statistic of interest) for samples of a given size. One such sam-

TABLE 13-2
Possible Outcomes From Testing a Null Hypothesis.

True	Decision	
State	Reject Null	Do not reject Null
Null false	Correct decision (power)	Type II error (β)
Null true	Type I error (α)	Correct decision

pling distribution is given in Figure 13-1; it is the sampling distribution for our coin toss experiment. It has a mean of 5 and a standard deviation (the standard error of the mean) of 0.4996, and it is normal in shape.

At this point, we should consider where null hypotheses come from. Suppose, for example, that we are government gambling inspectors investigating allegations that gambling devices involving coin tosses have a bias in favor of the house. Some disgruntled players have complained that casino operators have been using coins that tend to favor the casino. Our job is to collect a sample of coin tosses and decide whether the coins are fair. The rules of the game say that if a toss comes up five heads nobody wins; six or more heads is a win for the house, and four or fewer heads is a win for the player. What is the null hypothesis?

This example brings up an interesting and important issue in the statement of the null hypothesis: It is possible for the coins to be unfair in favor of the house or the player. A loose statement of the null is that the game is fair; this statement implies the population distribution with parameters $\mu = 5$ and $\sigma = 1.58$ because this is the theoretical distribution for a toss of ten coins. For samples of $N = 10$, this population yields a sampling distribution of the mean with $\mu_{\bar{x}} = 5$ and $\sigma_{\bar{x}} = 0.4996$; however, there are three different ways that we can consider this null to be wrong. As gambling investigators, we are probably only concerned that the public is not being cheated. Since the null is that the game is fair, the alternate hypothesis is that the game is not fair, but we are only interested in one type of unfairness. We don't care if the game is unfair in favor of

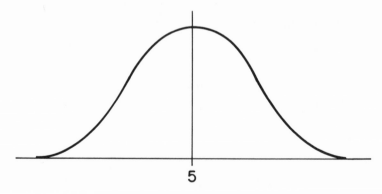

5

Figure 13-1   Sampling distribution of the mean when $\mu = 5$.

the public, only if it favors the house. Therefore, we shall reject the null only if our sample result favors the house by more than we would expect by chance. This is called a *one-tailed test* or a *one-tailed null hypothesis*.

The situation just outlined gives the following statement of the null hypothesis and its alternate:

H_0: $\mu \leq 5$

H_1: $\mu > 5$

We reject the null hypothesis in favor of its alternate H_1 if the results from our sample are unlikely to have occurred by chance from the population specified in the null hypothesis.

Here we must reintroduce α, the chance of a Type I error, the probability that we shall reject the null hypothesis when it is true. Consider Figure 13-2. In this figure, we again have the sampling distribution under the null. We can select any level of α that we wish, but in this case, we have chosen the 0.05 level; that is, we have decided to reject the null if the sample results are such as would occur in only 5 samples out of 100. The shaded part of the figure is that portion of the sampling distribution that falls in this *rejection region*. A sample result that falls in this region will cause us to reject the null hypothesis.

Now, consider the point of view of the casino operator. S/he wants to be certain that the coins used are not biased in favor of the players, but

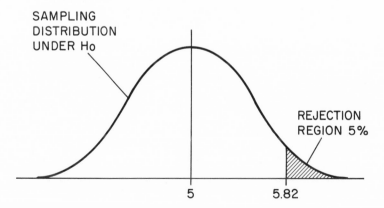

Figure 13-2 Five-percent rejection region for a one-tailed null hypothesis that $\mu \leq 5$.

coins that favor the house will be permitted. The operator's concern is that $\mu \geqslant 5$, so the null and alternate hypotheses would be

H_0: $\mu \geqslant 5$

H_1: $\mu < 5$.

These hypotheses imply the same sampling distribution as before, but the rejection region is located at the other end, as shown in Figure 13-3. As casino operator, we select $\alpha = 0.05$ and find the rejection region to be as shown. If the sample mean is less than 4.18, we shall decide to reject the null (and probably to get some new coins too!).

Suppose now that our only concern is to make the game fair to both parties; that is, we want to be certain that neither the casino operator nor the player has an advantage. In this case, we shall reject the null hypothesis if the sample results in too many heads *or* too few. That is, we shall have rejection regions at both ends of the sampling distribution, as shown in Figure 13-4. Using the same α-level (0.05), we put half of the rejection area in each tail of the sampling distribution. The null hypothesis is called a *two-tailed* null and the test of the null is a two-tailed test; the null and its alternative are symbolically stated as

H_0: $\mu = 5$

H_1: $\mu \neq 5$.

We can summarize our discussion by saying that null hypotheses may be either one-tailed or two-tailed. In a one-tailed test, the null is rejected

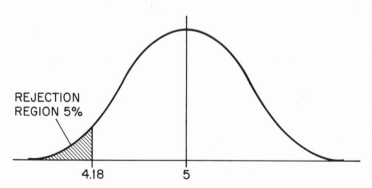

REJECTION REGION 5%

4.18   5

Figure 13-3   Five-percent rejection region for a one-tailed null hypothesis that $\mu \geqslant 5$.

only if the value of the sample mean (or other statistic) is in the predicted direction from the mean of the sampling distribution. If we use the symbol K to stand for the constant value of the null distribution ($K = 5$ in the example we have been using), the two forms of the one-tailed null hypothesis are

a. $\mu \geq K$

b. $\mu \leq K$,

while the two-tailed null has the general form

c. $\mu = K$.

In **a.**, we would reject the null only if $\bar{X} < K$; no value of $\bar{X}$ that is greater than K would lead to rejection of the null. Conversely, in **b.**, the only values of $\bar{X}$ that would lead to rejection are those greater than K. The two-tailed null is rejected whenever $\bar{X}$ is different enough from K in either direction to fall in the rejection region. The rejection region is that portion of the sampling distribution that falls beyond a *critical value*. The critical value is the value in the sampling distribution that cuts off a stated portion of the area under the curve. The stated portion is α, the value chosen for statistical significance. If the sample result exceeds the critical value of the statistic, it falls in the rejection region, and we conclude that the null hypothesis is false.

When the sampling distribution of the statistic is normal, as it is in our example, we can use the table of areas under the normal curve to compute critical values. Suppose that we set α at 0.05. Looking in Appendix Table

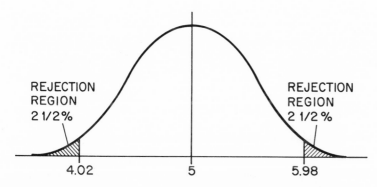

Figure 13-4   Rejection region for a two-tailed null hypothesis.

B-1 under "area beyond z," we find that 5 percent of the distribution falls beyond a z of 1.645. This means that the critical value *for a one-tailed hypothesis* is 1.645 standard deviations away from the mean. Whether it is above the mean or below it depends on the direction specified in the hypothesis. For null hypotheses of the form $\mu \geq K$, the 5 percent critical value is -1.645, while for the null $\mu \leq K$ the value is $+1.645$. This comparison is shown in Figure 13-5.

It is important to note that the values given in the figure are standard scores; that is, the distribution is expressed with a mean of zero and a standard deviation of 1. We can convert these values to the sampling distribution of our example by the usual linear transformation from z-scores to raw scores (equation 5.1). This yields

$$CV = (+1.645)(0.4996) + 5 = (+0.82) + 5 = 5.82$$

$$CV = (-1.645)(0.4996) + 5 = (-0.82) + 5 = 4.18,$$

where the standard deviation is the standard error of the mean (because we have a distribution of means), and the mean is as specified by the null ($K = 5$).

We are now ready to examine the second major difference between one-tailed and two-tailed hypotheses. The first difference was a logical one: Are you are interested in only one type of outcome?; the second difference is a quantitative one: How large is the critical value?. In a two-tailed hypothesis, we have rejection regions in both tails of the distribution. If we use one-tailed critical values ($+1.645$ and -1.645), we shall have 5 percent of the distribution in each tail and a total of 10 percent of the distribution in the rejection region. Thus, if our hypothesis is two-tailed, we must adjust our critical values. To keep 5 percent of the distribution in the total rejection region, we should put $2\frac{1}{2}$ percent in each tail.[3] Going to the normal curve table, we find the necessary values to be $+1.96$ and -1.96; these z's give us critical values of

$$CV_U = (+1.96)(0.4996) + 5 = (+0.98) + 5 = 5.98$$

$$CV_L = (-1.96)(0.4996) + 5 = (-0.98) + 5 = 4.02,$$

which are the values that appear in Figure 13-4.

---

[3]It is not necessary to put $2\frac{1}{2}$ percent in each tail. We could just as well put 4 percent in one tail and 1 percent in the other, but it would be difficult to justify this in most cases. It is conventional to put half the rejection region in each tail.

The consequence of stating our null as a two-tailed hypothesis should now be clear: The critical values are larger, and it is therefore more difficult to reject the null. This fact has led some people to be prejudiced against one-tailed null hypotheses. The reasoning is that if an effect is big enough to be meaningful, it should be big enough to exceed the larger critical value required by the two-tailed test. Unfortunately, the problem is not so simple as the size of the critical value. It is part of a debate that has been going on among statisticians and investigators who use statistics for over 50 years. The center of the debate is the proper use of null and alternate hypotheses. In Chapter 12, we saw that investigators in the physical sciences test their theories using inductive inference and research hypotheses derived from theories. Proving a research hypothesis

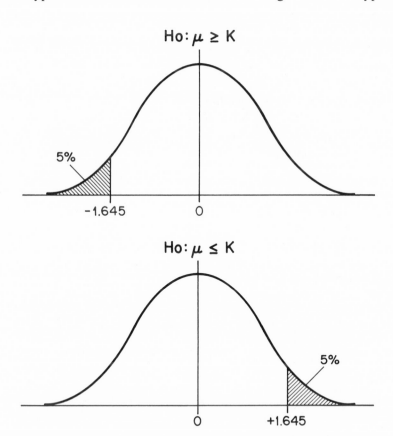

Figure 13-5   Critical values of z and 5-percent rejection regions for one-tailed null hypotheses.

to be false leads to modification and (hopefully) improvement of the theory.

It is clear that the research hypothesis in the physical sciences is equated with the null hypothesis of statistical inference. The test is performed in order to reject the research hypothesis. However, in the social and behavioral sciences, the most common practice is to cast hypotheses in such a way that the statistical alternate hypothesis is equated with the research hypothesis. The null hypothesis is stated as an outcome that would *not* be expected if the theory giving rise to the research hypothesis were true. The following is a slightly oversimplified example of the way that statistical inference is most frequently used in psychology.

Rita, an aspiring undergraduate psychology major, has a theory that larger rewards lead to faster learning. Before running a study to test this theory, she frames her hypotheses. Since she is using rats for subjects, a maze as her learning task, and food pellets as reward, her hypotheses will be stated in terms of pellet size and running time. Her research hypothesis is that the rats that receive larger pellets will run faster than those receiving smaller pellets. After consulting the research literature and her instructor, she forms the following null hypothesis: "There will be no difference in running speed between rats receiving large pellets and rats receiving small pellets."

This is a somewhat more complex problem than we have used up to now, involving, as it does, two groups of subjects. However, it is typical of the situations in which we find two-tailed null hypotheses used in practice. The theory makes a directional prediction that μ_L (the population mean running time for rats receiving larger pellets) is less than μ_S (the population mean running time for rats receiving smaller pellets). Clearly, the research hypothesis under the theory is

$$\mu_L < \mu_S,$$

the mean running time for large-pellet rats is smaller than the mean running time for small-pellet rats. But, the two-tailed hypothesis states that

$$\mu_L = \mu_S,$$

and if Rita rejects this hypothesis, she can conclude that

$$\mu_L \neq \mu_S,$$

but not that

$$\mu_L < \mu_S.$$

That is, a two-tailed test cannot be used to test a theory that makes a directional prediction because neither the null hypothesis nor its negation (the alternate) reflects on the truth or falsehood of the research hypothesis. In order to draw logical conclusions from research, we must frame our hypotheses to be logically consistent with our theories. There are two alternate outcomes; either we reject the null in favor of the alternate hypothesis or we do not reject the null. Formally, the alternative is the negation of the null; unless either the null or its negation is exactly equivalent to our research hypothesis, our study does not test the predictions made from our theory.

TYPE I AND TYPE II ERRORS

We must now return to the topic of errors in our decisions. We have seen that Type I error, a decision to reject the null when it is true, is directly related to the concept of statistical significance. The investigator can select and control the probability of a Type I error by her/his choice of a critical value. In fact, as we saw, the investigator actually chooses the probability of a Type I error first and then computes the critical value.

To see exactly what is involved in Type I error, let us consider again our population of coin tosses. Since this is a hypothetical example, we have the advantage of being able to specify what truth is. To start with, we set truth equal to the null hypothesis; that is, our population has the parameters $\mu = 5$ and $\sigma = 1.58$, yielding a sampling distribution of the mean for samples of $N = 10$ of $\mu_{\bar{X}} = 5$ and $\sigma_{\bar{X}} = 0.4996$.

Given this population, we would expect that if we repeated our experiment a large number of times, if we drew a large number of samples of size 10, 5 percent of them would have means of 5.82 or greater, and 5 percent would have means of 4.18 or smaller (see Figure 13-5). These results would be expected to occur by chance in the process of drawing random samples from the population. Another way to say this is that if we drew 100 random samples, we would expect about five of them to have means of 5.82 or greater and another five to have means at, or below, 4.18.

Suppose that we specify a one-tailed null hypothesis that $\mu \leq 5$ and an α (probability of a Type I error) of 0.05. Using the calculations just described, the critical value is 5.82, and our rejection region is the portion of the scale above the critical value. We shall reach the conclusion that the null is false if we obtain a sample result where $\bar{X} > 5.82$. Under the condition that the null is true, we would expect five samples in 100 to have means in this region. The chance that our sample is one of these five is 5/100, or 5 percent, the selected value for α. Each of these five samples would lead us to decide that the null is false. We would reach the incorrect decision five times and the correct decision 95 times. Since the decision to reject the null is a Type I error (remember, we know truth), we say that the Type I error rate is 5 percent.

In the real world, we do not draw 100 independent random samples; rather, we draw a single sample from the population and reach our conclusion on the basis of the results from that sample. The distribution specified by the null hypothesis yields a region that would contain 5 percent (or any other value we might choose for α) of the samples. The chance that our sample falls in the rejection region is 5 percent, the selected value for α. Therefore, the probability that we shall make a Type I error by rejecting the null hypothesis is also α (0.05 in this case).

Now let us consider what happens if the truth is something else. Suppose that each coin in the population has a probability of 0.60 of coming up heads. This means that if we tossed each coin a large number of times, each would come up heads on 60 percent of the tosses. For a set of ten coins such as this, the mean of the population of coin tosses is 6 and the standard deviation is 1.55.[4] Samples of size 10 from this population yield a sampling distribution of the mean with $\mu_{\bar{x}} = 6$ and $\sigma_{\bar{x}} = 0.4902$. If we assume that this distribution is normal (it isn't quite, but the approximation is very close due to the central limit theorem), we can use Appendix Table B-1 to represent areas under the curve. Our null hypothesis was that $\mu \leq 5$. If we were omniscient, we would know that H_0 is false and that the alternative ($H_1: \mu > 5$) is correct. However, we do not have such knowledge, so we must run an experiment and attempt to infer the true state of affairs from the results.

The two sampling distributions that we have described are shown in Figure 13-6. The one on the left is the sampling distribution that would exist if H_0 were true. The one on the right is the sampling distribution for $\mu_{\bar{x}} = 6$. This is one of the many sampling distributions that satisfies the negation of the null and, therefore, satisfies the alternate. A similar distribution could be drawn for $\mu_{\bar{X}} = 5.1$, $\mu_{\bar{X}} = 5.2$, and so on.

---

[4]Our coin-tossing problem is an example of a binomial experiment. In any binomial experiment, it is always true that $\mu = Np$ and $\sigma = \sqrt{Npq}$ where N is the number of coins tossed (number of binomial events), p is the probability that a coin will come up heads, and q is $(1 - p)$.

The 5 percent critical value for the null, 5.82, is shown in Figure 13-6; this value marks the decision point. A sample result to the left of (less than) this value will lead to the decision not to reject the null hypothesis. Since we now know (as abstract observers, not as practicing scientists) that $\mu_{\bar{X}} = 6$, the decision not to reject H_0 is an error; more specifically, it is a Type II error, a failure to detect a false null hypothesis.

Just as α is the probability of making a Type I error when the null hypothesis is true, β is the probability of making a Type II error *when a given alternative to the null is true*. We have seen that the investigator can specify α, so that the probability of a Type I error is under her/his control. This is so because there is only one sampling distribution specified by the null hypothesis. Since the alternate hypothesis does not specify a single distribution but a class of distributions and there is no way of knowing which of them is correct, it is not possible to specify or control β. It will have one value if $\mu_{\bar{X}} = 5.1$, another if $\mu_{\bar{X}} = 6.0$; there are as many different values for β as there are different values for $\mu_{\bar{X}}$.

We have seen that α is the proportion of the area of the null hypothesis sampling distribution that falls in the rejection region. β is the proportion of the area of a particular alternate sampling distribution (for example, $\mu_{\bar{X}} = 6$) that *does not* fall in the rejection region. In Figure 13-6, this is the proportion of the upper distribution that falls below 5.82.

The value of β can be calculated for a given alternative to the null. The procedure is to calculate the z-score of the null hypothesis critical value *in the alternate distribution* and look up the area beyond that z-score in

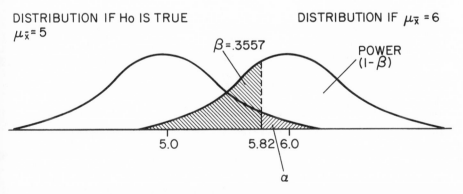

DISTRIBUTION IF Ho IS TRUE
$\mu_{\bar{x}} = 5$

DISTRIBUTION IF $\mu_{\bar{x}} = 6$

$\beta = .3557$

POWER
$(1-\beta)$

5.0   5.82 6.0

α

Figure 13-6   Power and the probabilities of type I (α) and type II (β) errors for a true μ of 6.

Appendix Table B-1. The value of β for the alternate $\mu_{\bar{x}} = 6$ is calculated as follows:

$CV = 5.82$ (from the null)

$$\mu_{\bar{x}} = 6 \qquad\qquad \sigma_{\bar{x}} = 0.4902$$

$$z_{5.82} = \frac{5.82 - 6}{0.4901} = \frac{-0.18}{0.4901} = -0.37$$

$$\beta = 0.3557.$$

This value can be interpreted to mean that if the true value of $\mu_{\bar{x}}$ is 6.0, there is about a 36 percent chance that our experiment with a sample of ten will fail to lead to the conclusion that the null hypothesis is false.

The value of β is the probability of making a Type II error; its complement $(1 - \beta)$ is called *power*. Power is the probability that a statistical test of an hypothesis will lead to a correct rejection of the null hypothesis (see Table 13-2). In the preceding example, the power of the test is $1 - 0.3557$ or 0.6443. Keep in mind that the power of a test varies inversely with β and that their relative magnitudes depend on the particular alternate distribution that is being considered *and* on the value of α chosen by the investigator. We can use variants of our example to illustrate these points.

The effect of changing α (for a constant alternate) is to change the critical value. Lowering α to 0.025 changes the needed z to 1.96 and the critical value to 5.98. The value of $z_{5.98}$ on the alternate distribution is

$$z_{5.98} = \frac{5.98 - 6}{0.4902} = \frac{-0.02}{0.4902} = -0.04$$

$$\beta = 0.484 \text{ and power is } 0.516.$$

Thus, reducing the chance of making a Type I error by $2\frac{1}{2}$ percent means that we must increase the chance of a Type II error by almost 13 percent and reduce the power of the test by that amount. The price to the investigator of reducing the probability of one kind of error is always an increase in the risk of making the other kind of error. In many practical situations, the choice of which error to minimize is dictated by the consequences of a wrong decision. This topic is beyond our scope, so we shall not discuss it further.

Consider now what happens when the alternate distribution (truth) is assumed to have $\mu_{\bar{x}} = 5.5$ and $\sigma_{\bar{x}} = 0.4975$. This does not in any way affect α or the critical value because these are defined on the null hypothesis distribution, but it has a profound effect on β. If $\alpha = 0.05$, the critical value returns to 5.82. The situation is diagramed in Figure 13-7. Calculating $z_{5.82}$ on the alternate distribution, we obtain

$$z_{5.82} = \frac{5.82 - 5.5}{0.4975} = \frac{+0.32}{0.4975} = +0.64$$

$\beta = 0.7389$ and power $= 0.2611$.

We are much less likely to detect the fact that the null hypothesis is false if the difference between truth and the null distribution is small.

SAMPLE SIZE

There is one other feature of the research design that is often under the investigator's control and that can have a considerable effect on the test of the null hypothesis. This factor is the number of observations collected, the sample size. The effect of sample size is readily apparent from equation 13.2, which reads

$$\sigma_{\bar{X}} = \frac{\sigma_X}{\sqrt{N}}.$$

For a constant population standard deviation (and, of course, it must be constant because parameters do not fluctuate), the standard error of the mean is reduced when sample size is increased. In the coin-tossing experiment, for example, an increase in sample size from $N = 10$ to $N = 25$ reduces the value of $\sigma_{\bar{X}}$ in the null hypothesis sampling distribution from 0.4996 $[(1.58)/\sqrt{10} = 0.4996]$ to 0.316 $[(1.58)/\sqrt{25} = 0.316]$. This in

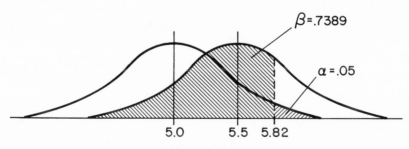

Figure 13-7   Power and the probabilities of type I (α) and type II (β) errors for a true μ of 5.5. Note the increase in β.

turn reduces the critical value for the one-tailed hypothesis with $\alpha = 0.05$ from 5.82 [0.4996 (1.645) + 5 = 5.82] to 5.52 [0.316 (1.645) + 5 = 5.52]. A further increase in sample size to $N = 100$ reduces $\sigma_{\bar{x}}$ to 0.158 [(1.58)/ $\sqrt{100} = 0.158$] and the critical value to 5.26 [0.158 (1.645) + 5 = 5.26].

Obviously, the effect of increasing sample size is to reduce variability among samples. The sampling distribution is still centered in the same location, but it shows reduced spread. The same effect occurs on the sampling distributions under the various alternate hypotheses. The result of increasing N, as computations from our coin-toss alternatives show, is that for constant α, β is reduced and power is increased.

For $N = 25$ and true $\mu = 6$, $\sigma_X = 1.549$

$$\sigma_{\bar{x}} = \frac{1.549}{\sqrt{25}} = 0.31.$$

With a critical value of 5.52, we calculate

$$z_{5.52} = \frac{5.52 - 6}{0.31} = \frac{-0.48}{0.31} = -1.55.$$

The proportion of the area of the alternate distribution that falls below the critical value is 0.0606; therefore,

$$\beta = 0.0606$$

and

$$\text{power} = 0.9394.$$

This compares favorably with the values of β (0.3557) and power (0.6443) that we obtained for $N = 10$.

The same calculations for our other alternative ($\mu = 5.5$, $\sigma_X = 1.57$) give the following results:

$$\sigma_{\bar{x}} = \frac{1.57}{\sqrt{25}} = 0.315.$$

The critical value is still 5.52, so

$$z_{5.52} = \frac{5.52 - 5.5}{0.315} = +0.0635.$$

The associated value of β is 0.52 with power = 0.48. For $N = 100$, the reduction in β and the increase in power would be even more substantial.

As a check on her/his own understanding of how to determine β and power, the student may wish to confirm that for $N = 100$, the β's for the two alternatives are 0.0000 and 0.0643, respectively.

The investigator's ability to control sample size provides indirect control over β. As we noted before, α is under direct control simply by changing the critical value; on the other hand, β depends in part on the true value of μ in the population. If we assume that truth is that $\mu \neq K$, then β is inversely proportional to N. By letting N get very large, we can reduce β to a small amount for any value of $\mu \neq K$. Thus, while we can never know the actual value of β, we can reduce it by taking a larger sample.

Let us now review briefly the process involved in testing a statistical hypothesis. First, we state a null hypothesis that is derived from a theory or belief. The null hypothesis implies a particular set of parameters for the population ($\mu_X = K$ and a particular value for σ_X). Next, we select values for N and α, which are used along with μ_X and σ_X to calculate a critical value for the test. This critical value is the value in the null hypothesis sampling distribution for the statistic of interest (usually the mean) that cuts off α percent of that distribution (called the rejection region) consistent with the negation of the null hypothesis. The rejection region may be in the upper tail, lower tail, or both tails of the sampling distribution, depending on the null hypothesis itself. Once we have determined the rejection region, we collect our data and compute the value of the statistic of interest. If the value of the statistic falls in the rejection region, we conclude that the null hypothesis is false or that the difference between μ and K (for example) is statistically significant.

Sample size occupies a very important place in this sequence of events due to its effect on the standard error of the sampling distribution. As sample size increases, the standard error decreases, bringing the critical value closer to the parameter specified in the null. (Remember that in our preceding example the effect of increasing N from 10 to 25 to 100 reduced the critical value from 5.82 to 5.52 to 5.26.) This means that smaller and smaller differences will be needed to lead to rejecting the null hypothesis.

We mentioned before that statistical significance refers to the probability that the difference between the hypothesized value of the parameter and our sample statistic would occur by chance. Statistical significance or the probability of a Type I error is related to the trustworthiness or reproducibility of the results, not their importance or meaningfulness. If we couple this understanding with the knowledge that increasing N will lead us to find smaller differences to be statistically significant, we can see that using large samples can result in meaningless and unimportant differences being found statistically significant; thus, there is a disadvantage (aside from the logistic problems of dealing with large sets of data) to using large samples.

The moral of this story is that we must use our heads as well as statistical analysis both in the design and in the interpretation of a study. If we are going to perform a study to test a hypothesis, the study should be designed with the statistical analyses in mind. We should know what major analyses will be performed before the data are collected, and sample size should be selected with a view to the size of difference that it is useful to interpret. After the statistical analyses have been completed, a logical analysis should be used to determine what the outcome of the study means for the hypotheses under test. Statistical analysis is a tool to be used to provide information, not decisions.

SUMMARY

Statistical inference involves using sampling distributions to test *statistical hypotheses*. A *sampling distribution* is the frequency distribution of values of a statistic that would be obtained from a large number of random samples of a given size drawn from a population. All statistics have sampling distributions.

The *standard error* of a statistic is the standard deviation of its sampling distribution; it is inversely related to sample size. The *central limit theorem* states that for large samples, the sampling distributions of most statistics approach the normal distribution, regardless of the shape of the population frequency distribution.

There are two kinds of statistical hypotheses. The *null hypothesis* states the characteristics of the population that are to be tested and usually includes a statement of the mean and standard deviation. The *alternate hypothesis* is the negation of the null, which may be *one-* or *two-tailed*.

Statistical inference proceeds by calculating a *critical value* for the statistic in its assumed sampling distribution. If the statistic computed from the sample data falls in the *rejection region*, the decision is made to reject the null hypothesis.

An experimental result is said to be *statistically significant* when it is unlikely that the sample result could have been obtained by chance from a population where the conditions specified in the null hypothesis are true; such a finding leads to a decision to reject the null. A *Type I error* occurs when the decision is reached to reject the null, but it is actually true. When the true situation is that the null is false, but the decision is reached not to reject it, a *Type II error* has been made. The *power* of an analysis refers to its ability to detect a false null hypothesis.

PROBLEMS

1. For each of the following examples, find the standard error of the mean and the probability of drawing a sample with a mean as large or larger than the X given:

*(a) $\mu = 20$	$\sigma = 3$	$N = 9$	$\bar{X} = 21$
(b) $\mu = 27$	$\sigma = 6$	$N = 36$	$\bar{X} = 28$
*(c) $\mu = 14.7$	$\sigma = 2.8$	$N = 25$	$\bar{X} = 15$
(d) $\mu = 248.6$	$\sigma = 29.3$	$N = 49$	$\bar{X} = 255$
*(e) $\mu = 75$	$\sigma = 4.2$	$N = 20$	$\bar{X} = 72$
(f) $\mu = 47$	$\sigma = 15.2$	$N = 70$	$\bar{X} = 44$

*2. What does the term statistically significant mean?

3. For the studies you looked up in Chapter 12, what were the authors' null hypotheses? Would rejecting these nulls support or refute the authors' theories?

*4. Define Type I and Type II errors.

5. What does it mean to say that a test is one-tailed? two-tailed? When is it appropriate to use a one-tailed test?

6. State the appropriate null and alternate hypotheses for each of the following research situations or statements:

*(a) Our theory predicts that at age 7 boys will weigh more than girls.

(b) Thordike's theory of euphoria states that blonds have more fun.

*(c) Republicans and Democrats hold different beliefs on price supports for farmers.

(d) Children in California and New York are equal in reading achievement.

*(e) Single men carry more auto insurance than do single women.

(f) The rain in Spain falls mainly on the plain.

*Answers to starred questions are found in Appendix D.

7. For each of the following situations, find the critical value and the power of the test for each alternative given:

*(a) Ho: $\mu \leq 10$ $\quad$ $\sigma = 2$ $\quad$ $N = 16$ $\quad$ $\alpha = 0.05$
alternatives of 10.5, 11, 12

(b) Ho: $\mu \geq 25$ $\quad$ $\sigma = 8$ $\quad$ $N = 25$ $\quad$ $\alpha = 0.05$
alternatives of 24, 23, 22

*(c) Ho: $\mu = 50$ $\quad$ $\sigma = 10$ $\quad$ $N = 64$ $\quad$ $\alpha = 0.01$
alternatives of 45, 48, 53, 56

(d) Ho: $\mu = 60$ $\quad$ $\sigma = 12$ $\quad$ $N = 49$ $\quad$ $\alpha = 0.01$
alternatives of 55, 58, 60, 63, 66

14

TESTING HYPOTHESES ABOUT MEANS

The majority of the hypotheses tested in the behavioral and social sciences concern the mean or means of one or more groups of subjects. The last chapter described in some detail the logical structure underlying the testing of statistical hypotheses. The general procedure described there was to select a test statistic, specify the sampling distribution of that statistic under the null hypothesis, calculate the value of the test statistic in the sample, and reject the null if the probability of obtaining that extreme a sample value of the test statistic was less than a chosen α-level. In this chapter, we first examine more closely what a test statistic really is, then apply the concept to a more realistic set of problems than coin tosses.

TEST STATISTICS

The term test statistic refers to the numerical indices used to test hypotheses. In Chapter 13, we were testing hypotheses about means, but the statistic upon which we based our decision to reject or not reject the null hypothesis was z; the test statistic was z, not $\bar{X}$. The test statistic is computed from the descriptive statistics of the sample using the conditions assumed by the null hypothesis, which may involve sample means, sample variances, or both. Sample correlations may be involved and the hypothesis may be about means, variances, correlations, or some other characteristics.

The test statistic in Chapter 13 is called the *critical ratio*. It was one of the early test statistics to be developed and was widely used prior to 1915. Since then, its use has dropped off markedly because it can only be properly used under very restricted conditions. It has been replaced by another test statistic, called t, that has the advantage of being appropriate for many research problems. t is quite similar to z, but, as we shall see, there are important differences. Other test statistics that we encounter briefly in later chapters are the F statistic and χ^2 (chi-square).

The choice of which test statistic to use to test a particular hypothesis depends on several things. First, what descriptive property of the sample is being used? Hypotheses about means may involve z, t, or F; hypotheses about variances generally use F or χ^2. Second, how much is known about the population?; the more we know about the population, the more powerful our test will be. Sample size and the number of samples in the analysis also affect our choice. Finally, the level of scale used to make measurements must be considered. Most of the popular procedures involving z, t, and F require the dependent variable to be measured on an interval scale. Test statistics that do not require this condition, such as some uses of χ^2, are generally called *nonparametric statistics*.

In the remainder of this chapter, we describe procedures that are appropriate when a null hypothesis is tested using the means of one or two samples. First, we cover the case where the standard deviation of the dependent variable X in the population is known; we then turn our attention to the more common case where we do not know the population standard deviation. Finally, the special case where the subjects in two groups are matched on some characteristic is examined.

WHEN σ IS KNOWN—1 SAMPLE z

Use of the critical ratio as a test statistic is restricted to those situations where the standard deviation of X in the population (σ_X) is known; this was the case in our coin-toss experiment. We know that

$$\sigma_X = \sqrt{Npq}$$

for any such situation. We can compute σ_X for any null hypothesis: $\mu_X = K$. The standard error of the mean is

$$\sigma_{\bar{X}} = \frac{\sigma_X}{\sqrt{N}},$$

and the sample critical ratio is

$$z = \frac{\bar{X} - \mu_{\bar{X}}}{\sigma_{\bar{X}}}. \tag{14.1}$$

The value of z is then used to determine whether the probability of z is less than α from the table of areas of the normal distribution.

Two other procedures essentially equivalent to this one are also frequently used. If the investigator uses one of the standard values of α (0.05 or 0.01), the required critical values of z (z_α) for a one- or two-tailed hypothesis can be looked up ahead of time. The z computed from the data can then be compared to the critical value of z and a decision reached about the hypothesis. Alternately, a critical value can be computed for $\bar{X}$,

$$\bar{X}_{CV} = z\,(\sigma_{\bar{X}}) + \mu$$

and the obtained mean compared to this critical value.

One point that should be kept in mind throughout this and future discussions of hypothesis testing is the difference between the population parameter and its sample estimate (in this case μ and $\bar{X}$) and the test statistic (here z). Our hypotheses are about the population parameters, but our decisions about those hypotheses are reached on the basis of test statistics. Just as there is a sampling distribution of the *sample statistic* around the population parameter, so, also, is there a sampling distribution of the *test statistic* around a value that would occur if the null hypothesis were true. The sampling distribution of $\bar{X}$ around μ is precisely paralleled by the sampling distribution of the critical ratio z around the value it would have (0) if the null hypothesis were true. This distinction was blurred in Chapter 13 to illustrate the relationship between sample statistics, probability, and decisions about hypotheses. In cases where only one or two samples are involved, it is easy to go back and forth between the two concepts. However, when we attack more complex problems, such as hypotheses involving three means, it is not possible to generate sample statistics from the test statistic. In these cases, it is the sampling distribution of the test statistic that is used to test the hypothesis, not the sampling distribution of the sample statistic around the parameter. This distinction will recur when appropriate throughout the remainder of our discussion.

WHEN σ IS KNOWN—2 SAMPLE z

There are relatively few research problems where it would be appropriate to use the one-sample critical ratio just described. Somewhat more frequently, we are interested in hypotheses involving two samples that differ in some way. This difference may involve status characteristics of the individuals, gender, for example, or it may involve some sort of manipulation; in either case, it is necessary to modify the critical ratio.

First, consider two different populations, males and females, for example, and a dependent or measured variable, perhaps score on an agility test. The male population has a frequency distribution on this test with mean μ_M and standard deviation σ_M. Likewise, the females have a frequency distribution with mean μ_F and standard deviation σ_F. For some strange reason known only to statisticians, we know σ_M and σ_F, but not μ_M and μ_F. Our task is to reach a decision about the relationship between the two population means.

We know that there is a sampling distribution of $\bar{X}_F$ around μ_F that is formed by taking samples of size N_F. This sampling distribution will have mean μ_F and standard deviation

$$\sigma_{\bar{X}_F} = \frac{\sigma_F}{\sqrt{N_F}} .$$

Likewise, there is a sampling distribution of $\bar{X}_M$ for samples of size N_M, which has μ_M as its mean and $\sigma_{\bar{X}_M}$ as its standard deviation.

Now, suppose we draw a sample of males and a sample of females, compute $\bar{X}_M$ and $\bar{X}_F$ and find the difference between them $(\bar{X}_M - \bar{X}_F)$, record this difference between the means, go back to the populations and draw another sample from each, compute the means and their difference, and repeat this process many, many times. We now have the material to make a frequency distribution of the difference between means. This frequency distribution is called the *sampling distribution of the differences between means*. The elements in the distribution are the differences $(\bar{X}_M - \bar{X}_F)$.

We express the mean of this sampling distribution as $\mu_{(\bar{X}_M - \bar{X}_F)}$. It is a mean of differences and it can be shown that

$$\mu_{(\bar{X}_M - \bar{X}_F)} = \mu_M - \mu_F;$$

that is, the mean of the sampling distribution of the differences between sample means is equal to the difference between the population means.

The sampling distribution has a standard deviation around its mean, which is known as the *standard error of the difference between means* and is symbolized $\sigma_{(\bar{X}_M - \bar{X}_F)}$

$$\sigma_{(\bar{X}_M - \bar{X}_F)} = \sqrt{\frac{\sigma_M^2}{N_M} + \frac{\sigma_F^2}{N_F}}.$$

In general, if we use the numerals 1 and 2 to designate the groups (note that this is a nominal scaling of the independent variable), the above equations become

$$\mu_{(\bar{X}_1 - \bar{X}_2)} = \mu_{\bar{X}_1} - \mu_{\bar{X}_2} \tag{14.2}$$

$$\sigma_{(\bar{X}_1 - \bar{X}_2)} = \sqrt{\frac{\sigma_{\bar{X}_1}^2}{N_1} + \frac{\sigma_{\bar{X}_2}^2}{N_2}}. \tag{14.3}$$

This process is shown graphically in Figure 14-1. It is the resulting sampling distribution of differences between means that is the basis for the test statistic.

An important feature of the sampling distribution of the difference between means is that it will be normal in shape, regardless of the shapes of the frequency distributions in the two populations if the samples are reasonably large. This is a result of the central limit theorem and makes it possible to use the critical ratio as a test statistic when σ_{X_1} and σ_{X_2} are known.

We have already seen that the general form of the critical ratio is that of a z-score in a sampling distribution. The critical ratio for a two-group comparison has exactly the same form, provided we remember that the sampling distribution is a distribution of *differences*. The equation is

$$z_{(\bar{X}_1 - \bar{X}_2)} = \frac{(\bar{X}_1 - \bar{X}_2) - (\mu_1 - \mu_2)}{\sigma_{(\bar{X}_1 - \bar{X}_2)}}, \tag{14.4}$$

where the quantities in parentheses are single quantities in the sampling distribution of differences.

The z computed in equation 14.4 is treated in the same way as the z in equation 14.1. We can use the normal curve table to find the probability that a z this large or larger would occur, and if this probability is less than our chosen α, we reject the null hypothesis. Of course, it is also possible to have determined the critical value of z or of $\bar{X}_1 - \bar{X}_2$ beforehand; then the decision can be reached without further reference to tables.

Before considering an example computing a two-sample critical ratio,

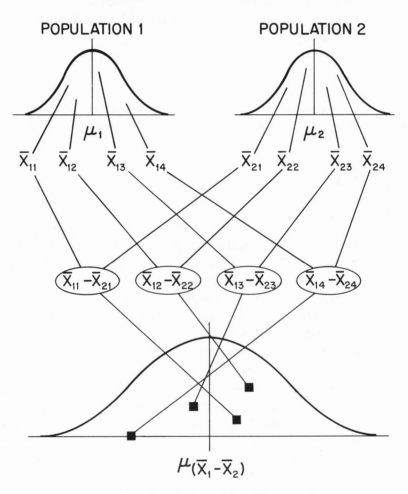

Figure 14-1   Sampling distribution of the differences between means.

we must discuss the hypothesis we are testing. Naturally, the hypothesis under test is a null hypothesis; it has the general form

$$H_0 \begin{cases} \mu_1 - \mu_2 \leqslant K \\ \mu_1 - \mu_2 \geqslant K \end{cases} \text{one-tailed} \\ \mu_1 - \mu_2 = K \end{cases} \text{two-tailed.}$$

That is, the null may state that the difference between population means is less than or equal to K, greater than or equal to K, or equal to K; and the value of K is chosen with reference to the theory that gave rise to the hypothesis.

There is an unfortunate tendency among investigators in the social and behavioral sciences to always choose the same value for K. In the vast majority of research studies, the proper value for K is not discussed; it is automatically chosen as zero. An hypothesis that $\mu_1 - \mu_2 = 0$ is equivalent to an hypothesis that $\mu_1 = \mu_2$; if this is a rational deduction from the theory, then the hypothesis is appropriate. However, in many cases, the theory does not predict the equality of means but a difference between them. As the theory becomes more refined, reasonable estimates of the magnitude of that difference become possible. These estimates can then be used to develop nonzero values for K that will make the outcome of the hypothesis test a more useful addition to knowledge.

Let us return briefly to our example of coin-tossing. (With coins, we have the advantage of knowing what the population parameters are.) As experimenters, we believe in the power of thought processes to alter events in the physical world. We have two sets of ten coins, and we are going to project a wish into these coins; for one set (A), we shall "think heads," and for the other set (B), we shall "think tails." We know that $\mu_A = 5$ and $\mu_B = 5$ if there is nothing to our theory; also, $\sigma_A = \sigma_B = 1.58$. At this stage in our research, we have no idea about the magnitude of effect to expect, but our theory clearly predicts that μ_A, the mean number of heads for the set of coins where we think heads, should exceed μ_B, the mean number of heads for the other set.

The appropriate null hypothesis in this example is that $\mu_A - \mu_B \leqslant 0$. The null value for μ_A and μ_B is 5, but our theory makes a directional prediction. A result in the opposite direction, no matter how big, is not support for our theory. We should not reject the null in favor of our theory unless μ_A is larger than μ_B by an amount that exceeds the critical value.

We now have the null hypothesis and its alternate.

H_0: $\mu_A - \mu_B \leq 0$

H_1: $\mu_A - \mu_B > 0$.

We decide to flip each set of coins ten times. With $\sigma_A = \sigma_B = 1.58$, we can calculate the standard error of the sampling distribution of differences. This value, which is also called simply the standard error of the difference, is, by equation 14.3,

$$
\begin{aligned}
\sigma_{(\bar{X}_1 - \bar{X}_2)} &= \sqrt{\frac{(1.58)^2}{10} + \frac{(1.58)^2}{10}} \\
&= \sqrt{\frac{2.4964}{10} + \frac{2.4964}{10}} \\
&= \sqrt{0.49928} \\
&= 0.7066.
\end{aligned}
$$

Knowing that there is a general unwillingness in the scientific community to accept the proposition that thoughts affect the physical world, we decide to guard quite carefully against a Type I error. We decide that there should be a risk of only one chance in 100 that we are in error if we decide to reject the null hypothesis. Therefore, choosing $\alpha = 0.01$ and going to Appendix Table B-1, we find that the smallest value for z for which the area beyond is no more than 0.01 is 2.326. (Had our hypothesis been two-tailed, we would have used $\alpha/2 = 0.005$ and arrived at $z = 2.576$.) The critical value for our test statistic is $z = +2.326$ because our rejection region is only in the upper tail of the sampling distribution.

We are now ready to conduct our experiment. The ten coins of group

TABLE 14-1
Outcomes of 20 Tosses of Ten Coins.

Group A		Group B	
5	7	4	3
6	5	3	4
6	6	6	4
4	8	5	6
5	7	5	4

A are placed in a shaker, and while they are shaken and dumped on the table, we earnestly "think heads". We keep on "thinking heads" for nine more trials, each time recording the number of heads. This is followed by ten observations of the ten coins in group B, only now we project a wish for tails. Our study is now complete. We obtained the data shown in Table 14-1. All that remains is to calculate the value of the test statistic and reach a decision about our null hypothesis.

The first thing we do is calculate the means for the two groups. We find that $\sum X_A = 59$ and $\sum X_B = 44$, which gives us 5.9 and 4.4 for the values of $\bar{X}_A$ and $\bar{X}_B$, respectively. Since we know that $\sigma_{(\bar{X}_A - \bar{X}_B)} = 0.7066$, we calculate z to be

$$z = \frac{(5.9 - 4.4)}{0.7066} = \frac{1.5}{0.7066}$$

$$z = +2.12$$

This value of z puts us in a bind because if we had used an α of 0.05, we would reject the null hypothesis and conclude that our wishing had affected the coins; however, z does not reach the value we specified for an α of 0.01. The probability that a difference this large would occur by chance is somewhere between 0.05 and 0.01. One solution to this problem that has become popular in recent years is to give the value of the test statistic and the probability that such a value would occur. If we were to adopt that approach, we would report that $z = 2.12$ and $\alpha < 0.02$. (The area beyond a z of 2.12 is given in Appendix Table B-1 as 0.0170. However, it is customary to specify α as less than some quantity and to give only one nonzero numeral.)

There is one advantage to this alternative, but there are two disadvantages. The advantage is that the reader of the research report has more information about the probability of a Type I error and can reach her/his own decision to reject or not reject the null hypothesis. The first, less serious disadvantage is that the formal logical structure of the hypothesis test has been violated by changing the rules after the fact. The second and more serious problem is that the level of significance has become a metric for judging the importance of a research finding. Results having a lower likelihood of Type I error are viewed by the unwary as more important. Relevance to the theory being tested, freedom from misinterpretation, and predictive power are more valuable criteria for judging research results, but they are often overlooked in favor of the simple number provided by the α-level. A further discussion of this topic is beyond our scope, but the interested reader should consult Meehl (1978).

In addition to the level of significance problem, this study has a major flaw in design that some readers may have identified. Remember that one of our goals in designing an experiment is to eliminate alternate explanations and provide a clear test of the research hypothesis. In the design of this study, one obvious plausible rival hypothesis was overlooked: a preexisting bias in the two sets of coins; it may be, and we have no way of knowing, that the coins in group A were biased to come up heads. A much better design that would have eliminated this alternative would have been to use the same ten coins for both conditions and alternate our treatment from trial to trial. Failure to eliminate this plausible rival hypothesis by properly designing the study would make the issue of α-level moot and the results of the study uninterpretable.

ESTIMATING σ

The two procedures described so far both assume that the population standard deviations are known by the investigator. This assumption is rarely met in practice, so it is usually necessary to estimate the population values from those found in the sample. This has some important consequences for the sampling distribution of the mean, as we shall see.

In Chapter 4, we learned that the standard deviation of a set of observations is

$$S_X = \sqrt{\frac{\sum x_i^2}{N}} = \sqrt{\frac{\sum (X_i - \bar{X})^2}{N}} .$$

This value is correct for the particular group, but it will tend to be smaller than the population standard deviation; that is, S_X is biased as an estimate of σ_X. It provides an underestimate of σ_X.

There are several explanations for why S_X underestimates σ_X. The one most useful to us involves the fact that we are also using $\bar{X}$ to estimate μ_X. The definition of σ_X is

$$\sigma_X = \sqrt{\frac{\sum (X - \mu_X)^2}{N}} .$$

If we knew μ_X and could use it to compute the standard deviation in the sample, the resulting value would be an unbiased estimate of σ_X; however, the sample mean is not always equal to the population mean. It is an unbiased estimate of μ_X, but it is also at the least squares center of the sample distribution. $\sum(X - \bar{X})^2$ will always be less than $\sum(X - \mu_X)^2$ unless $\bar{X} = \mu_X$. This will rarely be exactly true, so S_X will tend to be smaller than σ_X.

Degrees of Freedom. The amount of the bias is related to the size of the sample. When we use $\bar{X}$ to estimate μ_X, we are placing a numerical restriction on the data that is greater for small samples. This numerical restriction comes from the fact that while, in our sample

$$\sum x = \sum(X - \bar{X}) = 0,$$

$\sum(X - \mu_X)$ does not have to equal any particular value.

The consequence of this numerical restriction on $\sum x$ is that once $(N - 1)$ of the values have occurred, there is only one possible number for the last one. If the first nine deviation scores in a set of ten sum to -2.36, then the tenth can have no other value than $+2.36$. $(N - 1)$ of the values are free to vary without restriction, but the last is completely determined by the others. The general term used to refer to the number of values that are not restricted is *degrees of freedom*. When we consider a set of N deviation scores, $(N - 1)$ of them are not restricted, so there are $(N - 1)$ degrees of freedom.

We have encountered elsewhere the notion of a *sum-of-squares* or, more specifically, a sum of squared deviations from a mean; $\sum x^2$ is a sum-of-squares, as is its equivalent expression, $\sum(X - \bar{X})^2$. A sum-of-squares for a sample, divided by its degrees of freedom, provides an *unbiased estimate* of the variance in the population. If we use $\hat{S}_X^2$ to represent an unbiased estimate of the population variance σ_X^2, then

$$\hat{S}_X^2 = \frac{\sum(X - \bar{X})^2}{N - 1}, \tag{14.5}$$

and an estimate of σ_X is provided by[1]

$$\hat{S}_X = \sqrt{\frac{\sum(X - \bar{X})^2}{N - 1}}. \tag{14.6}$$

[1]Although $\hat{S}_X^2$ is an unbiased estimate of σ_X^2, $\hat{S}_X$ is not an unbiased estimate of σ_X (see Hays, 1973, or Lordahl, 1967, for a discussion). However, the bias in $\hat{S}_X$ is so small that we can safely ignore it and use $\hat{S}_X$ as a good estimate of σ_x.

It should be clear that the difference between S_X^2 and $\hat{S}_X^2$ is the difference between N and $(N - 1)$ in the denominator; in fact, a little algebra shows that since

$$S_X^2 = \frac{\sum(X - \bar{X})^2}{N} \longrightarrow NS_X^2 = \sum(X - \bar{X})^2$$

and

$$\hat{S}_X^2 = \frac{\sum(X - \bar{X})^2}{N - 1} \longrightarrow (N - 1)\hat{S}_X^2 = \sum(X - \bar{X})^2$$

$$\left.\begin{array}{c} (N - 1)\hat{S}_X^2 = N \ S_X^2 \\[2mm] \hat{S}_X^2 = \dfrac{N}{N - 1} S_X^2 \\[2mm] S_X^2 = \dfrac{N - 1}{N} \hat{S}_X^2. \end{array}\right\} \tag{14.7}$$

Clearly, as sample size becomes large, the ratio of N to $(N - 1)$ approaches 1, and S_X^2 approaches $\hat{S}_X^2$.

THE t DISTRIBUTION

We have just seen that $\hat{S}_X^2$ provides an unbiased estimate of σ_X^2. It would seem reasonable to use $\hat{S}_X$ in place of σ_X to describe the sampling distribution of the mean when σ_X is unknown. We can do this, and it is the proper thing to do; unfortunately, the addition of a second estimated value complicates the problem because the relationship between σ_X and $\hat{S}_X$ is related to the degrees of freedom for $\hat{S}_X$.

Because we must estimate both $\mu_{\bar{X}}$ and $\sigma_{\bar{X}}$ from the sample statistics $\bar{X}$ and $\hat{S}_X$, the sampling distribution of the mean no longer has the shape of the normal distribution. This fact was first discovered by an English statistician named Gossett who, writing under the pen name Student, published a description of the actual sampling distribution of the mean under these conditions. He showed that there is actually a unique sampling distribution for each possible number of degrees of freedom and that as $(N - 1)$ became very large (over about 120 for practical purposes), the sampling distribution approached the normal distribution. He called this family of distributions the *t* distribution.

The *t* distribution is an important concept in the practical application of statistics because it fits a wide variety of research problems. As we said, it is really a family of distributions, one for every possible number of degrees of freedom from 1 to infinity. Each curve can be used in exactly the same way that we use the normal curve to represent probabilities; that is, the area under the curve beyond a certain point is the probability that a value of the test statistic at least that large will occur. Likewise, the area between two values is the relative frequency with which we would expect events in that range to occur. The major difference between a *t* distribution (any one of them) and the normal curve is that the *t* distribution will have a greater proportion of its area in the tails of the distribution. This feature is illustrated in Figure 14-2.

The existence of all these different distributions would present quite a problem for users of statistics, were it not for the fact that interest has centered on the standard critical values appropriate for hypothesis testing. This narrowing of interest has made it feasible to put the most popular critical values for a range of degrees of freedom into a table such as Appendix Table B-2, part of which is reproduced here (Table 14-2). The entries across the top are the proportions of area in one or two tails of the distribution; entries in the left-hand column are degrees of freedom (*df*), and the elements in the body of the table are critical values of the test statistic *t* for that probability with the given degrees of freedom. The test statistic itself, which we cover in detail in the remaining sections of this chapter, is virtually identical to *z* in its computation and interpretation. The difference is that it applies to a different sampling distribution.

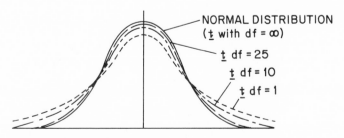

Figure 14-2   t distributions for various degrees of freedom.

Inspecting Table 14-2 shows clearly the relationship between degrees of freedom and the shape of the related *t* distribution. If we choose the 0.05 level of α (two-tailed), we see a value of 1.960 in the bottom row with infinite (∞) degrees of freedom. This is exactly the value of *z* that cuts off 5 percent of the area under the normal distribution for a two-tailed hypothesis. As we move up the column to 25 *df*, the critical value for *t* increases to 2.060. This means that we must be farther from the mean of the *t* distribution to contain 95 percent of the area under the curve between our two critical values. As *df* drops to 10, the critical value increases to 2.228, and in the extreme case of *df* = 1, we must go all the way to a *t* of ± 12.706 to encompass 95 percent of the distribution and leave only 2½ percent in each tail. This principle is illustrated in Figure 14-3.

WHEN σ IS UNKNOWN—1 SAMPLE *t*

The test statistic for an hypothesis involving one sample and one unknown population standard deviation is known as Student's *t*, after our

TABLE 14-2
Partial Table of the Critical Values for t Distributions.

		Levels of Significance (α)					
	One tail 0.10	0.05	0.025	0.01	0.005	0.0005	
df	Two tail 0.20	0.10	0.05	0.02	0.01	0.001	
1	3.078	6.314	12.706	31.821	63.657	636.619	
2	1.886	2.920	4.303	6.965	9.925	31.598	
.							
.							
.							
10	1.372	1.812	2.228	2.764	3.169	4.587	
.							
.							
.							
25	1.316	1.708	2.060	2.485	2.787	3.725	
.							
.							
.							
∞	1.282	1.645	1.960	2.326	2.576	3.291	

friend Gossett. It is identical in structure to the one-sample critical ratio and tests the same hypothesis, namely that $\mu = K$, $\mu \leq K$ or $\mu \geq K$

$$t = \frac{\bar{X} - \mu}{\hat{S}_{\bar{X}}} . \tag{14.8}$$

The numerator in t is the same as in z, but there is a difference in the denominator. Because we do not know the population standard error of the mean, we must estimate it from the sample data. This estimated standard error of the mean $\hat{S}_{\bar{X}}$, is found by substituting $\hat{S}_X$ for σ_X.

$$\hat{S}_{\bar{X}} = \frac{\hat{S}_X}{\sqrt{N}} . \tag{14.9}$$

The value of t obtained from equation 14.8 is just like a z; it is a deviation score divided by a standard deviation. In this case, the deviation score is the deviation of a sample mean from the mean of the sampling distribution, and the standard deviation is the unbiased estimate of the standard error of the mean. The difference between t and z lies in the shape of the sampling distribution of the test statistic. The critical ratio z has a sampling distribution that is normal in shape. The t statistic with $(N - 1)$ degrees of freedom has a sampling distribution that is the t distribution for that number of degrees of freedom.

The t statistic provides exactly the same hypothesis testing procedure that we encountered with z, except that we do not have to assume that we know σ_X. Suppose, for example, that we have a theory about learning that includes the proposition that plants cannot learn. To test this proposition

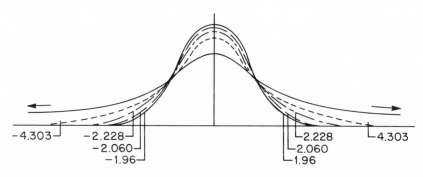

Figure 14-3   Critical values for several t distributions.

we must design a situation where plants might learn, expose a sample of plants to the appropriate stimuli, and measure their behavior.

There are plants, such as the Venus Flytrap, that emit measurable behaviors, so we decide to use a sample of five of them. The Flytrap closes on anything that stimulates its ingestive area, so we shall test our proposition by seeing whether we can train the plant to close to the sound of a bell. First, we pair the bell with a fly being placed on the plant, which is repeated 100 times. Then, we omit the fly and just ring the bell, at the same time measuring the amount of closure in millimeters by the plant.

Our null hypothesis is that no learning will take place or, stated in proper quantitative form, that the amount of closure at the sound of the bell is zero.

$\mu \leq 0$.

This must be a one-tailed test because it is not possible for there to be less than no closure. Note that the properties of the measurement scale (a ratio scale) combine with the prediction from the theory to make a two-tailed hypothesis inappropriate. The alternate hypothesis is, of course,

$\mu > 0$.

Since we do not know the population standard deviation, we must use a t test to reach a decision about our hypothesis. Our experiment provided the data shown in Table 14-3. The scores are millimeters of closure within ten seconds after ringing the bell.

The steps necessary to compute the quantities to test our hypothesis are also shown in the table. First, we compute $\bar{X}$ and find it to be 1.2, the mean millimeters of closure within ten seconds after ringing the bell. Next we must compute our estimate of σ. The computational formula

$$\hat{S}_X = \sqrt{\frac{N \sum X^2 - (\sum X)^2}{N(N - 1)}} \tag{14.10}$$

is very similar to the computational formula for S_X (note the substitution of $N(N - 1)$ for N^2 in the denominator) and yields a value of 1.3038. For the sake of comparison, we also compute S_X, $S_{\bar{X}}^2$ and $\hat{S}_{\bar{X}}^2$. The student may wish to satisfy her/himself that

$$\frac{N - 1}{N} \hat{S}_{\bar{X}}^2 = S_{\bar{X}}^2, \qquad \frac{N}{N - 1} S_{\bar{X}}^2 = \hat{S}_{\bar{X}}^2$$

Next, we compute $\hat{S}_{\bar{X}}$; equation 14.9 is used first and yields a value of 0.583. An algebraically equivalent equation that is preferred by some authors and is useful when only S_X has been computed is

$$\hat{S}_{\bar{X}} = \frac{S_X}{\sqrt{N-1}} \; ; \qquad\qquad (14.11)$$

obviously, it produces the same answer. Finally, we compute t and find it to be 2.058. We look up the critical value 0.05 in Appendix Table B-2 for four degrees of freedom and find it is 2.132 for a one-tailed test. We must conclude that we cannot reject the null hypothesis at the 0.05 level.

There is an additional important feature to this example. Note that if we had (improperly) used the critical ratio, we would have rejected our null hypothesis at the 0.05 level. The fact that we were using a small sample and did not know σ_X led us to use t, and this produced a proper decision according to the rules of inference. We have no way of knowing whether we made a Type II error, but we did use the correct statistic. Had we used the critical ratio, we would have committed what has been called

TABLE 14-3
Computing a One-Sample t.

Plant	Score X	X²
1	0	0
2	1	1
3	3	9
4	2	4
5	0	0
	$\sum X = 6$	$\sum X^2 = 14$

Calculations

$\hat{S}_{\bar{X}} = \dfrac{S_X}{\sqrt{N}} = \dfrac{1.3038}{\sqrt{5}} = 0.583$ $\qquad \bar{X} = 1.2$

$\qquad\qquad\qquad\qquad\qquad\qquad\qquad S_X = 1.1662$

$\hat{S}_{\bar{X}} = \dfrac{S_X}{\sqrt{N-1}} = \dfrac{1.1662}{\sqrt{4}} = 0.583$ $\qquad \hat{S}_X = 1.3038$

$\qquad\qquad\qquad\qquad\qquad\qquad\qquad S_X^2 = 1.36$

$t = \dfrac{\bar{X} - \mu}{\hat{S}_{\bar{X}}} = \dfrac{1.2 - 0}{0.583} = 2.058$ $\qquad \hat{S}_X^2 = 1.70$

a Type IV error; that is, we would have reached an incorrect conclusion because we used the wrong statistical test. (A Type III error occurs when we test a null hypothesis and decide to reject it on the basis of a statistically significant difference in the wrong direction. This would happen when $\mu_1 > \mu_2$, but $\bar{X}_1 < \bar{X}_2$. See McNemar [1969] for a complete description.) It is important to know whether our data fulfill the assumptions underlying our test statistic if we wish to reach sound decisions about our hypotheses.

TWO INDEPENDENT SAMPLES

Research situations where the population standard deviation is known are rare; so are situations where a design using a single sample provides a test of the hypothesis of interest. A much more normal situation is a research design involving two samples, where it is necessary to estimate the standard deviation in both of them. This problem is very much like the one we encountered with the two-sample critical ratio. Again, we are dealing with a sampling distribution that involves differences between means. Again, our decision whether to reject the null hypothesis will be based on the deviation, the difference between our samples $(\bar{X}_1 - \bar{X}_2)$, from the mean of the sampling distribution of differences under the assumptions of the null hypothesis. The difference is that the sampling distribution is a t distribution rather than the normal distribution.

Pooled Variance.   There was a fairly clear implication in the last section that the larger the degrees of freedom on which an estimate of the population standard deviation was based, the better the estimate. This principle becomes important in the case of two samples because an assumption underlying the null hypothesis is that the two samples both come from the same population. While it would be inappropriate to combine the two samples and use the deviations of $(N_1 + N_2)$ observations from a single mean to estimate the value of σ_X, we can pool the two separate estimates, pool their degrees of freedom, and obtain a better single estimate.

If we let $\hat{S}_1^2$ (based on N_1 observations) be the unbiased estimate of σ^2 in sample 1 and $\hat{S}_2^2$ (based on N_2 observations) be the unbiased estimate from sample 2, then the improved pooled estimate of σ^2 is

$$\hat{S}_p^2 = \frac{(N_1 - 1)\,\hat{S}_1^2 + (N_2 - 1)\,\hat{S}_2^2}{(N_1 - 1) + (N_2 - 1)}$$ (14.12)

$$\hat{S}_p^2 = \frac{(N_1 - 1)\,\hat{S}_1^2 + (N_2 - 1)\,\hat{S}_2^2}{N_1 + N_2 - 2}.$$

The pooled variance estimate $\hat{S}_p^2$ is based on $(N_1 - 1) + (N_2 - 1)$ or $(N_1 + N_2 - 2)$ degrees of freedom.

There are two other forms of $\hat{S}_p^2$ that are useful in certain situations. When only the sample standard deviations are available, equation 14.12 can be written

$$\hat{S}_p^2 = \frac{N_1 S_1^2 + N_2 S_2^2}{N_1 + N_2 - 2}.$$

If the computations are done on a calculator that stores sums-of-squares, we can use this information directly. In this case, the pooled variance estimate is equal to the pooled sum-of-squares divided by the pooled degrees of freedom

$$\hat{S}_p^2 = \frac{\left[N_1 \sum X_1^2 - (\sum X_1)^2\right] + \left[N_2 \sum X_2^2 - (\sum X_2)^2\right]}{(N_1 + N_2)(N_1 + N_2 - 2)}$$

$$\hat{S}_p^2 = \frac{\sum x_1^2 + \sum x_2^2}{N_1 + N_2 - 2}.$$

Once we have the pooled variance, it is used in exactly the same way as σ^2 to compute the estimated standard error of the difference between means. By substituting $\hat{S}_p^2$ for σ_1^2 and σ_2^2 in equation 14.3, we obtain

$$\hat{S}_{(\bar{X}_1 - \bar{X}_2)} = \sqrt{\frac{\hat{S}_p^2}{N_1} + \frac{\hat{S}_p^2}{N_2}}.$$ (14.13)

This standard error is then used to compute t, the test statistic

$$t = \frac{\bar{X}_1 - \bar{X}_2 - (\mu_1 - \mu_2)}{\hat{S}_{(\bar{X}_1 - \bar{X}_2)}}.$$ (14.14)

This t has $(N_1 + N_2 - 2)$ degrees of freedom, which means that we shall find the necessary critical values in the $(N_1 + N_2 - 2)^{th}$ row of Appendix Table B-2.

The data in Table 14-4 could have come from a typical two-group study. Suppose, for example, that we believe that the presence of soft background music will induce people to purchase more items in our store.

Since the audio system is fairly expensive, we decide to run a study to see whether our hunch is likely to be true. The first thing to do is set up our hypotheses. We decide to associate the null hypothesis with the negation of our expectation because we want to guard against going to the expense of installing the system if it will not result in more sales. We have direct control over the probability of a Type I error, so we control the probability of mistakenly installing the system by our choice of the null hypothesis. Loosely stated, our null is that the presence of music will *not* result in increased sales. We shall reject this null in favor of its alternative and

TABLE 14-4
Results of a Study of the Effects of Music on Purchasing Behavior.

Group 1	Group 2	Summary Statistics
3	6	
9	5	$\sum X_1 = 232$
7	2	$\sum X_2 = 181$
17	11	$\sum X_1^2 = 2584$
8	14	$\sum X_2^2 = 1773$
3	5	$\sum X_1 X_2 = 1884$
11	9	
10	15	$\bar{X}_1 = 9.28$
8	2	$\bar{X}_2 = 7.24$
4	3	$\hat{S}_{X_1} = 4.24$
9	9	$\hat{S}_{X_2} = 4.39$
14	9	$S_{X_1} = 4.15$
13	14	$S_{X_2} = 4.30$
13	13	
11	0	$\hat{S}_p = 4.31$
6	6	$\hat{S}_p^2 = 18.62$
9	9	
9	7	$\hat{S}^2_{(\bar{X}_1 - \bar{X}_2)} = 1.49$
17	5	$\hat{S}_{(\bar{X}_1 - \bar{X}_2)} = 1.22$
14	10	$r_{X_1 X_2} = 0.458$
13	8	
5	1	
12	10	
4	0	
3	8	

incur the expense of installing the audio system only if the probability that the null is true is sufficiently small. Note that there are several other null hypotheses that we could have chosen; for example, that the music would not reduce buying or that music would increase (or decrease) buying by a certain amount. The choice of null hypothesis is up to the investigator and should be carefully made to provide the most direct answer to the research question of interest.

The formal statement of our hypotheses is

H_0: $\mu_M - \mu_{NM} \leq 0$

H_1: $\mu_M - \mu_{NM} > 0.$

The mean dollar sales to people listening to music μ_M is contrasted to the mean dollar sales of people who are not listening to music μ_{NM} through sample estimates of the parameters $\bar{X}_M$ and $\bar{X}_{NM}$. A one-tailed hypothesis was chosen because we are not interested in the alternative that music reduces sales.

Next, we must consider some aspects of the design of our study. Since we have no population parameters available, we cannot use a critical ratio. Fluctuations in the economy make it unwise to compare our new condition (music) with average sales for the last six months. We decide to run a study using two groups of people with 25 shoppers in each group in order to have samples large enough to be representative of their respective populations. This means that we are going to analyze our data and test our hypothesis using a two-sample t test.

A two-sample t test with 50 observations has 48 degrees of freedom. We decide to use an α of 0.05, and since our hypothesis is one -tailed, we look in column 2 of Appendix Table B-2 to find the critical value. This leads us to the realization that beyond $df = 30$, most tables of the t distribution are incomplete. In general, the proper thing to do is to use the critical value for the next *lower df*. The tabled entry for $df = 40$ is 1.684, so we use this as our critical value. If the t obtained from the comparison $\bar{X}_M - \bar{X}_{NM}$ exceeds $+1.684$, we shall reject the null hypothesis, conclude that music increases sales, and install the audio system.

We randomly divided 50 people into two groups and admitted them to the store. Group 1 had background music, group 2 did not; the dollar sales volume for each customer is recorded in Table 14-4 along with the sums and sums-of-squares needed for computation. The means are found to be

$$\bar{X}_M = \frac{232}{25} = 9.28$$

$$\bar{X}_{NM} = \frac{181}{25} = 7.24.$$

The sample standard deviations are

$$S_M = \sqrt{\frac{25(2584) - (232)^2}{25^2}} = 4.15$$

and

$$S_{NM} = \sqrt{\frac{25(1773) - (181)^2}{25^2}} = 4.30,$$

while the estimates of the population standard deviation are

$$\hat{S}_M = \sqrt{\frac{25(2584) - (232)^2}{25(24)}} = 4.24$$

$$\hat{S}_{NM} = \sqrt{\frac{25(1773) - (181)^2}{25(24)}} = 4.39.$$

Either of these pairs of standard deviations can be used to compute the pooled variance and standard deviation (the difference in the results below is due to rounding).

$$\hat{S}_p^2 = \frac{25(4.15)^2 + 25(4.30)^2}{48} = 18.60$$

$$\hat{S}_p^2 = \frac{24(4.24)^2 + 24(4.39)^2}{48} = 18.62$$

$$\hat{S}_p = 4.31.$$

The value of $\hat{S}_p^2$ is then used to compute the standard error of the difference between means

$$\hat{S}_{(\bar{X}_M - \bar{X}_{NM})} = \sqrt{\frac{18.60}{25} + \frac{18.60}{25}} = 1.22,$$

which gives us a t of

$$t = \frac{9.28 - 7.24}{1.22} = \frac{+2.04}{1.22} = +1.672.$$

This value of t is not quite so large as the critical value we specified, so we would not reject the null hypothesis; however, the outcome was in the predicted direction. Depending on the cost of the audio system and the perceived long-term sales return, we may choose to let the matter drop and do research on some other theory, or we may repeat the study with a larger sample, thus increasing our degrees of freedom and reducing the critical value for *t*. Note that if our *df* had been 60, we would have rejected the null.

MATCHED PAIRS *t*

There is one other alternative that we could try instead of increasing our sample size. If it is reasonable under the research conditions to consider observations as occurring in pairs, it is possible to use a test statistic called the *matched pairs t* or the *t test for related observations*. This procedure has the advantage of reducing $\hat{S}_{(\bar{X}_1-\bar{X}_2)}$ in most situations, thereby making it possible to reject the null hypothesis with a smaller difference between the means.

The necessary condition for using a matched pairs *t* is that the observations be logically paired, which can be accomplished in three general ways. The first is to make a pair of observations on each person, one under each condition; in our example, this would involve observing each shopper once under the music condition and once under the no-music condition. The second procedure is to take naturally occurring pairs of individuals, identical twins, siblings, married couples, and so on, and assign one member of each pair to each condition; this technique is commonly used in genetic and social research. The third procedure is to form pairs by matching otherwise unrelated individuals on the basis of one or more status characteristics; it is common in educational research, for example, to form pairs by matching age, race, and economic status.

Once the pairs have been formed, the study is conducted in the usual way to test the same general hypothesis that would be tested using the *t* test for independent samples. The difference is that instead of using equation 14.13 to compute $\hat{S}_{(\bar{X}_1-\bar{X}_2)}$ we can use

$$\hat{S}_{(\bar{X}-\bar{X}_2)} = \sqrt{\frac{\hat{S}_1^2}{N_1} + \frac{\hat{S}_2^2}{N_2} - 2r_{X_1X_2}\left(\frac{\hat{S}_1}{\sqrt{N_1}}\right)\left(\frac{\hat{S}_2}{\sqrt{N_2}}\right)}. \qquad (14.15)$$

The difference between equations 14.13 and 14.15 is the term that is subtracted,

$$2r_{X_1X_2} \left(\frac{\hat{S}_1}{\sqrt{N_1}}\right) \left(\frac{\hat{S}_2}{\sqrt{N_2}}\right).$$

Any time the correlation between paired observations is positive, this quantity, which is two times the *covariance* of $\bar{X}_1$ and $\bar{X}_2$, will be positive, thereby reducing $\hat{S}_{(\bar{X}_1-\bar{X}_2)}$. Notice that if the correlation between the two variables is negative, equation 14.15 will yield a larger value than equation 14.13. Therefore, the matched pairs t should be used only when there is reason to believe that $r_{X_1X_2}$ is positive.

The consequences of matching can be illustrated using the data from Table 14-4. Suppose that we had actually observed each of 25 individuals twice. We compute the sum-of-crossproducts $\sum X_1 X_2$ to be 1884 and find

$$r_{X_1X_2} = \frac{25(1884) - 232\,(181)}{\sqrt{25(2584) - (232)^2}\,\sqrt{25(1773) - (181)^2}} = 0.458.$$

This value is combined with the necessary standard deviations to yield

$$\hat{S}_{(\bar{X}_1-\bar{X}_2)} = \sqrt{\frac{(4.24)^2}{25} + \frac{(4.39)^2}{25} - 2(0.458)\left(\frac{4.24}{\sqrt{25}}\right)\left(\frac{4.39}{\sqrt{25}}\right)} = 0.90.$$

Substituting this value into our equation for t, we obtain

$$t = \frac{9.28 - 7.24}{0.90} = 2.27.$$

This t is based on 25 pairs of observations; therefore, there are only 24 degrees of freedom associated with this test. (We shall use a different approach shortly to illustrate this principle.) Going to Appendix Table B-2 with $df = 24$, we find the 0.05 one-tailed critical value to be 1.711, leading us to conclude that we should reject the null hypothesis. In fact, our obtained t exceeds the one-tailed critical value for $\alpha = 0.025$.

The important thing to notice here is that the same data, the same set of numbers, can lead to different decisions, depending on the assumptions we make and the way we design our study. It is often possible to make a study more sensitive to differences between means by matching subjects or making multiple observations of subjects. It is usually desirable to design the study to be as sensitive as possible.

Paired observations offer us another way of looking at differences. Instead of grouping the observations and then finding the difference between groups, we can find the differences first and then compute statistics on the differences. This is sometimes called the direct difference method. It involves computing a simple difference score D_i for each individual

$$D_i = X_{1i} - X_{2i}$$

and performing our analyses on these difference scores. Using difference scores has the effect of changing our formal hypotheses, for example

$$H_0: \quad \mu_1 - \mu_2 = K \text{ becomes } \mu_D = K$$

$$H_1: \quad \mu_1 - \mu_2 \neq K \text{ becomes } \mu_D \neq K$$

These changes are slight and in most cases do not require a great change in our thinking. We now have a sample of D's rather than two samples of X's, so we are back to a one-sample problem. The mean $\bar{D}$ is our sample estimate of μ_D and the sampling distribution of D will have an estimated standard error,

$$\hat{S}_{\bar{D}} = \frac{\hat{S}_D}{\sqrt{N}} . \tag{14.16}$$

$\hat{S}_D$ is computed just like any other estimate of a population standard deviation

$$\hat{S}_D = \sqrt{\frac{N \sum D^2 - (\sum D)^2}{N(N-1)}} . \tag{14.17}$$

Of course, in both equations N refers to the number of D's or the number of pairs of original observations. The test of the null hypothesis ($H_0: \mu_D = K$) is a t test,

$$t = \frac{\bar{D} - K}{\hat{S}_{\bar{D}}} , \tag{14.18}$$

and it is easy to see that since $\hat{S}_D$ is based on N differences, the t test will have $(N - 1)$ degrees of freedom.

The data from Table 14-4 are repeated in Table 14-5 in the form of a direct difference analysis. Summing the values in the D column to get $\sum D = 51$ and dividing by $N = 25$ yields

$$\bar{D} = \frac{51}{25} = 2.04,$$

which, strangely, is exactly the value we obtained for $\bar{X}_1 - \bar{X}_2$. In fact, it will always be true that

$$\bar{D} = \bar{X}_1 - \bar{X}_2.$$

Next, we use $\sum D^2 = 589$ to compute

$$\hat{S}_D = \sqrt{\frac{25(589) - (51)^2}{25\,(24)}} = 4.495.$$

Using this result in equation 14.16 produces

$$\hat{S}_{\bar{D}} = \frac{4.495}{\sqrt{25}} = 0.899,$$

TABLE 14-5

Computing a Matched-Pairs t for the Data from Table 14-4.

Individual	X_1	X_2	D	D^2	Summary Statistics
1	3	6	−3	9	
2	9	5	4	16	$\sum D = 51$
3	7	2	5	25	$\sum D^2 = 589$
4	17	22	6	36	
5	8	14	−6	36	$\bar{D} = 2.04$
6	3	5	−2	4	$\hat{S}_D = 4.495$
7	11	9	2	4	$\hat{S}_{\bar{D}} = 0.899$
8	10	15	−5	25	
9	8	2	6	36	
10	4	3	1	1	
11	9	9	0	0	
12	14	9	5	25	
13	13	14	−1	1	
14	13	13	0	0	
15	11	0	11	121	
16	6	6	0	0	
17	9	9	0	0	
18	9	7	2	4	
19	17	5	12	144	
20	14	10	4	16	
21	13	8	5	25	
22	5	1	4	16	
23	12	10	2	4	
24	4	0	4	16	
25	3	8	−5	25	

which is within rounding error of the value 0.90 that we obtained for $\hat{S}_{(\bar{X}_1-\bar{X}_2)}$. The final step is to compute t with $df = 24$

$$t = \frac{2.04}{0.899} = 2.27.$$

Obviously, this is exactly the same value that we obtained before.

The two different procedures for computing t for matched pairs data are exactly equivalent; which one we use is a matter of convenience. The direct difference method has some appeal because the computations are less involved. However, there is the added step in data preparation of calculating the D's. Many modern hand calculators include built-in statistical routines that will compute $\bar{X}_1, \bar{X}_2, S_1, S_2,$ and $r_{X_1 X_2}$ automatically from the raw paired observations. If this feature is available, it may be simpler to compute t by equations 14.15 and 14.14 than by 14.16 and 14.18. Which computation we use is less important than how well we design and conduct our study.

SUMMARY

Hypotheses about group means are tested by comparing the value of a *test statistic* with a critical value for that statistic. The critical value of the statistic is the value that cuts off a chosen percent α of the sampling distribution that the statistic would have under the assumption that the null hypothesis is true. When the value of the test statistic exceeds the critical value, we can reject the null hypothesis with a risk no greater than α of being wrong.

In research situations where the population variance is known, the test statistic is a *critical ratio*. The sampling distribution of the critical ratio is the normal distribution. There is a critical ratio for single sample studies that involves the standard error of the mean, and there is a two-sample critical ratio where the standard error of the difference between means is used. In either case, the numerator is the difference between the sample result and that expected under the null hypothesis.

There are few research situations where the population variance is known. When the population variance is not known, it is necessary to use an *unbiased estimate* of the population variance. The unbiased estimate is obtained by dividing the *sum-of-squares* by its *degrees of freedom* and is used to estimate the standard error of the mean.

The sampling distribution that results when the difference between the sample mean and the hypothesized population value is divided by the estimated standard error of the mean is known as a *t* distribution and the test statistic is called *t*. There is a different *t* distribution for each possible number of degrees of freedom. As *df* gets large, the *t* distribution approaches the normal distribution.

A one-sample *t* is known as Student's *t*. When the study involves two independent samples, the two sample variances are pooled to obtain a better estimate of the population variance. The pooled variance estimate is used to compute an estimated standard error of the difference between means, and this is used to compute a *t* that has $df = N_1 + N_2 - 2$.

It is often possible to obtain a more sensitive test of our hypothesis by using related samples. This may be done by using naturally occurring pairs of subjects, by making observations of the same subjects under different conditions, or by matching subjects on status variables. The major benefit obtained from matching is a reduction in the standard error of the difference between means.

PROBLEMS

For each of the following sets of data, read the conditions given and select and perform the appropriate test of the hypothesis and state your decision:

*1. Ho: $\mu \leqslant 15$ $\sigma = 3$ $\alpha = 0.05$
13, 14, 17, 19, 19, 13, 19, 21, 18
  2. Ho: $\mu \geqslant 15$ $\sigma = 3$ $\alpha = 0.01$
14, 12, 13, 18, 13, 15, 9, 9, 10
*3. Ho: $\mu = 28$ $\alpha = 0.01$
25, 29, 25, 28, 26, 28, 22, 39, 36, 31, 20, 24, 26, 34, 22, 28, 21
  4. Ho: $\mu = 40$ $\alpha = 0.05$
40, 37, 36, 37, 37, 27, 43, 29, 30, 26, 39, 32, 45, 34, 34, 36, 46
*5. Ho: $\mu \leqslant 22$ $\alpha = 0.001$
14, 16, 17, 21, 17, 13, 18, 21, 19, 19, 18, 18, 23, 19, 16, 20, 16
  6. Ho: $\mu \geqslant 32$ $\alpha = 0.001$
34, 37, 33, 38, 33, 35, 37, 38, 37, 35

*Answers to starred questions are found in Appendix D.

*7. Ho: $\mu_1 \leqslant \mu_2$ $\sigma_1 = 3$ $\sigma_2 = 4$ $\alpha = 0.05$
Sample 1: 12, 8, 5, 11, 9, 6, 9, 9, 15
Sample 2: 13, 11, 15, 11, 12, 14, 9, 17, 9
   8. Ho: $\mu_1 \geqslant \mu_2$ $\sigma_1 = 7$ $\sigma_2 = 5$ $\alpha = 0.05$
Sample 1: 43, 40, 39, 40, 40, 28, 47, 30, 32, 27, 43, 34, 50, 36
Sample 2: 42, 36, 46, 52, 44, 40, 36, 40, 45, 40, 45, 43, 43, 47
   *9. Ho: $\mu_1 = \mu_2$ $\sigma_1 = 4$ $\sigma_2 = 6$ $\alpha = 0.01$
Sample 1: 29, 19, 24, 27, 19, 22, 22, 27
Sample 2: 21, 23, 24, 21, 39, 16, 31, 35, 20, 33, 19
   10. Ho: $\mu_1 = \mu_2$ $\sigma_1 = 6$ $\sigma_2 = 3$ $\alpha = 0.01$
Sample 1: 7, 10, 19, 10, 16, 15, 18
Sample 2: 19, 17, 16, 21, 18, 19, 16, 12, 13, 17, 15, 14, 15
   *11. Ho: $\mu_1 \leqslant \mu_2$ $\alpha = 0.05$
Sample 1: 11, 9, 7, 11, 10, 8
Sample 2: 19, 10, 10, 15, 13, 14, 17, 25, 11, 14, 13
   12. Ho: $\mu_1 = \mu_2$ $\alpha = 0.05$
Sample 1: 19, 16, 21, 18, 15, 21, 23, 17, 22
Sample 2: 26, 19, 28, 28, 18, 20, 21, 21, 15, 20, 16, 21, 20, 28
   *13. Ho: $\mu_1 = \mu_2$ $\alpha = 0.05$
First measurement: 23, 18, 17, 20, 23, 19
Second measurement: 25, 20, 22, 26, 26, 19
   14. Ho: $\mu_1 \leqslant \mu_2$ $\alpha = 0.05$
First measurement: 30, 36, 27, 26, 46, 33, 27, 32, 34, 32, 37
Second measurement: 30, 45, 27, 26, 46, 33, 25, 30, 18, 29, 29
   15. For each of the following conditions, create a set of data that yields a value of the test statistic that is statistically significant at the 0.05 level but not the 0.01 level.
   (a) Ho: $\mu \geqslant 8$ $\sigma = 3$ $N = 10$
   (b) Ho: $\mu = 10$ $\sigma = 2$ $N = 7$
   (c) Ho: $\mu = 15$ $N = 10$
   (d) Ho: $\mu_1 = \mu_2$ $\sigma_1 = 3$ $\sigma_2 = 4$ $N_1 = 5$ $N_2 = 7$
   (e) Ho: $\mu_1 \geqslant \mu_2$ $N_1 = 10$ $N_2 = 8$
   (f) Ho: $\mu_1 = \mu_2$
First measurement: 28, 22, 17, 27, 24, 19, 23, 24, 34, 22

15

INFERENCES ABOUT
OTHER INDICES

Our discussion in Chapter 14 concerned testing hypotheses about the mean. Depending on the nature of the study and whether we can assume to know the population variance, we can use the one- or two-sample form of the critical ratio or the t test to draw conclusions about means. In this chapter, we first discuss two additional sampling distributions and see how they can be applied in drawing inferences about variances. Next, we turn our attention to frequencies; and, finally, we consider the problem of drawing inferences about the correlation coefficient.

THE CHI-SQUARE DISTRIBUTION

Suppose that we have a normal distribution where all of the elements are in z-score form. The distribution has a mean of zero and a standard deviation of one. We draw a random sample of size N from this normally distributed population of z's; the resulting set of N z-scores is a set of deviation scores. Therefore, the variance in this sample of z's is

$$\sigma_z^2 = \frac{\sum\limits_{i=1}^{N} z_i^2}{N},$$

and the sum-of-squares of the z's is $\sum z_i^2$. Let us give the name χ^2 (capital Greek letter chi squared) to this sum of squared z's; that is,

$$\chi^2 = \sum z_i^2. \tag{15.1}$$

Now, suppose that we draw another sample and another and another from this normally distributed population. For each sample, we compute a value of χ^2 and place it in a frequency distribution of χ^2's. After we have collected a large number of these χ^2's, all based on N z-scores, we have a sampling distribution for the χ^2 statistic. We know from our work with the mean that sampling distributions depend on sample size. χ^2 is rather like t in this regard; not only the spread of the distribution, but also its shape and location depend on the sample size. As was the case with t, we can use the concept of degrees of freedom to indicate which of the many χ^2 distributions applies to a given problem.

There is another important feature to keep in mind concerning the χ^2 distribution, which involves sums-of-squares. Since sums-of-squares cannot be negative, the χ^2 distribution has zero as its minimum possible value. Figure 15-1 illustrates the nonnegative property of several χ^2 distributions. Note that with small df's, the curves show marked positive skew. As sample size increases, the curves shift to the right and become more nearly normal.

If χ^2 were limited in its interpretation to a distribution of sums-of-squares of z-scores, there would be little interest in the statistic and we would not include it. However, it turns out that many other quantities that describe sample results have the same or nearly the same distribution as χ^2. We cover some of these uses in this chapter, while others, special nonparametric statistics and applications in multivariate analysis, are beyond our scope. The χ^2 family of distributions probably has more different applications than any other sampling distribution.

Critical values of the χ^2 distribution are included in Appendix Table B-3. Because there is a family of curves, only a few selected values are given for each member of the family (each df value). The value at the head of each column is the proportion of the curve that falls to the right of the given value of χ^2. The first column, labeled df, indicates the degrees of freedom or which curve the critical values refer to. For example, the value 0.0642, which falls in the first row ($df = 1$) under the heading 0.80, is the value of χ^2 with $df = 1$ for which 80 percent of the distribution falls to the right; another way of looking at this value is that it cuts off the bottom 20 percent of the curve. Likewise, the value 11.07 in the 0.05 column, row 5, is the value of χ^2 that cuts off the top 5 percent of the distribution when $df = 5$. We can also say that 90 percent of this $df = 5$ curve is included between the values $\chi^2 = 1.145$ and $\chi^2 = 11.070$. Note that we are treating these values of χ^2 in exactly the same way that we treated the values in the t distribution.

The χ^2 table stops at $df = 30$ because the distribution is very nearly normal above this value. For larger df an approximate value for a critical ratio is computed by using the expression

$$z = \sqrt{2\chi^2} - \sqrt{2(N - 1) - 1}. \tag{15.2}$$

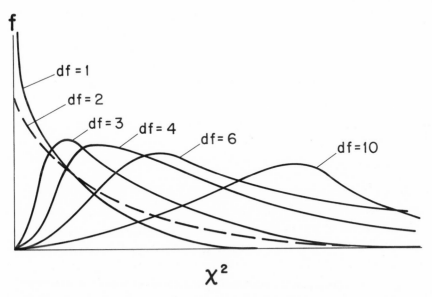

Figure 15-1   Examples of chi-square distributions. Note that all values are positive and that the distributions approach being normal in shape for large degrees of freedom.

The table for the normal distribution is then used to find the probability associated with z.

χ^2 AND VARIANCE

In Chapter 13, we described the concept of a sampling distribution and said that this concept applies to all sample descriptive statistics. We focused our attention on the sampling distribution of the mean in Chapter 14, but we also described the unbiased estimate of the population variance. This statistic,

$$\hat{S}_x^2 = \frac{\sum x_i^2}{N - 1}$$

also has a sampling distribution around its population parameter, σ_x^2. If we assume that we know the value of σ_x^2, we can develop a sampling distribution for drawing inferences about the variance.

First, we note that

$$(N - 1)\hat{S}^2 = \sum x_i^2.$$

Now, dividing both sides by σ_x^2

$$\frac{(N - 1)\hat{S}^2}{\sigma_x^2} = \frac{\sum x_i^2}{\sigma_x^2} = \sum \frac{x_i^2}{\sigma_x^2}.$$

But each of the x_i^2/σ_x^2 is a squared z-score. The right-hand term is $\sum z_i^2$; therefore, from the definition of χ^2 in equation 15.1, we conclude that

$$\chi^2 = \frac{(N - 1)\hat{S}_x^2}{\sigma_x^2} \tag{15.3}$$

with $(N - 1)$ degrees of freedom.

One benefit of this result is that it gives us an equivalent of the one-sample critical ratio that we can use to test hypotheses about variances. Assuming that we know the population variance, we can test the hypothesis that our sample was drawn at random from that population. For example, suppose we have drawn a sample of 25 individuals and computed the value of $\hat{S}^2$ to be 133. Our null hypothesis is that this is a random sample from a population with a variance of 300. We have no reason to make our null hypothesis directional, so we test a two-tailed null; that is,

H_0: $\sigma^2 = 300$

H_1: $\sigma^2 \neq 300$.

Selecting $\alpha = 0.02$ (1 percent of the distribution in each tail), we find the critical values for χ^2 with $df = 24$ to be 10.856 for the lower tail and 42.980 for the upper tail. We compute the value of χ^2 for our data to be

$$\chi^2 = \frac{24(133)}{300} = 10.64.$$

Since the sample result falls in the critical region (below the lower critical value), we decide to reject the null hypothesis and conclude that our sample is not a random sample from a population with a variance of 300. Note carefully that χ^2 uses variances, not standard deviations.

One-sample hypotheses involving known parameters occur no more frequently with variances than with means, so this use of χ^2 seldom occurs in the real world of research. However, the relationship between χ^2 and variance does allow us to use χ^2 and the value from our sample to calculate a confidence interval for the unknown parameter. The logic here is the same as it was for the mean and t. Just as we would expect 90 percent of the values of t to fall between the upper and lower 5 percent critical values, so would we also expect 90 percent of the χ^2's to fall between the upper and lower 5 percent critical values. Thus, we can set up the inequalities

$$\chi^2_{0.05} < \frac{(N-1)\hat{S}_x^2}{\sigma_x^2} < \chi^2_{0.95}.$$

By solving these inequalities for σ_x^2, we obtain

$$\frac{(N-1)\hat{S}_x^2}{\chi^2_{0.95}} < \sigma_x^2 < \frac{(N-1)\hat{S}_x^2}{\chi^2_{0.05}}. \tag{15.4}$$

For this example ($\hat{S}_x^2 = 133$), the 90 percent confidence interval for σ_x^2 is

$$\frac{24(133)}{36.415} < \sigma^2 < \frac{24(133)}{13.848}$$

$$87.656 < \sigma^2 < 230.5.$$

In other words, this confidence interval permits us to be confident (with 10 percent chance of error) that our sample was drawn from a population with a variance somewhere between 87.7 and 230.5.

THE *F* DISTRIBUTION

Another very useful distribution can be derived either from χ^2 or by direct definition. Suppose we have two independent estimates of the same population variance; this gives rise to two χ^2's

$$\chi_1^2 = \frac{(N_1 - 1)\hat{S}_1^2}{\sigma^2} , \qquad \chi_2^2 = \frac{(N_2 - 1)\hat{S}_2^2}{\sigma^2}$$

Since these χ^2's can be based on different degrees of freedom (and therefore refer to different χ^2 distributions), we must reduce them to the same scale by dividing each by its degrees of freedom. Doing this produces

$$\frac{\chi_1^2}{df_1} = \frac{\hat{S}_1^2}{\sigma^2} , \qquad \frac{\chi_2^2}{df_2} = \frac{\hat{S}_2^2}{\sigma^2} .$$

We can now define a function, call it *F*, as

$$F = \frac{\chi_1^2/df_1}{\chi_2^2/df_2} = \frac{\hat{S}_1^2/\sigma^2}{\hat{S}_2^2/\sigma^2} . \tag{15.5}$$

Under the assumption that both samples have been drawn from the same population, we simplify the fraction

$$F = \frac{\hat{S}_1^2}{\sigma^2} \cdot \frac{\sigma^2}{\hat{S}_2^2} = \frac{\hat{S}_1^2}{\hat{S}_2^2} . \tag{15.6}$$

It is also possible to obtain the result in equation 15.6 directly by definition; that is, we can define *F* as the ratio

$$F = \frac{\hat{S}_1^2}{\hat{S}_2^2} , \tag{15.7}$$

which is the ratio of two sample estimates of a population variance. Using our procedure of drawing a large number of samples (in this case, pairs of samples), computing the desired index for each, and making a frequency distribution, we can obtain a sampling distribution for *F* for samples of these sizes. It should be clear both from using the degrees of freedom terms with the χ^2's in equation 15.5 and from the fact the samples yielding $\hat{S}_1^2$ and $\hat{S}_2^2$ in the definition in equation 15.7 were not required to be the same size, that the sampling distribution of F is affected by two degrees-of-freedom terms. The numerator variance is based on df_1 and the denominator variance is based on df_2. Therefore, there is a unique sampling distribution of F for every possible combination of degrees of freedom.

Critical values for many of the sampling distributions of F can be found in Appendix Table B-4. Because there are so many distributions (900 possibilities for the combinations of df of 30 or less), only critical values for the conventional levels of α (0.05, 0.01, and 0.001) are included. Also, the F ratio is most frequently used in situations where the value of the numerator df is small, so only selected df values are included.

While each of the F distributions is a complete sampling distribution with extreme values at both the upper and lower ends, interest centers on the upper, or right side, of the distribution. This is possible because the decision as to which variance to call $\hat{S}_1^2$ in equation 15.7 is arbitrary. To save space, it has become conventional to place the larger of the two sample variances in the numerator, which has the effect of allowing us to deal only with the upper half of each F distribution. It also has the effect of making all hypotheses tested with F two-tailed hypotheses unless specific and careful logical steps are taken in constructing the hypotheses prior to the analysis. (We shall return to this point shortly; but first, a word about reading the table.)

The F table (Appendix Table B-4) is read from the two degrees-of-freedom values. The numerator degrees of freedom (df_1) is used to find the proper column and the denominator degrees of freedom (df_2) the proper row. The three values at the intersection of the df_1 column with the df_2 row are the 0.05, 0.01, and 0.001 upper critical values for the F distribution that has df_1 and df_2 as its degrees of freedom. For example, with df_1 of 10 and df_2 of 15, the critical values are 2.54, 3.80, and 6.08, respectively.

F AND VARIANCE

While χ^2 provided us with a way to test hypotheses about a single sample variance, F gives us a way to deal with two samples. If we assume that our two samples come either from the same population or from two populations with equal variances, the ratio of the sample estimates of those variances should be an F with $df_1 = (N_1 - 1)$ and $df_2 = (N_2 - 1)$. Thus, the condition that we assume to be true, our null hypothesis, can be stated as

H_0: $\sigma_1^2 = \sigma_2^2$.

If this condition is true, the ratio $\hat{S}_1^2/\hat{S}_2^2$ will have a sampling distribution of the appropriate F distribution. We determine the critical value of F by reference to Appendix Table B-4 with $df_1 = (N_1 - 1)$ and $df_2 = (N_2 - 1)$ and compute the ratio of the two sample variances, placing the larger variance in the numerator. If the value of F computed from the sample data exceeds the critical value from the table, we decide to reject the null hypothesis and conclude either that the two samples did not come from the same population (first assumption) or that the two populations do not have equal variances (second assumption).

Suppose we wish to test an hypothesis that the variances in scores on the statistics final exam are the same in the spring and fall semesters, which amounts to a null hypothesis that $\sigma_S^2 = \sigma_F^2$. We collect a sample of spring scores from 18 students and a sample of fall scores from 23 students. The two classes give us $\hat{S}_S^2 = 41.7$ and $\hat{S}_F^2 = 30.4$. Since we must put the larger variance in the numerator, $df_1 = 17$ and $df_2 = 22$. Assume that we set α at 0.01. Looking in the table, we find the 0.01 critical value for 15 and 22 degrees of freedom to be 2.98 (as with t, we go to the next lower df when our exact value is not in the table). We compute the value of F from our study and find

$$F = \frac{41.7}{30.4} = 1.37.$$

The F from our study does not exceed the critical value, so we conclude that we cannot reject the null hypothesis. Note, as with all tests of hypotheses, we cannot conclude that σ_S^2 and σ_F^2 *are* equal, only that we cannot reject the possibility that they are.

As previously stated, the values in the F table are for two-tailed hypotheses, which means that the 0.05 critical value 2.54 that we looked up earlier actually cuts off the upper $2\frac{1}{2}$ percent of the area of the F distribution for ten and 15 degrees of freedom, but since we arbitrarily place the larger variance in the numerator, we must double the probability. This is so because by arbitrarily placing the larger variance in the numerator of the F-ratio we are considering only the top half of the distribution, and $2\frac{1}{2}$ percent of the whole distribution is 5 percent of the top half of the same distribution. This doubling is taken care of in the labeling of Appendix Table B-4. However, there may be some rare occasions when it is proper to test a directional hypothesis concerning variances. Suppose, for example, that we want to test the proposition that there is greater variability among males in academic performance than there is among females. This prediction is clearly directional, calling for a one-tailed hypothesis. If our null assumption that $\sigma_M^2 = \sigma_F^2$ is true, the value of the ratio is 1, so we can state our hypotheses as

$$H_0: \quad \frac{\sigma_M^2}{\sigma_F^2} \leqslant 1$$

$$H_1: \quad \frac{\sigma_M^2}{\sigma_F^2} > 1.$$

Under our hypotheses, we do not have the option of arbitrarily placing the larger variance in the numerator. Therefore, the critical values found in Appendix Table B-4 would properly refer to α levels of 0.025, 0.005, and 0.0005, respectively.

FREQUENCY COMPARISONS

We mentioned that χ^2 has many uses other than forming confidence intervals for variances, the most widely known of which is its use in testing hypotheses about the relationship between nominal variables. Recall from our discussion in Chapter 1 that nominal variables do not contain any information about order or amount of the property under investigation. The numerals assigned to the categories of the variable are not quantitative and, therefore, cannot be used as scores in the sense that we have used that term. The only quantitative information that we can obtain from a nominal scale is information about the frequency with which each category occurs. For this reason, tests of hypothesis concerning nominal variables generally involve comparing the observed frequencies of the categories with those that would be expected to occur if the null hypothesis were true.

Nominal variables involve discrete categories. There are procedures available to calculate the exact probability associated with each amount of difference between the expected frequencies (the null hypothesis condition) and the observed frequencies; however, these probabilities are difficult and time-consuming to compute. It happens that the distribution of the discrepancies between observed and expected frequencies is very closely approximated by the χ^2 distribution. Where one or both of the variables has at least three categories, the approximation is very good; we must, however, introduce a correction when both variables are dichotomies. (The principle of substituting a continuous test statistic for a discrete set of events is one we have encountered before. Our coin-tossing examples produced discrete outcomes with calculable exact probabilities; however, we found that the normal distribution provided a good approximation of these probabilities. We are doing the same thing with χ^2 except that the distribution of exact probabilities is too complex for us to go into.)

The analysis of nominal variables involves preparing a *cross-tabulation table*, sometimes called a crosstab. It is prepared by setting up two axes, one for each variable. Each axis is divided into as many parts as there are categories of the variable. Each individual has a score on both variables, which is tabulated as a frequency in the appropriate cell of the table.

Suppose, for example, that we are conducting an investigation of marital status and voting preference. The categories of our two variables are shown in Table 15-1. For the purposes of this analysis, each observation yields two pieces of information about an individual: her/his marital status and stated voting preference. If Charlie states that he has never been married and is a Republican, a tally mark representing Charlie is placed in the upper left cell; Joyce, who is a married independent, would be tabulated in the middle-right cell, and all other people would be handled in a similar way, each contributing to the frequency in the appropriate cell. Some hypothetical data for our study are included in Table 15-1. The values in the cells are called the *observed cell frequencies*. The values at the right and at the bottom of the table are called the *marginal frequencies*.

The first thing that we must do to analyze the results of our study is to compute the *expected cell frequencies*. The marginal frequencies for each variable give the number of individuals in each category of each variable considered singly. If there is no relationship between the variables, we should expect the cell frequencies in each column to be proportional to the marginal frequencies on the right. Likewise, the cell frequencies in each row should be proportional to the marginals on the bottom.

At this point we must bring up for serious consideration an issue that we have generally avoided before, the issue of statistical independence and its relationship to probability. The application of χ^2 to crosstab tables is a test of the null hypothesis that the two variables are statistically independent or unrelated. We use "unrelated" here with much the same meaning that the term has in discussions of correlation. If two variables are unrelated, knowledge of a person's status on one does not reduce our uncertainty about his or her status on the other.

The marginal frequencies give us the probability distribution for each of the variables without consideration of the other. For example, the chance that a randomly selected individual will be a Democrat is 212/527 or 0.402277; likewise, the probability that a person will never have been married is 145/527 or 0.27514. The marginal frequencies, or probabilities, for the categories of one variable are independent of the marginals for the other variable.

If (and only if) the two variables are statistically independent, the cell frequencies within each row (or column) of the table will be proportional to the row (or column) marginal frequencies within random variations due to sampling. For example, if the two variables of voting preference and marital status are statistically independent, the cell frequencies in the never-married row should occur in the same proportions as the marginal frequencies at the bottom of the table. The same should hold true for the now-married and the divorced rows. Likewise, the cell frequencies for the Republican column should be proportional to the marginals on the right of the table, as should those for the Democrat and Independent columns.

Under the assumption (our null hypothesis) that the two variables are

TABLE 15-1

Cross Tabulation of Marital Status and Voting Preference.

Marital Status	Republican	Democrat	Independent	*Marginal Frequencies*
Never married	31	53	61	145
Now married	102	112	104	318
Divorced, widowed, etc.	10	47	7	64
Marginal Frequencies	143	212	172	527

unrelated, we can use the multiplication theorem of probability (see Chapter 7) to calculate the probability that a person will be both a Democrat and never married (that is, fall in the top-middle cell of the table). The probability is

$0.402277 \cdot 0.27514 = 0.11068.$

This is the probability, or relative frequency, with which we would expect to find never-married Democrats in our sample if the two variables are independent or unrelated. This relative frequency can be converted into an expected cell frequency by multiplying it by the total number of observations; in our example, the result is

$0.11068 \cdot 527 = 58.33.$

Expected cell frequencies can be computed directly from the marginals by the general equation

$$E_{RC} = \frac{f_R f_C}{N} , \tag{15.8}$$

where

E_{RC} is the expected frequency in cell RC,

f_R is the marginal frequency in row R,

f_C is the marginal frequency in column C

N is the total number of observations.

For our example, equation 15.8 yields

$$E = \frac{145(212)}{527} = 58.33,$$

which is the same value we obtained using probabilities. It is necessary to use equation 15.8 to compute an expected frequency for each cell of the table.

Expected frequencies are used with the observed frequencies to compute a value of χ^2 for the table. The formula for the χ^2 is

$$\chi^2 = \sum_R \sum_C \frac{(O_{RC} - E_{RC})^2}{E_{RC}} . \tag{15.9}$$

For each cell RC we find the squared difference between the observed cell frequency O_{RC} and the expected cell frequency E_{RC} and divide it by the expected cell frequency. These cell values are then summed for the entire table.

The steps for computing χ^2 in our example are shown in Table 15-2. The three numbers in each cell are the observed frequency, the expected frequency, and the value of $(O - E)^2/E$ for that cell. Thus, for the upper-left cell, we obtain

$$\frac{(31 - 39.35)^2}{39.35} = \frac{(-8.35)^2}{39.35} = \frac{69.7225}{39.35} = 1.772;$$

the same procedure is repeated for each cell in turn.

We must have a value for degrees of freedom in order to look up the critical values for χ^2. Remembering that in each row of the table, the cell entries must sum to the marginal frequency, we can see that if there are C (the number of columns in the table) cells in each row, $(C - 1)$ of the cells

TABLE 15-2
Computing Chi-Square for Data in Table 15-1

Marital Status	Republican	Democrat	Independent	Marginal Frequencies
Never married	$O = 31$ $E = 39.35$ 1.772	$O = 53$ $E = 58.33$ 0.487	$O = 61$ $E = 47.32$ 3.955	145
Now married	$O = 102$ $E = 86.29$ 2.860	$O = 112$ $E = 127.92$ 1.981	$O = 104$ $E = 103.79$ 0.00	318
Divorced, widowed, etc.	$O = 10$ $E = 17.37$ 3.127	$O = 47$ $E = 25.75$ 17.536	$O = 7$ $E = 20.89$ 9.236	64
Marginal Frequencies	143	212	172	527

Calculations

$\chi^2 = 1.772 + 0.487 + 3.955 + 2.860 + 1.981$

$\qquad + 0.00 + 3.127 + 17.536 + 9.236$

$\chi^2 = 40.954$

are free to vary. Once the first $(C - 1)$ cell frequencies have occurred, the value of the last is fixed. Given values of 31 and 53 for the first two cells in row 1, the last must be 61 in order for the sum to be 145.

The same principle holds in each column. All but one of the cells is free to vary. There are $(R - 1)$ degrees of freedom in each column and $(C - 1)$ degrees of freedom in each row. Since the total number of cells is given by the product $R \cdot C$, the degrees of freedom for the whole table is given by

$$df = (R - 1)(C - 1). \tag{15.10}$$

In our example, this value is

$$df = (3 - 1)(3 - 1) = 4.$$

Looking in Appendix Table B-3, we find the 0.05 critical value for χ^2 to be 9.488. The critical value for an α of 0.001 is 18.465. At this point we have to consider what hypothesis is being tested by the χ^2. Our reasoning proceeds as follows:

1. We assume that the marginal frequencies reflect the population with respect to the relative frequency of each category of each variable.

2. Our null hypothesis is that the two variables are independent.

3. If the null hypothesis is true, the relative cell frequencies in the population will be equal to the expected frequencies.

4. If the null hypothesis is true and we draw a very large (in theory, infinite) number of samples from the population and compute a value of χ^2 as defined by equation 15.9 for each sample, the frequency distribution of these sample statistics will have the shape of a χ^2 distribution with $(R - 1)(C - 1)$ degrees of freedom.

5. If the null hypothesis is true, the probability that we will draw a sample with a value in excess of the α critical value (for example, 0.01) is no greater than α.

6. If the sample value exceeds the critical value, we conclude that the null hypothesis is false.

The substantive conclusion that we reach upon rejecting the null hypothesis depends, of course, on the nature of our original research question. In the example just given, our research interest was in the relationship between voting preference and marital status. The null hypothesis was that the two variables were unrelated, which means that we expect to find no systematic tendency among people of a particular marital status to state a particular party preference. Since our obtained χ^2 of 40.954 exceeds the 0.001 critical value, we must reject the null and conclude that there is a relationship between the two variables. Inspecting the cells leads us to conclude that people who fall in the divorced/widowed category tend to state Democrat preference much more frequently and Republican or Independent much less frequently than we would expect. Also, there is a tendency for never-married people to call their voting preference independent. Uncovering the deeper meaning of these make-believe findings is left to the student.

It should be clear that χ^2 is a statistic that characterizes a sample, just as t and z are. Like t, χ^2 has a sampling distribution based on its degrees of freedom that would occur if the null conditions were true. A sample value that is unlikely to have come from that sampling distribution leads us to reject the null hypothesis.

CORRECTION FOR CONTINUITY

As we noted, the χ^2 computed by equation 15.9 provides a good approximation to the exact probability distribution when either variable has more than two categories. However, when both variables are dichotomous so that the χ^2 has only one degree of freedom, the accuracy of the approximation is not so satisfactory. The reason for this deterioration is that χ^2 is based on a continuous variable $\sum z^2$, and the variables in the crosstab table are discrete, causing the value of χ^2 to change in discrete jumps. The error between the exact probabilities and the χ^2 is large enough in this case to require correction.

The necessary correction is to subtract 0.5 from the absolute value (disregard sign) of the difference between the observed and expected frequencies. Equation 15.9 is rewritten as

$$\chi^2 = \sum \sum \left[\frac{(\,|O_{RC} - E_{RC}| - 0.5)}{E_{RC}} \right]^2. \tag{15.11}$$

This form of χ^2 is used only for $2 \cdot 2$ tables, those where χ^2 has one degree of freedom.

The effect of equation 15.11 is to reduce slightly the difference between observed and expected frequencies. One way to think about what is going on here is to view the expected frequency as a theoretically continuous variable. If we subtract 0.5 from $(O - E)$, we are using the real limit of the E-interval that is nearer zero, thereby making a more nearly continuous variable of the discrete frequencies. The correction for continuity has a substantial effect on χ^2 only when there is one or more small expected frequency.

There is one final note of caution we must mention with regard to χ^2. Small expected frequencies have an adverse effect on χ^2 because the value of the statistic is then greatly affected by sampling error. If any expected frequency is zero, the χ^2 is undefined and therefore unusable. However, most authors suggest that χ^2 not be used if any expected frequency is less than 5.

INFERENCES ABOUT CORRELATION

Like all other statistics, the correlation coefficient is subject to variation from sample to sample. For a given population, it has a sampling distribution around the population parameter ρ (rho), and this distribution has a standard error, σ_r. Unfortunately, the sampling distribution of r is much more complex than the other sampling distributions we have encountered.

Fisher's z-transformation. The most difficult problem that we face in dealing with the correlation coefficient is that the sampling distribution has a different shape, depending on the value of ρ. Remember that r is limited to the range of values between $+1$ and -1. If the value of ρ is about zero (that is, in the middle of this range), sample deviations can occur equally in either direction. However, as ρ departs from zero, this symmetry is lost because one end of the sampling distribution is more restricted than the other. For extreme values of ρ, the sampling distribution of r becomes markedly skewed due to the restriction of ± 1.0.

A solution to this problem was developed by R. A. Fisher, who proposed a transformation for r that involves logarithms. The resulting index

$$z_F = 1.1513 \log_{10} \left(\frac{1 + r}{1 - r} \right) \tag{15.12}$$

has the advantage that the distribution is almost exactly normal for any value of ρ and has a standard error of

$$\sigma_{z_F} = \frac{1}{\sqrt{N-3}} \, . \tag{15.13}$$

It is not really necessary to use equation 15.12 to compute z_F. Since there are a limited number of values that r can have, it is possible to prepare tables of the necessary values. Two tables are provided in Appendix B for the Fisher transformation; one, Table B-5, gives the value of z_F for any value of r and is used to transform r to z_F. The other, Table B-6, is used to reverse the transformation after any necessary computations have been completed.

There are several general situations that we may encounter in testing hypotheses concerning r; most frequently, we are faced with a test of the null hypothesis that $\rho = 0$. It is not necessary to use z_F in conjunction with this problem because the sampling distribution will be symmetrical. For large samples (N at least 100), an appropriate standard error for the test is

$$\sigma_r = \frac{1}{\sqrt{N}} \, , \tag{15.14}$$

which can then be used in a critical ratio formula

$$z = \frac{r}{\sigma_r} \, . \tag{15.15}$$

Note that this is a normal deviate or critical ratio z, not a Fisher's z. It is unfortunate that the same symbol has been applied to both indices, but the usage is so widespread and firmly entrenched that we must learn to live with it.

Testing the hypothesis that $\rho = 0$ using small samples ($N < 100$) involves using the t distribution. The index

$$t = \frac{r}{\sqrt{(1 - r^2)/(N - 2)}} \tag{15.16}$$

follows the t distribution with $(N - 2)$ degrees of freedom. That is, the quantity

$$\frac{r}{\sqrt{(1 - r^2)/(N - 2)}}$$

has a sampling distribution with the same shape as the t distribution with $(N - 2)$ degrees of freedom.

The null hypothesis tested by either equations 15.15 or 15.16 usually is that $\rho = 0$. If the value of the test statistic exceeds the critical value at the α (0.05 or 0.01) level, we reject the null at that level of confidence. Of course, a theory or prior experience may call for a one-tailed null hypothesis, in which case the critical value is determined accordingly.

A second situation that we occasionally encounter is the need to place a confidence interval for ρ on an observed r. Since this usually involves a nonzero r, it is generally necessary to use z_F. The procedure is to determine z_F for the obtained r from Appendix Table B-5, then calculate σ_{z_F}. Using the appropriate normal deviate z's (z_α) from Appendix Table B-1 (for example, ± 1.96 for the 95 percent confidence interval), compute the upper and lower limits for z_F

$$z_F - (z_\alpha)\sigma_{z_F} \text{ and } z_F + (z_\alpha)\sigma_{z_F}.$$

These limits are then transformed by Appendix Table B-6 back into correlation values.

For example, suppose we want to determine the 95 percent confidence interval around an r of 0.72 computed on a sample of 50 people. From Appendix Table B-5, we find z_F to be 0.908. The standard error of z_F is

$$\frac{1}{\sqrt{47}} = \frac{1}{6.856} = 0.146.$$

The upper- and lower-limit values for z_F are

$$0.908 + (1.96)(0.146) = 1.194$$

$$0.908 - (1.96)(0.146) = 0.622.$$

From Appendix Table B-6, we find the corresponding r's to be 0.83 and 0.55. Note that this confidence interval is symmetric in terms of probability and z_F, but not in r. The confidence interval goes from 0.55 to 0.83 with its center at 0.72, reflecting the fact that the sampling distribution of r in this region is negatively skewed. Had we used σ_r from equation 15.14 and not transformed to z_F, we would have obtained a very different and erroneous pair of limits.

The situation sometimes arises where we want to test a null hypothesis that two correlations are equal. If the two correlations involve the same variables in two different samples, z_F can be used. First, transform both r's to z_F's, then calculate the standard error of the difference between two z_F's

$$\sigma_{(z_{F_1} - z_{F_2})} = \sqrt{\frac{1}{N_1 - 3} + \frac{1}{N_2 - 3}}. \tag{15.17}$$

A critical ratio z then provides the test statistic for the hypothesis that $\rho_1 = \rho_2$.

We may, for example, have the correlation between midterm and final-examination scores for students in a statistics class. For the 17 men in the class, the correlation is 0.78, while for the 24 women, r is 0.55. The hypothesis that $\rho_M = \rho_F$ is tested by finding

$$\sigma_{(z_M - z_F)} = \sqrt{\frac{1}{17 - 3} + \frac{1}{24 - 3}} = \sqrt{0.119} = 0.345$$

$$z = \frac{0.78 - 0.55}{0.345} = \frac{+0.23}{0.345} = 0.67.$$

Clearly, we cannot reject the null hypothesis on the basis of these data.

The final situation that we cover is the problem of averaging correlations. The correlation coefficient does not represent an interval scale; the meaning of differences between correlations changes, depending on where we are in the range of possible values. For this reason, we cannot use simple averaging techniques with r's. We can, however, use z_F because it does represent an interval variable. Whenever it is necessary to find an average of several correlations, particularly when they differ by more than about 0.10, the appropriate procedure is to transform all r's to z_F's, find $\bar{z}_F$ (the mean of the z_F's), and then reverse the transformation using $\bar{z}_F$ to find the mean r.

When the correlations being averaged are based on samples of different sizes, it is necessary to compute a weighted average. Under these conditions,

$$\bar{z}_F = \frac{(N_1 - 3)z_{F_1} + (N_2 - 3)z_{F_2} + \cdots + (N_K - 3)z_{F_K}}{(N_1 - 3) + (N_2 - 3) + \cdots + (N_K - 3)} \tag{15.18}$$

produces the proper weighting. Hypotheses concerning this mean correlation should be tested using $\bar{z}_F$, which has a standard error of

$$\sigma_{\bar{z}_F} = \frac{1}{\sqrt{(N_1 - 3) + (N_2 - 3) + \cdots + (N_K - 3)}}.$$

To illustrate this procedure and the appropriate use of equations 15.15 and 15.16, imagine that we have the correlation between the midterm examination scores in statistics and final examination scores in history for each of three classes. The data are

$$r_1 = 0.61 \qquad N_1 = 10 \qquad z_{F_1} = 0.709$$

$$r_2 = 0.37 \qquad N_2 = 26 \qquad z_{F_2} = 0.389$$

$$r_3 = 0.15 \qquad N_3 = 107 \qquad z_{F_3} = 0.151$$

We can test the hypothesis that $\rho_3 = 0$ using equation 15.15

$$\sigma_r = \frac{1}{\sqrt{N}} = \frac{1}{\sqrt{107}} = \frac{1}{10.34} = 0.097$$

$$z = \frac{0.15}{0.097} = 1.55.$$

The correct test for the hypothesis $\rho_1 = 0$ uses equation 15.16

$$t = \frac{0.61}{\sqrt{(1 - 0.372)/(N - 2)}} = \frac{0.61}{\sqrt{0.63/8}} = \frac{0.61}{\sqrt{0.078}} = 2.18$$

$df = 8.$

Neither of these test statistics exceeds the 0.05 two-tailed critical value for its sampling distribution. Still, we may wish to find $\bar{r}$ and test the hypothesis that the mean correlation is zero. This is done by finding

$$\bar{z}_F = \frac{7(0.709) + 23(0.389) + 104(0.151)}{7 + 23 + 104} = 0.221$$

$$\bar{r} = 0.22$$

$$\sigma_{\bar{z}} = \frac{1}{\sqrt{134}} = 0.0864$$

$$z = \frac{0.221}{0.0864} = 2.56$$

from which we can conclude that the mean correlation of 0.22 does differ significantly from zero.

SUMMARY

It is possible to draw inferences about other statistics and parameters than the mean; the *chi-square* (χ^2) family of distributions is particularly useful or about frequencies. There is a unique χ^2 distribution for each number of degrees of freedom. When χ^2 is used with variances, the *df* value is the same as the *df* for the variance estimate itself. In testing hypotheses about frequencies in a *cross-tab table*, *df* is $(R - 1)(C - 1)$.

A second family of distributions that is useful in several hypothesis testing situations is called the *F distribution*. An *F* distribution with df_1 and df_2 degrees of freedom is the sampling distribution of the ratio of two χ^2's each divided by its *df*. It can also be viewed as the sampling distribution of the ratio of two independent, unbiased estimates of a population variance. An *F* distribution is used to test hypotheses about the equality of variances from two samples.

Hypotheses about correlation coefficients use the *Fisher z-transformation* to provide a sampling distribution that is normal in shape. A critical ratio or normal deviate *z* can be computed directly from *r* to test the hypothesis that $\rho = 0$ when sample size is larger than 100, while a *t* test is used for smaller samples. Confidence intervals and tests of hypotheses involving several correlations or situations where ρ is not zero require using Fisher's *z*. In addition, Fisher's *z* can be used to average correlation coefficients and to test hypotheses about the equality of correlations.

PROBLEMS

1. For each of the following values of *df*, find the values of χ^2 that fall at the 1, 10, 50, 95 and 99.9 percent points of the distribution.
 *(a) *df* = 2
 (b) *df* = 5
 *(c) *df* = 10
 (d) *df* = 25

2. We know that the standard deviation of intelligence-test scores in the population is 15. In each of the following cases, test the null hypothesis that the sample described is a random sample from this population at the 0.05 level, two-tailed
 *(a) $\hat{S}^2 = 100$ $N = 8$
 (b) $\hat{S}^2 = 336$ $N = 14$

---

*Answers to starred questions are found in Appendix D.

*(c) $S^2 = 100$ $N = 22$
(d) $S^2 = 348$ $N = 30$
*(e) $\hat{S} = 18.5$ $N = 20$
(f) $\hat{S} = 13$ $N = 15$
*(g) $S = 19.5$ $N = 12$
(h) $S = 10.2$ $N = 18$

3. For each of the situations in question 2, find the 90-percent confidence interval for σ^2.

4. Find the critical value of F for each of the following situations:

*(a) $df_1 = 3$ $df_2 = 8$ $\alpha = 0.01$
(b) $df_1 = 15$ $df_2 = 10$ $\alpha = 0.05$
*(c) $df_1 = 16$ $df_2 = 100$ $\alpha = 0.001$
(d) $df_1 = 100$ $df_2 = 100$ $\alpha = 0.05$
*(e) $df_1 = 19$ $df_2 = 75$ $\alpha = 0.01$
(f) $df_1 = 45$ $df_2 = 200$ $\alpha = 0.05$

*5. You have been conducting a study of the effects of food deprivation on learning. Children in group 1 ($N = 7$) were given candy just before the learning task; group 2 ($N = 8$) was given a morning snack two hours before the task, but no candy; group-3 ($N = 10$) children had nothing to eat since breakfast. The standard deviations were $\hat{S}_1 = 3.1$, $\hat{S}_2 = 5.7$, $\hat{S}_3 = 9.2$. Test the three possible hypotheses that these samples come from the same population.

*6. Using the data provided, test the hypothesis that gender and eye color are unrelated in these two groups.

(a)

	Eyes	
	Brown	Blue
Male	10	15
Female	12	13

(b)

	Eyes	
	Brown	Blue
Male	20	5
Female	9	16

How would you interpret results like these?

7. Widgitry is conducting a study of the effects of light intensity on its employees' performance. Some workers are getting high-intensity light, some average, and some low. Their performance is recorded as above or below average; the results were as follows:

Light Condition	Output	
	Above Average	Below Average
High	25	12
Average	15	16
Low	7	20

Test the hypothesis and interpret the results.

8. Transform each of the following correlations to z_F:

*(a) 0.73 $N = 25$
 (b) 0.82 $N = 20$
*(c) 0.36 $N = 37$
 (d) 0.27 $N = 60$
*(e) −0.15 $N = 386$
 (f) −0.55 $N = 20$

*9. Which of the six correlations in question 8 are statistically significant?

10. What is the average of the six correlations in question 8? Is this average r statistically significant?

16

ANALYSIS OF VARIANCE

To answer a number of research questions in the behavioral and social sciences, it is desirable or necessary to compare more than two groups. For example, studies of the effect of drugs on behavior often include a high-dose group, a low-dose group, and a group that is given a substance that is not the drug at all, but a neutral substance such as sugar or salt. In this chapter, we bring together ideas and principles from several other chapters and develop a method for testing hypotheses that involve the means of more than two groups. The method of analysis that we present here is one member of a family of analytic procedures that has the general name *analysis of variance*, ANOVA, for short.

Prior to the 1920s, if someone conducted a multiple group study (one involving more than two groups), it was common practice to test hypotheses by what has been called the multiple *t*-test method: Each group was paired with every other group, and a *t* test was performed to test the hypothesis that the means of the two groups were not different. The drug example we described would require three pairs of comparisons: high drug (H) with low drug (L), high drug (H) with no drug (N), and low drug (L) with no drug (N). In this case, the problem does not look too bad; however, in a study with ten groups, the number of required paired comparisons is 45.

Aside from the problems that one may encounter in attempting to interpret a large number of comparisons among means, there are two other factors that make the multiple t-test method inappropriate for testing hypotheses in the way that we have been doing it; both involve the risk of a Type I error—incorrectly rejecting the null hypothesis. Since Type I error has occupied a central position in the thinking of many statisticians and research methodologists for 50 years, it is to be expected that much attention has been focused on the problem.

The first difficulty is purely a matter of probability. The value we choose for α, the probability of a Type I error, is given in terms of a single study. It is the number of times we would expect to get a difference as large as the critical value if the null is true. For an α of 0.05, we would expect the sample results to exceed the critical value five times in 100 repetitions of the comparison. The chance that our study is one of those five is only 0.05; however, if we compute more than one t test (or critical ratio or χ^2 or any other test statistic), the probability that *at least* one of them will exceed the critical value is greater than 5 percent, and possibly much greater. For example, if the null hypothesis is exactly true and we conduct 45 t tests as just described, we would expect two or three of the obtained t's to exceed the 0.05 critical value.

A second problem compounds the first to make matters even worse: The t tests are not independent of each other, but involve overlapping pairs of means. For example, the three-group study yields three comparisons, H with L, H with N, and L with N, but these three comparisons are not independent; any two of them determines the third. If $H = 15$, $L = 10$, and $N = 5$, then $(H - L) + (L - N) = (H - N)$. We can even say, as we will shortly, that there are two degrees of freedom among these means, so that once two of the tests have been run, the value of the third is no longer unknown or free to vary. As the number of groups increases, this problem gets worse and combines with the first to so alter the probability of a Type I error that the result of any single comparison among means is uninterpretable.

PARTITIONING VARIANCE

We have already encountered the fundamental principle by which these problems were solved; it is a slight variation on the separation of total variance into predictable and unpredictable portions that we encountered in our discussion of correlation in Chapter 9. First, let us consider some hypothetical data for a drug study such as the one just described. We want to study the effects of drug X on learning a list of vocabulary words. We pretest a group of college students and determine that none of them knows any of the words; we then draw three random samples of five students. Each student is to learn a list of 20 words under one of the three conditions: Group H receives a high dose of the drug by injection, group L a low dose (but equal volume) of the drug, and group N is given an equivalent volume injection of saline. The students study the vocabulary words and later are tested to determine how many of the words they learned. Scores are the total number of words correctly defined. The results of the study are shown in Table 16-1.

Double Subscript Notation. We have collected data on 15 people, five in each of three groups. For the purpose of keeping track of the data, we introduce an extension of our summation-notation scheme; we use the subscript i to refer to a person within a group and j to identify the group. Thus, the general symbol for a score is X_{ij}, the score of the ith person in

TABLE 16-1
Data From a Three-Group Drug Study.

N-dimension (Subject)	J-dimension (Group)		
1	11	12	15
2	6	14	11
3	9	11	17
4	8	12	13
5	12	15	16
$\sum X =$	46	64	72
$\sum X^2 =$	446	830	1060
	$\bar{X}_1 = 9.2$	$\bar{X}_2 = 12.8$	$\bar{X}_3 = 14.4$

group j. A particular group is identified by substituting its number ($1 = H$, $2 = L$, $3 = N$) for the subscript j, while inserting numbers for both subscripts specifies a particular score; thus, the sum of scores for the high-drug group has the symbol

$$\sum_{i=1}^{5} X_{i1}$$

and has the numerical value 46. Likewise, X_{14} has the value 8 and X_{22} is 14.

This double subscript notation allows us to specify our summation operations more easily. A single $\sum$ involves summation over only one dimension of the table, while the double summation $\sum\sum$ means that we are using values from the entire table—summing across both the people dimension and the group dimension. We can then use our familiar formulas for means and variances, only changing the number of dimensions across which we sum.

We compute some statistics for our hypothetical data to see how the double summation system works. First, we find the mean of group 1 ($\bar{X}_1$)

$$\bar{X}_1 = \frac{\displaystyle\sum_{i=1}^{5} X_{i1}}{N_1} = \frac{46}{5} = 9.2;$$

likewise, the standard deviation for group 2 (S_2) is

$$S_2 = \sqrt{\frac{N_2 \displaystyle\sum_{i=1}^{5} X_{i2}^2 - \left(\displaystyle\sum_{i=1}^{5} X_{i2}\right)^2}{N_2^2}} = \sqrt{\frac{5(830) - (64)^2}{25}} = 1.47.$$

Note carefully that this is the sample standard deviation, *not* an estimate of σ, which would be $\hat{S}_2$.

The mean and variance for the total study can be computed in the same general way. We use the symbol $\bar{\bar{X}}$ to indicate that the value for the total group is a mean of the group means; S_T^2 is the total variance

$$\bar{\bar{X}} = \frac{\displaystyle\sum_{j=1}^{J} \sum_{i=1}^{N} X_{ij}}{JN} \tag{16.1}$$

$$S_T^2 = \frac{JN \sum\limits_{j=1}^{J} \sum\limits_{i=1}^{N} X_{ij}^2 - \left(\sum\limits_{j=1}^{J} \sum\limits_{i=1}^{N} X_{ij} \right)^2}{(JN)^2}. \qquad (16.2)$$

Both of these equations are written in a general form that allows for any number of groups. However, we have restricted the notations to groups of equal size by using JN for the number of scores. Procedures for groups of unequal size are found in more advanced texts. The other quantities involve finding the sum (either of X's or of X^2's) for each group and then summing across all groups. For the example in Table 16-1, we find $\overline{\overline{X}}$ to be

$$\overline{\overline{X}} = \frac{(46 + 64 + 72)}{(5 + 5 + 5)} = \frac{182}{15} = 12.13.$$

The total variance S_T^2 is

$$S_T^2 = \frac{(15)(1060 + 830 + 446) - (182)^2}{225}$$

$$= \frac{15(2336) - 33,124}{225} = 8.52$$

Partitioning a Score. Now, let us consider again the idea that a score may be composed of several parts. This proposition is illustrated in Figure 16-1. The scores of two individuals, X_{11} and X_{23}, are equal; both are 11. But, if we bring in the information that they belong to different groups, we can say that their scores are composed of three pieces. Everyone in the study contributes information to the total mean $\overline{\overline{X}}$, so we say that $\overline{\overline{X}}$ is a part of each person's score; this part is labeled (a) in the figure. Those people in group 1 contribute information to $\overline{X}_1$, so their scores caused $\overline{X}_1$ to be different from $\overline{\overline{X}}$. This difference $(\overline{X}_1 - \overline{\overline{X}})$, is part of everyone's score in group 1 and is labeled (b) in the figure. Finally, each person contributes something unique to her/his own score, something that makes it more or less different from the group mean; for score X_{11} this part $(X_{11} - \overline{X}_1)$ is labeled (c).

A person in group 3 shares the (a) effect with everyone else; however, the members of group 3 all contribute to the difference between their group mean $\overline{X}_3$ and the total mean $\overline{\overline{X}}$. This difference $(\overline{X}_3 - \overline{\overline{X}})$ is labeled (d). Score X_{23} differs from the group mean by an amount $(X_{23} - \overline{X}_3)$, labeled (e). Notice that (b) and (d) have the same meaning, the difference of a group mean from $\overline{\overline{X}}$, but different numerical values. Similarly, (c) and (e) both represent the difference between a single score and the group mean, but are numerically different.

We now have two scores that are each composed of three parts; in general, we have

$$X_{ij} = \overline{\overline{X}} + (\overline{X}_j - \overline{\overline{X}}) + (X_{ij} - \overline{X}_j). \tag{16.3}$$

The two cases in our example are

$$X_{11} = 11 = 12.13 + (9.2 - 12.13) + (11 - 9.2)$$

$$X_{23} = 11 = 12.13 + (14.4 - 12.13) + (11 - 14.4).$$

Each individual's score is composed of the overall mean plus the deviation of the group mean from the overall mean plus the deviation of the individual's score from the group mean.

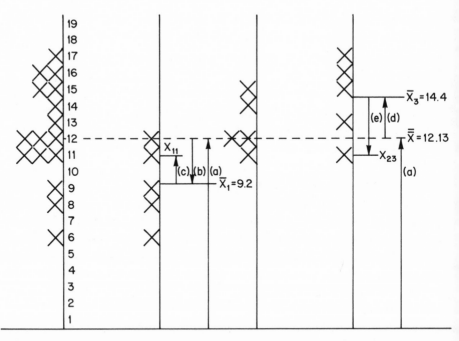

Figure 16-1 Frequency distribution of data from Table 16-1 showing that each score is composed of three parts.

By subtracting $\bar{\bar{X}}$ from both sides of equation 16.3, we can convert the equation to deviations from the overall mean. The deviation of individual X_{ij} from $\bar{\bar{X}}$ is $(X_{ij} - \bar{\bar{X}})$ and is composed of two parts, a deviation of the group mean from $\bar{\bar{X}}$ and the individual's deviation from the group mean. As an equation, this is

$$(X_{ij} - \bar{\bar{X}}) = (\bar{X}_j - \bar{\bar{X}}) + (X_{ij} - \bar{X}_j). \tag{16.4}$$

We know from Chapter 3 that the sum of the deviations of a set of scores from their mean is always zero, so if we take the sum of each of these terms across the JN people in our study, each will have a value of zero. However, we also recall, this time from Chapter 4, that the sum of *squared* deviations is not zero; rather, it is a sum of squares that can be used to calculate a variance. From our discussion of double subscript notation, we see that the sum of squares of all scores around $\bar{\bar{X}}$ can be obtained by summing over both subscripts,

$$SS_T = \sum_j \sum_i (X_{ij} - \bar{\bar{X}})^2.$$

The partitioning of deviations in equation 16.4 shows that this total sum of squares can be broken down into two parts, one part due to the effect of group means and a second part due to the deviations of individuals from the means of their groups.[1] (We shall use SS as a shorthand for sum of squares from now on.) Writing these sums of squared deviation terms out fully in an equation yields

$$\sum_{j=1}^{J} \sum_{i=1}^{N} (X_{ij} - \bar{\bar{X}})^2 = \sum_{j=1}^{J} \sum_{i=1}^{N} (\bar{X}_j - \bar{\bar{X}})^2 + \sum_{j=1}^{J} \sum_{i=1}^{N} (X_{ij} - \bar{X}_j)^2.$$

Notice that for every individual in group j the quantity $(\bar{X}_j - \bar{\bar{X}})$ is the same; therefore, we can substitute, as we have in equation 16.5, $N(\bar{X}_j - \bar{\bar{X}})^2$ for the summation over the N individuals in the group

$$\sum_{j=1}^{J} \sum_{i=1}^{N} (X_{ij} - \bar{\bar{X}})^2 = \sum_{j=1}^{J} \left[N(\bar{X}_j - \bar{\bar{X}})^2 \right] + \sum_{j=1}^{J} \left[\sum_{i=1}^{N} (X_{ij} - \bar{X}_j)^2 \right]. \tag{16.5}$$

The two quantities to the right of the equals sign in equation 16.5 are sums-of-squares. The first, which involves group means, includes only

---

[1] The derivation of this equation is identical to the one for equation 9.5. (See Appendix A.)

differences between or among groups; it is called the *between groups sum-of-squares* or SS_B. The second term contains the deviations of individuals within a group from their own group mean; therefore, it is called the *within groups sum-of-squares* or SS_W. We can now write equation 16.5 in the form

$$SS_T = SS_B + SS_W.$$

The total SS is equal to the sum of its two independent parts.

The null hypothesis. We should now consider what null hypothesis we are testing. Because ANOVA involves several groups, which usually means that the independent variable is a nominal scale, we cannot specify directional hypotheses in most cases. Special methods are needed if we want to test hypotheses about the order of differences among means. Such methods are available (see Winer, 1971) but are beyond our scope. Here, we limit our concern to nondirectional or two-tailed null hypotheses.

As we have seen, a two-tailed null hypothesis has the general form $\mu_1 = \mu_2$. When more than two groups are present in the study, the non-directional null hypothesis specifies the equality of all means. The null hypothesis that is appropriate for our three-group drug study is

$$\mu_H = \mu_L = \mu_N.$$

If the null hypothesis is true, then our three groups may be considered random samples from the same population (or from three populations with identical means and variances, which is essentially the same thing). A true null condition implies that differences among the groups are no greater than would be expected to occur by chance under the conditions of random sampling.

VARIANCE ESTIMATES

In Chapter 14, we discussed two ideas that are central to understanding ANOVA; the first of these is degrees of freedom and the second is that a sum-of-squares divided by its degrees of freedom is an unbiased estimate of the variance in the population from which the sample was drawn. Recalling this, we see that each of the terms in equation 16.5 can be converted into a variance estimate by dividing by the appropriate df. The variance estimates and df's appropriate to each sum-of-squares are

$$\hat{S}_T^2 = \frac{\sum_j \sum_i (X_{ij} - \bar{\bar{X}})^2}{JN - 1} = \frac{SS_T}{JN - 1}$$

$$\hat{S}_W^2 = \frac{\sum_j [\sum_i (X_{ij} - \bar{X}_j)^2]}{JN - J} = \frac{SS_W}{JN - J} \qquad (16.6)$$

$$\hat{S}_B^2 = \frac{\sum_j [N(\bar{X}_j - \bar{\bar{X}})^2]}{J - 1} = \frac{SS_B}{J - 1}.$$

These variance estimates are called mean squares or *MS*'s.

Note that while the *SS*'s in equation 16.5 are additive, the *MS*'s or variance estimates in equation 16.6 are not; that is, the *SS*'s form an equation, but $\hat{S}_T^2$ is not equal to the sum of $\hat{S}_W^2$ and $\hat{S}_B^2$. The equality is destroyed because the two sides of equation 16.5 are divided by different quantities to obtain the variance estimates in equation 16.6. The degrees of freedom, however, are additive

$$JN - 1 = (JN - J) + (J - 1)$$

$$df_{\text{total}} = df_{\text{within}} + df_{\text{between}}.$$

Under the assumptions that the null hypothesis is true and that our groups represent *J* random samples from a single population, we consider a population variance, σ^2. The best estimate that we have of σ^2 is $\hat{S}_T^2$, the variance estimate based on *JN* individuals that loses one *df* for the overall mean; however, we note that $\hat{S}_W^2$ is also an estimate of σ^2, but based on an average of several samples

$$\hat{S}_W^2 = \frac{\sum_j [\sum_i (X_{ij} - \bar{X}_j)^2]}{JN - J} = \frac{\sum \left[\frac{\sum_i (X_{ij} - \bar{X}_j)^2}{N - 1} \right]}{J}.$$

That is, assuming the null is true, each of the groups provides an unbiased estimate of σ^2 from

$$\frac{\sum_i (X_{ij} - \bar{X}_j)^2}{N - 1}.$$

Because the sum of deviations (*not* squared deviations) must be zero within each group, there are $(N - 1)$ degrees of freedom associated with the sum-of-squares within each group. But there are *J* independent groups, so the degrees of freedom associated with SS_W is $J(N - 1)$ or $(JN - J)$, and $\hat{S}_W^2$ is simply an average of these J unbiased estimates of σ^2. Therefore, $\hat{S}_W^2$ is an unbiased estimate of the same population variance σ^2. A null hypothesis that the samples are drawn from different populations but that the means and variances of these populations are the same gives us $\hat{S}_W^2$ as an estimate of each of these variances.

Now, let us turn our attention to $\hat{S}_B^2$. We note that $\hat{S}_B^2$ involves the division of a sum of deviations squared of means about their mean by their *df*. If we think of $\overline{\overline{X}}$ as a best estimate of μ, then we can view the sample means as deviating around this value. This looks rather like the situation that gave rise to the concept of the standard error of the mean; that is, in the data from our study, we have a variance of sample means around the overall mean. It is as though we had taken several samples from the population and were estimating the standard error of the mean in the population from the variability among the means of our samples. Viewed in this way, we find that $\hat{S}_{\overline{X}}^2$ is an unbiased estimate of the population variance $\sigma_{\overline{X}}^2$

$$\hat{S}_{\overline{X}}^2 = \frac{\sum(\overline{X}_j - \overline{\overline{X}})^2}{J - 1}.$$

Since

$$\hat{S}_B^2 = \frac{N \sum\limits_j (\overline{X}_j - \overline{\overline{X}})^2}{J - 1} = N \frac{\sum(\overline{X}_j - \overline{\overline{X}})^2}{J - 1},$$

then by substitution

$$\hat{S}_B^2 = N\hat{S}_{\overline{X}}^2.$$

We recall from Chapter 14 that the unbiased estimate of $\sigma_{\overline{X}}^2$ is given by

$$\hat{S}_{\overline{X}}^2 = \frac{\hat{S}_X^2}{N},$$

which means that

$$N\hat{S}_{\overline{X}}^2 = \hat{S}_X^2.$$

But $\hat{S}_B^2$ also equals $N\hat{S}_{\overline{X}}^2$, so we conclude that under the conditions specified by the null hypothesis, $\hat{S}_B^2$ is an unbiased estimate of σ^2 because $\hat{S}_X^2$ is an unbiased estimate of σ^2.

Notice, also, that $(J - 1)$ are the appropriate degrees of freedom for SS_B. Because

$$\sum_{j=1}^{J} (\bar{X}_j - \bar{\bar{X}}) = 0,$$

there are only $(J - 1)$ values of $\bar{X}_j$ that are free to vary. Therefore, any variance estimate based on SS_B can only have $(J - 1)$ degrees of freedom.

There is one additional feature of $\hat{S}_B^2$ and $\hat{S}_W^2$ that can help us see why we analyze variances to test hypotheses about means. Remember that all the statistics we have discussed to date have sampling distributions. Every sampling distribution has a mean that is known as the expected value of the statistic and denoted by the symbol $\mathscr{E}$. When the expected value of the statistic is the parameter, we say the statistic is unbiased; thus,

$$\mathscr{E}(\bar{X}) = \mu_X$$

$$\mathscr{E}(S_X^2) = \sigma_X^2.$$

It is possible to apply the concept of expected values to our present variance estimates. Using some algebra that need not concern us (see McNemar, 1969, pp. 292–301 for details), it is possible to show that

$$\mathscr{E}(\hat{S}_W^2) = \sigma_X^2 \tag{16.7}$$

but that

$$\mathscr{E}(\hat{S}_B^2) = \sigma_X^2 + N\sigma_{\mu_j}^2, \tag{16.8}$$

where $\sigma_{\mu_j}^2$ is the variance among the means of the populations from which our samples were drawn. If the conditions specified by either form of the null hypothesis that (1) all samples come from one population or (2) all population means are equal are true, then the value of $\sigma_{\mu_j}^2$ would be zero. Thus, we can restate our null hypothesis in a new form: The null hypothesis that $\mu_1 = \mu_2 = \mu_3$ is equivalent to the hypothesis

$$\sigma_{\mu_j}^2 = 0$$

or the variance among population means is zero. If this condition is true, $\hat{S}_B^2$ is the estimate of σ_X^2 that we developed earlier; if the null is true, $\hat{S}_B^2$ and $\hat{S}_W^2$ are both estimates of the same variance. Because $\sigma_{\mu_j}^2$ can never be negative, we can say that $\mathscr{E}(\hat{S}_B^2) \geq \mathscr{E}(\hat{S}_W^2)$. This gives us two quantities that under the null conditions, both estimate the same variance, but with one $(\hat{S}_B^2)$ always the larger variance.

In Chapter 15, we developed a test statistic F that is based on the ratio of two unbiased estimates of a variance. The sampling distribution of F was seen to be complex, depending on the degrees of freedom for the numerator variance and the degrees of freedom for the denominator variance. The F statistic itself was used to test the null hypothesis that the two variances were estimates of the same population variance or represented two samples drawn from populations with equal variances.

Let us take stock of where we are. We have converted our null hypothesis about means into one that involves variances. We have two variances, $\hat{S}_B^2$ with $(J - 1)$ degrees of freedom and $\hat{S}_W^2$ with $(JN - J)$, or $J(N - 1)$, degrees of freedom, both of which are estimates of the same population variance under the conditions of the null hypothesis. We have the F statistic as a means of testing a null hypothesis of the equality of two variances. Finally, we have the condition that $\mathscr{E}(\hat{S}_B^2) \geq \mathscr{E}(\hat{S}_W^2)$, which means that if we form an F ratio to test the null hypothesis, we *must* put $\hat{S}_B^2$ in the numerator to be consistent with our rule of putting the larger variance in the numerator.

Clearly, when we have $\hat{S}_B^2$ and $\hat{S}_W^2$ (or MS_B and MS_W, in more conventional ANOVA terminology), we can form an F ratio to test the hypothesis that the two variances are equal

$$F = \frac{\hat{S}_B^2}{\hat{S}_W^2} = \frac{MS_B}{MS_W} = \frac{SS_B/df_B}{SS_W/df_W} \ . \tag{16.9}$$

This F has $(J - 1)$ and $J(N - 1)$ for its numerator and denominator degrees of freedom, respectively. A study that yields a value of F exceeding the appropriate critical value will cause us to reject the null hypothesis that gave rise to the study. By substituting equations 16.7 and 16.8 in equation 16.9 we get

$$F = \frac{\sigma_X^2 + N\sigma_{\mu_j}^2}{\sigma_X^2} \ . \tag{16.10}$$

Thus, a statistically significant value of F can be interpreted to mean that the value of $\sigma_{\mu_j}^2$ is not zero, which implies that we must reject the hypothesis that the means are equal.

COMPUTING THE ANSWER

Definition equations. The general equations in 16.5 or 16.6 are sometimes used to compute the quantities needed to perform an analysis of variance. They are repeated here for convenience and will be used to illustrate the necessary computations in Table 16-1. (It should now be clear why the procedures described in this chapter are called analysis of variance even though the basic null hypothesis involves means. We have broken down the total variance into its component parts and tested our hypothesis with these components.) From equations 16.5 and 16.6

$$SS_T = \sum_j \sum_i (X_{ij} - \bar{\bar{X}})^2$$

$$SS_B = N \sum_j (\bar{X}_j - \bar{\bar{X}})^2$$

$$SS_W = \sum_j \sum_i (X_{ij} - \bar{X}_j)^2$$

$$MS_B = \frac{SS_B}{df_B} = \frac{N \sum_j (\bar{X}_j - \bar{\bar{X}})^2}{J - 1}$$

$$MS_W = \frac{SS_W}{df_W} = \frac{\sum_j \sum_i (X_{ij} - \bar{X}_j)^2}{J(N - 1)} \, .$$

Calculations using these formulas are quite straightforward, although often somewhat time consuming. SS_T is found by subtracting $\bar{\bar{X}}$ from the score of every individual in every group, squaring each difference, and summing over all observations; thus,

$$SS_T = (11 - 12.13)^2 + (6 - 12.13)^2 + (9 - 12.13)^2 + (8 - 12.13)^2$$
$$+ \ldots + (17 - 12.13)^2 + (13 - 12.13)^2 + (16 - 12.13)^2$$
$$= 127.73.$$

SS_B is computed from the group means and $\bar{\bar{X}}$

$$SS_B = 5(9.2 - 12.13)^2 + 5(12.8 - 12.13)^2 + 5(14.4 - 12.13)^2$$
$$= 5[(9.2 - 12.13)^2 + (12.8 - 12.13)^2 + (14.4 - 12.13)^2]$$
$$= 5(8.5849 + 0.4489 + 5.1529)$$
$$= 5(14.1867) = 70.9335.$$

SS_W can be computed either by the computational formula

$$SS_W = [(11 - 9.2)^2 + (6 - 9.2)^2 + (9 - 9.2)^2 + (8 - 9.2)^2$$
$$+ (12 - 9.2)^2] + [(12 - 12.8)^2 + (14 - 12.8)^2 + \ldots$$

$$+ (15 - 12.8)^2] + [(15 - 14.4)^2 + (11 - 14.4)^2 + \ldots$$
$$+ (16 - 14.4)^2]$$
$$= 56.8.$$

or by subtraction from the relationship

$$SS_W = SS_T - SS_B$$
$$SS_W = 127.73 - 70.93$$
$$= 56.8.$$

We next calculate the necessary mean squares

$$MS_B = \frac{70.93}{2} = 35.465$$

$$MS_W = \frac{56.8}{12} = 4.733.$$

Inserting these MS's in the equation for F yields

$$F = \frac{35.465}{4.773} = 7.49,$$

which has $df_B = 2$ and $df_W = 12$. Looking in Appendix Table B-4, we find that the 0.01 critical value for an F with two and 12 degrees of freedom is 6.93. Since our obtained F exceeds this value, we would probably decide to reject the null hypothesis.

Computational Formulas. We would not use definitional equations for most problems because they require working with decimals. There are several alternatives that allow us to work with sums and sums-of-squares computed directly from the data table. For all of them, the needed quantities can be obtained from the $\sum X$ and $\sum X^2$ for each group.

The computational scheme presented here is known as the *df*-components method. This name comes from the fact that there is a particular sum that is associated with each term in the degrees of freedom, and these sums are used exactly as specified in the formula for degrees of freedom.

First, let us consider the various df terms; we have $df_T = JN - 1$, $df_B = J - 1$, and $df_W = JN - J$. There are three unique components here: JN, J, and 1. There is also a sum associated with each, and the expressions for df tells us how to combine them. There are two dimensions to our data table in 16-1. There is a J dimension that refers to groups and an N dimension that refers to people. Each of the *df* components involves these dimensions and tells us which quantities to square and sum. For each component, we sum across the dimensions not mentioned in the component, then we square each of the resulting sums, divide by the number of things summed, and sum across the dimensions that are included in the component. All this sounds complicated, but it is really quite simple once we get the hang of it. (So are high-wire walking and stunt car driving!) The trick is to lay the data out so that we can see what needs to be calculated.

Table 16-2 contains the data on our drug experiment with more complete computations. The first thing to do is find $\sum X$ and $\sum X^2$ in each cell of the table (that is, for each group); these values are given at the end of the table.

As a general rule, we must square as many things as are specified in the component; the 1 component involves squaring a single quantity, the J component involves squaring J (in this case, three) quantities, while the JN component requires 15 items ($J \cdot N = 3 \cdot 5$) in our example. Our rules are as follows:

1. Sum across the dimensions that *are not* mentioned in the component.
2. Square each of the resulting sums.
3. Divide by the number of things summed.
4. Sum across the dimensions that *are* mentioned in the component.

TABLE 16-2
Computing Sums and Sums-of-Squares

Subject N	High	Low	None	
1	11	12	15	
2	6	14	11	
3	9	11	17	
4	8	12	13	
5	12	15	16	
N totals				*JN totals*
$\sum X =$	46	64	72	$182 = \sum \sum X$
$\sum X^2 =$	446	830	1060	$2336 = \sum \sum X^2$

Let us now see how these rules apply to our data. In the 1 component, both the J dimension and the N dimension are not mentioned; therefore, we sum over both of them, which is $\sum \sum X_{ij}$. In fact, we can say that the 1 component always involves the total sum of scores. When we have found the sums for the cells, we sum these to get

$$\sum \left(\sum X \right) = 46 + 64 + 72 = 182.$$

The next two rules tell us to square this result and divide by the number of things summed. This yields

$$\frac{\left(\sum_j \sum_i X_{ij} \right)^2}{JN} = \frac{(182)^2}{15} = \frac{33,124}{15} = 2,208.27.$$

Since there is only 1 in the component, we do not have to sum in the last step, and 2,208.27 is the quantity associated with the 1 df component.

The JN component mentions both dimensions; therefore, we are dealing with single scores and have no unmentioned dimension to sum over. There are $15 X_{ij}^2$'s, and since each is a single number, we need not divide. Rule 4 tells us to sum over the remaining dimensions, which yields

$$\sum_j \sum_i X_{ij}^2 = 2336.$$

This sum is easily computed by summing the $\sum X^2$'s for each group. In general, we can say that the df component that includes all dimensions (JN in this case) always involves the sum of the squares of all the individual scores.

Finally, we have the J component. Since N is not specified in the component, we must sum over this dimension, which gives us a value of $\sum_i X_{ij}$

for each group. These sums are then squared and divided by the number of things summed

$$\sum_{i=1}^{N} X_{i1} = 46 \qquad \sum_i X_{i2} = 64 \qquad \sum_i X_{i3} = 72$$

$$\frac{(\sum X_{i1})^2}{N} = \frac{(46)^2}{5} = \frac{2116}{5} = 423.2$$

$$\frac{(\sum X_{i2})^2}{N} = \frac{(64)^2}{5} = \frac{4096}{5} = 819.2$$

$$\frac{(\sum X_{i3})^2}{N} = \frac{(72)^2}{5} = \frac{5184}{5} = 1036.8.$$

In the last step, we add these values together

$$\sum_{j=1}^{J} \frac{(\sum_i X_{ij})^2}{N} = 423.2 + 819.2 + 1036.8 = 2279.2.$$

We summarize the degrees-of-freedom components as shown in Table 16-3. Each value is obtained from relatively simple computations involving a minimum of division and no $\bar{X}$'s.

Now comes the magic and hocus-pocus. We take the expression for the degrees of freedom for each variance estimate and substitute the values we computed for the *df* components to obtain the sums-of-squares.

TABLE 16-3
Computing Sums and Sums-of-Squares.

df Component	*Computational Formula*	*Numerical Value*
1	$\dfrac{\left(\sum\limits_j \sum\limits_i X_{ij}\right)^2}{JN}$	2208.27
JN	$\sum\limits_j \sum\limits_i X_{ij}^2$	2336
J	$\sum\limits_{j=1}^{J} \dfrac{\left(\sum\limits_{i=1}^{N} X_{ij}\right)^2}{N}$	2279.2

Calculations

$$SS_T \quad \rightarrow \quad JN - 1 \quad \rightarrow \quad \sum_j \sum_i X_{ij}^2 - \frac{\left(\sum_j \sum_i X_{ij}\right)^2}{JN}$$

$$SS_B \quad \rightarrow \quad J - 1 \quad \rightarrow \quad \sum_{j=1}^{J} \frac{\left(\sum_{i=1}^{N} X_{ij}\right)^2}{N} - \frac{\left(\sum_j \sum_i X_{ij}\right)^2}{JN}$$

$$SS_{\text{H}} \quad \rightarrow \quad JN - J \quad \rightarrow \quad \sum_j \sum_i X_{ij}^2 - \sum_{j=1}^{J} \frac{\left(\sum_{i=1}^{N} X_{ij}\right)^2}{N}$$

The df_T is given by $(JN - 1)$, so we subtract the 1 component from the JN component

$SS_T(JN - 1) = 2336 \quad - 2208.27 = 127.73.$

Treating the other two SS's in the same way, we get

$SS_B(J - 1) = 2279.2 - 2208.27 = \quad 70.93$

$SS_W(JN - J) = 2336 \quad - 2279.2 \quad = \quad 56.8.$

The value of this procedure is threefold: First, it is quick and easy (a little like making an omelet: Telling how takes longer than doing it). Second, it is completely general. Analysis of variance can involve very complex designs with multiple independent variables; nevertheless, the rules for computing and combining df components apply in every case. Third, the procedure provides a handy mnemonic for remembering what goes where. The complete computational formulas for the sums-of-squares are included at the end of Table 16-3.

PRESENTING AND INTERPRETING RESULTS

The results of an analysis of variance are presented in a table called a Summary Table. The Summary Table for our example is given in Table 16-4 and includes five columns. The column labeled source specifies which source of variance or which variance estimate is being summarized in each row. The between-groups source is shown in the first row; the within-groups source in the second; and total in the last row. Column 2, labeled SS, gives the values of the sums-of-squares; the df column gives the degrees of freedom associated with each source. The values in the MS, or mean square column, are, of course, the SS's divided by their degrees of freedom; since MS_{total} is not used in any computations, it is generally omitted. The F column gives the value of the F statistic, MS_B/MS_W; it is not uncommon for asterisks (*) to be used to indicate F's that exceed the standard critical values.

While the purpose of the analysis of variance is the same as the t test, testing hypotheses about the equality of population means, its interpretation is considerably more complex. A statistically significant value for t is interpreted to mean that the difference between the two sample means is greater than would be expected by chance under the conditions specified by the null hypothesis. A statistically significant value for F implies that the variance due to the differences among the several group means is greater than would be expected by chance under the null hypothesis conditions. Unfortunately, neither the F itself nor any of the mean squares give us information about which mean differences are responsible for the statistical significance. We cannot tell from Table 16-4 which means differ from which.

The solution to this problem involves going back to a point that is closer to the original data. First, we can go to the cell or treatment-group means. Graphs of the means, such as the one in Figure 16-2, often help interpretation, particularly when the number of means to be considered is large. From this graph, it is easy to see that the low-drug group is more similar to the no-drug group than it is to the high-drug group. Also, from the graph and direct inspection of the group means, we would probably be safe in concluding that the high-drug-group mean is statistically significantly different from the no-drug mean and that this difference is at least part of the cause of the significant F.

We begin to encounter real difficulties when we attempt to extend our interpretations. Can we conclude that the difference between any other pair of means is statistically significant? Unfortunately, we can not draw such conclusions from the ANOVA itself; in fact, even our apparently safe decision about μ_H and μ_N is not entirely secure. In order to reach conclusions about specific pairs of means after a significant F, we must perform what are called *post hoc contrasts*.

Post hoc contrasts. The principle that gives rise to post hoc, or after the fact, contrasts is that we can get a clear interpretation only when we compare pairs of things. For example, if we compare the high-drug-group

TABLE 16-4
Summary Table for an Analysis of Variance.

Source	SS	df	MS	F
Between	70.93	2	35.465	7.49
Within	56.8	12	4.733	
Total	127.73	14		

mean with the low-drug-group mean and obtain a statistically significant result, we can make a clear interpretation of the relationship between the two drug dosages and behavior.

One way to attack the problem could be to compute t tests for pairs of means; unfortunately, this is improper for the same reasons that caused us to develop the methods of ANOVA in the first place. Even if we only compared the two most extreme means, computing only one t, that t is suspect simply because we chose the largest of the several possible differences; we biased the comparison in our favor.

A number of statisticians have developed procedures for dealing with this problem. Some are appropriate under certain conditions, others under different conditions; some analyze pairs of means, while others can be used in more complex situations. Many of these methods are described in Winer (1971) and other more advanced texts. Here, we present a method for post hoc comparisons developed by Scheffé (1959). It has the advantage that it is easy to understand and compute, applies to most situations, and is conservative (that is, if a comparison is significant using this procedure, you can be confident that the relationship it represents would have been found to be significant if you had designed the original study to make only this comparison).

Before we begin, we must dispose of an item of terminology. The mean square within groups is often called the error mean square or MS_E. This MS_E is exactly like the pooled variance estimate that we used to make our

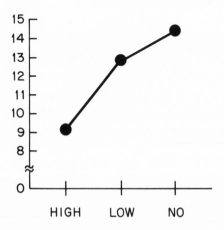

Figure 16-2   Plot of group means for drug study.

two group t tests in Chapter 14 (they are identical for two groups); thus, we can use this MS_E just like an $\hat{S}_p^2$, where the pooling has involved more than two groups.

First, we must define a contrast. A contrast C is the difference between two selected means or averages of means. We may, for example, wish to form a contrast between the high-drug group and the average of the low- and no-drug groups. The general form for such contrasts is

$$(16.11)$$

$$C = \frac{N_a\bar{X}_a + N_b\bar{X}_b + \ldots + N_k\bar{X}_k}{N_a + N_b + \ldots + N_k} - \frac{N_l\bar{X}_l + N_m\bar{X}_m + \ldots + N_z\bar{X}_z}{N_l + N_m + \ldots + N_z}$$

That is, the value of the contrast C is the difference between the weighted average of the means on one side of the comparison and the weighted average of the means on the other side. Each mean is weighted by its sample size. For the contrast proposed above, this would be

$$C = \frac{N_H\bar{X}_H}{N_H} - \frac{N_L\bar{X}_L + N_N\bar{X}_N}{N_L + N_N}$$

$$C = \frac{5(9.2)}{5} - \frac{5(12.8) + 5(14.4)}{5 + 5} = 9.2 - \frac{12.8 + 14.4}{2} = -4.4.$$

Next, we must compute the standard error of the contrast. Recalling that MS_E or MS_W is equivalent to $\hat{S}_p^2$, we can compute a variance error for C from the general equation

$$\hat{S}_C^2 = MS_E \left(\frac{1}{N_a + N_b + \ldots + N_k} + \frac{1}{N_l + N_m + \ldots + N_z} \right). \quad (16.12)$$

The square root of equation 16.12 gives the necessary standard error. For our problem this gives

$$\hat{S}_C^2 = 4.733 \left(\frac{1}{5} + \frac{1}{5 + 5} \right) = 4.733 \, (0.2 + 0.1) = 1.4199$$

$$\hat{S}_C = \sqrt{1.4199} = 1.1916.$$

As we noted, the Scheffé procedure is used after finding a significant F. The procedure uses the critical value of F to calculate what we might call a corrected critical value for t. We then compute a t in the ordinary way using C and $\hat{S}_C$.

$$t = \frac{C}{\hat{S}_C}. \quad (16.13)$$

If this t exceeds the corrected critical value for t, we conclude that the difference between the two portions of the contrast is statistically significant.

The corrected critical value is found by multiplying the critical value of the appropriate F by the between groups degrees of freedom and taking the square root of the resulting product; that is, we look up the F at the chosen α for df_B and df_W. For our example with $df_B = 2$ and $df_W = 12$ and $\alpha = 0.01$, the appropriate F is 6.93. This is then multiplied by df_B to give 13.86, which has a square root of 3.723

$$t_{\substack{\text{corrected} \\ \text{critical}}} = \sqrt{(df_B)} \, (F_{df_B, df_W}). \tag{16.14}$$

This corrected critical t has the same α level as the F.

The final step is to use equation 16.13 to compute a t for the contrast. For our data this gives

$$t = \frac{-4.4}{1.1916} = -3.693,$$

which is only slightly smaller than the critical value. Our post hoc contrast does not lead us to reject the null hypothesis that the high-drug group is not different from the average of the other two. Of course, if we had selected the 0.05 level for α, we would have reached a different conclusion.

One of the advantages of the Scheffé procedure is that it can be used repeatedly with the same data, so that we can test other contrasts easily and without violating our chosen α level. For example, the contrast between the high and no-drug groups would proceed as follows:

$$C = 9.2 - 14.4 = -5.2$$

$$\hat{S}_C = \sqrt{4.733 \left(\frac{1}{5} + \frac{1}{5}\right)} = \sqrt{1.8932} = 1.376$$

$$t = \frac{-5.2}{1.376} = -3.779.$$

The corrected critical value for t remains the same for all contrasts from the study, so we would reject the null hypothesis that $\mu_H = \mu_N$ at the $\alpha = 0.01$ level on the basis of these data.

SUMMARY

Many research problems in the behavioral and social sciences require a study design using more than two groups. Results of such studies should not ordinarily be analyzed by comparing pairs of means because t tests so computed are not independent of each other. The results of one comparison affect the magnitude of others; also, multiple t tests increase the risk of making a Type I error.

The alternative to multiple t tests is the *analysis of variance* or *ANOVA*. ANOVA involves partitioning the total variance among scores into two parts: a variance due to differences between groups and a variance within groups. These two variances are both independent estimates of the population variance under the conditions specified in the null hypothesis. The F ratio with degrees of freedom of $(J - 1)$ and $(JN - J)$ is used to test the equality of the two variances. A significant value for F leads to rejecting the null hypothesis and the conclusion that the variance among means is greater than would be expected by chance.

ANOVA requires computing SS_B and SS_W (which sum to SS_T). The df component method can be used for these calculations. The sums-of-squares are then divided by their degrees of freedom to produce the mean squares: $F = MS_B/MS_W$.

Interpreting results is aided by graphs of means and by performing *post hoc contrasts*, which involve combinations of means. MS_W is used as a pooled variance to compute a standard error for the contrast. A corrected critical value for t, computed from the F and df_B, is used for all post hoc contrasts in the study.

PROBLEMS

1. A student decided to measure the masculinity of participants in several college sports. The student believed that participants in more violent sports (football and wrestling) would have higher masculinity scores than would participants in nonviolent sports (tennis and track). The results for four subjects in each group were:

Football	Wrestling	Tennis	Track
31	26	18	14
20	27	13	15
27	31	15	17
22	25	20	19

Answer the following questions with respect to these data:
(a) What is the numerical value for each of the following?

$*$i X_{24} ii X_{13}

$*$iii $\sum\limits_{i=1}^{4} X_{i1}$ iv $\sum\limits_{i=1}^{4} X_{i4}$

$*$v $\sum\limits_{i=1}^{4} (X_{i1} - \bar{X}_1)^2$ vi $\sum\limits_{i=1}^{4} (X_{i3} - \bar{X}_3)^2$

$*$vii $\sum\limits_{j=1}^{4} \sum\limits_{i=1}^{4} X_{ij}$ viii $\sum\limits_{j=1}^{4} \sum\limits_{i=1}^{4} X_{ij}^2$

$*$(b) What is the overall null hypothesis?

$*$(c) Perform the analysis of variance on the data given using deviation formulas 16.6.

$*$(d) Repeat the analysis using the *df*-component formulas from Table 16-3. Are the results identical? Why might you expect some differences?

$*$(e) Prepare a summary table of your results and interpret them.

$*$(f) For element X_{24}, show that $(X_{ij} - \bar{\bar{X}}) = (X_{ij} - \bar{X}_j) + (\bar{X}_j - \bar{\bar{X}})$.

$*$(g) The original hypothesis could have been stated as a contrast between football and wrestling, on one hand and tennis and track, on the other.

i State the hypothesis for this contrast.

ii Perform the contrast as a post-hoc contrast and interpret your results.

iii Perform any other contrasts that might be of interest.

$*$(h) Are we justified in inferring a causal relationship? Explain your answer.

$*$Answers to starred questions are found in Appendix D.

2. The superintendent of a large city school system has decided to find out whether any one of the four algebra books available to the system is better than the others. There are 20 algebra classes available for study, so the superintendent randomly assigns classes to books. Each book is used by five classes.

(a) What is the sampling unit in this study? What are the degrees of freedom?

(b) Discuss the concept of a treatment population in a study such as this.

The score for each class was the class mean on a common final exam. The results for the 20 classes are given. Answer questions $1a–1f$ and $1h$ with respect to this study. Run any appropriate post-hoc comparisons.

Book A	Book B	Book C	Book D
107	106	108	135
111	112	114	131
99	105	106	138
97	105	95	129
106	109	114	121

PART IV

APPENDICES

Appendix A

ALGEBRA SUPPLEMENT: SELECTED DERIVATIONS

CONTENTS

The material presented in this section is not essential for understanding and using the data analysis procedures described in the text. In fact, many students find that too much mathematical detail in statistics interferes with understanding the application of formulas to practical problems. However, other students find that their understanding is enhanced if they can trace the development of equations from the definition to the usable forms. For those students who desire the algebraic details development of selected equations is given in detail, in this section.

Rules for the Algebra of Summations.

Rule I. Summing a constant: summing a constant C over N observations is equivalent to multiplying the constant by N

$$\sum_{i=1}^{N} C = NC.$$

Rule II. Distributing the summation sign: summing the sums or differences of two or more variables is equivalent to taking the sum or difference of their sums

(sum) $$\sum_{i=1}^{N} (X_i + Y_i + Z_i) = \sum_{i=1}^{N} X_i + \sum_{i=1}^{N} Y_i + \sum_{i=1}^{N} Z_i$$

(difference) $$\sum_{i=1}^{N} (X_i - Y_i) = \sum_{i=1}^{N} X_i - \sum_{i=1}^{N} Y_i.$$

Rule III. Product of a constant and variable: Summing the product of a constant and a variable is equivalent to multiplying the sum of the variable by the constant

$$\sum_{i=1}^{N} CX_i = C \sum_{i=1}^{N} X_i.$$

Rule IV. Equivalence of division and multiplication: It will occasionally be helpful to make use of the fact that

$$\frac{X}{Y} = \frac{1}{Y} (X).$$

Computational formulas for S^2 (all summations are $i = 1, N$).

STEP	JUSTIFICATION
1. $S^2 = \dfrac{\sum (X - \bar{X})^2}{N}$	Definition of S^2
2. $= \dfrac{1}{N} \sum (X - \bar{X})^2$	Rule IV
3. $= \dfrac{1}{N} \sum (X^2 - 2X\bar{X} + \bar{X}^2)$	Squaring $(X - \bar{X})$
4. $= \dfrac{1}{N} (\sum X^2 - \sum 2X\bar{X} + \sum \bar{X}^2)$	Rule II
5. $= \dfrac{1}{N} (\sum X^2 - 2\bar{X} \sum X + N\bar{X}^2)$	Rules I and III
6. $= \dfrac{1}{N} \left[\sum X^2 - 2\left(\dfrac{\sum X}{N}\right) \sum X + N \left(\dfrac{\sum X}{N}\right)^2 \right]$	Substituting definition of $\bar{X}$
7. $= \dfrac{1}{N} \left[\sum X^2 - 2\dfrac{(\sum X)^2}{N} + N \dfrac{(\sum X)^2}{N^2} \right]$	$(\sum X)(\sum X) = (\sum X)^2$ $\left(\dfrac{\sum X}{N}\right)^2 = \dfrac{(\sum X)^2}{N^2}$
8. $= \dfrac{1}{N} \left[\sum X^2 - 2\dfrac{(\sum X)^2}{N} + \dfrac{(\sum X)^2}{N} \right]$	Canceling N's in last term

STEP	JUSTIFICATION
9. $= \dfrac{1}{N}\left[\sum X^2 - \dfrac{(\sum X)^2}{N}\right]$	Adding
10a. $= \dfrac{\sum X^2}{N} - \dfrac{(\sum X)^2}{N^2}$	Distributing $\dfrac{1}{N}$
11a. $S^2 = \dfrac{\sum X^2}{N} - \bar{X}^2$	$\dfrac{(\sum X)^2}{N^2} = \left(\dfrac{\sum X}{N}\right)^2 = \bar{X}^2$ Reversing Rule IV
10b. $= \dfrac{\sum X^2 - \dfrac{(\sum X)^2}{N}}{N}$	
11b. $= \dfrac{N\left[\sum X^2 - \dfrac{(\sum X)^2}{N}\right]}{N(N)}$	Multiplying numerator and denominator by N
12b. $S^2 = \dfrac{N\sum X^2 - (\sum X)^2}{N^2}$	Distributing and canceling N's

The mean as a least squares value $\left(\text{all } \sum\text{'s are } \sum\limits_{i=1}^{N} \right)$.

STEP	JUSTIFICATION
1. $K = \bar{X} \pm a \; (a \neq 0)$	Defining K as any value other than $\bar{X}$
2. $x' = X - K$	Defining deviation score as x'
3. $x' = X - (\bar{X} \pm a)$	Substituting definition of K
4. $x' = (X - \bar{X}) \pm a$	Rearranging parentheses
5. $x'^2 = [(X - \bar{X}) \pm a]^2$	Squaring both sides
6. $\sum x_i'^2 = \sum [(X_i - \bar{X}) \pm a]^2$	Summing both sides ($i = 1, N$)
7. $\sum x_i'^2 = \sum (X_i - X)^2 \pm 2a \sum (\bar{X}_i - \bar{X}) + Na^2$	Squaring right side and using Rules I, II, and III
8. $\sum x_i'^2 = \sum (X - \bar{X})^2 + Na^2$	$\sum (X - \bar{X}) = 0$

Since Na^2 cannot be negative or zero, $\sum x_i'^2$ must be greater than $\sum x_i^2$, and the sum of squared deviations is less about the mean than about any other value.

Subtracting a constant $\left(\text{all } \sum\text{'s are } \sum_{i=1}^{N}\right)$.

STEP	JUSTIFICATION
1. $R_i = X_i - C$	Defining R_i as X_i minus constant C
2. $\sum R_i = \sum (X_i - C)$	Summing both sides over i
3. $\sum R_i = \sum X_i - \sum C$	Rule II
4. $\sum R_i = \sum X_i - NC$	Rule I
5. $\dfrac{\sum R_i}{N} = \dfrac{\sum X_i}{N} - \dfrac{NC}{N}$	Dividing both sides by N
6. $\bar{R} = \bar{X} - C$	Canceling N's and substituting

Multiplying by a constant (all summations are $i = 1, N$).

STEP	JUSTIFICATION
1. $\quad R_i = CX_i$	Defining R_i as X_i times constant C
2. $\quad \sum R_i = \sum (CX_i)$	Summing both sides over i
3. $\quad \dfrac{\sum R_i}{N} = \dfrac{\sum (CX_i)}{N}$	Dividing both sides by N
4. $\quad \dfrac{\sum R_i}{N} = C \dfrac{\sum X_i}{N}$	Rule III and rearranging terms
5. $\quad \bar{R} = C\bar{X}$	Substituting $\bar{X}$ and $\bar{R}$
6. $\quad \dfrac{\sum (R - \bar{R})^2}{N} = \dfrac{\sum (CX - C\bar{X})^2}{N}$	Definition of variance of R and its equivalent CX
7. $\quad\quad\quad = \dfrac{\sum (C^2X^2 - 2\widehat{CX}C\bar{X} + C^2\bar{X}^2)}{N}$	Multiplying term on the right

	STEP	JUSTIFICATION
8.	$= \dfrac{C^2 \sum X^2 - 2C^2 N\bar{X}\sum X + C^2 N\bar{X}^2}{N}$	Rules I, II, and III
9.	$= \dfrac{C^2(\sum X^2 - 2N\bar{X}\sum X + N\bar{X}^2)}{N}$	Factoring out C^2
10.	$= \dfrac{C^2\left[\sum (X - \bar{X})^2\right]}{N}$	Factoring remaining numerator
11.	$= C^2 \dfrac{\sum (X - \bar{X})^2}{N} = C^2 S_X^2$	Rearranging terms and substituting
12.	$\sqrt{\dfrac{\sum (R - \bar{R})^2}{N}} = \sqrt{C^2 \dfrac{\sum (X - \bar{X})^2}{N}}$	Taking square root of both sides
13.	$S_R = C \sqrt{\dfrac{\sum (X - \bar{X})^2}{N}} = C\, S_X$	Simplifying and substituting

Combinations of $N(=10)$ coins yielding $r(=0, 10)$ heads.

$$_NC_r = \frac{N!}{r!(N-r)!}$$

$r = 0$ $_{10}C_0 = \dfrac{10!}{0!(10!)} = 1$ $(0! = 1)$

$r = 1$ $_{10}C_1 = \dfrac{10!}{1!(9!)} = \dfrac{(10)\cdot(9\cdot8\cdot7\cdot6\cdot5\cdot4\cdot3\cdot2\cdot1)}{(1)(9\cdot8\cdot7\cdot6\cdot5\cdot4\cdot3\cdot2\cdot1)} = 10$

$r = 2$ $_{10}C_2 = \dfrac{10!}{2!(8!)} = \dfrac{(10\cdot9)\cdot(8\cdot7\cdot6\cdot5\cdot4\cdot3\cdot2\cdot1)}{(2\cdot1)(8\cdot7\cdot6\cdot5\cdot4\cdot3\cdot2\cdot1)} = \dfrac{10\cdot9}{2\cdot1} = 45$

$r = 3$ $_{10}C_3 = \dfrac{10!}{3!(7!)} = \dfrac{(10\cdot9\cdot8)\cdot(7\cdot6\cdot5\cdot4\cdot3\cdot2\cdot1)}{(3\cdot2\cdot1)(7\cdot6\cdot5\cdot4\cdot3\cdot2\cdot1)} = \dfrac{10\cdot9\cdot8}{3\cdot2\cdot1} = 120$

$r = 4$ $_{10}C_2 = \dfrac{10!}{4!(6!)} = \dfrac{(10\cdot9\cdot8\cdot7)\cdot(6\cdot5\cdot4\cdot3\cdot2\cdot1)}{(4\cdot3\cdot2\cdot1)(6\cdot5\cdot4\cdot3\cdot2\cdot1)} = \dfrac{10\cdot9\cdot8\cdot7}{4\cdot3\cdot2\cdot1} = \dfrac{10\cdot3\cdot7}{1} = 210$

$r = 5$ See p. 145

$r = 6$ $_{10}C_6 = \dfrac{10!}{(6!)(4!)} = \dfrac{10!}{(4!)(6!)} = _{10}C_4 = 210$

$r = 7$ $_{10}C_7 = _{10}C_3 = 120$

$r = 8$ $_{10}C_8 = _{10}C_2 = 45$

$r = 9$ $_{10}C_9 = _{10}C_1 = 10$

$r = 10$ $_{10}C_{10} = _{10}C_0 = 1$

Equation for computing $b_{y \cdot x}$, the slope of the least-squares regression line (all summations are $i = 1, N$).

STEP	JUSTIFICATION
1. $\hat{y}_i = b_{y \cdot x} x_i$	Definition
2. $F = \sum (y_i - \hat{y}_i)^2 = \text{minimum}$	Principle of least squares
3. $F = \sum (y_i - bx_i)^2$	Substituting from 1

The simplest way to find the minimum of this expression is to use calculus. We want to find the value of b that will cause this expression to have its minimum value. This is accomplished by taking the derivative of the function with respect to b and setting this derivative equal to zero.

STEP	JUSTIFICATION
4. $\dfrac{dF}{db} = -2 \sum x_i (y_i - bx_i)$	Derivative of equation 3
5. $0 = -2 \sum x_i (y_i - bx_i)$	Evaluating the minimum of equation 4
6. $0 = \sum (x_i y_i - bx_i^2)$	Dividing both sides by -2 and multiplying
7. $0 = \sum x_i y_i - b \sum x_i^2$	Rules II and III
8. $b \sum x_i^2 = \sum x_i y_i$	Adding $b \sum x^2$ to both sides
9. $b = \dfrac{\sum x_i y_i}{\sum x_i^2}$	Dividing both sides by $\sum x_i^2$
10. $x_i = (X_i - \bar{X}); \quad y_i = (Y_i - \bar{Y})$	Definition

11. $b = \dfrac{\sum(X_i - \bar{X})(Y_i - \bar{Y})}{\sum(X_i - \bar{X})^2}$ Substituting

12. $= \dfrac{\sum(X_iY_i - X_i\bar{Y} - Y_i\bar{X} + \bar{X}\bar{Y})}{\sum(X_i^2 - 2X_i\bar{X} + \bar{X}^2)}$ Multiplying

13. $= \dfrac{\sum X_iY_i - \bar{Y}\sum X_i - \bar{X}\sum Y_i + N\bar{X}\bar{Y}}{\sum X_i^2 - 2\bar{X}\sum X_i + N\bar{X}^2}$ Rules I, II, and III

14. $= \dfrac{\sum X_iY_i - (\sum Y_i/N)\sum X_i - (\sum X_i/N)\sum Y_i + N\left(\dfrac{\sum X_i}{N}\right)\left(\dfrac{\sum Y_i}{N}\right)}{\sum X_i^2 - 2\sum X(\sum X_i)/N + N(\sum X_i)^2/N^2}$ Substituting

15. $= \dfrac{\sum XY - (\sum Y\sum X)/N - (\sum X\sum Y)/N + N(\sum X\sum Y)/N^2}{\sum X^2 - 2(\sum X)^2/N + N(\sum X)^2/N^2}$ Reversing Rule IV (subscripts omitted for clarity)

$\sum X\sum Y = \sum Y\sum X$

16. $= \dfrac{\sum XY - 2(\sum X\sum Y)/N + (\sum X\sum Y)/N}{\sum X^2 - 2(\sum X)^2/N + (\sum X)^2/N}$ Canceling N's

17. $= \dfrac{\sum XY - (\sum X\sum Y)/N}{\sum X^2 - (\sum X)^2/N}$ Simplifying

18. $= \dfrac{N\sum XY - \sum X\sum Y}{N\sum X^2 - (\sum X)^2}$ Multiplying numerator and denominator by N

Equation for the intercept of the regression line.

STEP	JUSTIFICATION
1. $\hat{y} = b_{yx}x$	Definition
2. $\hat{Y} - \bar{Y} = b(X - \bar{X})$	Substituting raw score equivalents
3. $\hat{Y} = \bar{Y} + b(X - \bar{X})$	Solving for $\hat{Y}$
4. $A = \hat{Y}$ when X is zero	
5. $A = \bar{Y} + b(0 - \bar{X})$	
6. $A = \bar{Y} - b\bar{X}$	Definition of A

Summation of z scores (all summations are $i = 1, N$).

STEP	JUSTIFICATION
1. $z_i = \dfrac{(X_i - \bar{X})}{S_x}$	Definition of z
2. $\sum z_i^2 = \sum \left(\dfrac{(X - \bar{X})}{S_x} \right)^2$	Substituting from equation 1
3. $ = \sum \dfrac{(X - \bar{X})^2}{S_x^2}$	
4. $ = \dfrac{\sum(X - \bar{X})^2}{S_x^2}$	
5. $S_x^2 = \dfrac{\sum(X - \bar{X})^2}{N}$	Definition of variance
6. $NS_x^2 = \sum(X - \bar{X})^2$	Multiplying by N
7. $\sum z_i^2 = \dfrac{NS_x^2}{S_x^2}$	Substituting from equation 6
8. $\sum z_i^2 = N \dfrac{S_x^2}{S_x^2}$	Rule IV
9. $\sum z_i^2 = N$	$\dfrac{S_x^2}{S_x^2} = 1$

Predictable and Error Portions of Variance.

STEP	JUSTIFICATION
1. $(Y_{ij} - \bar{Y}) = (\bar{Y}_j - \bar{Y}) + (Y_{ij} - \bar{Y}_j)$	Definition in eq. 9.4
2. $(Y_{ij} - \bar{Y})^2 = [(\bar{Y}_j - \bar{Y}) + (Y_{ij} - \bar{Y}_j)]^2$	Square step 1
3. $= (\bar{Y}_j - \bar{Y})^2 + (Y_{ij} - \bar{Y}_j)^2 + \; 2(Y_{ij} - \bar{Y}_j)(\bar{Y}_j - \bar{Y})$	Multiplying step 2
4. $\displaystyle\sum_{j=1}^{J}\sum_{i=1}^{N_j}(Y_{ij} - \bar{Y})^2 = \sum_{j=1}^{J}\sum_{i=1}^{N_j}\left[(\bar{Y}_j - \bar{Y})^2 + (Y_{ij} - \bar{Y}_j)^2 + \; 2(Y_{ij} - \bar{Y}_j)(\bar{Y}_j - \bar{Y})\right]$	Summing both sides over i and j
5. $\displaystyle = \sum_{j=1}^{J}\sum_{i=1}^{N_j}(\bar{Y}_j - \bar{Y})^2 + \sum_{j=1}^{J}\sum_{i=1}^{N_j}(Y_{ij} - \bar{Y}_j)^2 + \; 2\sum_{j=1}^{J}\sum_{i=1}^{N_j}(Y_{ij} - \bar{Y}_j)(\bar{Y}_j - \bar{Y})$	Rule II

Looking at the last term we notice that for each individual i in group j the value $(\bar{Y}_j - \bar{Y})$ is a constant. Using Rule III we may rewrite this term

$$2 \sum_{j=1}^{J} \sum_{i=1}^{N_j} (\bar{Y}_j - \bar{Y})(Y_{ij} - \bar{Y}_j) = 2 \sum_{j=1}^{J} (\bar{Y}_j - \bar{Y}) \sum_{i=1}^{N_j} (Y_{ij} - \bar{Y}_j).$$

But, $\sum_{i=1}^{N_j} (Y_{ij} - \bar{Y}_j)$, over the members of group j, must be zero for every group (see Chapter 4); therefore, the entire term is zero and

6. $\displaystyle \sum_{j=1}^{J} \sum_{i=1}^{N_j} (Y_{ij} - \bar{Y})^2 = \sum_{j=1}^{J} \sum_{i=1}^{N_j} (\bar{Y}_j - \bar{Y})^2 + \sum_{j=1}^{J} \sum_{i=1}^{N_j} (Y_{ij} - \bar{Y}_j)^2$

Dividing both sides by the total sample size, $\sum N_j$, yields

7. $\displaystyle \frac{\sum_{j=1}^{J} \sum_{i=1}^{N_j} (Y_{ij} - \bar{Y})^2}{\sum_{j=1}^{J} N_j} = \frac{\sum_{j=1}^{J} \sum_{i=1}^{N_j} (\bar{Y}_j - \bar{Y})^2}{\sum_{j=1}^{J} N_j} + \frac{\sum_{j=1}^{J} \sum_{i=1}^{N_j} (Y_{ij} - \bar{Y}_j)^2}{\sum_{j=1}^{J} N_j}$

Computational formula for r, raw scores (all summations are $i = 1, N$).

STEP	JUSTIFICATION
1. $\quad r = \dfrac{\sum xy}{N S_x S_y}$	Definition of r (equation 9.21)
$\quad x = (X - \bar{X}); y = (Y - \bar{Y})$	Definition of terms
2. $\quad S_x = \sqrt{\dfrac{N\sum X^2 - (\sum X)^2}{N^2}}\ ; S_y = \sqrt{\dfrac{N\sum Y^2 - (\sum Y)^2}{N^2}}$	Definition of terms
3. $\quad r = \dfrac{\sum(X - \bar{X})\,(Y - \bar{Y})}{N\sqrt{[N\sum X^2 - (\sum X)^2]/N^2}\,\sqrt{[N\sum Y^2 - (\sum Y)^2]/N^2}}$	Substituting terms from equation 2 into equation 1
4. $\quad = \dfrac{\sum(XY - X\bar{Y} - \bar{X}Y - \bar{X}\bar{Y})}{N(1/N)\sqrt{N\sum X^2 - (\sum X)^2}\,\sqrt{N\sum Y^2 - (\sum Y)^2}}$	Multiplying numerator Rule IV in denominator
5. $\quad = \dfrac{\sum XY - \bar{Y}\sum X - \bar{X}\sum Y - N\bar{X}\bar{Y}}{\sqrt{N\sum X^2 - (\sum X)^2}\,\sqrt{N\sum Y^2 - (\sum Y)^2}}$	Distributing $\sum$ (Rule II) $N\left(\dfrac{1}{N}\right) = 1$

By applying the same steps to the numerator in equation 5 that we used for the raw score form of b, we get

$$r = \frac{N\sum XY - \sum X\sum Y}{\sqrt{N\sum X^2 - (\sum X)^2}\,\sqrt{N\sum Y^2 - (\sum Y)^2}}.$$

Relationship of r to $S_{y \cdot x}$ (summations are $i = 1, N$).

STEP	JUSTIFICATION
1. $\quad S_{y \cdot x}^2 = \dfrac{1}{N} \sum (y_i - b x_i)^2$	Definition of $S_{y \cdot x}^2$
2. $\quad b_{y \cdot x} = r_{xy} \dfrac{S_y}{S_x}$	Equation 9.20
3. $\quad S_{y \cdot x}^2 = \dfrac{1}{N} \sum \left(y - r\, \dfrac{S_y}{S_x}\, x \right)^2$	Substituting equation 2 in equation 1
4. $\quad = \dfrac{1}{N} \sum \left(y^2 - 2r\, \dfrac{S_y}{S_x}\, xy + r^2\, \dfrac{S_y^2}{S_x^2}\, x^2 \right)$	Squaring equation 3
5. $\quad = \dfrac{1}{N} \left(\sum y^2 - 2r\, \dfrac{S_y}{S_x} \sum xy + r^2\, \dfrac{S_y^2}{S_x^2} \sum x^2 \right)$	Distributing $\sum$ (Rule II)
6. $\quad = \dfrac{\sum y^2}{N} - 2r\, \dfrac{S_y}{S_x}\, \dfrac{\sum xy}{N} + r^2\, \dfrac{S_y^2}{S_x^2}\, \dfrac{\sum x^2}{N}$	Distributing $\dfrac{1}{N}$

STEP	JUSTIFICATION
7. $\dfrac{\sum y^2}{N} = S_y^2$; $\dfrac{\sum x^2}{N} = S_x^2$	Definition of S_y^2; S_x^2
8. $S_{y\cdot x}^2 = S_y^2 - 2r\,\dfrac{S_y}{S_x}\,\dfrac{\sum xy}{N} + r^2\,\dfrac{S_y^2}{S_x^2}\,S_x^2$	Substituting from equation 7
9. $\dfrac{\sum xy}{N} = rS_yS_x$	Equation 9.22
10. $S_{y\cdot x}^2 = S_y^2 - 2r\,\dfrac{S_y}{S_x}\,rS_yS_x + r^2\,\dfrac{S_y^2 S_x^2}{S_x^2}$	Substituting from equation 9
11. $\phantom{S_{y\cdot x}^2} = S_y^2 - 2r^2\,\dfrac{S_y^2 S_x}{S_x} + r^2\,\dfrac{S_y^2 S_x^2}{S_x^2}$	Commutative property
12. $\phantom{S_{y\cdot x}^2} = S_y^2 - 2r^2 S_y^2 + r^2 S_y^2$	$\dfrac{S_x}{S_x} = 1$; $\dfrac{S_x^2}{S_x^2} = 1$
13. $S_{y\cdot x}^2 = S_y^2 - r^2 S_y^2$	Simplifying

Partitioning observed-score variance (all summations are $i = 1, N$).

	STEP	JUSTIFICATION
1.	$x_i = t_i + e_{ij}$	Definition
2.	$S_x^2 = \dfrac{\sum x_i^2}{N}$	Definition
3.	$S_x^2 = \dfrac{1}{N} \sum (t + e)^2$	Substituting equation 1 in equation 2; Rule IV
4.	$= \dfrac{1}{N} \sum (t^2 + 2\,te + e^2)$	Squaring equation 3
5.	$= \dfrac{1}{N} \sum t^2 + 2 \left(\dfrac{1}{N} \sum te \right) + \dfrac{1}{N} \sum e^2$	Distributing $\dfrac{1}{N}$ and $\sum$ (Rule II)
6.	$2 \left(\dfrac{1}{N} \sum te \right) = 2\,\dfrac{\sum te}{N}$	Reversing Rule IV
7.	$= 2 r_{te} S_t S_e$	Equation 9.22
8.	$r_{te} S_t S_e = 0$	Assumption of model
9.	$S_x^2 = \dfrac{1}{N} \sum t^2 + \dfrac{1}{N} \sum e^2$	Using equation 8 in equation 5
10.	$S_x^2 = \dfrac{\sum t^2}{N} + \dfrac{\sum e^2}{N}$	Reversing Rule IV
11.	$S_x^2 = S_t^2 + S_e^2$	$\sum t^2$ and $\sum e^2$ are sums of squared deviation scores. Their means are variances by definition.

Mean and Variance—True Score Model.

STEP		JUSTIFICATION
1.	$X_{ij} = T_i + e_{ij}$	Definition
2.	$\dfrac{\sum\limits_{j=1}^{N_j} X_{ij}}{N_j} = \dfrac{\sum\limits_{j=1}^{N_j} T_i}{N_j} + \dfrac{\sum\limits_{j=1}^{N_j} e_{ij}}{N_j}$	Summing both sides over j and dividing by N_j
3.	$\bar{X}_i = \dfrac{\sum\limits_{j=1}^{N_j} T_i}{N_j} + \dfrac{\sum\limits_{j=1}^{N_j} e_{ij}}{N_j}$	Substituting $\bar{X}_i$ for the operations that define it
4.	$\bar{X}_i = \dfrac{N_j T_i}{N_j} + \bar{e}_i$	Rule 1 and substituting; by assumption T_i is constant
5.	$\bar{X}_i = T_i$	By assumption, $\bar{e} = 0$; $\dfrac{N_j}{N_j} = 1$

6. $$\bar{X}_{ij} - \bar{X}_i = (T_i + e_{ij}) - \bar{X}_i$$

Subtracting $\bar{X}_i$ from both sides of equation 1

7. $$\frac{1}{N}\sum(X_{ij} - \bar{X}_i)^2 = \frac{1}{N}\sum[(T_i - \bar{X}_i) + (e_{ij} - \bar{X}_j)]^2$$

Squaring, summing, and dividing both sides by N

8. $$\frac{1}{N}\sum(X_{ij} - \bar{X}_i)^2 = \frac{1}{N}\sum[(T_i - T_i) + (e_{ij} - \bar{X}_i)]^2$$

Substituting from equation 5

9. $$\frac{1}{N}\sum(X_{ij} - \bar{X}_i)^2 = \frac{1}{N}\sum(e_{ij} - \bar{X}_i)^2$$

Simplifying $(T_i - T_i) = 0$

10. $$S^2_{X_{ij}} = S^2_{e_{ij}}$$

Substituting—each term defines a variance

Appendix B

TABLE B-1

Areas under unit normal distribution $z = \dfrac{X - \bar{X}}{S_X}$

z	Area Between z and X̄	Area Beyond z	z	Area Between z and X̄	Area Beyond z	z	Area Between z and X̄	Area Beyond z
0.00	¹0000	¹5000	0.21	0832	4168	0.42	1628	3372
0.01	0040	4960	0.22	0871	4129	0.43	1664	3336
0.02	0080	4920	0.23	0910	4090	0.44	1700	3300
0.03	0120	4880	0.24	0948	4052	0.45	1736	3264
0.04	0160	4840	0.25	0987	4013	0.46	1772	3228
0.05	0199	4801	0.26	1026	3974	0.47	1808	3192
0.06	0239	4761	0.27	1064	3936	0.48	1844	3156
0.07	0279	4721	0.28	1103	3897	0.49	1879	3121
0.08	0319	4681	0.29	1141	3859	0.50	1915	3085
0.09	0359	4641	0.30	1179	3821	0.51	1950	3050
0.10	0398	4602	0.31	1217	3783	0.52	1985	3015
0.11	0438	4562	0.32	1255	3745	0.53	2019	2981
0.12	0478	4522	0.33	1293	3707	0.54	2054	2946
0.13	0517	4483	0.34	1331	3669	0.55	2088	2912
0.14	0557	4443	0.35	1368	3632	0.56	2123	2877
0.15	0596	4404	0.36	1406	3594	0.57	2157	2843
0.16	0636	4364	0.37	1443	3557	0.58	2190	2810
0.17	0675	4325	0.38	1480	3520	0.59	2224	2776
0.18	0714	4286	0.39	1517	3483	0.60	2257	2743
0.19	0753	4247	0.40	1554	3446	0.61	2291	2709
0.20	0793	4207	0.41	1591	3409	0.62	2324	2676

z	Area Between z and X̄	Area Beyond z	z	Area Between z and X̄	Area Beyond z	z	Area Between z and X̄	Area Beyond z
0.63	2357	2643	0.89	3133	1867	1.15	3749	1251
0.64	2389	2611	0.90	3159	1841	1.16	3770	1230
0.65	2422	2578	0.91	3186	1814	1.17	3790	1210
0.66	2454	2546	0.92	3212	1788	1.18	3810	1190
0.67	2486	2514	0.93	3238	1762	1.19	3830	1170
0.68	2517	2483	0.94	3264	1736	1.20	3849	1151
0.69	2549	2451	0.95	3289	1711	1.21	3869	1131
0.70	2580	2420	0.96	3315	1685	1.22	3888	1112
0.71	2611	2389	0.97	3340	1660	1.23	3907	1093
0.72	2642	2358	0.98	3365	1635	1.24	3925	1075
0.73	2673	2327	0.99	3389	1611	1.25	3944	1056
0.74	2704	2296	1.00	3413	1587	1.26	3962	1038
0.75	2734	2266	1.01	3438	1562	1.27	3980	1020
0.76	2764	2236	1.02	3461	1539	1.28	3997	1003
0.77	2794	2206	1.03	3485	1515	1.29	4015	0985
0.78	2823	2177	1.04	3508	1492	1.30	4030	0968
0.79	2852	2148	1.05	3531	1469	1.31	4049	0951
0.80	2881	2119	1.06	3554	1446	1.32	4066	0934
0.81	2910	2090	1.07	3577	1423	1.33	4082	0918
0.82	2939	2061	1.08	3599	1401	1.34	4099	0901
0.83	2967	2033	1.09	3621	1379	1.35	4115	0885
0.84	2995	2005	1.10	3643	1357	1.36	4131	0869
0.85	3023	1977	1.11	3665	1335	1.37	4147	0853
0.86	3051	1949	1.12	3686	1314	1.38	4162	0838
0.87	3078	1922	1.13	3708	1292	1.39	4177	0823
0.88	3106	1894	1.14	3729	1271	1.40	4192	0808

TABLE B-1 (*Continued*)

Areas under unit normal distribution $z = \dfrac{X - \bar{X}}{S_X}$

z	Area Between z and $\bar{X}$	Area Beyond z	z	Area Between z and $\bar{X}$	Area Beyond z	z	Area Between z and $\bar{X}$	Area Beyond z
1.41	4207	0793	1.63	4484	0516	1.82	4656	0344
1.42	4222	0778	1.64	4495	0505	1.83	4664	0336
1.43	4236	0764	1.645	4500	0500	1.84	4671	0329
1.44	4251	0749				1.85	4678	0322
1.45	4265	0735	1.65	4505	0495	1.86	4686	0314
1.46	4279	0721	1.66	4515	0485	1.87	4693	0307
1.47	4292	0708	1.67	4525	0475	1.88	4699	0301
1.48	4306	0694	1.68	4535	0465	1.89	4706	0294
1.49	4319	0681	1.69	4545	0455	1.90	4713	0287
1.50	4332	0668	1.70	4554	0446	1.91	4719	0281
1.51	4345	0655	1.71	4564	0436	1.92	4726	0274
1.52	4357	0643	1.72	4573	0427	1.93	4732	0268
1.53	4370	0630	1.73	4582	0418	1.94	4738	0262
1.54	4382	0618	1.74	4591	0409	1.95	4744	0256
1.55	4394	0606	1.75	4599	0401			
1.56	4406	0594	1.76	4608	0392	1.96	4750	0250
1.57	4418	0582	1.77	4616	0384			
1.58	4429	0571	1.78	4625	0375	1.97	4756	0244
1.59	4441	0559	1.79	4633	0367	1.98	4761	0239
1.60	4452	0548	1.80	4641	0359	1.99	4767	0233
1.61	4463	0537	1.81	4649	0351	2.00	4772	0288
1.62	4474	0526				2.01	4778	0222

z	Area Between z and $\overline{X}$	Area Beyond z	z	Area Between z and $\overline{X}$	Area Beyond z	z	Area Between z and $\overline{X}$	Area Beyond z
2.02	4783	0217	2.28	4887	0113	2.51	4940	0060
2.03	4788	0212	2.29	4890	0110	2.52	4941	0059
2.04	4793	0207	2.30	4893	0107	2.53	4943	0057
2.05	4798	0202	2.31	4896	0104	2.54	4945	0055
2.06	4803	0197	2.32	4898	0102	2.55	4946	0054
2.07	4808	0192				2.56	4948	0052
2.08	4812	0188	2.326	4890	0100	2.57	4949	0051
2.09	4817	0183						
2.10	4821	0179	2.33	4901	0099	2.576	4950	0050
2.11	4826	0174	2.34	4904	0096			
2.12	4830	0170	2.35	4906	0094	2.58	4951	0049
2.13	4834	0166	2.36	4909	0091	2.59	4952	0048
2.14	4838	0162	2.37	4911	0089	2.60	4953	0047
2.15	4842	0158	2.38	4913	0087	2.61	4955	0045
2.16	4846	0154	2.39	4916	0084	2.62	4956	0044
2.17	4850	0150	2.40	4918	0082	2.63	4957	0043
2.18	4854	0146	2.41	4920	0080	2.64	4959	0041
2.19	4857	0143	2.42	4922	0078	2.65	4960	0040
2.20	4861	0139	2.43	4925	0075	2.66	4961	0039
2.21	4864	0136	2.44	4927	0073	2.67	4962	0038
2.22	4868	0132	2.45	4929	0071	2.68	4963	0037
2.23	4871	0129	2.46	4931	0069	2.69	4964	0036
2.24	4875	0125	2.47	4932	0068	2.70	4965	0035
2.25	4878	0122	2.48	4934	0066	2.75	4970	0030
2.26	4881	0119	2.49	4936	0064			
2.27	4884	0116	2.50	4938	0062			

TABLE B-1 *(Continued)*

Areas under unit normal distribution $z = \dfrac{X - \bar{X}}{S_X}$

z	Area Between z and $\bar{X}$	Area Beyond z	z	Area Between z and $\bar{X}$	Area Beyond z	z	Area Between z and $\bar{X}$	Area Beyond z
2.80	4974	0026	3.10	4990	0010	3.60	4998	0002
2.81	4975	0025	3.15	4992	0008	3.70	4999	0001
			3.20	4993	0007	3.80	4999	0001
			3.25	4994	0006	3.90	49995	00005
2.85	4978	0022	3.30	4995	0005	4.00	49997	00003
2.90	4981	0019	3.35	4996	0004			
2.95	4984	0016	3.40	4997	0003			
3.00	4987	0013	3.45	4997	0003	4.25	49999	00001
3.05	4989	0011	3.50	4998	0002			

SOURCE: Values in table computed by using the normal distribution program in the standard library of the TI-58 calculator.
¹Decimal points omitted.

TABLE B-2
Critical Values of t Distributions

Degrees of Freedom	One Tail	.10	.05	.025	.01	.005	.0005
	Two tails	.20	.10	.05	.02	.01	.001
1		3.078	6.314	12.706	31.821	63.657	636.619
2		1.886	2.920	4.303	6.965	9.925	31.598
3		1.638	2.353	3.182	4.541	5.841	12.941
4		1.533	2.132	2.776	3.747	4.604	8.610
5		1.476	2.015	2.571	3.365	4.032	6.859
6		1.440	1.943	2.447	3.143	3.707	5.959
7		1.415	1.895	2.365	2.998	3.499	5.405
8		1.397	1.860	2.306	2.896	3.355	5.041
9		1.383	1.833	2.262	2.821	3.250	4.781
10		1.372	1.812	2.228	2.764	3.169	4.587
11		1.363	1.796	2.201	2.718	3.106	4.437
12		1.356	1.782	2.179	2.681	3.055	4.318
13		1.350	1.771	2.160	2.650	3.012	4.221
14		1.345	1.761	2.145	2.624	2.977	4.140
15		1.341	1.753	2.131	2.602	2.947	4.073
16		1.337	1.746	2.120	2.583	2.921	4.015
17		1.333	1.740	2.110	2.567	2.898	3.965
18		1.330	1.734	2.101	2.552	2.878	3.922
19		1.328	1.729	2.093	2.539	2.861	3.883
20		1.325	1.725	2.086	2.528	2.845	3.850
21		1.323	1.721	2.080	2.518	2.831	3.819
22		1.321	1.717	2.074	2.508	2.819	3.792
23		1.319	1.714	2.069	2.500	2.807	3.767
24		1.318	1.711	2.064	2.492	2.797	3.745
25		1.316	1.708	2.060	2.485	2.787	3.725
26		1.315	1.706	2.056	2.479	2.779	3.707
27		1.314	1.703	2.052	2.473	2.771	3.690
28		1.313	1.701	2.048	2.467	2.763	3.674
29		1.311	1.699	2.045	2.462	2.756	3.659
30		1.310	1.697	2.042	2.457	2.750	3.646
40		1.303	1.684	2.021	2.423	2.704	3.551
60		1.296	1.671	2.000	2.390	2.660	3.460
120		1.289	1.658	1.980	2.358	2.617	3.373
∞		1.282	1.645	1.960	2.326	2.576	3.291

SOURCE: Pearson and H. O. Hartley (eds.), *Biometrika Tables for Statisticians*, vol. II, 1972. Reprinted by permission of the Trustees of *Biometrika*.

TABLE B-3

Selected Values of Chi-Square Distribution.

df \ P[1]	.999	.990	.950	.900	.800	.700	.600	.500	.400	.300	.200	.100	.050	.010	.001
1[2]	0.0⁵157	0.0³157	0.0³393	0.016	0.064	0.148	0.275	0.455	0.708	1.074	1.642	2.706	3.841	6.635	10.828
2	0.002	0.020	0.103	0.211	0.446	0.713	1.022	1.386	1.833	2.408	3.219	4.605	5.991	9.210	13.816
3	0.024	0.115	0.352	0.584	1.005	1.424	1.869	2.366	2.946	3.665	4.642	6.251	7.815	11.341	16.266
4	0.091	0.297	0.711	1.064	1.649	2.195	2.753	3.357	4.045	4.878	5.989	7.779	9.488	13.277	18.467
5	0.210	0.554	1.145	1.610	2.343	3.000	3.656	4.351	5.132	6.064	7.289	9.236	11.070	15.086	20.515
6	0.381	0.872	1.635	2.204	3.070	3.828	4.570	5.348	6.211	7.231	8.558	10.645	12.592	16.812	22.458
7	0.598	1.239	2.167	2.833	3.822	4.671	5.493	6.346	7.283	8.383	9.803	12.017	14.067	18.475	24.322
8	0.857	1.646	2.733	3.490	4.594	5.527	6.423	7.344	8.351	9.524	11.030	13.362	15.507	20.090	26.124
9	1.152	2.088	3.325	4.168	5.380	6.393	7.357	8.343	9.414	10.656	12.242	14.684	16.919	21.666	27.877
10	1.479	2.558	3.940	4.865	6.179	7.267	8.295	9.342	10.473	11.781	13.442	15.987	18.307	23.209	29.588
11	1.834	3.053	4.575	5.578	6.989	8.148	9.237	10.341	11.530	12.899	14.631	17.275	19.675	24.725	31.264
12	2.214	3.571	5.226	6.304	7.807	9.034	10.182	11.340	12.584	14.011	15.812	18.549	21.026	26.217	32.910
13	2.617	4.107	5.892	7.042	8.634	9.926	11.129	12.340	13.636	15.119	16.985	19.812	22.362	27.688	34.528
14	3.041	4.660	6.571	7.790	9.467	10.822	12.078	13.339	14.685	16.222	18.151	21.064	23.685	29.141	36.123
15	3.483	5.229	7.261	8.545	10.307	11.721	13.030	14.339	15.733	17.322	19.311	22.307	24.996	30.578	37.697
16	3.942	5.812	7.962	9.312	11.152	12.624	13.983	15.338	16.780	18.418	20.465	23.542	26.296	32.000	39.252

df															
17	4.416	6.408	8.672	10.085	12.002	13.531	14.937	16.338	17.824	19.511	21.615	24.769	27.587	33.409	40.790
18	4.905	7.015	9.390	10.865	12.857	14.440	15.893	17.338	18.868	20.601	22.760	25.898	28.869	34.805	42.312
19	5.407	7.633	10.117	11.651	13.716	15.352	16.850	18.338	19.910	21.689	23.900	27.204	30.144	36.191	43.820
20	5.921	8.260	10.851	12.443	14.578	16.266	17.809	19.337	20.951	22.775	25.038	28.412	31.410	37.566	45.315
21	6.447	8.897	11.591	13.240	15.445	17.182	18.768	20.337	21.992	23.858	26.171	29.616	32.671	38.932	46.797
22	6.983	9.542	12.338	14.042	16.314	18.101	19.729	21.337	23.031	24.939	27.302	30.813	33.924	40.289	48.268
23	7.529	10.196	13.090	14.848	17.186	19.021	20.690	22.337	24.069	26.018	28.429	32.007	35.172	41.638	49.728
24	8.085	10.856	13.848	15.659	18.062	19.943	21.652	23.337	25.106	27.096	29.553	33.196	36.415	42.980	51.179
25	8.649	11.524	14.611	16.473	18.940	20.867	22.616	24.337	26.143	28.172	30.675	34.382	37.652	44.314	52.618
26	9.222	12.198	15.379	17.292	19.820	21.792	23.579	25.336	27.179	29.246	31.795	35.563	38.885	45.642	54.052
27	9.803	12.878	16.151	18.134	20.703	22.719	24.544	26.336	28.214	30.319	32.912	36.741	40.113	46.963	55.476
28	10.391	13.565	16.928	18.939	21.588	23.648	25.509	27.336	29.249	31.391	34.027	37.916	41.337	48.278	56.892
29	10.986	14.256	17.708	19.768	22.475	24.577	26.475	28.336	30.282	32.461	35.319	39.088	42.557	49.588	58.301
30	11.588	14.954	18.493	20.599	23.364	25.508	27.442	29.336	31.316	33.530	36.250	40.256	43.773	50.892	59.703

SOURCE: E. S. Pearson and H. O. Hartley (ed.), *Biometrika Tables for Statisticians*, vol. II, 1972. Reprinted by permission of the Trustees of *Biometrika*.

[1]Tabled values are the values of chi square above which a given portion P of the distribution lies. Thus, for $df = 3$ 0.001 of the chi-square distribution lies *below* the value of 0.024, while 0.999 of the distribution lies *above* this value. Forty percent of the distribution lies *above* this value. Forty percent of the same distribution lies above the value 2.946 and 5 percent lies above 7.815. For df greater than 30, the expression $\sqrt{2\chi^2} - \sqrt{2(df-1)}$ yields a value essentially equivalent to a z-score.

Probabilities associated with this statistic are found in Table B-1.

[2]Superscripts indicate the number of zeroes before the first nonzero value.

TABLE B-4
Critical Values of F Distribution.

df_2	df_1	1	2	3	4	5	6	7	8	9	10	12	15	20	30	∞
1	0.05	161.4	199.5	215.7	224.6	230.2	234.0	236.8	238.9	240.5	241.9	243.9	245.9	248.0	250.1	254.3
	0.01[1]	40.52	50.00	54.03	56.25	57.64	58.59	59.28	59.81	60.22	60.56	61.06	61.57	62.09	62.61	63.66
	0.001[2]	40.53	50.00	54.04	56.25	57.64	58.59	59.29	59.81	60.23	60.56	61.07	61.58	62.09	62.61	63.66
2	0.05	18.51	19.00	19.16	19.25	19.30	19.33	19.35	19.37	19.38	19.40	19.41	19.43	19.45	19.46	19.50
	0.01	98.50	99.00	99.17	99.25	99.30	99.33	99.36	99.37	99.39	99.40	99.42	99.43	99.45	99.47	99.50
	0.001	998.50	999.00	999.17	999.25	999.30	999.33	999.36	999.37	999.39	999.40	999.42	999.43	999.45	999.47	999.50
3	0.05	10.13	9.55	9.28	9.12	9.01	8.94	8.89	8.85	8.81	8.79	8.74	8.70	8.66	8.62	8.53
	0.01	34.12	30.82	29.46	28.71	28.24	27.91	27.67	27.49	27.34	27.23	27.05	26.87	26.69	26.50	26.12
	0.001	167.03	148.50	141.11	137.10	134.58	132.85	131.58	130.62	129.86	129.25	128.32	127.37	126.42	125.45	123.47
4	0.05	7.71	6.94	6.59	6.39	6.26	6.16	6.09	6.04	6.00	5.96	5.91	5.86	5.80	5.75	5.63
	0.01	21.20	18.00	16.69	15.98	15.52	15.21	14.98	14.80	14.66	14.55	14.37	14.20	14.02	13.84	13.46
	0.001	74.14	61.25	56.18	53.44	51.71	50.52	49.66	49.00	48.48	48.05	47.41	46.76	46.10	45.43	44.05
5	0.05	6.61	5.79	5.41	5.19	5.05	4.95	4.88	4.82	4.77	4.74	4.68	4.62	4.56	4.50	4.36
	0.01	16.26	13.27	12.06	11.39	10.97	10.67	10.46	10.29	10.16	10.05	9.89	9.72	9.55	9.38	9.02
	0.001	47.18	37.12	33.20	31.08	29.75	28.83	28.16	27.65	27.24	26.92	26.42	25.91	25.40	24.87	23.78
6	0.05	5.99	5.14	4.76	4.53	4.39	4.28	4.21	4.15	4.10	4.06	4.00	3.94	3.87	3.81	3.67
	0.01	13.74	10.92	9.78	9.15	8.75	8.47	8.26	8.10	7.98	7.87	7.72	7.56	7.40	7.23	6.88
	0.001	35.51	27.00	23.70	21.92	20.80	20.03	19.46	19.03	18.69	18.41	17.99	17.56	17.12	16.67	15.74
7	0.05	5.59	4.74	4.35	4.12	3.97	3.87	3.79	3.73	3.68	3.64	3.57	3.51	3.44	3.38	3.23
	0.01	12.25	9.55	8.45	7.85	7.46	7.19	6.99	6.84	6.72	6.62	6.47	6.31	6.16	5.99	5.65
	0.001	29.24	21.69	18.77	17.20	16.21	15.52	15.02	14.63	14.33	14.08	13.71	13.32	12.93	12.53	11.70

	α															
8	0.05	2.93	3.08	3.15	3.22	3.28	3.35	3.39	3.44	3.50	3.58	3.69	3.84	4.07	4.46	5.32
	0.01	4.86	5.20	5.36	5.52	5.67	5.81	5.91	6.03	6.18	6.37	6.63	7.01	7.59	8.65	11.26
	0.001	9.33	10.11	10.48	10.84	11.19	11.54	11.77	12.05	12.40	12.86	13.48	14.39	15.83	18.49	25.42
9	0.05	2.71	2.86	2.94	3.01	3.07	3.14	3.18	3.23	3.29	3.37	3.48	3.63	3.86	4.26	5.12
	0.01	4.31	4.65	4.81	4.96	5.11	5.26	5.35	5.47	5.61	5.80	6.06	6.42	6.99	8.02	10.56
	0.001	7.81	8.55	8.90	9.24	9.57	9.89	10.11	10.37	10.70	11.13	11.71	12.56	13.90	16.39	22.86
10	0.05	2.54	2.70	2.77	2.84	2.91	2.98	3.02	3.07	3.14	3.22	3.33	3.48	3.71	4.10	4.96
	0.01	3.91	4.25	4.41	4.56	4.71	4.85	4.94	5.06	5.20	5.39	5.64	5.99	6.55	7.56	10.04
	0.001	6.76	7.47	7.80	8.13	8.44	8.75	8.96	9.20	9.52	9.93	10.48	11.28	12.55	14.90	21.04
11	0.05	2.40	2.57	2.65	2.72	2.79	2.85	2.90	2.95	3.01	3.09	3.20	3.36	3.59	3.98	4.84
	0.01	3.60	3.94	4.10	4.25	4.40	4.54	4.63	4.74	4.89	5.07	5.32	5.67	6.22	7.21	9.65
	0.001	6.00	6.68	7.01	7.32	7.63	7.92	8.12	8.35	8.66	9.05	9.58	10.35	11.56	13.81	19.69
12	0.05	2.30	2.47	2.54	2.62	2.69	2.75	2.80	2.85	2.91	3.00	3.11	3.26	3.49	3.89	4.75
	0.01	3.36	3.70	3.86	4.01	4.16	4.30	4.39	4.50	4.64	4.82	5.06	5.41	5.95	6.93	9.33
	0.001	5.42	6.09	6.40	6.71	7.00	7.29	7.48	7.71	8.00	8.38	8.89	9.63	10.80	12.97	18.64
13	0.05	2.21	2.38	2.46	2.53	2.60	2.67	2.71	2.77	2.83	2.92	3.03	3.18	3.41	3.81	4.67
	0.01	3.17	3.51	3.66	3.82	3.96	4.10	4.19	4.30	4.44	4.62	4.86	5.21	5.74	6.70	9.07
	0.001	4.97	5.63	5.93	6.23	6.52	6.80	6.98	7.21	7.49	7.86	8.35	9.07	10.21	12.31	17.82
14	0.05	2.13	2.31	2.39	2.46	2.53	2.60	2.65	2.70	2.76	2.85	2.96	3.11	3.34	3.74	4.60
	0.01	3.00	3.35	3.51	3.66	3.80	3.94	4.03	4.14	4.28	4.46	4.70	5.04	5.56	6.51	8.86
	0.001	4.60	5.25	5.56	5.85	6.13	6.40	6.58	6.80	7.08	7.44	7.92	8.62	9.73	11.78	17.14
15	0.05	2.07	2.25	2.33	2.40	2.48	2.54	2.59	2.64	2.71	2.79	2.90	3.06	3.29	3.68	4.54
	0.01	2.87	3.21	3.37	3.52	3.67	3.80	3.89	4.00	4.14	4.32	4.56	4.89	5.42	6.36	8.68
	0.001	4.31	4.95	5.25	5.54	5.81	6.08	6.26	6.47	6.74	7.09	7.57	8.25	9.34	11.34	16.59
16	0.05	2.01	2.19	2.28	2.35	2.42	2.49	2.54	2.59	2.66	2.74	2.85	3.01	3.24	3.63	4.49
	0.01	2.75	3.10	3.26	3.41	3.55	3.69	3.78	3.89	4.03	4.20	4.44	4.77	5.29	6.23	8.53
	0.001	4.06	4.70	4.99	5.27	5.55	5.81	5.98	6.20	6.46	6.80	7.27	7.94	9.01	10.97	16.12

TABLE B-4 (*Continued*)
Critical Values of F Distribution.

df_2	df_1	1	2	3	4	5	6	7	8	9	10	12	15	20	30	∞
17	0.05	4.45	3.59	3.20	2.96	2.81	2.70	2.61	2.55	2.49	2.45	2.38	2.31	2.23	2.15	1.96
	0.01	8.40	6.11	5.18	4.67	4.34	4.10	3.93	3.79	3.68	3.59	3.46	3.31	3.16	3.00	2.65
	0.001	15.72	10.66	8.73	7.68	7.02	6.56	6.72	5.96	5.75	5.58	5.32	5.05	4.78	4.48	3.85
18	0.05	4.41	3.55	3.19	2.93	2.77	2.66	2.58	2.51	2.46	2.41	2.34	2.27	2.19	2.11	1.92
	0.01	8.29	6.01	5.09	4.58	4.25	4.01	3.84	3.71	3.60	3.51	3.37	3.23	3.08	2.92	2.57
	0.001	15.38	10.39	8.49	7.46	6.81	6.36	6.02	5.76	5.56	5.39	5.13	4.87	4.59	4.30	3.67
19	0.05	4.38	3.52	3.13	2.90	2.74	2.63	2.54	2.48	2.42	2.38	2.31	2.23	2.16	2.07	1.88
	0.01	8.18	5.93	5.01	4.50	4.17	3.94	3.77	3.63	3.52	3.43	3.30	3.15	3.00	2.84	2.49
	0.001	15.08	10.16	8.28	7.27	6.62	6.18	5.85	5.59	5.39	5.22	4.97	4.70	4.43	4.14	3.51
20	0.05	4.35	3.49	3.10	2.87	2.71	2.60	2.51	2.45	2.39	2.35	2.28	2.20	2.12	2.04	1.84
	0.01	8.10	5.85	4.94	4.43	4.10	3.87	3.70	3.56	3.46	3.37	3.23	3.09	2.94	2.78	2.42
	0.001	14.82	9.95	8.10	7.10	6.46	6.02	5.69	5.44	5.24	5.08	4.82	4.56	4.29	4.00	3.38
21	0.05	4.32	3.47	3.07	2.84	2.68	2.57	2.49	2.42	2.37	2.32	2.25	2.18	2.10	2.01	1.81
	0.01	8.02	5.78	4.87	4.37	4.04	3.81	3.64	3.51	3.40	3.31	3.17	3.03	2.88	2.72	2.36
	0.001	14.59	9.77	7.94	6.95	6.32	5.88	5.56	5.31	5.11	4.95	4.70	4.44	4.17	3.88	3.26
22	0.05	4.30	3.44	3.05	2.82	2.66	2.55	2.46	2.40	2.34	2.30	2.23	2.15	2.07	1.98	1.78
	0.01	7.95	5.72	4.82	4.31	3.99	3.76	3.59	3.45	3.35	3.26	3.12	2.98	2.83	2.67	2.31
	0.001	14.38	9.61	7.80	6.81	6.19	5.76	5.44	5.19	4.99	4.83	4.58	4.33	4.06	3.78	3.15
23	0.05	4.28	3.42	3.03	2.80	2.64	2.53	2.44	2.37	2.32	2.27	2.20	2.13	2.05	1.96	1.76
	0.01	7.88	5.66	4.76	4.26	3.94	3.71	3.54	3.41	3.30	3.21	3.07	2.93	2.78	2.62	2.26
	0.001	14.20	9.47	7.67	6.70	6.08	5.65	5.33	5.09	4.89	4.73	4.48	4.23	3.96	3.68	3.05

df	α															
24	0.05	4.26	3.40	3.01	2.78	2.62	2.51	2.42	2.36	2.30	2.25	2.18	2.11	2.03	1.94	1.73
	0.01	7.82	5.61	4.72	4.22	3.90	3.67	3.50	3.36	3.26	3.17	3.03	2.89	2.74	2.58	2.21
	0.001	14.03	9.34	7.55	6.59	5.98	5.55	5.23	4.99	4.80	4.64	4.39	4.14	3.87	3.59	2.97
25	0.05	4.24	3.39	2.99	2.76	2.60	2.49	2.40	2.34	2.28	2.24	2.16	2.09	2.01	1.92	1.71
	0.01	7.77	5.57	4.68	4.18	3.86	3.63	3.46	3.32	3.22	3.13	2.99	2.85	2.70	2.54	2.17
	0.001	13.88	9.22	7.45	6.49	5.89	5.46	5.15	4.91	4.71	4.56	4.31	4.06	3.79	3.52	2.89
26	0.05	4.23	3.37	2.98	2.74	2.59	2.47	2.39	2.32	2.27	2.22	2.15	2.07	1.99	1.90	1.69
	0.01	7.72	5.53	4.64	4.14	3.82	3.59	3.42	3.29	3.18	3.09	2.96	2.82	2.66	2.50	2.13
	0.001	13.74	9.12	7.36	6.41	5.80	5.38	5.07	4.83	4.64	4.48	4.24	3.99	3.72	3.44	2.82
27	0.05	4.21	3.35	2.96	2.73	2.57	2.46	2.38	2.31	2.25	2.20	2.13	2.06	1.97	1.88	1.67
	0.01	7.68	5.49	4.60	4.11	3.78	3.56	3.39	3.26	3.15	3.06	2.93	2.78	2.63	2.47	2.10
	0.001	13.61	9.02	7.27	6.33	5.73	5.31	5.00	4.76	4.57	4.41	4.17	3.92	3.66	3.38	2.75
28	0.05	4.20	3.34	2.95	2.71	2.56	2.45	2.36	2.29	2.24	2.19	2.12	2.04	1.96	1.87	1.65
	0.01	7.64	5.45	4.57	4.07	3.75	3.53	3.36	3.23	3.12	3.03	2.90	2.75	2.60	2.44	2.06
	0.001	13.50	8.93	7.19	6.25	5.66	5.24	4.93	4.69	4.50	4.35	4.11	3.86	3.60	3.32	2.69
29	0.05	4.18	3.33	2.93	2.70	2.55	2.43	2.35	2.28	2.22	2.18	2.10	2.03	1.94	1.85	1.64
	0.01	7.60	5.42	4.54	4.04	3.73	3.50	3.33	3.20	3.09	3.00	2.87	2.73	2.57	2.41	2.03
	0.001	13.39	8.85	7.12	6.19	5.59	5.18	4.87	4.64	4.45	4.29	4.05	3.80	3.54	3.27	2.64
30	0.05	4.13	3.32	2.92	2.69	2.54	2.42	2.33	2.27	2.21	2.16	2.09	2.01	1.93	1.84	1.62
	0.01	7.56	5.39	4.51	4.02	3.70	3.47	3.30	3.17	3.07	2.98	2.84	2.70	2.55	2.39	2.01
	0.001	13.29	8.77	7.05	6.12	5.53	5.12	4.82	4.58	4.39	4.24	4.00	3.75	3.49	3.22	2.59
40	0.05	4.08	3.23	2.84	2.61	2.45	2.34	2.25	2.18	2.12	2.08	2.00	1.92	1.84	1.74	1.51
	0.01	7.31	5.18	4.31	3.83	3.51	3.29	3.12	2.99	2.89	2.80	2.66	2.52	2.37	2.20	1.80
	0.001	12.61	8.25	6.59	5.70	5.13	4.73	4.44	4.21	4.02	3.87	3.64	3.40	3.14	2.87	2.23
60	0.05	4.00	3.15	2.76	2.53	2.37	2.25	2.17	2.10	2.04	1.99	1.92	1.84	1.75	1.65	1.39
	0.01	7.08	4.98	4.13	3.65	3.34	3.12	2.95	2.82	2.72	2.63	2.50	2.35	2.20	2.03	1.60
	0.001	11.97	7.77	6.17	5.31	4.76	4.37	4.09	3.86	3.69	3.54	3.32	3.08	2.83	2.55	1.89

TABLE B-4 (*Continued*)
Critical Values of F Distribution.

df_2	df_1	1	2	3	4	5	6	7	8	9	10	12	15	20	30	∞
120	0.05	3.92	3.07	2.68	2.45	2.29	2.18	2.09	2.02	1.96	1.91	1.83	1.75	1.66	1.55	1.25
	0.01	6.85	4.79	3.95	3.48	3.17	2.96	2.79	2.66	2.56	2.47	2.34	2.19	2.03	1.86	1.38
	0.001	11.38	7.32	5.78	4.95	4.42	4.04	3.77	3.55	3.38	3.24	3.02	2.78	2.53	2.26	1.54
∞	0.05	3.84	3.00	2.60	2.37	2.21	2.10	2.01	1.94	1.88	1.83	1.75	1.67	1.57	1.46	1.00
	0.01	6.63	4.61	3.78	3.32	3.02	2.80	2.64	2.51	2.41	2.32	2.18	2.04	1.88	1.70	1.00
	0.001	10.83	6.91	5.42	4.62	4.10	3.74	3.47	3.27	3.10	2.96	2.74	2.51	2.27	1.99	1.00

SOURCE: E. S. Pearson and H. O. Hartley (ed.), *Biometrika Tables for Statisticians*, vol. II, 1972. Reprinted by permission of the Trustees of *Biometrika*.

[1]Entries in this row must be multiplied by 100.
[2]Entries in this row must be multiplied by 10,000.

TABLE B-5

Transformation of r to z_F = (Fisher's z).

r	.00	.01	.02	.03	.04	.05	.06	.07	.08	.09
0.0	0.000	0.010	0.020	0.030	0.040	0.050	0.060	0.070	0.080	0.090
0.1	0.100	0.110	0.121	0.131	0.141	0.151	0.161	0.172	0.182	0.192
0.2	0.203	0.213	0.224	0.234	0.245	0.255	0.266	0.277	0.288	0.299
0.3	0.310	0.321	0.332	0.343	0.354	0.366	0.377	0.388	0.400	0.412
0.4	0.424	0.436	0.448	0.460	0.472	0.485	0.497	0.510	0.523	0.536
0.5	0.549	0.563	0.577	0.590	0.604	0.618	0.633	0.648	0.663	0.678
0.6	0.693	0.709	0.725	0.741	0.758	0.775	0.793	0.811	0.829	0.848
0.7	0.867	0.887	0.908	0.929	0.950	0.973	0.996	1.020	1.045	1.071
0.8	1.099	1.127	1.157	1.188	1.221	1.256	1.293	1.333	1.376	1.422
0.9	1.472	1.528	1.589	1.658	1.738	1.832	1.946	2.092	2.298	2.647
0.99	2.647	2.700	2.759	2.826	2.903	2.995	3.106	3.250	3.453	3.800

SOURCE: Values in table computed by using the equation

$$z_F = 1.1513 \log_{10} \frac{1 + r}{1 - r}$$

TABLE B-6

Transformation of z_F = (Fisher's z) to r.

z_F	.00	.01	.02	.03	.04	.05	.06	.07	.08	.09
0.0	0.00	0.01	0.02	0.03	0.04	0.05	0.06	0.07	0.08	0.09
0.1	0.10	0.11	0.12	0.13	0.14	0.15	0.16	0.17	0.18	0.19
0.2	0.20	0.21	0.22	0.23	0.24	0.24	0.25	0.26	0.27	0.28
0.3	0.29	0.30	0.31	0.32	0.33	0.34	0.35	0.35	0.36	0.37
0.4	0.38	0.39	0.40	0.41	0.41	0.42	0.43	0.44	0.45	0.45
0.5	0.46	0.47	0.48	0.49	0.49	0.50	0.51	0.52	0.52	0.53
0.6	0.54	0.54	0.55	0.56	0.56	0.57	0.58	0.58	0.59	0.60
0.7	0.60	0.61	0.62	0.62	0.63	0.64	0.64	0.65	0.65	0.66
0.8	0.66	0.67	0.68	0.68	0.69	0.69	0.70	0.70	0.71	0.71
0.9	0.72	0.72	0.73	0.73	0.74	0.74	0.74	0.75	0.75	0.76
1.0	0.76	0.77	0.77	0.77	0.78	0.78	0.79	0.79	0.79	0.80
1.1	0.80	0.80	0.81	0.81	0.81	0.82	0.82	0.82	0.83	0.83
1.2	0.83	0.84	0.84	0.84	0.85	0.85	0.85	0.85	0.86	0.86
1.3	0.86	0.86	0.87	0.87	0.87	0.87	0.88	0.88	0.88	0.88
1.4	0.89	0.89	0.89	0.89	0.89	0.90	0.90	0.90	0.90	0.90
1.5	0.91	0.91	0.91	0.91	0.91	0.91	0.92	0.92	0.92	0.92
1.6	0.92	0.92	0.92	0.93	0.93	0.93	0.93	0.93	0.93	0.93
1.7	0.94	0.94	0.94	0.94	0.94	0.94	0.94	0.94	0.94	0.95
1.8	0.95	0.95	0.95	0.95	0.95	0.95	0.95	0.95	0.95	0.96
1.9	0.96	0.96	0.96	0.96	0.96	0.96	0.96	0.96	0.96	0.96
2.0	0.96	0.96	0.97	0.97	0.97	0.97	0.97	0.97	0.97	0.97
2.1	0.97	0.97	0.97	0.97	0.97	0.97	0.97	0.97	0.97	0.98
2.2	0.98	0.98	0.98	0.98	0.98	0.98	0.98	0.98	0.98	0.98
2.3	0.98	0.98	0.98	0.98	0.98	0.98	0.98	0.98	0.98	0.98
2.4	0.98	0.98	0.98	0.98	0.98	0.99	0.99	0.99	0.99	0.99

SOURCE: Values obtained by interpolation from Table B-5.

Appendix C
EQUATION SUMMARIES

CHAPTER 3

Median for raw data

$$\text{Mdn} = LL_i + \left[\frac{N/2 - cf_{i-1}}{f_i}\right] \tag{3.1}$$

Median for grouped data

$$\text{Mdn} = LL_i + \left(\frac{N/2 - cf_{i-1}}{f_i}\right)I \tag{3.3}$$

Mean for raw data

$$\bar{X} = \frac{\sum_{i=1}^{N} X_i}{N} \tag{3.2}$$

Mean for grouped data

$$\bar{X} = \frac{\sum\limits_{j=1}^{J} f_j X_j}{\sum\limits_{j=1}^{J} f_j} \tag{3.4}$$

Quartiles for grouped data

$$Q_1 = LL_{0.25} + \left[\frac{0.25N - cf_{0.25-1}}{f_{.25}}\right]I$$

$$Q_3 = LL_{0.75} + \left[\frac{0.75N - cf_{0.75-1}}{f_{0.75}}\right]I \tag{4.2}$$

Definition of the variance

$$S_X^2 = \frac{\sum\limits_{i=1}^{N} (X_i - \bar{X})^2}{N}$$

Definition of the standard deviation

$$S_X = \sqrt{\frac{\sum\limits_{i=1}^{N} (X_i - \bar{X})^2}{N}}$$

Computational formulas for raw data

$$S = \sqrt{\frac{\sum\limits_{i=1}^{N} X_i^2}{N} - \bar{X}^2} \tag{4.7}$$

$$S = \sqrt{\frac{N \sum\limits_{i=1}^{N} X_i^2 - \left(\sum\limits_{i=1}^{N} X_i\right)^2}{N^2}} \tag{4.8}$$

Computational formula for grouped data

$$S = \sqrt{\frac{\left(\sum\limits_{j=1}^{J} f_j\right)\left(\sum\limits_{j=1}^{J} f_j X_j^2\right) - \left(\sum\limits_{j=1}^{J} f_j X_j\right)^2}{\left(\sum\limits_{j=1}^{J} f_j\right)^2}} \tag{4.11}$$

CHAPTER 5

Definition of standard score

$$z_i = \frac{X_i - \bar{X}}{S_X} \tag{5.2}$$

Mean of transformed scores—grouped data

$$\text{Mean}_T = \frac{\sum\limits_{j=1}^{J} [f_j(T_j)]}{\sum\limits_{j=1}^{J} (f_j)} \tag{5.3}$$

Standard deviation of transformed scores—grouped data

$$S_T = \sqrt{\frac{[\sum(f_j)]\left[\sum\limits_{j=1}^{J} [f_j(T_j^2)]\right] - \left[\sum\limits_{j=1}^{J} [f_j(T_j)]\right]^2}{\left[\sum\limits_{j=1}^{J} (f_j)\right]^2}} \tag{5.4}$$

CHAPTER 6

Calculation of percentile p—grouped data

$$P_p = LL_i + \left[\frac{pN - cf_{i-1}}{f_i}\right] \cdot I \tag{6.1}$$

Percentile rank of score i

$$PR_i = \frac{cf_{i-1} + \frac{1}{2}f_i}{N} \tag{6.2}$$

Linear transformation to an arbitrary mean and standard deviation

$$X_{A_i} = z_i(S_A) + \bar{X}_A \tag{6.3}$$

Probability of outcome H

$$P_H = \frac{N_H}{N} \tag{7.1}$$

Number of combinations of N things in groups of r

$$_NC_r = \frac{N!}{r!(N-r)!} \tag{7.2}$$

Raw-score, linear-regression equation

$$\hat{Y}_i = BX_i + A \tag{8.2}$$

Deviation-score, linear-regression equation

$$\hat{y}_i = bx_i \tag{8.5}$$

Definitional equation for the regression slope

$$b_{y \cdot x} = \frac{\displaystyle\sum_{i=1}^{N} x_i y_i}{\displaystyle\sum_{i=1}^{N} x_i^2} \tag{8.6}$$

Computational equation for the regression slope

$$b_{y \cdot x} = \frac{N(\sum X_i Y_i) - (\sum X_i)(\sum Y_i)}{N(\sum X_i^2) - (\sum X_i)^2} \tag{8.8}$$

Computation of the intercept

$$A_{y \cdot x} = \bar{Y} - b_{y \cdot x} \bar{X} \tag{8.9}$$

Definition of the standard error of estimate

$$S_{y \cdot x} = \sqrt{\frac{\sum\limits_{i=1}^{N} (Y_i - \hat{Y}_i)^2}{N}} \tag{8.3}$$

CHAPTER 9

Partitioning total variance into predictable and error portions

$$\frac{\sum\limits_{j=1}^{J} \sum\limits_{i=1}^{n_j} (Y_{ji} - \bar{Y})^2}{\sum\limits_{j=1}^{J} n_j} = \frac{\sum\limits_{j=1}^{J} \sum\limits_{i=1}^{n_j} (\bar{Y}_j - \bar{Y})^2}{\sum\limits_{j=1}^{J} n_j} + \frac{\sum\limits_{j=1}^{J} \sum\limits_{i=1}^{n_j} (Y_{ji} - \bar{Y}_j)^2}{\sum\limits_{j=1}^{J} n_j} \tag{9.5}$$

Definition of the correlation ratio

$$\eta^2 = \frac{S_{\hat{y}}^2}{S_y^2} = 1 - \frac{S_{y \cdot x}^2}{S_y^2} \tag{9.9}$$

$$\eta^2 = \frac{\sum\limits_{j=1}^{J} \sum\limits_{i=1}^{n_j} (\bar{Y}_j - \bar{Y})^2}{\sum\limits_{j=1}^{J} \sum\limits_{i=1}^{n_i} (Y_{ji} - \bar{Y})^2} = 1 - \frac{\sum\limits_{j} \sum\limits_{i} (Y_{ji} - \bar{Y}_j)^2}{\sum\limits_{j} \sum\limits_{i} (Y_{ji} - \bar{Y})^2} \tag{9.10}$$

Definition of the squared-correlation coefficient as a variance ratio

$$r_{xy}^2 = \frac{S_{\hat{y}}^2}{S_y^2} = 1 - \frac{S_{y \cdot x}^2}{S_y^2} \tag{9.16}$$

Definition of the correlation coefficient in standard scores

$$r_{yx} = \frac{\sum z_y z_x}{N} \tag{9.18}$$

Relationship between the regression slope and the correlation coefficient

$$b_{y \cdot x} = r_{yx} \frac{S_y}{S_x} \tag{9.20}$$

Definition of the correlation coefficient in deviation scores

$$r_{xy} = \frac{\sum\limits_{i=1}^{N} \dfrac{x_i}{S_x} \dfrac{y_i}{S_y}}{N} = \frac{\sum x_i y_i}{N S_x S_y} \tag{9.21}$$

Computational formula for the correlation coefficient

$$r = \frac{N\left[\sum(XY)\right] - \sum X(\sum Y)}{\sqrt{N\sum X^2 - (\sum X)^2} \sqrt{N\sum Y^2 - (\sum Y)^2}} \tag{9.23}$$

Computational formula for the variance error of estimate

$$S_{y\cdot x}^2 = S_y^2(1 - r_{xy}^2) \tag{9.24}$$

CHAPTER 10

Total (observed) score is composed of true score and error of measurement

$$X_{ij} = T_i + e_{ij} \tag{10.1}$$

Total variance is composed of true-score variance and error-score variance

$$S_{X_1}^2 = S_T^2 + S_{e_1}^2 \tag{10.3}$$

Definition of the reliability coefficient

$$r_{x_1 x_2} = \frac{S_T^2}{S_x^2} \tag{10.7}$$

Computational formula for the standard error of measurement

$$S_e = S_x \sqrt{1 - r_{xx}} \tag{10.8}$$

CHAPTER 13

Standard error of the mean

$$\sigma_{\bar{x}} = \frac{\sigma}{\sqrt{N}} \tag{13.2}$$

Critical ratio for one sample hypothesis

$$z_{\bar{X}} = \frac{\bar{X} - \mu}{\sigma_{\bar{X}}} \qquad (13.3)$$

Ways of making Type I and Type II errors

		Decision	
		Reject Null	*Do not reject Null*
True	Null False	Correct decision (power)	Type II error (β)
State	Null True	Type I error (α)	Correct decision

One-tailed null hypotheses

$\mu \geq K$

$\mu \leq K$

Two-tailed null hypothesis

$\mu = K$

CHAPTER 14

Mean of the differences is equal to the difference between means

$$\mu_{(\bar{X}_1 - \bar{X}_2)} = \mu_{\bar{X}_1} - \mu_{\bar{X}_2} \qquad (14.2)$$

Standard error of the difference between means

$$\sigma_{(\bar{X}_1 - \bar{X}_2)} = \sqrt{\frac{\sigma_{\bar{X}_1}^2}{N_1} + \frac{\sigma_{\bar{X}_2}^2}{N_2}} \qquad (14.3)$$

Two-sample critical ratio

$$z_{(\bar{X}_1 - \bar{X}_2)} = \frac{(\bar{X}_1 - \bar{X}_2) - (\mu_1 - \mu_2)}{\sigma_{(\bar{X}_1 - \bar{X}_2)}} \qquad (14.4)$$

Unbiased estimate of the population variance—definitional formula

$$\hat{S}_X^2 = \frac{\sum (X - \bar{X})^2}{(N - 1)} \qquad (14.5)$$

Estimate of the population standard deviation—definitional formula

$$\hat{S}_X = \sqrt{\frac{\sum(X - \bar{X})^2}{(N - 1)}} \qquad (14.6)$$

Relationship between the sample variance and the unbiased population variance

$$\hat{S}_X^2 = \frac{N}{(N - 1)} S_X^2 \qquad (14.7)$$

Estimate of the standard error of the mean

$$\hat{S}_{\bar{X}} = \frac{\hat{S}_X}{\sqrt{N}} \qquad (14.9)$$

Computational formula for the estimate of the population variance

$$\hat{S}_X = \sqrt{\frac{N\sum X^2 - (\sum X)^2}{N(N - 1)}} \qquad (14.10)$$

Computing the standard error of the mean from the sample standard deviation

$$\hat{S}_{\bar{X}} = \frac{S_X}{\sqrt{N - 1}} \qquad (14.11)$$

One-sample t-test

$$t = \frac{\bar{X} - \mu}{\hat{S}_{\bar{X}}} \qquad (14.8)$$

Formulas for two independent samples:

Pooled estimate of the population variance

$$\hat{S}_p^2 = \frac{(N_1 - 1)\,\hat{S}_1^2 + (N_2 - 1)\,\hat{S}_2^2}{N_1 + N_2 - 2} \qquad (14.12)$$

Standard error of the difference from the pooled estimate of the variance

$$\hat{S}_{(\bar{X}_1 - \bar{X}_2)} = \sqrt{\frac{\hat{S}_p^2}{N_1} + \frac{\hat{S}_p^2}{N_2}} \qquad (14.13)$$

Two-sample t-test

$$t = \frac{\bar{X}_1 - \bar{X}_2 - (\mu_1 - \mu_2)}{\hat{S}_{(\bar{X}_1 - \bar{X}_2)}} \qquad (14.14)$$

Formulas for matched pairs or related samples:

Standard error of the difference between means

$$\hat{S}_{(\bar{X}_1 - \bar{X}_2)} = \sqrt{\frac{\hat{S}_1^2}{N_1} + \frac{\hat{S}_2^2}{N_2} - 2r_{X_1 X_2}\left(\frac{\hat{S}_1}{\sqrt{N_1}}\right)\left(\frac{\hat{S}_2}{\sqrt{N_2}}\right)} \tag{14.15}$$

Two-sample t-test for matched or related samples

$$t = \frac{\bar{X}_1 - \bar{X}_2 - (\mu_1 - \mu_2)}{\hat{S}_{(\bar{X}_1 - \bar{X}_2)}} \tag{14.14}$$

Formulas for the direct difference method with matched or related pairs:

Standard error of the difference—computational formula

$$\hat{S}_D = \sqrt{\frac{N\sum D^2 - (\sum D)^2}{N(N-1)}} \tag{14.17}$$

Standard error of the mean of differences

$$\hat{S}_{\bar{D}} = \frac{\hat{S}_D}{\sqrt{N}} \tag{14.16}$$

t-test for the significance of the difference

$$t = \frac{\bar{D} - K}{\hat{S}_{\bar{D}}} \tag{14.18}$$

CHAPTER 15

Definition of chi square and test of hypotheses about a single sample variance

$$\chi^2 = \frac{(N-1)\hat{S}_x^2}{\sigma_x^2} \tag{15.3}$$

Confidence interval for the population variance

$$\frac{(N-1)\hat{S}_x^2}{\chi_{0.95}^2} < \sigma_x^2 < \frac{(N-1)\hat{S}_x^2}{\chi_{0.05}^2} \tag{15.4}$$

Definition of F as a ratio of chi-square variables

$$F = \frac{\chi_1^2/df_1}{\chi_2^2/df_2} = \frac{\hat{S}_1^2/\sigma^2}{\hat{S}_2^2/\sigma^2} \tag{15.5}$$

Definition of F as a ratio of two-variance estimates and test of hypotheses concerning variances of two samples

$$F = \frac{S_1^2}{S_2^2} \tag{15.7}$$

Chi-square tests for frequencies:

Computation of expected frequency

$$E_{RC} = \frac{f_R f_C}{N} \tag{15.8}$$

Chi-square test of independence for $df > 1$

$$\chi^2 = \sum_R \sum_C \frac{(O_{RC} - E_{RC})^2}{E_{RC}} \tag{15.9}$$

Chi-square test of independence with Yates correction for $df = 1$

$$\chi^2 = \sum \left[\frac{(\, |O_{RC} - E_{RC}\,| - 0.5)^2}{E} \right] \tag{15.11}$$

Tests of hypotheses about correlations:

Fisher's z transformation

$$z_F = 1.1513 \log_{10} \left(\frac{1 + r}{1 - r} \right) \tag{15.12}$$

Standard error of Fisher's z

$$\sigma_{z_F} = \frac{1}{\sqrt{N - 3}} \tag{15.13}$$

Standard error of the correlation coefficient for large samples

$$\sigma_r = \frac{1}{\sqrt{N}} \tag{15.14}$$

Critical ratio test of the hypothesis $r = 0.00$ for large samples

$$z = \frac{r}{\sigma_r} \tag{15.15}$$

t-test of the hypothesis that $r = 0.00$ for small samples

$$t = \frac{r}{\sqrt{(1 - r^2)/(N - 2)}} \tag{15.16}$$

Standard error of the difference between correlations using Fisher's *z*

$$\sigma_{(z_{F_1} - z_{F_2})} = \sqrt{\frac{1}{N_1 - 3} + \frac{1}{N_2 - 3}} \tag{15.17}$$

CHAPTER 16

Partitioning total sum of squares into between and within portions

$$\sum_{j=1}^{J} \sum_{i=1}^{N} (X_{ij} - \bar{\bar{X}})^2 = N \left[\sum_{j=1}^{J} (\bar{X}_j - \bar{\bar{X}})^2 \right] + \sum_{j=1}^{J} \left[\sum_{i=1}^{N} (X_{ij} - \bar{X}_j)^2 \right] \tag{16.5}$$

Definitional equations for sums of squares

$$SS_T = \sum_j \sum_i (X_{ij} - \bar{\bar{X}})^2$$

$$SS_B = N \sum_j (\bar{X}_j - \bar{\bar{X}})^2$$

$$SS_W = \sum_j \sum_i (X_{ij} - \bar{X}_j)^2$$

Definitional equations for mean squares

$$S_T^2 = \frac{\sum_j \sum_i (X_{ij} - \bar{\bar{X}})^2}{JN - 1} = \frac{SS_T}{JN + 1} = MS_T$$

$$\hat{S}_W^2 = \frac{\sum_j \left[\sum_i (X_{ij} - \bar{X}_j)^2 \right]}{JN - J} = \frac{SS_W}{JN - J} = MS_W \tag{16.6}$$

$$\hat{S}_B^2 = \frac{\sum_j [N(\bar{X}_j - \bar{\bar{X}})^2]}{J - 1} = \frac{SS_B}{J - 1} = MS_B$$

df Component	Computational Formula
1	$\dfrac{\left(\sum\limits_{j}\sum\limits_{i} X_{ij}\right)^2}{JN}$
JN	$\sum\limits_{i}\sum\limits_{j} X_{ij}^2$
J	$\sum\limits_{j=1}^{J} \dfrac{\left(\sum\limits_{i=1}^{N} X_{ij}\right)^2}{N}$

Computational formulas for sums of squares

$$SS_T = \sum_{j}\sum_{i} X_{ij}^2 - \frac{\left(\sum\limits_{j}\sum\limits_{i} X_{ij}\right)^2}{JN}$$

$$SS_B = \sum_{j=1}^{J} \frac{\left(\sum\limits_{i=1}^{N} X_{ij}\right)^2}{N} - \frac{\left(\sum\limits_{j}\sum\limits_{i} X_{ij}\right)^2}{JN}$$

$$SS_W = \sum_{j}\sum_{i} X_{ij}^2 - \sum_{j=1}^{J} \frac{\left(\sum\limits_{i=1}^{N} X_{ij}\right)^2}{N}$$

F-test of the hypothesis of the equality of several group means

$$F = \frac{MS_B}{MS_W} \tag{16.9}$$

Tests for posterior contrasts:

General equation for the definition of a contrast

$$\tag{16.11}$$

$$C = \frac{N_a\bar{X}_a + N_b\bar{X}_b + \ldots + N_k\bar{X}_k}{N_a + N_b + \ldots + N_k} - \frac{N_\ell\bar{X}_\ell + N_m\bar{X}_m + \ldots + N_z\bar{X}_z}{N_\ell + N_m + \ldots + N_z}$$

Standard error of contrast C

$$\hat{S}_c^2 = MS_W \left(\frac{1}{N_a + N_b + \ldots + N_k} + \frac{1}{N_\ell + N_m + \ldots + N_z} \right) \quad (16.12)$$

Value of t for contrast C

$$t = \frac{C}{\hat{S}_C} \quad (16.13)$$

Corrected critical value for t for use with posterior contrasts

$$t_{\substack{\text{corrected} \\ \text{critical}}} = \sqrt{(df_B)(F_{df_B df_W})} \quad (16.14)$$

Appendix D
Answers to Selected Problems

		tallies	f	
1. a.	Cedar	卌	5	
	Pine	卌 卌 ‖‖	14	
	Hemlock	卌	5	
	Tamarack	‖‖‖	4	
	Dogwood	‖	2	

2.a.				
	20	‖	1	20
	19		0	19
	18	卌	5	19
	17	卌	5	14
	16	卌‖	6	9
	15	‖	1	3
	14	‖	1	2
	13	‖	1	1

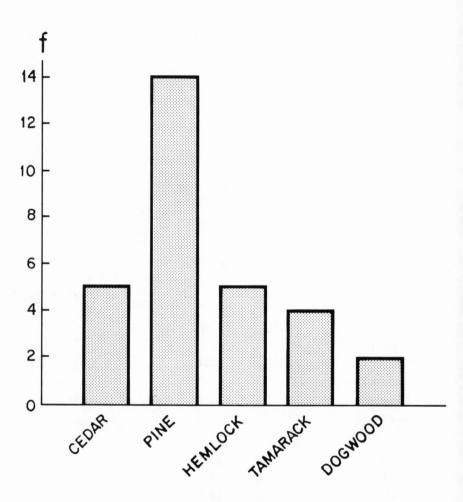

		tallies	*f*	*cf*
b.	63	||	2	20
	62		0	18
	61	|	1	18
	60		0	17
	59		0	17
	58		0	17
	57		0	17
	56		0	17
	55	|	1	17
	54	|	1	16
	53	||	2	15
	52	|	1	13
	51	||	2	12
	50	||	2	10
	49	|	1	8
	48	|	1	7
	47		0	6
	46		0	6
	45	|	1	6
	44		0	5
	43	|	1	5
	42	|	1	4
	41		0	3
	40		0	3
	39		0	3
	38		0	3
	37		0	3
	36		0	3
	35		0	3
	34		0	3
	33	||	2	3
	32		0	1
	31		0	1
	30		0	1
	29		0	1
	28	|	1	1

3.a. Not appropriate

b.

Interval	Midpoint	tallies	f	cf
63-65	64	||	2	20
60-62	61	|	1	18
57-59	58		0	17
54-56	55	||	2	17
51-53	52	ⅢⅠ	5	15
48-50	49	||||	4	10
45-47	46	|	1	6
42-44	43	||	2	5
39-41	40		0	3
36-38	37		0	3
33-35	34	||	2	3
30-32	31		0	1
27-29	28	|	1	1

b. Alternative

Interval	Midpoint	tallies	f	cf
60-64	62	|||	3	20
55-59	57	|	1	17
50-54	52	ⅢⅠ ||||	9	16
45-49	47	|||	3	8
40-44	42	||	2	5
35-39	37		0	3
30-34	32	||	2	3
25-29	27	|	1	1

4. Because the scores go from 59 to 86, there are 28 possible score values. You should therefore convert the data to a grouped frequency distribution with an interval width of 3 and construct your frequency polygon from this distribution.

Interval	X	f	Interval	X	f
84-86	85	2	69-71	70	8
81-83	82	4	66-68	67	2
78-80	79	10	63-65	64	1
75-77	76	8	60-62	61	1
72-74	73	13	57-59	58	1

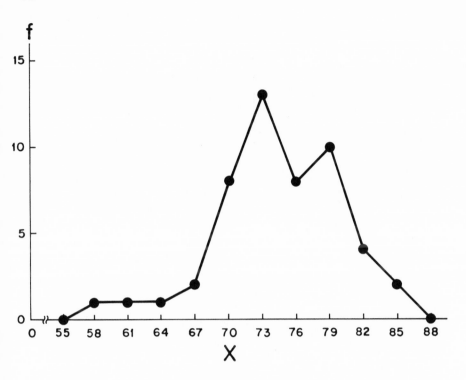

6. With 39 possible score values we must again group the data.

Interval	X	f
96-98	97	1
93-95	94	3
90-92	91	0
87-89	88	8
84-86	85	0
81-83	82	10
78-80	79	9
75-77	76	11
72-74	73	6
69-71	70	7
66-68	67	0
63-65	64	2
60-62	61	1

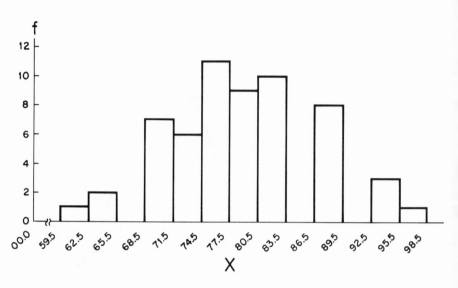

8.a.   First group the date using an interval of 3.

Interval	X	f	cf
27-29	28	1	35
24-26	25	3	34
21-23	22	4	31
18-20	19	3	27
15-17	16	9	24
12-14	13	4	15
9-11	10	9	11
6- 8	7	0	2
3- 5	4	2	2

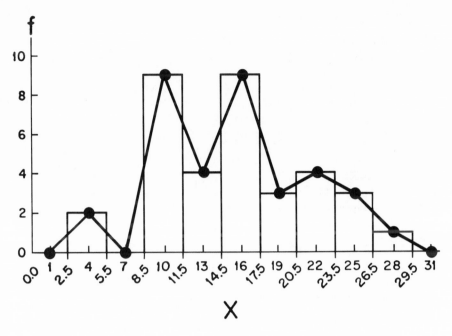

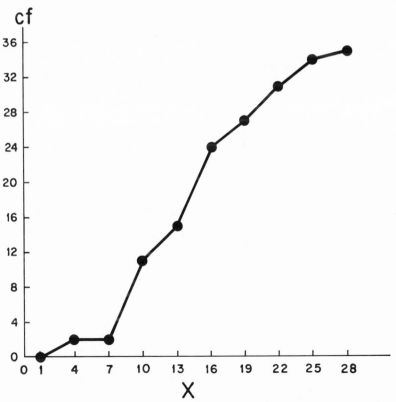

9.a.   With an interval of two

Interval	X	tallies	f	cf
88-89	88.5	|	1	50
86-87	86.5	|	1	49
84-85	84.5	|	1	48
82-83	82.5	||	2	47
80-81	80.5	卌	5	45
78-79	78.5	卌 |	6	40
76-77	76.5	卌 卌	10	34
74-75	74.5	||||	4	24
72-73	72.5	卌 ||||	9	20
70-71	70.5	|||	3	11
68-69	68.5	卌 |	6	8
66-67	66.5	||	2	2

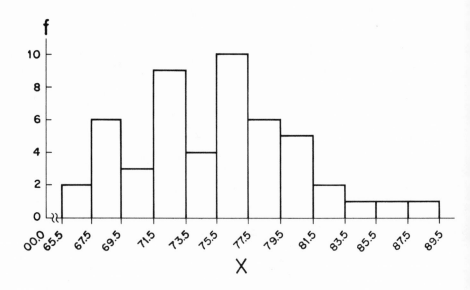

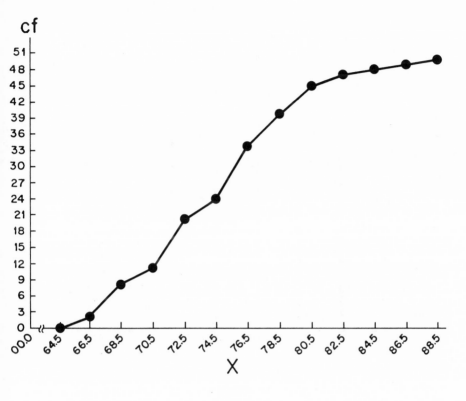

With an interval of three

87-89	88	│	1	50
84-86	85	‖	2	49
81-83	82	ЦНТ	5	47
78-80	79	ЦНТ │││	8	42
75-77	76	ЦНТ ЦНТ ‖	12	34
72-74	73	ЦНТ ЦНТ │	11	22
69-71	70	ЦНТ ‖	7	11
66-68	67	‖‖	4	4

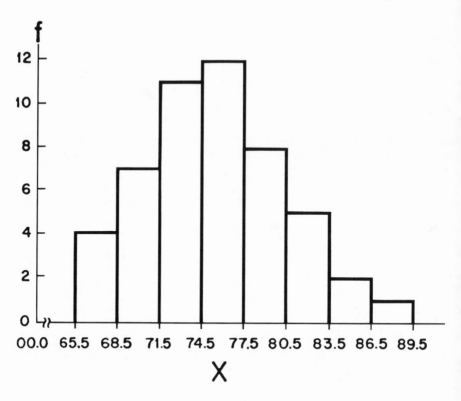

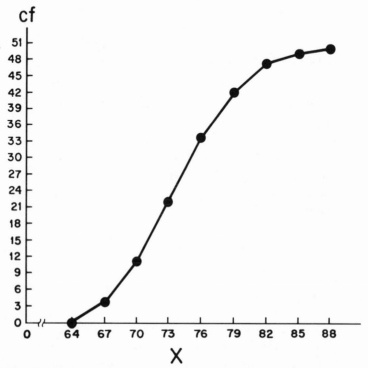

9.c.

Interval	X	tallies	f	cf
96-98	97	I	1	25
93-95	94	II	2	24
90-92	91	I	1	22
87-89	88	I	1	21
84-86	85	I	1	20
81-83	82	III	3	19
78-80	79	I	1	16
75-77	76	I	1	15
72-74	73	IIII	4	14
69-71	70	HIT I	6	10
66-68	67	II	2	4
63-65	64	I	1	2
60-62	61	I	1	1

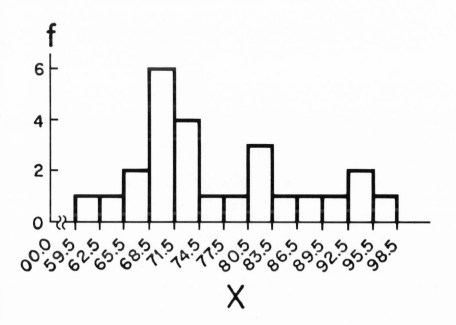

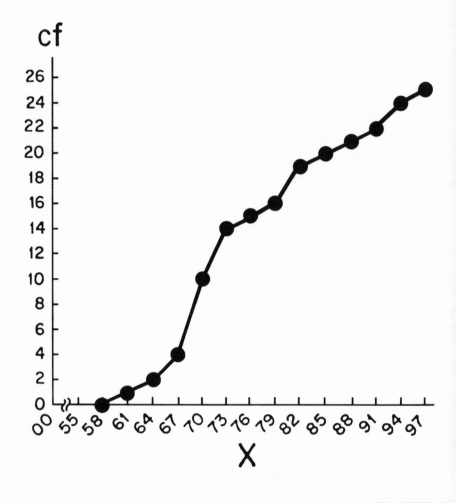

3.a.

X	f	cf	
20	1	15	
19	0	14	$.5N = 7.5$
18	5	14	
17	3	9	$LL_i = 16.5$
16	2	6	
15	1	4	$\text{Mdn} = 16.5 + \dfrac{7.5 - 6}{3}$
14	1	3	
13	0	2	$= 16.5 + \dfrac{1.5}{3}$

12	1	2		$= 17.0$
11	0	1		
10	1	1	$\Sigma X = 244$	
			$\overline{X} = 16.27$	

c.　Mdn $= 100$　　　　　　$\overline{X} = 103.13$

4.a.　$.5N = 17.5$　　　　　　$\Sigma X = 570$
　　　$LL_i = 16.5$　　　　　　$\overline{X} = 16.29$
　　　Mdn $= 16.5 + \dfrac{17.5 - 17}{5}$

　　　　　　$= 16.5 + \dfrac{.5}{5}$

　　　　　　$= 16.6$

5.a.　$.5N = 25$　　　　　　$\Sigma X = 3,731$
　　　$LL_i = 73.5$　　　　　　$\overline{X} = 74.62$
　　　Mdn $= 73.5 + \dfrac{25 - 22}{4}$

　　　　　　$= 73.5 + 3/4$
　　　　　　$= 74.25$

6.a.　Since there are 50 scores, the median falls half way between the 25th (483) and 26th (516). This value is 499.5.
　　　$\Sigma X = 25,316$　　　　　　　　　　$\overline{X} = 506.32$

b.

Interval	X	tallies	f	cf	fX
700-749	724.5			1	50	724.5
650-699	674.5	||||	4	49	2,698
600-649	624.5	ЖҬ	5	45	3,122.5
550-599	574.5	ЖҬ ||||	9	40	5,170.5
500-549	524.5	ЖҬ|	6	31	3,147
450-499	474.5	ЖҬЖҬ	10	25	4,745
400-449	424.5	ЖҬ	5	15	2,122.5
350-399	374.5	ЖҬ|	6	10	2,247
300-349	324.5	||	2	4	649
250-299	274.5	||	2	2	549

c. $.5N = 25$ $\Sigma fx = 25{,}175$

      $LL_i = 449.5$ $\overline{X} = \quad 503.5$

$$\text{Mdn} = 449.5 + \frac{25 - 15}{10} \cdot 50$$

$$= 449.5 + \frac{10}{10} \cdot 50$$

$$= 499.5$$

7.

X	f	cf	fX
5.02	1	20	5.02
5.01	6	19	30.12
5.00	7	13	35.00
4.99	4	6	19.96
4.98	2	2	9.96

Mode $= 5.00$ Median $= 4.9993$ $\overline{X} = 5.003$

8.

X (grams)	Y (mg)
267	.267
264	.264
252	.252
247	.247
247	.247
243	.243
242	.242
241	.241
239	.239
238	.238

$\Sigma Y = 2.480$ mg.

$\overline{Y} = \ .248$ mg

Mode $= \ .247$

$\overline{X} = 248$ grams

Mdn $= 245$ grams

The median is more representative.

10.   There are many possible sets of scores that will solve this problem.
The scores must add to 80 ($\Sigma X = 80$). Some possible solutions are
5, 5, 6, 6, 7, 8, 9, 9, 10, 16
5, 6, 7, 7, 7, 8, 9, 10, 10, 11
0, 0, 0, 0, 5, 10, 10, 10, 10, 35

CHAPTER 4

1. Range $= (69 - 53) + 1 = 17$

    $.25N = 3.75$ $\qquad\qquad$ $.75\,N = 11.25$

    $LL_i = 56.5$ $\qquad\qquad$ $LL_i = 63.5$

    $Q_1 = 56.5 + \dfrac{3.75 - 3}{1}$ $\qquad$ $Q_3 = 63.5 + \dfrac{11.25 - 11}{2}$

    $Q_1 = 57.25$ $\qquad\qquad$ $Q_3 = 63.625$

    Interquartile range $= Q_3 - Q_1 = 6.375$

    $\overline{X} = 60.5$

3. $\Sigma X^2 = 289.75$ $\qquad\qquad$ $S = 4.395$

5.a. $R = (15 - 3) + 1 = 13$ $\qquad$ $Q_1 = 7.375$ $\quad$ $Q_3 = 11.625$

    Interquartile range $= 4.25$ $\qquad\qquad$ Mdn $= 9.83$

    $\overline{X} = 9.32$ $\qquad\qquad\qquad$ $S = 3.18$

 c. $R = (22 - 2) + 1 = 21$ $\qquad$ $Q_1 = 7.25$ $\quad$ $Q_3 = 16.75$

    Interquartile range $= 9.5$ $\qquad\qquad$ Mdn $= 11.25$

    $\overline{X} = 12.05$ $\qquad\qquad\qquad$ $S = 5.79$

 e. $R = 16$ $\qquad\qquad\qquad\qquad$ $Q_1 = 9.375$ $\quad$ $Q_3 = 15.625$

    Interquartile range $= 6.25$ $\qquad\qquad$ Mdn $= 12.25$

    $\overline{X} = 12.74$ $\qquad\qquad\qquad$ $S = 3.81$

6.a. The set of scores 5, 6, 6, 7, 7, 7, 8, 10, 12, 12, 12, 12, 12, 13, 13, 14, 15, 16, 17, 17, 18, 20, 25, 25, 26 is one of a large number of possible answers.

 c. To solve problems of this kind you need to reason backward from the answer. Since $S = 3, S^2 = 9$. Also, $S^2 = \Sigma x^2/N$, so $\Sigma x^2 = NS^2 = 90$. Therefore, we must find a set of 10 squared deviations that sum to 90. A trivial answer is to have all of them be 9. The set 16, 16, 16, 9, 9, 9, 9, 4, 1, 1 also solves the problem, yielding deviation scores of 4, 3, 2 and 1. Some of these must be positive and some negative because their sum must be zero (remember, $\Sigma x = 0$). The set of deviation scores 4, -4, 4, -3, -3, -3, 3, 2, 1, -1 satisfies the necessary conditions that $\Sigma x = 0$ and $\Sigma x^2 = 90$. Raw scores are obtained by adding any mean you choose.

 e. The solution to this problem follows the same steps as 6.c., but the mean is 8. One solution is the set 11, 11, 11, 10, 10, 10, 9, 9, 9, 8, 7, 7, 7, 7, 6, 6, 6, 6, 5, 5.

7.a.

$\overline{X}$	f	fX	X^2	fX^2	cf
20	1	20	400	400	20
19	0	0	361	0	19
18	5	90	324	1,620	19
17	5	85	289	1,445	14
16	6	96	256	1,536	9
15	1	15	225	225	3
14	1	14	196	196	2
13	1	13	169	169	1

$\overline{X} = 16.65$ $Q_1 = 15.83$ $Q_3 = 17.70$

Interquartile range $= 1.87$ $S^2 = 2.33$ $S = 1.53$

8.a. $Q_1 = 28.875$ $Q_3 = 42.714$ Interquartile range $= 13.839$
     $S = 10.51$

9. $Q_1 = 78.89$ $Q_3 = 85.42$ Interquartile range $= 6.53$
     $S^2 = 37.75$ $S = 6.14$

11.a.   Interquartile range $= 17.5$ Mdn $= 98.0$
     $\overline{X} = 99.71$ $S = 14.89$
     Using an interval width of 5 with the bottom interval 65-69, the same
     statistics are: Interquartile range 18.85
     Mdn $= 99.0$ $\overline{X} = 99.43$ $S = 15.18$

CHAPTER 5

1.a.   813, 843, 893, 923, 933, 933, 943, 953, 973, 983, 1,003, 1,013, 1,013, 1,023, 1,023, 1,033, 1,033, 1,053, 1,083, 1,093, 1,133, 1,143, 1,153, 1,163, 1,163, 1,203

   b.   23, 33, 33, 43, 43, 43, 53, 53, 53, 53, 53, 53, 53, 53, 63, 63, 63, 63, 63, 63, 73, 73, 73, 83, 83, 83, 83, 83, 83, 83, 83, 83, 93, 93, 103

2.a. $\overline{X} = 101.69$ $S = 9.999$ $\overline{X}_T = 1,019.9$ $S_T = 99.99$
   c. $\overline{X} = 6.2$ $S = 1.894$ $\overline{X}_T = 65.0$ $S_T = 18.94$

3.a.   167, 172, 187, 217, 217, 232, 232, 247, 247, 247, 262, 267, 272, 277, 282, 292, 297, 312, 332, 332

   c.   37, 42, 47, 52, 57, 62, 67, 72, 77

     Mdn $= 50.5$ $\overline{X} = 50.5$ $Q = 12.5$ $S = 9.31$

4.a. $\text{Mdn}_T = 254.5$ $\overline{X}_T = 254.5$ $Q_T = 62.5$ $S_T = 46.55$

c.

X	X'	f	fX	fX'	fX²	fX'²	cf
15	77	2	30	308	450	11,858	50
14	72	5	70	360	980	25,920	48
13	67	5	65	335	845	22,445	43
12	62	6	72	372	864	23,064	38
11	57	14	154	798	1,694	45,486	32
10	52	8	80	416	800	21,632	18
9	47	6	54	282	486	13,254	10
8	42	2	16	84	128	3,528	4
7	37	2	14	74	98	2,738	2

$\overline{X} = 11.1$ $\text{Mdn} = 11.0$ $Q = 2.6$ $S = 1.92$

$\overline{X}_T = 57.5$ $\text{Mdn} = 57.0$ $Q = 13$ $S = 9.60$

5.a. -0.277 c. -2.191

     1.426 -1.553

     0.362 -0.064

    -1.766 1.000

CHAPTER 6

1.a. $P_{25} = 15.75$ $P_{47} = LL_i + \dfrac{.47N - cf_{i\ 1}}{f_i}$

$$= 16.5 + \frac{4.7 - 4}{3}$$

    $P_{08} = 12.3$ $= 16.73$

c. $P_{25} = 65.0$ $P_{47} = 74.33$ $P_{08} = 57.167$

2.a. $PR_{17} = \dfrac{cf_{i-1} + \frac{1}{2}f_i}{N}$ c. $PR_{117} = 94$

$$= \frac{2 + \frac{1}{2}(1)}{10}$$

$$= 25$$

3.a. -1.00 c. 1.92

    -0.25 0.25

     0.50 -2.25

5.a. $P_{30} = 72.75$ $P_{45} = 76.0$ $P_{55} = 78.0$ $P_{70} = 80.0$

b. $PR_{68} = 13$ $PR_{70} = 18$ $PR_{75} = 40$ $PR_{79} = 63$ $PR_{87} = 98$

c. $\overline{X} = 75.88$ $S = 5.965$

d. $z_{68} = -1.32$ $z_{75} = -0.148$ $z_{79} = 0.523$ $z_{87} = 1.864$

e. 78.88 $\qquad$ 97.632 $\qquad$ 108.368 $\qquad$ 129.824

CHAPTER 7

1.a. $N = 500$ $N_{\text{males}} = 225$ $P_{male} = 0.45$

c. $P_{F \text{ or } S} = P_F + P_S = 0.08 + 0.36 = 0.44$

e. $P_{M \text{ and } S} = P_M \cdot P_S = 0.36 \cdot 0.45 = 0.162$

Gender and class must be independent.

2.a. 0.25 $\quad$ c. 0.50 $\quad$ e. 25

f. 1) $z_{20} = -1.15$ $\quad p = 0.125$ $\qquad$ 3) $z_{22} = -0.69$ $\quad p = 0.755$

$\quad$ 5) $p = 0.51$ $\qquad$ 7) $p = 0.49$

$\quad$ 9) $p = 0.6733$ $\qquad$ 11) $p = 0.0929$

4.a. 0.1587 $\qquad$ c. 0.0505

e. 0.4987 $\qquad$ g. 0.8664

5.a. 0.00 $\quad$ c. -0.995 $\quad$ e. 2.576 $\quad$ g. 1.28

7. 155

9.a. 89 $\quad$ c. 59

11. 82.75 $\quad$ 117.25

CHAPTER 8

2.a. classification $\qquad$ b. placement $\quad$ c. classification

d. selection $\qquad$ e. selection

3.b. You must find the mean for each class. There are seven freshmen, and their mean attitude score is 7.14.

$\overline{X}_{Soph} = 5.14$ $\qquad \overline{X}_J = 2.86$ $\qquad \overline{X}_S = 6.43$

c. 1.245 (the standard deviation of the 7 juniors' scores)

d. 2.02 to 3.70

e. The class variable does not represent an interval scale and, more importantly, the relationship is definitely not linear.

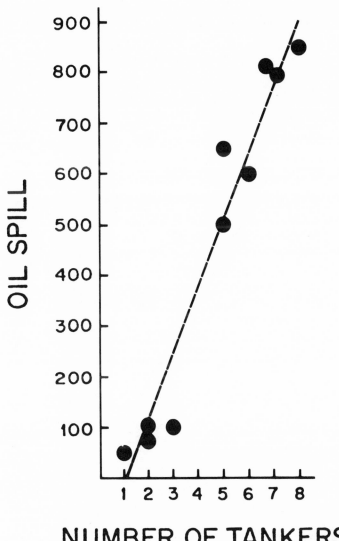

NUMBER OF TANKERS

5.a.

  b. $\hat{Y} = bX + A$ $\hat{Y} = 132.3\,X - 154.5$

  c. 5, 11, 2 or 3 (2.4!)

6.b. $b_{y \cdot x} = 6.26$ $A_{y \cdot x} = -6.05$ $S_{y \cdot x} = 3.26$

  d. $b_{y \cdot x} = 0.18$ $A_{y \cdot x} = 2.94$ $S_{y \cdot x} = 0.565$

7.b. $b_{y \cdot x} = -0.643$ $A_{y \cdot x} = 8.367$

      $\hat{Y} = -0.643\,X + 8.367$

  c. Johnny is 5.58 years old

      $\hat{Y} = -0.643\,(5.58) + 8.367$

      $\hat{Y} = 4.78$

  d. $S_{y \cdot x} = 1.56$

  e. 2.21 to 7.35

CHAPTER 9

1. $\Sigma(Y_{i1} - \overline{Y}_1)^2 = 61.5 \qquad \Sigma(Y_{i2} - \overline{Y}_2)^2 = 35.2 \qquad \Sigma(Y_{i3} - \overline{Y}_3)^2 = 90.8$

   $\Sigma n_j(\overline{Y}_j - \overline{Y})^2 = 54.25 \qquad \Sigma\Sigma(Y_{ij} - \overline{Y}_j)^2 = 187.5$

   $\Sigma\Sigma(\overline{Y}_{ij} - \overline{Y})^2 = 241.75$

   $S_y^2 = 15.11 \qquad S_{\hat{y}}^2 = 3.39 \qquad\qquad\qquad S_{y\cdot x}^2 = 11.72$

   $\eta^2 = \dfrac{3.39}{15.11} = 1 - \dfrac{11.72}{15.11} = .224$

   $\Sigma\Sigma(Y_{ij} - Y)^2 = 2{,}103.43 \qquad \Sigma n_j(Y_j - \overline{Y})^2 = 13.00$

   $\Sigma\Sigma(Y_{ij} - Y_j)^2 = 2{,}090.43$

   $S_y^2 = 131.46 \qquad\quad S_{\hat{y}}^2 = 0.81 \qquad\quad S_{y\cdot x}^2 = 130.65$

   $\eta^2 = 0.006$

3.a. $r = 0.968 \qquad\quad r^2 = 0.938 \qquad\quad b_{y\cdot x} = 0.121$

   This is a very high degree of relationship

   $S_{y\cdot x} = 0.815 \qquad\quad S^{x\cdot y} = 6.55$

   c. $r = 0.159 \qquad\quad r^2 = 0.025 \qquad\quad b_{y\cdot x} = 0.005$

   low relationship

   $S_{x\cdot y} = 3.81 \qquad\quad S^{x\cdot y} = 111.88$

   e. $r = -0.308 \qquad\quad r^2 = 0.095 \qquad\quad b_{y\cdot x} = -0.046$

   $S_{y\cdot x} = 3.98 \qquad\quad S^{x\cdot y} = 26.90 \qquad$ low to moderate relationship

4. There are two features of this problem that require careful attention. First, as the scatter plot below shows, the relationship is not linear. This means that the least-squares line of fit for these data is not a straight line and that the correlation coefficient of -0.347, which reflects the accuracy of prediction from a straight line, will under-estimate the actual relationship between the variables. The correlation ratio will give a better indication of the relationship, but you will probably want to reduce the number of motivation categories to three or four by grouping.

   The second factor to keep in mind is the meaning of a larger number on the performance variable. These scores are for items missed, so larger numbers mean poorer performance. Although the correlation coefficient is -0.347, the relationship between motivation and performance is positive.

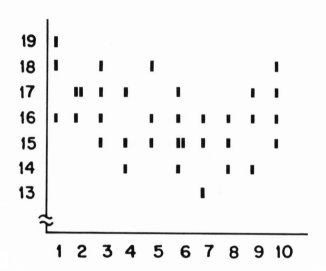

CHAPTER 10

1. Yes, the test-retest reliability is 0.90.
3. The new test has *negative* concurrent validity ($r = -0.56$) with the longer test. If we assume that the longer test has content validity, the shorter test should not be substituted for the longer one.
5.a. Concurrent and, perhaps, construct validity
   c. Concurrent and construct validity
   e. Concurrent

2.a. Sampling population—male white rats
   Treatment population—all rats (and perhaps other animals) exposed to one or the other treatment.
   c. Sampling population—students at college X.
4. A random sample is a) drawn from a defined sampling population; b) in such a way that each member of the population has an equal chance of being in the sample; c) so that the selection of one individual is independent of the selection of another. The most important characteristic for the sample is representativeness.

5.a. 31

  d. 17

  f. 7 or 8

Remember that these answers all assume that the different categories of each variable are independent so the probability of being a male varsity athlete is the product of P_{male} and $P_{\text{var. ath.}}$. If this is not the case, you would have to find the frequency of each specific type in the population.

CHAPTER 12

These are thought questions.

CHAPTER 13

1.a. $\sigma_x = \dfrac{\sigma}{\sqrt{N}} = \dfrac{3}{\sqrt{9}} = 1.0, \quad z_x = \dfrac{21 - 20}{1} = +1.0, \quad p \leq 0.159$

  c. $\sigma_x = 0.56 \qquad\qquad z_x = \quad 0.54 \qquad\qquad p \leq 0.295$

  e. $\sigma_x = 0.939 \qquad\qquad z_x = -3.19 \qquad\qquad p \leq 0.0008$

2. Statistically significant means unlikely to occur under conditions of random sampling from the population specified in the null hypothesis.

4. Type I error—reaching the conclusion that the null hypothesis is false when it is really true.

   Type II error—failing to conclude that the null hypothesis is false when it is really false; failing to detect the fact that the null hypothesis is false.

6.a. $H_0: \mu_{boys} \leq \mu_{girls}$ $\qquad\qquad$ $H_1: \mu_{boys} > \mu_{girls}$

  c. $H_0: \mu_R = \mu_D$ $\qquad\qquad\qquad$ $H_1: \mu_R \neq \mu_D$

  e. $H_0: \mu_m \leq \mu_w$ $\qquad\qquad\quad$ $H_1: \mu_m > \mu_w$

7.a. $\sigma_x = 0.50$, 0.05 critical value is $10.82\,(10.0 + 1.645 \cdot 0.5)$ for all conditions. Power for the three alternatives are 0.2611, 0.6406, and 0.9909. Note, this is a one-tailed hypothesis.

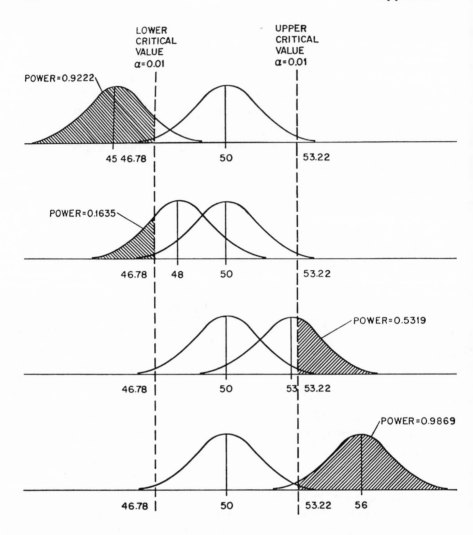

c. $\sigma_{\bar{x}} = 1.25$. This is a two-tailed hypothesis, so the upper critical value is 53.22 (50.0 + 1.25·2.576) and the lower critical value is 46.78 (50.0 − 1.25·2.576). Values for power are 0.9222, 0.1635, 0.5319 and 0.9868.

CHAPTER 14

1. σ is known, so the appropriate test is a one-sample, one-tailed z-test where $z = \dfrac{17 - 15}{3/\sqrt{9}} = \dfrac{17 - 15}{1} = +2.0$

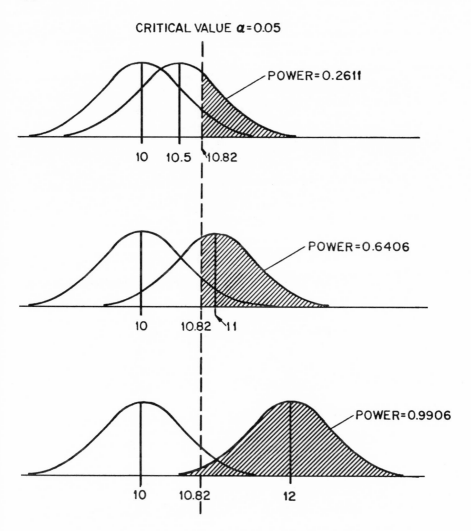

CRITICAL VALUE $\alpha = 0.05$

POWER = 0.2611

10   10.5   10.82

POWER = 0.6406

10   10.82   11

POWER = 0.9906

10   10.82   12

The critical value of z is $+1.645$; therefore, we reject the null hypothesis.

3. σ is not known, the hypothesis is two-tailed, and a value is specified for μ. The proper test is a one-sample t with 16 degrees of freedom. $\overline{X} = 27.29$, $\hat{S}_x = 5.30$, $\hat{S}_{\overline{x}} = 1.286$, critical value of t is ± 2.921, $t = -0.55$.
    Do not reject the null.

5. This should be a one-sample, one-tailed t-test with $df = 16$. The 0.005 critical value is $+2.921$. $\overline{X} = 17.94$.

$$\hat{S}_x = 2.56 \qquad \hat{S}_{\overline{x}} = 0.62 \qquad t = \frac{17.94 - 22}{0.62} = -6.55$$

Do not reject the null hypothesis because the direction of the difference is opposite that specified in the alternate and in the direction specified in the null.

7. Because the population variances are known, we calculate

$$\sigma_{\overline{x}_1 \, \overline{x}_2} = \sqrt{\frac{\sigma_1^2}{N_1} + \frac{\sigma_2^2}{N_2}} = \sqrt{\frac{9}{9} + \frac{16}{9}} = \sqrt{2.78} = 1.67$$

$$\overline{X}_1 = 9.33, \overline{X}_2 = 12.33, z = \frac{9.33 - 12.33}{1.67} = -1.80$$

We do not reject our one-tailed hypothesis because z does not exceed the critical value $+1.645$.

9. $$\sigma_{\overline{x}_1 - \overline{x}_2} = \sqrt{\frac{16}{8} + \frac{36}{11}} = \sqrt{5.27} = 2.30$$

$$z = \frac{23.625 - 25.636}{2.30} = -0.87$$

Do not reject H_0.

11. $\hat{S}_1^2 = 2.67 \qquad \hat{S}_2^2 = 19.45 \qquad \hat{S}_p^2 = 13.86$

$\overline{X}_1 = 9.33 \qquad \overline{X}_2 = 14.64 \qquad \hat{S}_{\overline{x}_1 - \overline{x}_2} = 1.89$

$$t = \frac{9.33 - 14.64}{1.89} = \frac{-5.31}{1.89} = -2.81 \qquad df = 15$$

critical value for $t = 1.753$

Do not reject H_0. Note that if this had been a two-tailed hypothesis we would have rejected it.

13. This is a related measures t, two-tailed test.
$\Sigma D = -18, \overline{D} = -3, \hat{S}_D = 2.19, \hat{S}_{\overline{D}} = 0.89$

$$t = \frac{D}{\hat{S}_{\overline{D}}} = \frac{-3}{0.89} = -3.35 \qquad df = 5$$

Critical value $= \pm 2.571$
Reject the null hypothesis.

If you chose to use equation 14.15, you should have the following results:

$\overline{X}_1 = 20 \qquad \overline{X}_2 = 23 \qquad \hat{S}_1 = 3.10 \qquad \hat{S}_2 = 2.53$

$$\hat{S}_{x_1\ x_2} = \sqrt{\frac{9.61}{6} + \frac{6.40}{6} - 2(.71)\left(\frac{3.10}{\sqrt{6}}\right)\left(\frac{2.53}{\sqrt{6}}\right)}$$

$$= \sqrt{1.60 + 1.07 - 1.86} = .90$$

$$t = \frac{20 - 23}{.90} = -3.33 \text{ with the difference of 0.02 due to}$$

rounding errors.

CHAPTER 15

1.a. 0.020, 0.211, 1.386, 5.991, 13.816

   c. 2.558, 4.865, 9.342, 18.307, 29.588

2.a. $X^2 = \dfrac{(8 - 1) \cdot 100}{15^2} = \dfrac{700}{225} = 3.11 \qquad df = 7$

   The 0.02 critical values for X^2 are 1.239 and 18.475. Do not reject the null.

   b. S^2 must first be converted to $\hat{S}^2$. $\hat{S}^2 = \dfrac{22}{21}(100) = 104.76$

   $$X^2 = \frac{2200}{225} = 9.78 \qquad df = 21$$

   Do not reject H_0 at the 0.02 level. (You would have been able to reject H_0 at the 0.05 level one-tailed.)

   e. $X^2 = \dfrac{19(18.5^2)}{225} = 28.9 \qquad df = 18 \qquad$ Do not reject H_0

   g. $\hat{S}^2 = \dfrac{12}{11}(19.5^2) = 414.8 \qquad X^2 = \dfrac{11(414.8)}{225} = 20.28$

   $df = 11$. Do not reject H_0.

3.a. The critical values of X^2 are 2.167 and 14.067

   $\dfrac{700}{14.067} < \sigma^2 < \dfrac{700}{2.167} \qquad$ e. $\dfrac{6502.75}{30.144} < \sigma^2 < \dfrac{6502.75}{10.177}$

   $49.76 < \sigma^2 < 3.03 \qquad\qquad 215.72 < \sigma^2 < 638.97$

   c. $\dfrac{2200}{32.617} < \sigma^2 < \dfrac{2200}{11.591} \qquad$ g. $\dfrac{4563}{19.675} < \sigma^2 < \dfrac{4563}{4.575}$

   $67.45 < \sigma^2 < 189.80 \qquad\qquad 231.92 < \sigma^2 < 997.38$

4.a.   7.59   c. 1.84   e. 2.35

5.   The three possible null hypotheses are: $\sigma_1^2 = \sigma_2^2$, $\sigma_1^2 = \sigma_3^2$, and $\sigma_2^2 = \sigma_3^2$. Each may be tested with an F. We shall use $\alpha = .05$. $F_{12} = \dfrac{\hat{S}_2^2}{\hat{S}_1^2} = \dfrac{32.49}{9.61} = 3.38$ with $df_1 = 7$ and and $df_2 = 6$. The .05 critical value is 3.87. Do not reject the null hypothesis that $\sigma_1^2 = \sigma_2^2$.

   b. $F_{13} = \dfrac{9.2^2}{3.1^2} = 8.81$. With $df_1 = 9$ and $df_2 = 6$ the critical value is 4.10. Reject the hypothesis that $\sigma_1^2 = \sigma_3^2$.

   c. $F_{23} = 2.61$ with $df_1 = 9$ and $df_2 = 7$. Do not reject H_0.

6.a.   Expected frequencies

11	14	25
11	14	25
22	28	50

$$X^2 = \frac{(10 - 11 - .5)^2}{11} + \frac{(12 - 11 - .5)^2}{11} + \frac{(15 - 14 - .5)^2}{14} +$$

$$\frac{(13 - 14 - .5)^2}{14} = .08$$

Do not reject H_0.

   b.   Expected frequencies

14.5	10.5	25
14.5	10.5	25
29	21	50

$X^2 = 1.72 + 1.72 + 2.38 + 2.38 = 8.20$

Reject the null hypothesis.

8.a.   0.929   c. 0.377   e. -0.151

9.a. $\sigma_{z_f} = \dfrac{1}{\sqrt{22}} = 0.2132$ $z = \dfrac{0.73}{0.2132} = 3.42$ $p < 0.01$

   c. $\sigma_{z_f} = 0.1715$ $z = 2.10$ $p < 0.05$

   e. $\alpha_{z_f} = 0.051$ $z = -2.94$ $p < 0.01$

CHAPTER 16

1.a. 1) 15   3) 100
    5) 74   7) 340

b. $\mu_f = \mu_w = \mu_t = \mu_{tr}$

c.

	Football	Wrestling	Tennis	Track	Total
ΣX_i	100	109	66	65	340
ΣX_i^2	2,574	2,991	1,118	1,071	7,754
X	25	27.25	16.5	16.25	21.25

$SS_T = \Sigma\Sigma(X_{ij} - \overline{\overline{X}})^2 = 529$ $\hat{S}_T^2 = 35.267$

$SS_W = \Sigma[\Sigma(X_{ij} - \overline{X}_j)^2] = 138.5$ $\hat{S}_W^2 = 11.542$

$SS_B = \Sigma[N_j(X_j = \overline{\overline{X}})^2] = 390.5$ $\hat{S}_B^2 = 130.167$

$$F = \frac{\hat{S}_B^2}{\hat{S}_W^2} = 11.28 \qquad df_1 = 3 \qquad df_2 = 12$$

Reject H_0 even if you set α at 0.001.

d.

df component	Numerical value
1	7225
JN	7754
J	7615.5

SS_T $JN - 1 \rightarrow 7754 \quad - 7225 \quad = 529$

SS_B $J \;\; - 1 \rightarrow 7615.5 - 7225 \quad = 390.5$

SS_W $JN - J \rightarrow 7754 \quad - 7615.5 = 138.5$

The remaining steps are identical to those in c.

e.

Source	SS	df	MS	F
Between	390.5	3	130.167	11.28
Within	138.5	12	11.542	
Total	529	15		

f. $(15 - 21.25) = (15 - 16.25) + (16.25 - 21.25)$
      $- \;\; 6.25 \;\; = \quad - \;\; 1.25 \;\; + (-5)$
      $- \;\; 6.25 \;\; = \quad - \;\; 6.25$

g.   1) H_0: $\dfrac{\mu_f + \mu_w}{2} = \dfrac{\mu_t + \mu_{tr}}{2}$ $\alpha = 0.01$

2) $C = \dfrac{4(25) + 4(27.25)}{8} - \dfrac{4(16.5) + 4(16.25)}{8}$

$C = \dfrac{209}{8} - \dfrac{131}{8} = 26.125 - 16.375 = 9.75$

$\hat{S}_C^2 = MS_w \left(\dfrac{1}{8} + \dfrac{1}{8} \right) = 11.542 \,(.25) = 2.8855$

$\hat{S}_C = 1.6987$

$t = \dfrac{C}{\hat{S}_C} = \dfrac{9.75}{1.6987} = 5.75$

$t_{cc} = \sqrt{df_B(F_{df_B,\, df_w})} = \sqrt{3(5.95)} = \sqrt{17.85} = 4.22$

Reject the null hypothesis. The data support your alternate hypothesis that participants in more violent sports have higher masculinity scores.

BIBLIOGRAPHY

GENERAL

Cronbach, L. J., Gleser, G. C., Nanda, H., and Rajaratnam, N. *The dependability of behavioral measurements: Theory of generalizability for scores and profiles*. New York: Wiley, 1972.

Cronbach, L. J., and Meehl, P. E. "Construct validity in psychological tests." *Psychological Bulletin*, **52** (1955): 281–302.

Hays, W. L. *Statistics for the social sciences*. 2d ed. New York: Holt, Rinehart, and Winston, 1973.

Huff, D. *How to lie with statistics*. New York: Norton, 1954.

Lindquist, E. F. *Design and analysis of experiments in psychology and education*. Boston: Houghton Mifflin, 1953.

Lordahl, D. S. *Modern statistics for the behavioral sciences*. New York: Ronald Press, 1967.

MacCorquodale, K., and Meehl, P. E. "On the distinction between hypothetical constructs and intervening variables." *Psychological Review*, **55** (1948): 95–107.

McNemar, Q. *Psychological statistics*. 4th ed. New York: Wiley, 1969.

Meehl, P. E. "Theoretical risks and tabular asterisks: Sir Karl, Sir Ronald, and the slow progress of soft psychology." *Journal of Consulting and Clinical Psychology*, 46 (1978): 806–834.

Rand Corporation. *A million random digits with 100,000 normal deviates*. New York: Free Press, 1955.

Scheffe, H. A. *The analysis of variance*. New York: Wiley, 1959.

Siegel, S. *Nonparametric statistics for the behavioral sciences*. New York: McGraw-Hill, 1956.

Stevens, S. S. "On the theory of scales of measurement." *Science*, 103 (1946): 677–680.

Thorndike, R. L. *Personnel selection*. New York: Wiley, 1949.

Torgerson, W. S. *Theory and methods of scaling*. New York: Wiley, 1958.

Tukey, J. W. *Exploratory data analysis*. Reading, Mass: Addison-Wesley, 1977.

Whaley, D. L. *Psychological testing and the philosophy of measurement*. Kalamazoo: Behaviordelia, 1973.

Winer, B. J. *Statistical principles in experimental design*. 2d ed. New York: McGraw-Hill, 1971.

EXPERIMENTAL DESIGN AND THE INTERPRETATION OF RESULTS

Agnew, N. McK., and Pyke, S. W. *The science game*. 2d. ed. Englewood Cliffs, N.J.: Prentice-Hall, 1978.

Campbell, S. K. *Flaws and fallacies in statistical thinking*. Englewood Cliffs, N.J.: Prentice-Hall, 1974.

Campbell, D. T., and Stanley, J. C. *Experimental and quasi-experimental designs for research*. Chicago: Rand McNally, 1963.

Cook, T. D., and Campbell, D. T. *Quasi-experimentation: Design and analysis issues for field settings*. Chicago: Rand McNally, 1979.

Huck, S. W., and Sandler, H. M. *Rival hypotheses: Alternative interpretations of data-based conclusions*. New York: Harper & Row, 1979.

Stern, P. C. *Evaluating social science research*. New York: Oxford University Press, 1979.

RESEARCH METHODS

Christensen, L. B. *Experimental Methodology.* Boston: Allyn and Bacon, 1977.

Cozby, P. C. *Methods in behavioral research.* Palo Alto, Calif.: Mayfield, 1977.

Johnson, H. H., and Solso, R. L. *An introduction to experimental design in Psychology: A case approach.* 2d ed. New York: Harper & Row, 1978.

Kerlinger, F. N. *Foundations of behavioral research.* 2d ed. New York: Holt, Rinehart, and Winston, 1973.

Mason, E. J., and Bramble, W. J. *Understanding and conducting research.* New York: McGraw-Hill, 1978.

Plutchik, R. *Foundations of experimental research.* 2d ed. New York: Harper & Row, 1974.

Sax, G. *Foundations of educational research.* Englewood Cliffs, N. J.: Prentice-Hall, 1979.

Wiersma, W. *Research methods in education.* Philadelphia: Lippincott, 1969.

MEASUREMENT TOPICS

Anastasi, A. *Psychological testing.* 4th ed. New York: Macmillan, 1976.

Bolton, B. *Handbook of measurement and evaluation in rehabilitation.* Baltimore: University Park Press, 1976.

Coombs, C. H. *A theory of data.* New York: Wiley, 1964.

Lord, F. M., and Novick, M. R. *Statistical theories of mental test scores.* Reading, Mass.: Addison-Wesley, 1968.

Nunnally, J. C. *Psychometric theory.* 2d ed. New York: McGraw-Hill, 1978.

Sax, G. *Principles of educational and psychological measurement and evaluation.* 2d ed. Belmont, Calif.: Wadsworth, 1980.

Thorndike, R. L. *Educational Measurement.* 2d ed. Washington: American Educational Research Council, 1971.

Thorndike, R. L., and Hagen, E. *Measurement and evaluation in psychology and education.* 4th ed. New York: Wiley, 1977.

Torgerson, W. S. *Theory and methods of scaling.* New York: Wiley, 1958.

STATISTICAL METHODS

Hays, W. L. *Statistics for the social sciences.* 2d ed. New York: Holt, Rinehart, and Winston, 1973.

Keppel, G. *Design and analysis: A researcher's handbook.* Englewood Cliffs, N.J.: Prentice-Hall, 1973.

Novick, M. R., and Jackson, P. H. *Statistical methods for educational and psychological research.* New York: McGraw-Hill, 1974.

Winer, B. J. *Statistical principles in experimental design.* 2d ed. New York: McGraw-Hill, 1971.

NONPARAMETRIC STATISTICS

Bishop, Y. M. M., Fienberg, S. E., and Holland, P. W. *Discrete multivariate analysis.* Cambridge, Mass: The MIT Press, 1975.

Siegel, S. *Nonparametric statistics for the behavioral sciences.* New York: McGraw-Hill, 1956.

Tukey, J. W. *Exploratory data analysis.* Reading, Mass: Addison-Wesley, 1977.

MULTIVARIATE ANALYSIS AND CORRELATION

Bock, R. D. *Multivariate statistical methods in behavioral research.* New York: McGraw-Hill, 1975.

Harman, H. H. *Modern factor analysis.* 3d ed. Chicago: University of Chicago Press, 1976.

Kerlinger, F. N., and Pedhazur, E. J. *Multiple regression in behavioral research.* New York: Holt, Rinehart, and Winston, 1973.

Thorndike, R. M. *Correlational procedures for research.* New York: Gardner Press, 1978.

INDEX

475